An AMERICAN HERITAGE Guide

GREAT
HISTORIC
PLACES

An AMERICAN HERITAGE Guide

GREAT HISTORIC PLACES

BY THE EDITORS OF
AMERICAN HERITAGE

EDITOR IN CHARGE
BEVERLEY DA COSTA

INTRODUCTION BY
RICHARD M. KETCHUM

PUBLISHED BY American Heritage Publishing Co., Inc., New York
Book Trade Distribution by McGraw-Hill Book Company

Staff for this Book

EDITOR
Beverley Da Costa

ASSOCIATE EDITOR
Margot Brill Higgins

CONTRIBUTING EDITORS
Bruce Bohle
Angela Weldon

COPY EDITOR
Helen C. Dunn

DESIGNER
Sara Krizmanich

PICTURE EDITOR
Ellen F. Zeifer

RESEARCHERS
Candace Carr Atkinson
Donna Whiteman

American Heritage
Publishing Co., Inc.

PRESIDENT AND PUBLISHER
Paul Gottlieb

EDITOR-IN-CHIEF
Joseph J. Thorndike

SENIOR EDITOR, BOOK DIVISION
Alvin M. Josephy, Jr.

EDITORIAL ART DIRECTOR
Murray Belsky

GENERAL MANAGER, BOOK DIVISION
Kenneth W. Leish

Library of Congress Cataloging in Publication Data

Main entry under title:

An American heritage guide.

1. Historic sites—United States. 2. National
parks and reserves—United States. I. Da Costa,
Beverley, ed. II. American heritage. III. Title:
Great historic places.
E159.A39   917.3′04′9   73–8836
ISBN   0–07–001171–0

HALF-TITLE PAGE: *a 19th-century weathervane representing Columbia*
TITLE PAGE: *Monticello in Charlottesville, Virginia*
COPYRIGHT PAGE: *San Jacinto Battlefield Monument near Houston, Texas*

Introduction

Americans have made history in an infinite variety of ways. Because the age-old pull of land had brought so many of them to this continent in the first place, the westering instinct was there from the beginning, luring them ever onward to the next hill, the next valley—on toward a destiny whose nature no one could possibly guess. They made an enduring mark on the countryside, quite often, simply by settling in a place where no man had lived before. They fought over the land—with Indians, with other settlers, with British and French and Spanish and Mexicans, with fellow citizens of their own divided nation. They built homes, churches, schools, forts, and manufactories. And in a state of perpetual restlessness, they explored everything that piqued their curiosity—from the ancient monuments of the red man to the mysteries of the mind, of science, and of the stars themselves.

A characteristic of the American is, and has always been, his urge to improve things, to make them better (or at least different), and one consequence of this determination has been the continuing destruction or alteration of what other nations might regard as inviolable historic landmarks. Yet enough of them survive, in all the fifty states, to enable us—if we will pause long enough and allow our imaginations to work—to see what the conditions of life must have been like three decades or three centuries ago.

It is a good thing for Americans of today to take stock of such matters now and again. It is well that we wander across the sloping fields of the Saratoga battlefield and remind ourselves what it was that caused those thousands of brave men to shed so much blood. It is worth standing for a long time in the main street of Deerfield, Massachusetts, to admire the grace and beauty of those old houses and ask ourselves if we have not lost something precious by settling for dwellings that are not both utilitarian *and* beautiful. It is important that we walk through the silent, towering redwoods of the Muir National Forest, absorbing the sense of timelessness that characterizes that cathedral-like place, and consider how we will make it possible for future generations to enjoy the wonders of open space and the beneficence of nature.

This little book holds a key to what was and is best about America, but because it is merely a guide it demands something on the part of the reader—a willingness to participate with open mind and active imagination and to dream awhile of a day that has passed but must not be forgotten.

There are listed, within these pages, more than a thousand historic sites, arranged alphabetically by state and by town. In most instances the days and hours that sites are open to visitors are indicated; these are, of course, subject to change, and it is wise to confirm them before a visit. Of particular interest during the celebration of the Bicentennial of the Revolution are those entries marked in the left-hand margin with the Liberty Bell symbol, designating the site as a Revolutionary War landmark. And the letters "NR," appearing at the end of an entry, mean that the building is listed in the *National Register of Historic Places*. Because of space limitations it has not been possible to include all historic houses; many others appear in *An American Heritage Guide to Historic Houses of America*, published in 1971.

—R. M. K.

ALABAMA

BIRMINGHAM

ARLINGTON HOME AND GARDENS, *331 Cotton Avenue, SW*

This Greek Revival plantation house, the oldest structure in Birmingham (1822–42), is the sole mansion in the South's leading steel center to survive the Civil War and the city's phenomenal industrial growth. In 1865 the mansion was used by Union General James H. Wilson for his headquarters; here he issued orders to burn the University of Alabama, the furnaces and foundries at Tannehill, Oxmoor, and Irondale, and the arsenal at Selma (*see*). According to legend, the "spy" poetess Mary Gordon Duffee was hiding in the attic at the time; she then walked 15 miles to Tannehill to warn the Confederates of Union plans. NR
Open: Tues–Sat 9–5, Sun 1–6. Admission: adults $1.50

DEMOPOLIS, *westcentral Alabama, on U.S. 43*

In 1817 a small band of exiled followers of Napoleon Bonaparte sailed up the Tombigbee River from Mobile and landed at **White Bluff** (NR) to settle the town that would become Demopolis, or "city of the people." They had received a land grant of several thousand acres in the Demopolis area from the United States government on the condition that they establish vineyards and olive groves. Their colony was a failure, however, and after a few years most of the French refugees left Demopolis. Between 1830 and 1860 a plantation society developed and many fine mansions were built in and around Demopolis. Two of the outstanding ones that may be visited today are **Gaineswood** and **Bluff Hall** (both NR).
Gaineswood open: Tues–Sat 9–5, Sun and holidays 1–5. Admission: adults $1, children 50¢. Bluff Hall open: Sun 2–5

Top: First White House of the Confederacy in Montgomery and Jefferson Davis. Below: an exhibit at the Space and Rocket Center in Huntsville

EUFAULA, *southeast Alabama, on U.S. 82 and 431, on the Chattahoochee*
Eufaula was established early in the 19th century as a center for
trading with the Lower Creek Indians. Known as Irwinton, the
riverfront settlement soon enjoyed an era of great affluence when
thousands of bales of cotton were shipped yearly down the Chattahoochee to the Gulf of Mexico. The first permanent structure, **The
Tavern** (NR), was built in 1836; it served as a Confederate hospital
during the Civil War. The oldest residence, the **Sheppard Cottage**
(NR), dates from 1837 and is a fine example of a Southern adaptation
of a Cape Cod cottage. The **McNab Bank Building** (NR) was built
by John McNab, a Scottish financier, early in the 1850s to house his
Eastern Bank of Alabama. The oldest standing bank building in
Alabama, it has a beautiful cast-iron façade. In April, during the
Eufaula Pilgrimage, many beautiful ante-bellum mansions here
are open to the public.

FORT MITCHELL SITE, *on State 165, on the Chattahoochee River*
One of the first military garrisons in the middle Chattahoochee
Valley, Fort Mitchell played a significant role in the history of U.S.
relations with the Creek Indians. It was built in the fall of 1813
following the national outcry over the massacre at Fort Mims (*see
Tensaw*). After the Battle of Horseshoe Bend (*see*) assured white
settlers peace in the area, the fort was used as a center for trade
with the Creeks. From 1821 to 1836 the **Creek Indian Agency** was
located here. In 1836 the Indians assembled at the fort when the
U.S. government forced them to move to Oklahoma and Kansas.
Excavations of the fort, trading factory, and agency are planned. NR

FORT PAYNE, *northeast Alabama, on U.S. 11, I-59*
The **Alabama Great Southern Railroad Depot·**(NR) and the **Fort
Payne Opera House** (NR) are remnants of the boom-town period of
the 1890s in northern Alabama. In 1889 the Fort Payne Iron and
Coal Company raised a million dollars in five days, mainly from
New England investors who then moved into the area. By the turn
of the century, when neither coal nor iron was found in great
quantities, the boom had ended.

HORSESHOE BEND NATIONAL MILITARY PARK, *eastcentral Alabama,
about 12 miles north of Dadeville on State 49*
Horseshoe Bend, a 100-acre peninsula formed by a large loop in the
Tallapoosa River, was the site of Andrew Jackson's decisive victory
over the Creek Nation on March 27, 1814, which ended the Creek
War. This battle, the culmination of his campaign against the warring Upper Creeks, or "Red Stick" faction, broke Creek power in
the southeastern United States and opened for settlement Creek
lands comprising most of the southern parts of Alabama and Georgia.
Approximately 900 warriors were killed in the fierce fighting. The
150-acre military park contains a visitor center that houses exhibits
on Creek culture, frontier life, and the Creek War. The 3-mile road,
which loops through the battlefield connecting key sites, has trails
and markers designed to enhance the visitor's understanding of
the battle. NR
For further information write: Box 63, Daviston, AL 36256

HUNTSVILLE, *northern Alabama, on U.S. 72*
During the Civil War Huntsville played a strategic role as the
eastern headquarters of the vital Confederate east-west rail link
between the Mississippi River and the Atlantic Ocean. The **Mem-**

phis and Charleston Railroad Depot (NR)—built in 1860, the oldest rail terminal still standing in Alabama—was the target of Union General O. M. Mitchell's attack on Huntsville on April 11, 1862. When the city fell, the depot served as a temporary Federal prison for about 200 Confederate soldiers. At this same depot in 1950 Dr. Werner von Braun arrived in Huntsville to build the U.S. space program. Working at **Redstone Arsenal,** Dr. von Braun and a team of scientists developed the Jupiter C rocket, which blasted the first U.S. satellite into orbit in 1958. *Freedom VII*, which hurled the nation's first astronaut, Navy Commander Alan B. Shepard, Jr., into outer space in 1961, was also designed at Redstone. A space exposition center at Tranquility Base is open to visitors.

Space and Rocket Center open: June–Aug 9-6, Sept–May 9-5. Admission: adults $1.75, children (6–12) 75¢

MOBILE AND VICINITY

CHURCH STREET EAST HISTORIC DISTRICT

The structures in this district reflect the ante-bellum history of Mobile; the district also contains the site of the founding of the city early in the 1700s (*see Fort Condé-Charlotte*), as well as four other National Register properties of historic interest. The **Raphael Semmes Home** commemorates a famous naval hero of the Civil War—Admiral Semmes, commander of the Confederate raiders *Sumter* and *Alabama*. The **Barton Academy** (built in 1836) became the state's first public school in 1852. The **Bishop Portier Home** from 1833 until 1914 served as the residence of the ranking prelates of the Catholic Church in Alabama. The **City Hospital** (in operation 1831–1966) housed wounded Confederates during the Battle of Mobile Bay in 1864 (*see Fort Morgan*) and Mobilians during the yellow fever epidemics from 1839 to 1897.

DAUPHIN ISLAND, *at entrance of Mobile Bay, access via bridge*

In 1699 Pierre le Moyne, Sieur d'Iberville, became the first European to visit this island. His brother, Jean Baptiste le Moyne, Sieur de Bienville, established a post on the island in 1702. He called it Massacre Island because of the number of bleached human bones found on its beaches. The island served as port of entry to the French settlement at Fort Louis de la Mobile, 30 miles upriver. In 1711 Bienville renamed the island "Dauphine" in honor of the wife of Dauphin Louis, Duke of Burgundy. In spite of hurricanes and attacks by British privateers, the Dauphin Island colony survived, serving as the main port for the Mobile area until about 1820. The most notable existing historic site on the island is **Fort Gaines,** located on the eastern tip. The long-silent cannon on its ramparts and the 5-foot-thick outer walls offer mute testimony to the role that this citadel played in the defense of Mobile Bay during the Civil War, when it guarded the western entrance to the bay, and Fort Morgan (*see*), the eastern entrance. A museum, located in the former officers' quarters, houses the wheel from Admiral David Farragut's flagship, the *Hartford*.

Fort open daily 8–sunset. Admission: adults 50¢, children 25¢

FORT CONDE-CHARLOTTE, *104 Church Street*

On this site stood two forts which protected the early French settlement that became Mobile. In 1711 Sieur de Bienville built a wooden stockade on this site and named it Fort Louis de la Mobile. In 1717 it was rebuilt in brick and three years later it was renamed Fort Condé de la Mobile. In 1763 the British took over Fort Condé and renamed it in honor of their queen, Charlotte. The Spanish took Mobile in 1780 and held the fort until 1813, when they were ousted by American troops. After the purchase of Florida in 1819, Fort Charlotte was of no further importance to American security and it was sold. Today the Fort Condé-Charlotte House, a two-story brick structure covered with smooth white stucco, stands on the site of the historic forts. The house, built about 1820 by Jonathan Kirkbridge, contains part of what is alleged to be Fort Condé-Charlotte's original wall. Bienville Square, in the business district of Mobile, contains a French cannon from Fort Condé and a British one from Fort Charlotte. NR

Open: Jan–May, Oct–Nov, Mon–Fri 1–4; Feb–Mar, Mon–Sat 10–5, Sun 1–5. Admission: adults $1, children 50¢

FORT MORGAN NATIONAL HISTORIC LANDMARK, *about 20 miles west of Gulf Shores via State 180*

Fort Morgan, a mainstay in the Confederate defense of Mobile Bay, stands on Mobile Point, at the end of a spit of land that juts into the bay. During the War of 1812 **Fort Bowyer**, a small wooden structure, stood on the site; it was destroyed by a storm in 1819. The present fort was built in 1833–34 according to the famous star-shaped design of Michelangelo. With its fine brick arches, this massive stronghold is one of the best examples of military architecture in North America. Between 1861 and 1864, together with Fort Gaines on Dauphin Island (*see*), Fort Morgan guarded Mobile Bay against the Federal fleet that was blockading it, its guns protecting the Confederate blockade-runners. On August 5, 1864, the Battle of Mobile Bay, one of the fiercest naval actions of the Civil War, was fought off Mobile Point. In the early hours of the day, Union Admiral David G. Farragut, commanding a fleet of 4 ironclad monitors and 18 wooden warships, forced entrance into the bay through a passage protected by Fort Morgan, the Confederate ironclad *Tennessee*, and 3 small wooden gunboats. When the Federal monitor *Tecumseh* was sunk by mines, Farragut issued his famous command: "Damn the torpedoes—full speed ahead!" All his vessels, some disabled, reached the bay, where a fierce battle ensued. Finally at 10 A.M. the *Tennessee* surrendered and Mobile Bay was lost to the Confederacy. When Fort Morgan surrendered on August 23, the city of Mobile was completely blockaded. NR

U.S.S. *ALABAMA* BATTLESHIP MEMORIAL, *berthed 2½ miles east of Mobile on U.S. 90*

During World War II this mighty battleship served in every major engagement in the Pacific and received nine battle stars. Visitors can stride its decks, step into the turrets of its 15″ guns, and slip into the seats of its 40mm antiaircraft guns. The admission price also includes a tour of the famous World War II submarine U.S.S. *Drum*, which is docked alongside.

Open daily 8–sunset. Admission: adults $2, children (6–11) 75¢

MONTGOMERY, *central Alabama, on U.S. 80, I-65, I-85*

Known as the Cradle of the Confederacy, Montgomery was the first capital established by the seceding states. One of the city's most important landmarks is the **Alabama State**, or **First Confederate, Capitol** (NHL), a magnificent Greek Revival building constructed in 1851 and similar in design to the National Capitol. In January, 1861, a fiery Secession Convention met in the capitol's house of representatives chamber and voted Alabama out of the

Union. Early the next month the secessionists met in the capitol's senate chamber to adopt the Provisional Constitution of the Confederacy and to elect Jefferson Davis president of the Confederacy. On February 18, 1861, Davis took the oath of office on the capitol's west portico. Opposite the state capitol stands the **First White House of the Confederacy**—the home of Jefferson Davis and his family when Montgomery was the capital of the Confederacy. It contains original Davis furniture and relics of the War Between the States. There are several fine ante-bellum mansions and town houses and two ante-bellum churches in the **Perry Street Historic District** (NR)—**St. Peter's Catholic Church** (1850) and **First Presbyterian Church** (mid-1840s). The **Ordeman-Shaw Historic District** (NR) encompasses one of the finest complexes of urban restoration in the nation.

State Capitol open daily 8–5. White House of the Confederacy open daily 9–4:30; both closed national holidays

OLD CAHABA, *about 14 miles southeast of Selma via State 22*
Built on the site of an old Indian village and a French trading post, Cahaba, now in ruins, served as Alabama's first permanent state capital from 1819 until 1826, when floods forced the removal of the state government to Tuscaloosa. By 1828 Cahaba was practically abandoned. Within a few years, however, it had been rebuilt and was the most important shipping point on the Alabama River. Cahaba was subsequently inundated and rebuilt several times, and in 1850 it reached its peak population of, it is estimated, some 5,000 inhabitants. During the Civil War the town was the site of a Confederate prison. Today only a few chimneys and columns remain, and a monument marks the site of the old State House.

RUSSELL CAVE NATIONAL MONUMENT, *8 miles west of Bridgeport on U.S. 72 and County 91 and 75*
Containing a record of 8,000 years of man's life on the North American continent, this limestone cliff shelter was first inhabited by prehistoric Indians who arrived about 7000 to 6500 B.C. The Indians of the Archaic Period (7000–500 B.C.) used the rock shelter as their winter home, camping along the shores of the Tennessee River in the summer. During the Woodland Period (500 B.C.–A.D. 1000) the inhabitants of Russell Cave began to use pottery and practice primitive agriculture. Today there is an archaeological excavation in the cave and exhibits in the visitor center. NR
For further information write: Bridgeport, AL 35740

ST. STEPHENS SITE, *off U.S. 43, on the Tombigbee River*
The hamlet of St. Stephens stands on the site of a fort erected by the Spanish in 1789, six years after the Treaty of Paris, ending the Revolutionary War, granted Florida and the Mobile area to Spain. The United States took possession of the fort after the area was ceded by the Spanish in 1795. The town that grew up around the fort became the trading center of the eastern Mississippi Territory. In 1804 the first American court in Alabama convened at St. Stephens. And in 1807 Aaron Burr was arrested nearby and escorted from St. Stephens to Richmond to stand trial for treason. This hamlet served as the territorial capital of Alabama (1817–19) and declined rapidly after it lost its political importance. NR

SELMA, *central Alabama, on U.S. 80*
With its arsenal, powder mill, shot and shell foundry, and navy

Indians defending their village against American soldiers during the Creek War

yard, Selma was a vital Confederate army depot. On April 2, 1865, the day Richmond fell, it was the scene of the Battle of Selma. In spite of the valiant efforts of General Nathan Bedford Forrest, the distinguished Confederate cavalry leader, and his forces, who fortified the city with earthworks, Selma was captured by Union General James H. Wilson and his "raiders." They plundered the city, burning Confederate facilities and many homes, and then moved on to Montgomery.

TALLADEGA, *northeast Alabama, on U.S. 231A*
Founded in 1834, Talladega is one of the oldest towns in the interior of Alabama. On November 9, 1813, during the Creek War, it was the site of the Battle of Talladega, in which Andrew Jackson led the Tennessee Volunteers and friendly Indians to victory over the hostile Red Stick faction of the Creeks.

TENSAW VICINITY
FORT MIMS SITE, *4 miles west of Tensaw off State 59*
Fort Mims was built in July, 1813, as a stockade that Samuel Mims, an early settler in Alabama, erected around his farm. The next month, fearing a Creek Indian uprising in retaliation for a white attack at Burnt Corn Creek, some 500 white and part-Indian settlers took shelter in the stockade, which soon became known as Fort Mims. On August 30 of that year a group of Creeks stormed the stockade, killing all but 36 of the soldiers and settlers. This brutal massacre spurred military action against the Creeks and marked the beginning of the Creek War (1813–14).

TUSCALOOSA AND VICINITY
GORGAS-MANLY HISTORIC DISTRICT, *University of Alabama campus*
In the heart of the University of Alabama campus, the historic district encompasses 8 buildings of architectural distinction. The **Gorgas Home,** built in 1829, was the only building from the original campus to survive the Civil War. Today the Federal-style house

serves as a memorial to the Gorgas family. Dr. William Gorgas (1854–1920) helped rid the Canal Zone of yellow fever during the construction of the Panama Canal and became Surgeon General of the U.S. Army during World War I. NR
House open: Mon–Sat 10–2 and 2–5, Sun 3–5

MOUNDVILLE NATIONAL HISTORIC LANDMARK, *17 miles south of Tuscaloosa on State 69, then 1 mile west*
This 320-acre state monument features 40 huge earthen mounds— including a restored 58½-foot-high temple mound—which mark the site of an Indian metropolis that flourished about A.D. 1000–1500. An archaeological museum contains artifacts from the ancient village and houses exhibits dealing with the Moundville Indians.
Open daily 9–5. Admission: adults $1, children 50¢

TUSCUMBIA
HELEN KELLER SHRINE, *300 West North Common Street*
The birthplace in 1880 of Helen Keller, Ivy Green was the scene of her heroic childhood struggle to overcome deafness and blindness. The shrine is a flower-filled 10-acre tract that includes the main house, built by Miss Keller's grandfather in 1820, and the tiny cottage where Helen and her teacher, Anne Sullivan, lived. NR
Open: Mon–Sat 8:30–4:30, Sun 1–4:30. Admission: adults $1, children (6–12) 50¢

TUSKEGEE
TUSKEGEE INSTITUTE NATIONAL HISTORIC LANDMARK, *U.S. 80*
Chartered by the state of Alabama in 1881, this pioneer Negro educational institution has furthered black economic progress through vocational and industrial training. Its founder and first president was Booker T. Washington, a former slave who became a distinguished educator and reformer. In 1896 George Washington Carver became head of the institute's agricultural department. His achievements include the development of 300 products from peanuts and 118 from sweet potatoes. The **Carver Museum** houses exhibits of the scientist's experiments with farm and forest products. The major portion of **The Oaks,** which was Dr. Washington's home, is used as offices, but the educator's study has been preserved with his original furnishings. NR
House open: Mon–Fri 8–12 and 1–4:30; admission: $1.00. Museum open: Mon–Fri 10–5, Sat 9–5, Sun 1–5

WETUMPKA VICINITY
FORT TOULOUSE NATIONAL HISTORIC LANDMARK, *about 5 miles southwest of Wetumpka off U.S. 231*
This fort, built in 1717, was the eastern outpost of the French province of Louisiana until the end of the French and Indian War in 1763. Strategically located at the confluence of the Coosa and Tallapoosa rivers, it protected the French settlements from Mobile Bay westward to New Orleans. It also served as a spearhead when the French attempted to wrest control of the present southeastern United States from the Spanish and English. In 1763 the French surrendered Fort Toulouse to the British, who used it until the end of the Revolutionary War and then destroyed it. In 1814 Andrew Jackson built **Fort Jackson** on the site of the old fort, and it was here, in August of that year, that the treaty ending the first Creek War was signed. Today all that remains of the forts are the ruins of a powder magazine. NR

ALEUTIAN ISLANDS
CHURCH OF THE HOLY ASCENSION NATIONAL HISTORIC LANDMARK, *village of Unalaska*
The central portion of this church probably dates from the original construction of 1825–26, making it the oldest Russian-built church still standing in the United States. It is also the finest Alaskan example of a 19th-century Russian Orthodox church constructed in the cruciform ground plan. The church is in active use. NR

WORLD WAR II BATTLE SITES
On June 3, 1942, Japanese carrier-borne aircraft bombed the village of **Dutch Harbor** on Amaknak Island, inflicting some casualties but only minor damage. This was the first Japanese attack on the Aleutian Islands. Several days later Japanese troops landed on the Aleutian islands of **Attu** and **Kiska,** conquering both quite easily. Japanese submarines then began patrolling the Aleutians and the North Pacific coast. On May 11, 1943, U.S. forces, handicapped by lack of information about Aleutian topography, landed on Attu. After three weeks of some of the bloodiest fighting in World War II the Americans retook the island. When U.S. and Canadian forces moved onto Kiska on August 15, 1943, they were surprised to discover that the Japanese had retreated from the island under cover of fog. From then on the Allies used the Aleutians for air bases.

ANAKTUVUK PASS ARCHAEOLOGICAL DISTRICT, *in Endicott Mountains*
This pass—one of the few existing corridors through the Brooks Range—was one of the routes by which primitive hunters first reached parts of the Western Hemisphere more than 20,000 years

Top left: Russian Orthodox Church at Sitka. Right: totem pole near Ketchikan.
Below: a Yukon stern-wheeler passes an Indian fish trap.

ago. Their first point of entry was western Alaska, which was linked to Siberia by a land bridge during glacial times. There are archaeological sites scattered over nearly 24 square miles at the mouth of the pass, but few have been investigated. NR nominee

EAGLE HISTORIC DISTRICT, *interior Alaska, on the Yukon River*
Eagle is situated on the Yukon River, on the U.S.–Canadian boundary. Located in the heart of the Yukon gold region (*see also Fort Yukon*), it served as a fur-trading post and supply center for goldmining operations in the 1890s. Here Judge James Wickersham—author, pioneer judge, and congressional delegate—established the first U.S. court in the interior of Alaska (*see also Juneau*). Visitors may see the ruins of **Fort Egbert**, abandoned in 1911. NR

FAIRBANKS, *central Alaska*
Situated near the geographical center of Alaska, Fairbanks was founded in August, 1909, when Captain E. T. Barnette, a river-boat operator, established a trading post on the banks of the Chena River. The next year the area experienced a gold-mining boom, and the settlement was renamed after the Vice President of the United States, Charles Fairbanks. Today Fairbanks is the transportation, market, and military hub of central Alaska. The **George C. Thomas Memorial Library** (NR), 901 First Avenue, is a log structure that dates from 1909 and commemorates the work of Episcopal missionaries. At nearby **Alaskaland,** site of the Alaska '67 centennial exposition (two miles west of State 2 on Airport Road), the S.S. **Nenana** (NR nominee) is moored. This stern-wheeler is typical of the river boats that carried people and supplies down the Yukon and Tanana rivers.

FORT YUKON, *interior Alaska, 140 miles northeast of Fairbanks*
This Athabascan Indian village is located just one mile north of the Arctic Circle, at a point where the Yukon River is almost 3 miles wide. Founded as a trading post in 1847 by the Hudson's Bay Company in agreement with the Russians, Fort Yukon is the oldest English-speaking settlement in Alaska. For over 20 years it was one of the British company's major posts before it passed into American hands. The town of Fort Yukon was a heavily used Yukon River port during the gold rush days. Today Fort Yukon is the largest village and trading post on the Yukon; it is famous for its fine native craftwork and furs.

JUNEAU, *southeast Alaska, near Yukon border in the Panhandle region*
Alaska's capital city, Juneau became the official capital of the territory of Alaska in 1900, although the government offices were not moved here from Sitka until 1906. When Joe Juneau and Richard Harris discovered gold here in 1880 they started the first gold rush in American Alaska. Within months a colony of about 100 miners had grown up on the site of the present city. Until they stopped operating, the famous Alaska-Juneau and Alaska-Treadwell gold mines produced more than 20,000 tons of ore daily. In summer visitors may take ore-train trips through the Alaska-Juneau Gold Mine, which terminated operations in 1944. There are also daily tours of the famous **House of Wickersham,** home of Judge James Wickersham, the historian and pioneer judge who went to Alaska in 1900 to establish the first courts and government in the interior (*see Eagle Historic District*).
Wickersham House open daily 11:30–7:30

KENAI, *southcentral Alaska, Kenai Peninsula, east shore of Cook Inlet*
One of the oldest permanent settlements in Alaska, Kenai was the site of **Fort, or Redoubt, St.** Nicholas, a fortified Russian fur-trading post built in August of 1791 at the mouth of the Kenai River on Cook Inlet. The fort was established by Grigor Konovalof of the Lebedef-Lastochkin Company. In April, 1869, **Fort Kenay,** one of Alaska's first U.S. Army posts, was built here; the village of Kenai derived its name from the fort. The village is also the site of the **Church of the Assumption of the Virgin Mary** (NHL), a Russian Orthodox mission church dating from 1894 and still in use.

KETCHIKAN VICINITY
TOTEM BIGHT STATE HISTORIC SITE, *10 miles north on Tongass Highway*
This state wayside includes a replica community house and a collection of totem poles carved in Haida and Tlingit styles. The house represented is a 19th-century chieftain's dwelling. Inside is one large room with a central fireplace and living quarters for several families, who shared the common fire. NR

KODIAK ISLAND
CITY OF KODIAK AND VICINITY, *northeast corner of Kodiak Island*
Kodiak Island was first discovered in 1763 by Russian explorer-traders who were lured there in search of the sea otter. In 1784 the Russians established a community at Three Saints Bay (*see*), in the southeast part of the island; this settlement served as a base of operations for Russia's fur-trading enterprises. The city of Kodiak was established in 1792 by Alexander Baranof after the earlier settlement at Three Saints Bay had been destroyed by an earthquake and a tidal wave. Baranof moved the headquarters of the Shelekof-Golikof Company to the new city, then known as Pavlovsk, and even today several of the original Russian buildings still stand. The most famous of these is the **Erskine House** (NHL), near the corner of Main Street and Mission Road. Built about 1793 by Baranof as an office and fur warehouse, it is the oldest standing Russian structure in the United States. The building was considerably remodeled in subsequent years and in 1912 became known as the Erskine House after its owner, William J. Erskine. It was acquired in 1965 by the Kodiak and Aleutian Islands Historical Society, Inc., which operates it as a museum. The **Fort Abercrombie State Historic Site** (NR), a half mile northeast of Kodiak, is the site of a World War II defense base.
Erskine House open: June–Sept, daily 10–3; winter, Wed, Fri, Sat, Sun 1–3

THREE SAINTS BAY ARCHAEOLOGICAL SITE, *Wildlife Refuge, Harbor of Three Saints*
The artifacts found in the layers of this archaeological site help to illuminate two distinct phases in Alaska history and culture. Eskimo stone artifacts, fishing gear, and items of personal adornment found at the first layer date from the first ten centuries A.D. The second layer consists of the remains of Three Saints Bay—the first permanent Russian settlement in Alaska. In August, 1784, Gregori Shelekof, part owner of the Shelekof-Golikof trading company, arrived in the area with 3 ships; after a pitched battle with the natives an understanding was reached, and the Russians constructed several small houses and a commercial building in the area. By 1785 what is believed to have been the first school in Russian

America was holding classes at Three Saints Bay. In 1791, when Alexander Baranof, who would later control all of Russian America, arrived at the bay, it was still the principal Russian settlement in Alaska. However, the following year Baranof moved his headquarters to a new location on Chiniak Bay, to the site of present-day Kodiak (*see*), which became the administrative center of Alaska. NR

METLAKATLA, ON ANNETTE ISLAND

FATHER DUNCAN'S COTTAGE, *Fifth Avenue and Atkinson Street*
This cottage was built about 1891 by Tsimshian Indians for Father William Duncan, an Anglican missionary who was pastor and leader of their society from 1857 until his death in 1919. In 1887 Father Duncan and some 400 Indians came to New Metlakatla from their settlement in British Columbia. By an act of 1891 a reservation was established here, and in 1895 Father Duncan founded the Metlakatla Industrial Company, a cooperative that lasted until 1905. NR

NOME, *Arctic Alaska, on south shore of Seward Peninsula*
The main supply center for the neighboring mining districts and native villages, Nome was the site of a now-legendary gold rush. The rush began when the first large gold placer strike was made in September, 1898, at Anvil Creek, about 4 miles north of present-day Nome. At the time of the strike, Nome (then called Anvil City) had a population of about 1,700. A gold rush camp quickly sprang up in a tent city extending for 15 miles along the Nome beach. By June, 1900, the U.S. Census showed 12,488 people in Nome, and in the next 2 years mining activities spread to the entire Seward Peninsula. Average daily recovery was from $20 to $100 per man. Since then others have mined these beaches with varying results, but 1899 was the banner year with $1 million of gold dust mined. Today Nome's population has shrunk to about 2,000 people. With its unpaved streets and wooden sidewalks, the town retains the "frontier" atmosphere of its gold rush days. The actual **Anvil Creek Gold Discovery Site** (NHL) has long been abandoned.

POINT HOPE PENINSULA

IPIUTAK NATIONAL HISTORIC LANDMARK, *adjacent to Point Hope*
This site, situated on the westernmost point of Alaska's Arctic Slope, contains the remains of an extraordinarily large Eskimo community, which flourished here about A.D. 300. Ipiutak Site encompasses approximately 200 acres of tundra and consists of some 800 house ruins, arranged in 5 long avenues, and a cemetery. The houses were typically Eskimo, built of driftwood logs supplemented with stones and moss and constructed partly beneath the surface of the ground. Other findings include the burial area, consisting of multiple burials in log tombs accompanied by grave offerings. Art objects related to the Scytho-Siberian style have also been discovered here. The most remarkable aspect of Ipiutak culture is that the several thousand inhabitants of this enormous town on the shores of the Arctic were able to procure enough food to feed themselves. They killed seal, walrus, and fish and went far inland to hunt migrating caribou. NR

PORT CHILKOOT

FORT WILLIAM H. SEWARD, *neck of Chilkat Peninsula*
Fort William H. Seward, also known as Chilkoot Barracks, was established next to a Tlingit Indian village by executive order in 1898. It was the last of 11 police garrisons constructed throughout

Left: Russian outpost at Sitka. Right: White Pass and Yukon Railway

the territory of Alaska to keep order during the Alaska gold rush of 1897–1904. It never contained any fortifications and was designed only as a means of imposing order on the booming, often lawless, gold rush frontier. At the end of World War II the fort was bought by private individuals, who incorporated it as the town of Port Chilkoot, which subsequently evolved into the nonprofit Alaska Indian Arts, Inc. Fort Seward originally had some 85 buildings, including officers' quarters that surrounded the parade grounds. Most of the buildings are privately owned; the parade grounds, which may be visited, contain **Totem Village** with a reproduction of a Chilkat tribal house, a replica trapper's cabin, and several large totems. NR

SITKA AND VICINITY

AMERICAN FLAG RAISING SITE NATIONAL HISTORIC LANDMARK, *Castle Hill*

Castle Hill, which overlooks the harbor, was claimed by the Tlingit Indians as their ancestral home. Here early in the 19th century the first Russian governor, Alexander Baranof, built his mansion. At this site on October 18, 1867, against the background of a booming cannon salute, the Russian flag was lowered and the American flag raised over Alaska for the first time. The place where the flagpole stood is marked by a plaque; on the grass-covered site 6 Russian cannon stand pointing out to sea. NR

OLD SITKA SITE NATIONAL HISTORIC LANDMARK, *6 miles north on Starrigavan Bay*

On July 7, 1799, Alexander Baranof, general manager of the Russian-American Trading Company, and a party of Russian fur hunters founded a fortified trading post on this site. At that time the Russians were eager to prevent American, British, and Spanish penetration of southeastern Alaska. By the following year Old Sitka, known also as Redoubt St. Michael, boasted a 2-story building, a blacksmith's shop, Baranof's residence, accommodations for officers and servants, a bathhouse, and a kitchen. In June, 1802, the Tlingit Indians destroyed the settlement in a surprise attack and temporarily frustrated Baranof's attempt to colonize the Alexander Archipelago. NR

ALASKA

RUSSIAN MISSION ORPHANAGE NATIONAL HISTORIC LAND-MARK, *Lincoln and Monastery streets*

Built in 1842 as a mission building, this is a fine example of Russian colonial architecture. The building also served as a school for the children of Russian-American Company employees and as a seminary. The National Parks Service has plans to restore it and open it to visitors. NR

SITKA NATIONAL MONUMENT, *in Sitka*

The monument preserves the site of the 1804 Battle of Sitka—the last stand of the Tlingit Indians against the Russian fur traders—and contains a record of native art and culture. When the Tlingit Indians destroyed the Russian settlement of Old Sitka (*see*) in 1802, its founder, Alexander Baranof, determined to re-establish the colony elsewhere. Two years later Baranof led about 1,000 men to present-day Sitka, roughly 6 miles south of the earlier settlement. As the Russians approached, the Indians withdrew from their village on Castle Hill to a stronger fort near the mouth of Indian River. The Russians besieged the fort for several days; when the Indians fled, they destroyed the fort. Within a short time the town of Sitka, then known as New Archangel, became the flourishing capital of Russian America. Under Baranof's leadership, docks, shipyards, and warehouses were built. All these structures were dominated by the governor's residence, known as **Baranof's Castle.** Below in the town the largest building was **St. Michael's Cathedral** (NR), built between 1848 and 1850 under the direction of Bishop Innocent Veniaminov, first bishop of Alaska. (This Russian Orthodox church, with its characteristic onion domes, was destroyed by fire in 1966, but it is already being restored according to the original designs.) Eventually the Tlingits returned to Sitka and built houses near the Russian settlement, which remained a thriving fur-trading center for over 60 years. Near the monument's visitor center is a valuable collection of Alaskan Indian totem poles that were exhibited at the 1904 St. Louis Exposition. The site of the Tlingit fort is outlined by white stakes; there is a self-guiding trail through the site.
For further information write: Superintendent, Box 738, Sitka, AK 99835

SKAGWAY HISTORIC DISTRICT AND WHITE PASS NATIONAL HISTORIC LANDMARK, *southeast Alaska, head of Taiya Inlet on Lynn Canal*

The town of Skagway grew up as a result of gold discoveries in the Upper Yukon Valley and the Klondike region during the icy winter of 1897–98. Prior to the news of the 1896 gold strike on Klondike Creek, which reached the United States in June, 1897, only one cabin stood on the site of Skagway. Soon hordes of eager would-be prospectors swarmed ashore at Skagway, strategically located on a direct route into the gold-bearing region via the Chilkoot Trail or the White Pass routes. Within a few months Skagway was a thriving city with hotels, saloons, stores, and dance halls, and a population of between 15,000 and 20,000 people. Skagway was also the terminus for the **White Pass and Yukon Route Railway,** completed in 1900. (This picturesque narrow-gauge railway still serves as an important overland link to Whitehorse, Canada.) The historic district contains about 100 buildings, which constitute the largest example of an Alaska frontier mining town. The old Federal court building is now the **Trail of '98 Museum.** White Pass, which is northeast of Skagway, is about 45 miles long with a maximum elevation of 2,880 feet. NR

TANGLE LAKES ARCHAEOLOGICAL DISTRICT, *40 miles west of Paxson on Denali Highway*

This archaeological district, which covers some 460,000 acres, is still much as it was before the first Euro-Americans entered the region and contains more archaeological sites than any other area of comparable size in the American subarctic. Archaeologists speculate that this region may have supported human occupation extending back 12,000–15,000 years, and that some of the earliest men to live in North or South America lived in the Tangle Lakes area. Many artifacts from Tangle Lakes sites show affinities with those from Central Siberia, where early man presumably began his migrations. NR

WRANGELL, *southeast Alaska, on Inside Passage near the mouth of the Stikine River*

One of Alaska's oldest white settlements, Wrangell was founded in 1834 as a Russian fort and trading post. Originally called Redoubt St. Dionysius, Wrangell was named for Baron Ferdinand Petrovich von Wrangell (1794–1870), a Russian explorer who served as governor general of Russian America from 1829 to 1834. The Russian fort was subsequently occupied by the British Hudson's Bay Company, and in 1867, after the Alaska Purchase, it became the U.S. Army's **Fort Wrangell.** The settlement was touched by 2 gold rushes: in 1870 it served as an outfitting center when gold was discovered in the rich Cassier district of Canada, and in 1897–1900 the stampeders went through Wrangell to utilize the Stikine River route to the Klondike.

One of the most interesting places to visit is the **Chief Shakes Historic Site** (NR) on Shakes Island in Wrangell Harbor. A footbridge leads from the mainland to the island. Visitors can see the **Tribal House of the Bear,** a replica of the community house built by the Tlingit Indians, a group of seafaring tribes inhabiting the southern coast of Alaska and northern British Columbia. The ancient Indian carvings in the house and the surrounding totem poles are painted with tribal designs; some are 200 years old.

YAKUTAT

NEW RUSSIA ARCHAEOLOGICAL SITE, *in Tongass National Forest*

These ruins tell the story of New Russia, which the Russians founded in 1796 in an effort to create a more stable base for the settlement of Alaska than that provided by several existing fur-trading posts. New Russia, at the center of a fine otter-hunting region, was also intended as an agricultural and shipbuilding center. The Yakutat colony played another important historical role. Between 1796 and 1805 Russian-Tlingit relations were strained, marked by the Indian destruction of Old Sitka (*see*) in 1802. In 1804 New Russia was a strategic point in the Russians' successful attempt to take the site of present-day Sitka from the Tlingits (*see Sitka National Monument*). In 1805 the Tlingits attacked and burned the colony of New Russia, which at that time reportedly consisted of 7 buildings within a stockade and 5 outside. A subsequent attempt by the Tlingits to destroy another Russian post farther north, on Hinchinbrook Island, led to the Russian massacre of the Indians who had destroyed New Russia. However, in spite of the slaughter of many of their warriors, the Tlingits of the Yakutat region were strong enough to keep white intruders out of the area for almost a century. Today the only evidence that men once occupied New Russia are earth depressions. NR

19

ARIZONA

CAMP VERDE AND VICINITY

FORT VERDE STATE PARK, *east of I-17 in central Arizona*

During the 1870s campaign to subdue the northern Apaches, this military post served as the main base for General George Crook's cavalry patrols, pack trains, and Indian scouts. Three buildings, including the **Pioneer Days Museum,** are open to visitors.

MONTEZUMA CASTLE NATIONAL MONUMENT, *northeast of Camp Verde off I-17*

One of the Southwest's best-preserved Indian ruins, Montezuma Castle nestles high in a limestone cliff overlooking Beaver Creek, a tributary of the Verde River. About A.D. 1100 a tribe of Sinagua Indians migrated from the Flagstaff area to the Verde Valley, where they erected small communal stone pueblos, farmed, and mixed with the local Hohokam Indians. By 1250 the Sinagua were building large structures on hilltops or in cliffs. The sheltering cavernlike recesses of the cliffs above Beaver Creek provided an ideal natural setting for the 5-story apartment clusters, which were constructed of limestone chunks and river boulders bound with adobe mortar and contained 20 rooms that were said to house 50 persons. Another group of dwellings to the west, known as **Castle A,** consisted of 45 rooms that accommodated 200 people. These habitations were occupied for 2 centuries. NR

For further information write: Camp Verde, AZ 86322

CANYON DE CHELLY NATIONAL MONUMENT, *headquarters at Chinle off State 63*

Built directly into or nestled at the base of the sheer red sandstone cliffs of Canyon de Chelly and its offshoots—Canyon del Muerto

Left: Montezuma Castle cliff dwelling. Above: the OK Corral at Tombstone. Below: San Xavier del Bac Mission near Tucson

and Black Rock and Monument canyons—are ruins of several hundred Pueblo Indian villages. Erected between A.D. 350 and 1300, these settlements represent four periods of Indian culture. The earliest tribe, the Basket Makers, or early Anasazi, lived in individual circular houses constructed over pits dug in the ground. From approximately 700 to 1300, Pueblos, or later Anasazi, occupied the area in large apartment-style cliff houses of stone masonry that were connected in compact villages. About 1300 a severe drought forced the Pueblos to migrate to other parts of the Southwest. The canyons were subsequently occupied by the Hopi Indians, relatives of the Pueblos, who cultivated the canyon bottoms. About 1700, warlike Navajo Indians swept down from northern New Mexico and made Canyon de Chelly their chief stronghold. In 1805 a detachment of Spanish troops under Lieutenant Antonio Narbona defeated a band of Navajos who had hidden themselves in a rock shelter now known as **Massacre Cave**. And in 1864 Kit Carson, leading a U.S. cavalry unit, defeated the Navajos and removed the survivors to new lands in New Mexico. This reservation experiment failed, and eventually the Navajos were permitted to return. Today the Navajos keep their summer homes—circular structures of poles and logs called hogans—here. The best known of of the cliff dwellings is **White House**, the only site within the monument that tourists may visit without guides. Other ruins are the **Mummy Cave, Antelope House,** and **Standing Cow.** NR
For further information write: Box 588, Chinle, AZ 86503

COOLIDGE

CASA GRANDE NATIONAL MONUMENT, *2 miles north on State 87*
The 4-story tower of packed earthen walls that dominates these ruins in the Gila Valley was built in approximately A.D. 1350 by Hohokam Indian farmers. Although the purpose of this remarkable structure is unknown, Casa Grande may have served as a fortress or ceremonial building. Surrounding the tower are the remains of a walled village of 60 to 90 individual single-room houses of mud and brush. The Hohokam settled in the arid Gila Valley as early as 400 B.C.; their most notable achievement was the construction of a complex irrigation system with over 600 miles of canals—evidences of which can still be seen—that enabled them to grow cotton, corn, beans, and squash. By 1450 Casa Grande and its village had been abandoned. In 1694 Father Eusebio Francisco Kino became the first European to discover this site, which was by then in partial ruins, and he gave the tower its present name, the Spanish words for "big house." NR
For further information write: Superintendent, Coolidge, AZ 85228

CORONADO NATIONAL MEMORIAL, *30 miles west of Bisbee off State 92*
Spanish nobleman Francisco Vásquez de Coronado, leader of the first major European expedition to explore the American Southwest, crossed from Mexico into what is now the United States near this site. In February, 1540, Coronado, with a contingent of cavalry, foot soldiers, priests, and Mexican-Indian allies—totaling some 1,350 people—set out from Mexico City in quest of the Seven Cities of Cíbola. After 5 months of rugged travel, Coronado's company came upon one of the fabled cities, which in reality turned out to be the rock-masonry pueblos of a village named Háwikuh, inhabited by Zuñi Indians and located near the present town of Gallup, New Mexico. Undaunted, Coronado and his men continued their quest for wealth, this time journeying as far east as the plains of

central Kansas. Returning to Mexico City in 1542 with no treasure and only a remnant of his once formidable force, Coronado was deemed a failure. However, his expedition provided useful information about the territories north of Mexico when exploration of these' regions was finally resumed 40 years later. At this memorial one may take a foot trail to Coronado Peak, which provides a view of the route the Spaniards took across the San Pedro Valley before entering this country. NR

For further information write: Star Route, Hereford, AZ 85615

FLAGSTAFF VICINITY

TUZIGOOT NATIONAL MONUMENT, *about 33 miles southwest of Flagstaff off U.S. 89A*

The remnants of this extensive fortified pueblo occupy the summit and higher terraces of a long limestone ridge 120 feet above the Verde Valley. About A.D. 1125 Sinagua Indian farmers began to erect a small cluster of masonry dwellings—about 15 or 20 rooms—that accommodated approximately 50 people. The structure changed little over the next century. However, severe droughts occurring between 1215 and 1299 caused farmers from the nearby valley flats to come to this area, with its permanent spring-fed streams and a working system of irrigation ditches. Thus the population of Tuzigoot quadrupled, and additions to the pueblo were made; by the end of the drought, Tuzigoot boasted 2 stories and 92 rooms, averaging 12 by 18 feet. During the 1300s Tuzigoot attained its present size of 110 rooms. By 1450 this pueblo and others in the Verde Valley had been abandoned, possibly as a result of overpopulation, inadequate arable land, and strife. NR

For further information write: Box 68, Clarkdale, AZ 86324

WALNUT CANYON NATIONAL MONUMENT, *8 miles east of Flagstaff via I-40*

Built into recesses along the walls of this 400-foot-deep canyon are the remains of over 300 Sinagua cliff dwellings. The Sinagua, who migrated here from northcentral Arizona in 1065, utilized the canyon's cavelike recesses and projecting limestone ledges to create homes protected from the elements. Skilled masons, they made front walls, room, and house partitions out of double slabs of limestone filled with mud. Mud was also used as mortar, and packed and dried for flooring. After living in Walnut Canyon for 150 years, the Sinagua evacuated their snug homesites for reasons unknown. NR

For further information write: Box 790, Flagstaff, AZ 86001

WUPATKI NATIONAL MONUMENT, *about 45 miles northeast of Flagstaff via U.S. 89*

More than 800 Indian ruins, representing a variety of cultures and ranging from small earth lodges on mesa tops to large pueblos, are contained within this monument. When the nearby Sunset Crater erupted in 1065, a layer of volcanic ash was deposited for hundreds of miles, transforming the soil into excellent farmland. News of this fertile area spread, and Indians, including Pueblo dry farmers from the northeast, Hohokam irrigation farmers from central Arizona, Mogollon tribes to the southeast, and the Cohonino to the west, flocked to the region already inhabited by the Sinagua, which became the most densely populated part of northern Arizona. Here between 1100 and 1225 they erected and occupied several villages. Wupatki, the Hopi word for "tall house," was the largest pueblo in the area with 100 rooms and parts consisting of 3 stories. Adjacent

to Wupatki are an open-air amphitheater, probably used for cere-
monials, and a stone-masonry ball court, one of the 2 found in
Arizona. Wind erosion of the volcanic ash and a severe drought in
1215 combined to force the Indians to desert this site by 1225. NR
For further information: Tuba Star Route, Flagstaff, AZ 86001

FORT BOWIE NATIONAL HISTORIC SITE, *13 miles south of Bowie off State
86*

From the 1860s through the 1880s, this stronghold in **Apache Pass**
offered protection to travelers crossing the Chiricahua Mountains.
Apache Indians would conceal themselves in the heights of this
4-mile-long gorge and ambush passing wagon trains and mail
couriers. During the Civil War, in 1862, California Volunteers
erected this fort near a running stream not far from an old stage
station. The post soon became a major base in the government's
wars against the Apaches. Troops garrisoned at Fort Bowie succeeded, in 1872, in forcing the Indian leader Cochise to accept a
truce. Other rebel chieftains were exiled from Arizona. By 1894
peace reigned over Apache Pass, and Fort Bowie was abandoned.
Today ruins of the old fort and stage station, as well as remnants of
the wagon-rutted **Butterfield Trail,** may be visited. NR
*For further information write: c/o Chiricahua National Monument,
Dos Cabezas Star Route, Willcox, AZ 85643*

GANADO
HUBBELL TRADING POST NATIONAL HISTORIC SITE, *1 mile west
off State 264*

This trading post on the Navajo Indian reservation, the oldest extant
post of its kind, was established in 1878 by John Lorenzo Hubbell.
Hubbell encouraged the Navajos to produce fine handicrafts—
especially rugs and silver jewelry. He also acted as mentor, writing
and translating letters for the Indians, explaining government
policy, and settling disputes. A legendary host, Hubbell entertained
leading personalities of the day—Theodore Roosevelt dubbed the
merchant "Lorenzo the Magnificent." Today Navajos still purchase
their supplies at the post, where fine examples of craftsmanship
are on display. NR
For further information write: Box 388, Ganado, AZ 86505

. **GILA BEND VICINITY**
PAINTED ROCKS STATE HISTORIC PARK, *15 miles west of Gila Bend
on I-8, 10 miles north on Painted Rocks Road*

Indian petroglyphs cover 50-foot-high rocks for nearly an acre in
this park. These remarkable drawings of snakes, turtles, birds, men,
and other figures were probably made in historic times to demarcate
the boundary between territories of the Yuma and Maricopa Indians.

JEROME HISTORIC DISTRICT NATIONAL HISTORIC LANDMARK,
on U.S. 89A

Almost a ghost town today, Jerome once was one of the great copper-
mining centers of the world. In 1883 the United Verde Mine
incorporated to develop the area, which was named after Eugene
Jerome, the company's major backer. Gradually, despite periodic
fires, a community of picturesque frame buildings on stilts grew up
along narrow, steep streets on the side of Cleopatra Mountain.
Jerome reached its peak as a copper-producing complex in 1929,
boasting a population of 15,000. In 1952 declining copper prices
and the exhaustion of ore deposits led to the closing of the main

mine and a population exodus. NR. The **James H. Douglas Mansion** in Jerome State Historic Park houses a mining museum.

NAVAJO NATIONAL MONUMENT, *32 miles southwest of Kayenta off State 64*
Three of the largest and most elaborate of the pueblo cliff dwellings are preserved at this site in the high plateau country of the Southwest. In the early part of the 12th century, the Anasazi farmers of the San Juan basin began to combine their hamlets into large villages; these cliff dwellings, built between A.D. 1225 and 1300, along with a variety of artifacts—especially pottery—of the same period, represent the culmination of Anasazi culture. **Betatakin** (Navajo for "lodge house") is the most accessible ruin and the site of monument headquarters. This structure contains 135 rooms—living quarters, courts, storage areas, granaries, and a kiva, or ceremonial room. Constructed between 1240 and 1282, **Keet Seel** (Navajo for "broken pottery") is the largest of the cliff dwellings, with 350 rooms. **Inscription House** consists of 75 rooms. By 1300 drought and erosion had caused the Anasazi to abandon these homes. Navajos settled in the region in the 19th century. NR
For further information write: Superintendent, Tonalea, AZ 86044

NOGALES VICINITY
PETE KITCHEN MUSEUM, *about 3 miles north of Nogales off U.S. 89*
From his fortress-ranch in the Santa Cruz Valley, the rugged settler Peter Kitchen held the fierce Apaches at bay for 25 years. Kitchen established his ranch in 1854, and although such formidable Apache adversaries as Cochise and Geronimo stole or killed his horses and cattle and scalped his son, Kitchen refused to be driven from his ranch. Armed sentries stood watch from the rooftop, while the house itself was a veritable arsenal. Over the years the ranch developed a reputation for being the safest place on the long road from Tucson to Mexico. Today a replica of the oldest continuously occupied ranch in Arizona has been made into a museum that contains relics of the region's colorful past. The adjacent **Kino Chapel** houses precious relics associated with the Jesuit missions.

Left: an 1890s photograph showing John Lorenzo Hubbell trading for a Navajo blanket. Right: an interior view of his trading post near Ganado

TUMACACORI NATIONAL MONUMENT, *18 miles north on U.S. 89*
The frontier mission of San José de Tumacacori represents the northernmost outpost of the Sonora mission chain, founded by Jesuit priests in the 17th century. In 1691 Father Eusebio Francisco Kino converted the Pima Indians of Tumacacori village and introduced ranching to the area. Father Kino's successors regularly visited Tumacacori, where they held services. After the Pima rebellion of 1751 the settlement was moved a few miles to its present site, where a small mission was erected and renamed San José de Tumacacori. When the Franciscans took over the Sonora mission chain in 1768, Tumacacori became the most important mission in the region. During the height of mission activity, between 1790 and the end of Spanish rule in 1821, the baroque church currently occupying the site was constructed. After 1821 the newly independent Mexican government stopped providing funds to support the frontier missions, and the last resident priest at Tumacacori departed before 1840. Apache raids made conditions in the region so intolerable that the devout Indian converts abandoned the mission in 1848, taking the church furnishings with them to San Xavier del Bac, near Tucson (*see*). Today, although the living quarters, granaries, and other buildings surrounding the courtyard have fallen into ruin, the church still stands—a sturdy symbol of the mission period. NR
For further information write: Box 67, Tumacacori, AZ 85640

ORAIBI
OLD ORAIBI NATIONAL HISTORIC LANDMARK, *3 miles west on State 264*
Old Oraibi vies with Acoma, New Mexico, as being the oldest continuously occupied pueblo in the Southwest. Since about 1150 the village has been inhabited by Hopi Indians, the only ancient Pueblo tribe to flourish in modern times. Situated atop a narrow, rocky mesa, this pueblo comprises 7 rows of 3- or 4-story houses of stone masonry with adobe mortar, 13 ceremonial kivas, and several enclosed courts. Gradually a newer pueblo grew up around the base of the mesa. NR

PHOENIX AND VICINITY
HOHOKAM-PIMA IRRIGATION SITES NATIONAL HISTORIC LANDMARK, *Park of the Four Waters*
The sophisticated system of irrigation developed by the Pima and Hohokam peoples of the Gila and Salt river regions is revealed at these sites. Constructed with hand tools between A.D. 1200 and 1400, this maze of canals and ditches was effectively watering thousands of acres of farmland when Spanish explorers first visited the area in 1687. Some of the canals are still functioning today in conjunction with modern irrigation systems. NR

PUEBLO GRANDE RUIN NATIONAL HISTORIC LANDMARK, *Pueblo Grande City Park*
Today enveloped by modern Phoenix, this Hohokam ruin, built between A.D. 900 and 1450, includes a large house mound surrounded by jacal and caliche-walled houses some 20 feet below on the desert floor. NR

STATE CAPITOL, *Washington Street and 17th Avenue*
Completed in 1900, this building served as the territorial capitol, and later as the State House after Arizona joined the Union in 1912.

James Riley Gordon of San Antonio designed the Roman Revival structure, which was built almost entirely of materials indigenous to Arizona: the malpais foundation is from the Camelback Mountain area; the upper walls are of porous tufa stone from the mountains of Yavapai County; and the first floor is of gray granite from the Salt River Mountains. Wings were added to the capitol in 1918 and 1939. A museum contains Indian artifacts and murals, painted by Jay Datus, depicting Arizona history.

Guided tours: weekdays at 10 and 2:30

PIPE SPRING NATIONAL MONUMENT, *15 miles southwest of Fredonia off U.S. 89 via State 389*

The historic fort and museum within this monument commemorate the Mormon pioneers who explored, settled, and developed this picturesque region just south of the Arizona-Utah border. Late in 1858 a party of Mormon missionaries led by Jacob Hamblin discovered a flowing spring on the Moccasin terrace of the Markagunt Plateau. Tradition has it that the site was named when William "Gunlock" Hamblin exhibited his marksmanship here by shooting the bottom out of a smoking pipe—hence "Pipe Spring." During the next few years, stockmen began migrating to the area and established ranches on the grasslands. In 1866, however, marauding bands of Navajos, pursued by the U.S. Army, claimed the lives of several ranchers, and the settlement was temporarily evacuated. By the spring of 1867 the Utah territorial militia was conducting its campaign against the Indians from Pipe Spring. Three years later Brigham Young and other elders of the Mormon church dispatched Anson Perry Winsor to Pipe Spring to establish a cattle and dairy ranch and build a fort to protect the homesteaders. NR

For further information write: Moccasin, AZ 86022

PRESCOTT, *central Arizona, off U.S. 89*

Prescott, the first capital of the Arizona territory, was born in May, 1864, when Governor John N. Goodwin removed the seat of government from a walled tent at Fort Whipple to a site 18 miles to the southwest. A sturdy log residence built by Goodwin was used simultaneously as the governor's office, state capitol, and military commandant's headquarters. In 1867 the territorial capital was transferred to Tucson; from 1877 to 1889 the capital returned to Prescott, after which time it was removed permanently to Phoenix. The world's first rodeo was held in Prescott on July 4, 1888. The event is still celebrated annually. The **Old Governor's Mansion** (NR) is now maintained as the Sharlot Hall Museum, housing Indian artifacts and Victorian furnishings. Nearby stands **Old Fort Misery,** a reconstruction of Prescott's first cabin. Other early structures may be seen around **Pioneer Square.**

TOMBSTONE HISTORIC DISTRICT NATIONAL HISTORIC LANDMARK, *off U.S. 80*

Known today as the Town Too Tough to Die, Tombstone earned an unparalleled reputation in the 1880s for its lawlessness and violence. In 1877 the prospector Ed Schieffelin, despite warnings that the only mineral wealth to be found would be his tombstone, ventured into the inhospitable reaches of southeastern Arizona, where he struck a rich silver lode that he named Tombstone. Almost overnight a community of tents, hastily constructed shacks, dance halls, and saloons sprang up around Schieffelin's claim. By 1881 the boom town boasted a population of 7,000 that during the decade more than doubled. Although Tombstone inevitably attracted a large percentage of desperados and gamblers, the town was perhaps the most cultivated city of its day in the Southwest: it featured its own opera house, where some of the world's best actors and musicians performed. Built in 1882, **St. Paul's Episcopal Church** (NR) was the first Protestant church to be erected in Arizona. Floods occurring in 1886 and 1887 finally forced the mines to shut down, and by 1900 the city was nearly deserted. Today many old landmarks serve to revivify the community's colorful past. They include the **Bird Cage Theatre**, with its 14 private boxes, which seated the town's leading citizens, suspended from the ceiling; the **Crystal Palace Gambling Casino**, now restored to its former splendor; the **OK Corral** (site of the famous Earp-Clanton gunfight in 1881) and nearby stagecoach house and stable; the **Wyatt Earp Museum**, housing that family's mementos; and the **Tombstone Courthouse**, an imposing Victorian structure dating from 1882 that has been converted into a museum. Near Tombstone's northern limits is the desolate **Boothill Graveyard.** NR

TONTO NATIONAL MONUMENT, *28 miles northwest of Globe on State 88*
Situated high above Roosevelt Lake on the scenic Apache Trail, these cliff dwellings were built in the mid-1300s by the Salado Indian inhabitants of the rugged Tonto Basin. They represent the best-preserved, most accessible structures of their kind in south-central Arizona. A sedentary tribe residing in the Tonto Basin since well before A.D. 900, the Salado cultivated crops in the nearby Salt River Valley. They erected their cliff dwellings, now known as **Upper Ruin, Lower Ruin,** and **Lower Ruin Annex,** comprising 40, 19, and 12 rooms respectively, in 2 natural caves. These homes were constructed of unshaped blocks of quartzite laid in adobe mortar, with roofs of large poles overlaid with smaller poles and a layer of adobe. Artifacts found in the Tonto ruins indicate that the Salado were skilled craftsmen; they produced excellent plain pottery as well as a distinctive type known as Salado polychrome, vessels with intricate designs in their interiors. Remnants of exquisitely woven cotton fabrics have also been discovered. After 1400, as part of a general exodus of Pueblo tribes from the mountains, the Salado abandoned Tonto Basin. NR
For further information write: Superintendent, Roosevelt, AZ 85545

TUCSON AND VICINITY
FREMONT (CARILLO) HOUSE, *145–153 South Main Street*
John C. Frémont, military commander of the U.S. forces invading California during the Mexican War, is believed to have resided in this house while serving as fifth territorial governor of Arizona from 1878 to 1882. This fine example of Mexican-Spanish architecture was constructed as early as 1858. In 1878 Leopoldo Carrillo, a leading Tucson businessman and landowner, acquired the property; he remodeled the house 2 years later. The Arizona Historical Society maintains the building as a public museum. NR
Open: Mon, Wed, Fri 9–1

SAN XAVIER DEL BAC MISSION NATIONAL HISTORIC LANDMARK, *9 miles south via Mission Road*
This mission has been celebrated as the most beautiful as well as the best-preserved example of mission architecture in the Spanish Southwest. In 1692 the Jesuit missionary Father Eusebio Francisco Kino (*see also Nogales, Tumacacori National Monument*) came

upon a Pima Indian village in southern Arizona that he named after his patron saint, Francis Xavier. Kino subsequently introduced cattle ranching to the community and in 1700 he established a mission, which was later destroyed in the Pima Indian revolt of 1751. After 1767 Franciscans took over the mission and attended, from 1783 to 1797, to the construction of the profusely ornamented present church of stucco-covered brick. The church fell into neglect after the Mexican government secularized its missions in 1821. San Xavier del Bac became United States property in the Gadsden Purchase of 1853 and was eventually restored. Today the church is a thriving parish on the San Xavier Indian Reservation. NR

TUBAC PRESIDIO STATE HISTORIC PARK, *45 miles south of Tucson on I-19*

Since it was founded in the Santa Cruz Valley in 1752, this military post has successively flown the Spanish, Mexican, and American flags. After 1776 the Spanish garrison was transferred to Tucson, and the local inhabitants were left to fend for themselves. Under Mexican government auspices, troops were restationed in 1828 to protect a nearby silver mine. A party of Mormons on the way to California encamped at the presidio from 1850 to 1851, but 3 years later it was reported abandoned. The arrival of Charles DeBrille Poston with some 300 Texas miners in 1856 temporarily revived the fort. The presidio was again deserted during the Civil War; it fell prey to the Apaches and was almost totally in ruins by 1908. Today remains of the presidio and a museum can be visited. NR

YUMA AND VICINITY

SANGUINETTI HOUSE (CENTURY HOUSE AND GARDENS), *240 Madison Avenue*

The Arizona Historical Society operates this old adobe structure as a museum depicting the early history of Yuma. It was the home of one of the town's early merchants, Eugene F. Sanguinetti.

YUMA CROSSING AND ASSOCIATED SITES NATIONAL HISTORIC LANDMARK, *on the banks of the Colorado River on U.S. 95*

This site on the Colorado River was important in Spanish colonial times, as well as during the period of American westward expansion, as a transportation and communication gateway to California. In 1540 Fernando de Alarçon, while exploring the Colorado River, became the first white man to pass through what is now the town of Yuma. About 1700 Father Eusebio Kino, in his search for a route to California, also visited this area. After gold was discovered in California, the United States obtained permission from Mexico to establish an emigrant route here—the **Gila River Trail**. A passenger ferry began operating in 1849, and the following year **Fort Yuma** was founded on the California side of the river. In the 1850s the Butterfield Overland Mail sped through here. Meanwhile, on the Arizona side, a small community began to grow that was originally named Colorado City, but was officially designated Yuma by the territorial legislature in 1873. Yuma soon became the most important community in southwestern Arizona. In 1876 the first **Territorial Prison** was erected on a bluff overlooking the river; some of the Old West's most dangerous desperados were confined in its dungeons and cell blocks until the prison shut down in 1909. Today the ruins of Fort Yuma, the **Yuma Charterhouse Depot**, opposite the fort, as well as the nearby prison—now **Yuma Territorial Prison State Park**—may be visited. NR

ARKANSAS

ARKANSAS POST NATIONAL MEMORIAL, 8 *miles southeast of Gillett off State 1 and 169*

In 1686 Henri de Tonti established a French settlement in this vicinity—the first European outpost in the region. Little is known about the sites of the first 2 French forts built in the Arkansas Post area; however, the site of a third fort, built by Lieutenant Chevalier de la Houssaye in 1752, is included within this 62-acre national memorial. For 11 years **De la Houssaye's Fort** served as a fur-trading center, church mission, and mustering station for France's Indian allies. In 1762 Spain gained control of the territory and 16 years later built **Fort San Carlos III** at the site of De la Houssaye's post. The new fort protected a thriving farming community, which had grown to more than 60 families by 1800. Then after 1803, when the Louisiana Purchase made Arkansas Post an American village, settlers poured into the area and the post became the first capital of Arkansas Territory in 1819. The town prospered as a trading center and Arkansas River port and was also the starting point for the first overland road into the interior. The *Arkansas Gazette,* still an important newspaper, was first published here in 1819. During the Civil War the Confederates built **Fort Hindman** at Arkansas Post. On January 10, 1863, Federal troops under General John A. McClernand attacked the fort, defended by General Thomas Churchill. A Federal fleet under Admiral David D. Porter sailed up the Arkansas River to give support to McClernand. The post soon fell to the 2-pronged Union assault. The advent of the railroads late in the 19th century marked the decline of steamboat commerce and with it, the town. NR

For further information write: Supervisor, Gillett, AR 72055

Left: the Louisiana Purchase survey marker. Right: the First State Capitol at Little Rock

ARKANSAS

CAMDEN VICINITY
POISON SPRINGS BATTLEFIELD STATE PARK, *18 miles northwest off State 24*

This park is at the site of a Confederate victory that helped stop the Union invasion of Texas during the Civil War. At Poison Springs on April 18, 1864, Confederate forces commanded by General John S. Marmaduke attacked and routed a large Federal supply train commanded by Colonel James M. Williams. After heavy fighting the Federals withdrew, abandoning about 200 wagons. This was a severe blow to the Union attempt to join the Red River campaign of 1864, in which Federal troops under General N. Prentiss Banks unsuccessfully tried to move into Texas. NR

EUREKA SPRINGS
EUREKA SPRINGS HISTORIC DISTRICT

One of the oldest health resorts in the Ozark region, Eureka Springs still preserves much of its late-19th-century flavor. The historic district consists of approximately 2 square miles in what was once the commercial and residential section of the town. The original wooden commercial structures were destroyed by fire in 1883 and were rebuilt in stone between 1883 and 1900. Most of the buildings in the district remain as they were then. The overall architectural style shows strong elements of the American Renaissance style popular in the East. NR

HATCHET HALL, *31 Steel Street*

Carry A. Nation, the ardent prohibitionist who became famous for chopping up saloons with her hatchet, lived here for the last 3 years of her life, 1908–11. The frame building was built in 1883 as a boarding house. Next door Mrs. Nation ran an academy for training young prohibitionists. Hatchet Hall now houses a small art museum.
Open: summer weekdays, 9:30–5:30. Admission: 50¢

FAYETTEVILLE AND VICINITY
HEADQUARTERS HOUSE (TEBBETTS HOUSE), *118 East Dickson Street*

This Greek Revival frame house was built about 1853 by Jonas Tebbetts, a wealthy lawyer, judge, and member of the state legislature. A Union sympathizer during the Civil War, Tebbetts fled to Missouri in 1862. The residence is so named because it was used as headquarters by Union Colonel M. LaRue Harrison prior to and during the Battle of Fayetteville, on April 18, 1863. It was during this battle that a hole, still visible today, was shot through one of the doors. When Harrison and his troops departed after the battle, Confederate General W. L. Cabell, who had led the Confederates in the Battle of Fayetteville, used the Tebbetts House as his headquarters. NR
Open: June 1–Oct 31, Tues–Sun 2–4

OLD MAIN, *Arkansas Avenue, on University of Arkansas campus*

Founded in 1871, the University of Arkansas now has 40 buildings on its 140-acre campus. Old Main, the administrative building completed in 1879, continues to be the identifying landmark of the university. A 4-story brick building, it was designed by Chicago architect John M. Van Osdel as an approximate copy of the Old Main at the University of Illinois. The **University Museum** is on the fourth floor. NR

PRAIRIE GROVE BATTLEFIELD PARK, *10 miles southwest via U.S. 62*
This park embraces 65 acres in the heart of the battlefield where
on December 7, 1862, Civil War hostilities in northwest Arkansas
were renewed on a major scale for the first time since the Battle of
Pea Ridge (*see*) in March. On November 28, 1862, General James G.
Blunt's Federal army, which held northwest Arkansas, had been
attacked by the newly organized Arkansas defense troops under
Confederate General Thomas Hindman. In response to Blunt's
request for reinforcements, General Francis J. Herron marched
down from Springfield, Missouri. On December 7 Herron and his
army were met at Prairie Grove by Hindman, determined to anni-
hilate the Federal reinforcements before they could reach Blunt.
However, Blunt's unexpected arrival at the battlefield during the
afternoon saved the day for the Union. That night the Confederates,
low on supplies and ammunition, withdrew to Van Buren. Visitors
can see the battle lines, which have been marked, and the restored
buildings of **Vineyard Village,** an Arkansas pioneer settlement
dating from the mid-19th century. The **Hindman Hall Museum**
contains Civil War relics. NR

FORDYCE VICINITY

MARKS' MILLS BATTLEFIELD PARK, *about 10 miles southeast off
State 8*
The Battle of Marks' Mill occurred here on April 25, 1864, when
Confederate troops under General James Fagan attacked and cap-
tured a Federal supply train urgently needed by General Frederick
Steele. Steele had been attempting to move his troops south-
westward from Little Rock toward Shreveport. He got as far as
Camden, Arkansas, where he awaited the arrival of a supply train
due from Pine Bluff. At Marks' Mill Fagan surprised the supply
train, capturing 240 wagonloads and many prisoners. Steele, whose
men were left without food and ammunition, headed back toward
Little Rock. Another skirmish took place 5 days later while Steele's
forces were crossing the Saline River at Jenkins' Ferry (*see
Sheridan*). NR

FORT SMITH NATIONAL HISTORIC SITE, *on Rogers Avenue between 2nd and 3rd streets*

Established in 1817 as one of the first U.S. military posts in the
Louisiana Territory, Fort Smith remained the center of law and
order for a vast area of untamed western frontier during some 80
years. Here one can see the stone foundations of the first fort (1817–
39) built on this site. An unimposing wooden structure, it was
situated at Belle Point, a rocky bluff overlooking the confluence
of the Poteau and Arkansas rivers. Its purpose was twofold: to
prevent warfare between the native Osage Indians and the
Cherokees, who were new arrivals from the southern Appalachians;
and to prevent white men from encroaching on Indian lands. The
garrison was successful in keeping the peace, and in 1839 the Army
abandoned it. In 1836, when Arkansas was admitted to the Union,
the citizens demanded protection from possible Indian uprisings.
Thus in 1839 the Army commenced building a new Fort Smith near
the earlier one. But the frontier had already moved farther west,
and the fort soon came to be used merely as a supply depot. During
the Civil War Fort Smith served as a hospital. In 1872 the Federal
Court for the Western District of Arkansas (which included 74,000
miles of Indian territory) established quarters in the former barracks
building of Fort Smith. Here from 1875 until his death in 1896, the

famous "Hanging Judge," Isaac C. Parker, presided over a court, keeping peace in the lawless territory. The only significant remains of the second fort are the old stone **Commisary Building** and **Judge Parker's Courtroom,** which has been restored. NR

For further information write: Box 1406, Fort Smith, AR 72902

LITTLE ROCK AND VICINITY

FIRST STATE CAPITOL, *300 West Markham Street*
This fine example of ante-bellum architecture, often called the Old State House, served as the state capitol from 1836 until 1911. In September, 1863, when Little Rock was occupied by Union forces, the state government fled from this building to the town of Washington *(see),* where the Confederate state capitol remained until the end of the Civil War. Early in 1864, however, a Union state government was organized in the Old State House, and in 1865 this government extended its authority over the entire state. Many of the rooms of the capitol have been restored with period antiques. NR

Open: Mon–Fri 8–4:30, Sat–Sun 1–5

THE "LITTLE ROCK," *foot of Rock Street*
The "Little Rock," from which the capital city takes its name, was discovered in 1722 by Benard de la Harpe, one of the first Europeans to ascend the Arkansas River to this site. At present only a portion of the original rock remains, but the remnant is quite large, rising about 18 feet above the level of the river and extending for a distance of about 40 feet along the south riverbank. The Little Rock, at one time probably taller than the riverbank, served as a landmark for travelers approaching the site from downstream. The rock was used as the beginning point of the Quapaw line—the western boundary of the Quapaw Indian lands, which were surveyed in 1818. It was also the starting point for most of the land surveys south of the Arkansas River. NR

OLD ARSENAL, *9th and Commerce streets, in MacArthur Park*
The Old Arsenal, or "Tower Building," a 2-story brick structure with an octagonal crenelated tower, was built by the U.S. Army Corps of Engineers as a military post to protect frontier Arkansas and as a storage place for arms and ammunition. The Little Rock Arsenal, completed in 1840, was originally a complex of 27 buildings. Today only the **Tower Building** remains. In August of 1862 the Little Rock Arsenal became an official Confederate ordnance station. After the Civil War the arsenal functioned as a peacetime military post. General Douglas MacArthur was born here on January 26, 1880, some 10 years before the post was deactivated. The Old Arsenal now houses the **Museum of Science and Natural History.** NR

Museum open: Tues–Sat 10–5, Sun 2–5

TEN MILE HOUSE, *10 miles southwest on east side of State 5*
This 2-story brick house, often called Stagecoach House, was built sometime between 1822 and 1835. Route 5, on which the residence stands, was once a part of the **Old Southwest Trail.** When Little Rock was occupied by Federal troops in September of 1863, General Frederick Steele's forces used the house as an outpost. It was here that David Owen Dodd, boy martyr of the Confederacy, was held prisoner after his capture by Federal troops. Dodd was executed as a spy at the age of 17. NR

TERRITORIAL CAPITOL RESTORATION, *Cumberland and 3rd streets*
This state-financed historical museum comprises 13 structures on a half block of land in downtown Little Rock. The restoration re-creates the appearance of Little Rock in the spirited prestatehood era. The **Territorial Capitol,** a hand-hewn cypress log house built in 1820 and sometimes known as The Tavern or Jesse Hinderliter House, was the meeting place of the last territorial legislature, October 5 to November 16, 1835. The **Noland House,** built early in the 1830s, was the home of the man who was officially delegated to deliver Arkansas' first constitution to Washington, D.C. The **Con-way House,** also dating from the 1830s, was the home of Elias N. Conway, territorial auditor and fifth governor of Arkansas (1852–60). The **Woodruff Group,** in the northeast corner of the restoration, was the home and office of William E. Woodruff and the second home of the *Arkansas Gazette,* the oldest continuously published news-paper west of the Mississippi.
Open: Apr 1–Oct 1, Tues–Sat 9:30–5; Sun, Mon 1–5. Oct 1–Apr 1, Tues–Sat 10–4:30; Sun, Mon 1–4:30. Admission: adults 30¢

LOUISIANA PURCHASE SURVEY MARKER, *at junction of Lee, Monroe, and Phillips counties*
This marker, which stands in a grove of cypress trees in the middle of a swamp in eastern Arkansas, indicates the point from which surveys of the newly acquired Louisiana Purchase of 1803 were determined. The marker is still the starting point from which all townships and section lines in Arkansas, Missouri, Iowa, and Minnesota are based. NR

NEWPORT
JACKSONPORT STATE PARK, *3 miles northwest of Newport on State 69*
Situated on the banks of the White River, this 90-acre park features the **Jacksonport Courthouse** (1861), the only extant structure of what was a thriving river town between 1833 and the coming of the railroad in 1872. The courthouse, which has been restored, has a mansard roof and 3-foot-thick brick walls built to withstand the floods at high water. Inside is a museum commemorating the court-house as one of the main mustering points for the Confederate Army of Northern Arkansas. The *Mary Woods II,* last of the steamboats to ply the river, is permanently berthed along the riverbank here. NR

NORFORK VICINITY
MAJOR JACOB WOLF HOUSE, *on State 5, 16 miles south of Mountain Home*
Reputed to be the first 2-story log home built in Arkansas Territory, this house was erected about 1809 by Major Jacob Wolf, an Indian agent for this part of the territory who may have been the first white man to settle here. The cabin served as the first courthouse in Arkansas, as one of the first post offices, and as a post for trading with the Indians. Wolf built a ferry, a blacksmith shop, and a saw and gristmill.
Open: Mon–Sat 12–4, Sun 2–6. Admission: adults 50¢, children 25¢

PEA RIDGE NATIONAL MILITARY PARK, *11 miles northeast of Rogers, adjacent to U.S. 62*
Pea Ridge, just south of the Missouri border, was the site of the Federal victory that secured Missouri for the Union and influenced the course of the Civil War throughout the Mississippi Valley. This park preserves the entire battlefield where, on March 7–8, 1862, this

decisive Civil War action took place. Brigadier General Samuel R. Curtis, who was in charge of the Union mission to gain control of Missouri, began his campaign in southwestern Missouri late in December, 1861. By February, 1862, Curtis' Federals had forced the Confederates of the Missouri state guard to retreat into Arkansas. By the end of the month the inadequate Confederate army had been enlarged with regular troops and was encamped in the Boston Mountains about midway between Fayetteville and Fort Smith (*see*). On March 3 Major General Earl Van Dorn, grandnephew of Andrew Jackson, took command of the Confederate forces. Early in the day of March 7, 1862, 2 areas of battle developed: one near **Elkhorn Tavern,** the other 2 miles away near a little hamlet called **Leetown.** The 2 areas were separated by Round Top Mountain and other high ground. On the first day the Confederate army, which included an Indian brigade, won at Elkhorn Tavern but was decisively beaten at Leetown. The next day most of the fighting was in the tavern vicinity. A lack of ammunition forced most of the Confederates to retreat, and the Battle of Pea Ridge ended in overall Federal victory. The Confederates went to Van Buren, Arkansas, and after gathering their scattered forces they moved on into Tennessee, arriving too late to participate in the bloody Battle of Shiloh. Visitors can see the restored tavern and follow a self-guiding auto tour of the battlefield. NR

For further information write: Superintendent, Pea Ridge, AR 72751

POTTSVILLE
POTTS INN, *Main and Center streets*

Built between 1850 and 1856 by Kirkbride Potts, this fine example of pioneer architecture is one of the best-preserved stagecoach stations on the Butterfield Overland Mail Route between Memphis,

A Union charge against the Confederates and their Cherokee allies at Pea Ridge

Tennessee, and Fort Smith, Arkansas. The inn also served as the Potts family home and as the first post office in the area. NR
Open: Apr 1–Dec 1, Sat and Sun 1–5

POWHATAN

POWHATAN COURTHOUSE, *northeast Arkansas, off U.S. 63*
The former seat of government for Lawrence County, Powhatan Courthouse was built in 1888 in the prevailing Victorian style. It contains a set of records dating back to 1815, when the county included most of northern Arkansas and part of Missouri. Many of the names are French, indicating the large number of French hunters and trappers who wandered over northern Arkansas. NR

SHERIDAN VICINITY

JENKINS' FERRY BATTLEGROUND STATE PARK, *about 12 miles southwest via State 46*
The Battle of Jenkins' Ferry took place on April 30, 1864, shortly after Union General Frederick Steele's supply train had been captured by Confederate forces at Marks' Mills (*see Fordyce*). Steele was retreating to Little Rock when Confederate troops attacked him as he attempted to cross the Saline River at Jenkins' Ferry. The skirmish, which lasted all day, was bloody but indecisive; both sides suffered considerable losses. Steele and his men were finally able to cross the river on pontoons and make their way back to Little Rock. NR

WASHINGTON

CONFEDERATE STATE CAPITOL, *off State 4*
One of the most historic villages in Arkansas, Washington served as a center of pioneer travel and communications. The Confederate state capitol, built in 1828–33 as the Hempstead County Courthouse, was the Confederate seat of state government from 1863 to 1865. When General Frederick Steele and his Union forces occupied Little Rock in September, 1863, Confederate Governor Harris Flanagin transferred his records and government to the town of Washington.
Open: Mon–Sat 9–5, Sun 1–5

OLD WASHINGTON, *on State 4, 9 miles northwest of Hope*
The Pioneer Washington Restoration Foundation has preserved and opened to the public several Old Washington landmarks that illustrate local history. These include the **Tavern,** dating from 1824, a stopping place for General Sam Houston, Davy Crockett, and Stephen F. Austin, as well as for many other travelers, settlers, and soldiers on their way to Texas. This tavern was a meeting place for the First Regiment of Arkansas Cavalry before it fought in the 1847 Battle of Buena Vista in northern Mexico. The **Blacksmith Shop,** an authentic log blacksmith shop, was reconstructed in 1960. It was here that the famous Bowie knife was invented by blacksmith James Black and James Bowie, hero of the Texas revolution. The **Block-Catts House,** built in 1828–32, is said to be one of the oldest 2-story houses in Arkansas, and the **Trimble House,** completed in 1847, contains items brought to Washington by river boats and ox-drawn wagons. The **Grandison D. Royston House,** built about 1830, was the home of the U.S. district attorney under President Tyler. The **Garland House,** built in 1836, was the home of Augustus H. Garland, who was attorney general under Grover Cleveland. NR
Open: Mon–Sat 9–5, Sun 1–5. Small admission fees for houses

CALIFORNIA

ANZA-BORREGO DESERT STATE PARK, *about 60 miles east of Oceanside via State 78*

The vast reaches of the Colorado Desert encompassed by this park contain two historic trails that played a significant role in the settlement of California. Lieutenant Pedro Fages became the first white man to cross the **Anza Trail,** via Coyote Canyon, in 1772. Captain Juan Bautista de Anza, in the fall of 1775, departed from Sonora with the first party of colonists to come overland to the Pacific Coast; the expedition of 240 soldiers and colonists and 1,000 head of cattle followed Fages's route and went on to colonize San Francisco. In 1847 the Mormon Battalion chopped a passage through the rocky walls of Box Canyon and thus opened the first road into southern California—the **Southern Emigrant Trail.**

AUBURN

OLD AUBURN HISTORIC DISTRICT, *northern inland region on I-80*

Situated in the Mother Lode region, Auburn grew up after gold was discovered here in May, 1848. First called Wood's Dry Diggins, the mining camp was renamed a year later by miners who had come from Auburn, New York. Auburn soon became an important trading post and stage terminal as well as a mining community. The advent of a railroad in 1865, and the growth of a profitable orchard industry during the 1880s and 1890s, prevented Auburn from becoming a ghost town after gold in the area was exhausted. The Old Town section at the head of Auburn Ravine preserves some buildings of the 1850s. NR

Top: San Diego de Alcalá, the first California mission, and the Cabrillo National Monument overlooking the entrance to San Diego Bay. Below: the gold-mining ghost town at Bodie

CALIFORNIA

BEAR FLAG MONUMENT. *See* SONOMA PUEBLO

BENICIA CAPITOL STATE HISTORICAL MONUMENT, 6 *miles southeast of Vallejo via U.S. 680*
> Built about 1852, this handsome structure of brick, faced with Doric columns made from masts of abandoned sailing ships, served as California's state capitol building from February 24, 1853, until February 28, 1854. NR
> *Open daily 10–5*

BODIE HISTORIC DISTRICT NATIONAL HISTORIC LANDMARK, 7 *miles south of Bridgeport*
> The town of Bodie grew up after Waterman S. Body found gold at this site in 1859. Within 20 years Bodie was a bustling, lawless metropolis of some 10,000 miners, gamblers, and other entrepreneurs. During the boom Bodie's mines yielded $400,000 in bullion per month, for an overall total of $100 million in gold. Today Bodie is a ghost town, but 170 original buildings still stand, maintained in a state of "arrested decay." NR

CARMEL
> CARMEL MISSION NATIONAL HISTORIC LANDMARK, *off State 1 at Rio Road*
>> San Carlos Borroméo de Carmelo was the second of 9 mission parishes established by Father Junípero Serra, the Franciscan president of the California missions. The present church was constructed between 1793 and 1797 and underwent extensive restoration in 1884. Father Serra and his successor, Father Fermín Francisco de Lasuén, are buried here. NR

COLOMA HISTORIC DISTRICT NATIONAL HISTORIC LANDMARK, 7 *miles northwest of Placerville on State 49*
> At 7:30 A.M. on January 24, 1848, James Wilson Marshall came upon glittering particles in the tailrace of a sawmill belonging to John Sutter, on the south fork of the American River. Marshall exclaimed, "Boys, I believe I have found a gold mine!" Reports of this strike precipitated the California gold rush of 1848–49, when some 80,000 people flocked to the gold fields. The community of Coloma (NR), which grew up around Marshall's discovery site, became known as the Queen of the Mines. Today visitors may see a replica of the sawmill, Marshall's wooden cabin, a historical museum, and ruins of many old structures.

COLUMBIA HISTORIC DISTRICT NATIONAL HISTORIC LANDMARK, 4 *miles north of Sonora off State 49*
> Situated in the foothills of the Sierra Nevada, in the heart of the Mother Lode country, Columbia in its heyday was known as the Gem of the Southern Mines. On March 27, 1850, Dr. Thaddeus Hildreth discovered gold near the site. Within a month 5,000 prospectors swarmed into the area, which soon became a thriving town. Between 1850 and 1880 some $87 million in gold was extracted from placer mines in this vicinity. Columbia began to decline rapidly after 1860 with the exhaustion of easily mined placer gold, and a general exodus ensued. However, the town always maintained a population of about 500 and never became a ghost town. Many of the edifices erected after a fire in 1857, covering about 12 blocks of the old business district, have been restored or reconstructed. NR

CALIFORNIA

DEATH VALLEY NATIONAL MONUMENT, *headquarters at Furnace Creek*
This great desert basin on the California-Nevada border received its present name from forty-niners who made a nearly disastrous trek across it on their way to the gold fields. Indians had occupied the valley for hundreds of years, as evidenced by the numerous petroglyphs, campsites, and foot trails found throughout the region. When the first covered wagons entered the valley on Christmas Day, 1849, the area was inhabited by the Panamint Indians. Although many pioneers nearly starved or died of thirst while crossing this inhospitable terrain, only one man actually perished. For decades prospectors flocked to Death Valley in search of silver or other metals. Death Valley's peak period occurred in the 1880s with the production of borax, the "white gold of the desert," which was hauled out by the 20-mule-team trains of high-wheeled wagons. Today ghost towns like Skidoo are reminders of once-thriving mining communities.
For further information write: Superintendent, Death Valley, CA 92328

DONNER CAMP NATIONAL HISTORIC LANDMARK, *2.6 miles west of Truckee, Nevada, on U.S. 40*
This state park commemorates the ill-fated Donner expedition of 1846–47. In the spring of 1846 a wagon train composed of more than 100 families headed west. Among the organizers of this journey were the brothers George and Jacob Donner and James F. Reed. The Donner party left the main body of the wagon train at Little Sandy River, Wyoming, and proceeded to take a vaguely defined short cut to California, blazing a trail across the rugged Wasatch Mountains—it took 21 days to cover 26 miles—and crossing the Great Salt Desert, which exacted a heavy toll in oxen, wagons, and supplies. An early winter closed in as the emigrants reached the Sierra Nevada, where they were trapped near the crest by snow. The party encamped, devising rude shelters, at the east end of Donner Lake. When 15 members of the group attempted to cross the summit on improvised snowshoes, 5 persons died and the others ate the dead. Before the snowbound group back at the camp was rescued early in 1847, they too resorted to cannibalism. Forty-two persons died of starvation or cold that fateful winter; there were only 47 survivors. NR

EL CAMINO REAL (KING'S HIGHWAY), *southern coastal to northern coastal region via U.S. 101*
This old Spanish trail linked the chain of 21 mission settlements established by the Franciscan fathers between 1769 and 1823. Extending from the border of Baja California some 500 miles to the north, the missions were located 20 to 30 miles apart—about a day's journey on horseback. Today the great express route U.S. 101 roughly follows El Camino Real and, in sections, bears its name.

ENCINO
LOS ENCINOS STATE HISTORIC PARK, *16756 Moor Park Street*
In August, 1769, an expedition led by Gaspar de Portolá became the first group of white men to pass through this part of the San Fernando Valley. About 25 years later Francisco Reyes, former mayor of the Pueblo de Los Angeles, established a small rancho in the vicinity. Three years later the Franciscan fathers of the nearby San Fernando Mission (*see*) gave Reyes the 4,460-acre Encino Rancho in exchange for his land. During the 1800s Encino Rancho

changed hands a number of times. Don Vincente de la Osa built the 9-room **Osa Adobe** in the mission style here in 1849; in 1858 the rancho was converted into a station for the Butterfield Stage lines. The **Garnier House**, a French-style limestone structure, was built in 1872 by Eugene Garnier, a merino sheep rancher. NR

Open: Wed–Sun 1–4

EUREKA
FORT HUMBOLDT STATE HISTORIC PARK, *on U.S. 101, 3431 Fort Avenue*

Brevet Lieutenant R. C. Buchanan and members of the Fourth United States Infantry established this fort in the redwood region of Humboldt Bay in January, 1853, to protect settlers from the local Indians. Ulysses S. Grant served here from 1853 to 1854, and Fort Humboldt was a base of operations for the Indian wars of the next decade. By 1870 the fort had been abandoned; today logging exhibits are on display.

FORT ROSS NATIONAL HISTORIC LANDMARK, *13 miles north of Jenner on State 1*

In 1812 the Russian-American Company sent approximately 95 Russian and 40 Aleutian fur traders from Alaska to northern California. They erected a stockaded trading post and fort out of redwood on this small elevated coastal plateau at the site of a Pomo Indian village. For the next 29 years the Russians hunted fur seals and sea otters along the California coast and stored the pelts at Fort Ross before shipment to China, Manchuria, and European ports. In 1821 the Tsar's attempt to close the Pacific coast north of San Francisco to any but Russian ships precipitated a diplomatic controversy which resulted in that part of the Monroe Doctrine (of 1823) prohibiting Europeans from extending their holdings in the New World. By 1839 the Russians had virtually decimated the herds of fur seals and sea otters, and in 1841 they negotiated the sale of their outpost to Captain John A. Sutter for $30,000 in gold and produce. Within the present monument, visitors may see the restored **Russian Orthodox Chapel**, stockade, blockhouse, and **Commander's House** (NHL), an outstanding and almost unaltered example of a Russian log house. NR

FORT TEJON STATE HISTORIC PARK, *Grapevine Canyon, 36 miles south of Bakersfield on U.S. 99*

In 1852 General Edward F. Beale, Commissioner of Indian Affairs in California and Nevada, oversaw the founding of this military post, strategically located at a pass in the Tehachapi Mountain Range. Becoming the regimental headquarters of the First Dragoons, the fort dispatched patrols to ride supply routes from Los Angeles, provide escorts to Salt Lake City, and generally maintain law and order in the southern part of California. NR

FORT YUMA. *See* YUMA CROSSING, ARIZONA

FREMONT
MISSION SAN JOSE DE GUADALUPE, *State 238 and Washington Blvd*

Father Fermín Francisco de Lasuén, accompanied by soldiers under Sergeant Pedro Amador, established this mission in the San Jose valley on June 11, 1797. An earthquake in 1868 completely demolished the mission except for the adobe fathers' quarters, which now contain mementos.

CALIFORNIA

GLEN ELLEN
LONDON RANCH NATIONAL HISTORIC LANDMARK, *1 mile west off State 12*

Located on a knoll surrounded by redwood, Douglas fir, and live oak, the "House of Happy Walls" was erected in 1919 as a memorial to Jack London, one of the world's best-loved and most prolific authors, by his widow, Charmian K. London. This memorial contains London's South Sea collection, brass bed, writing equipment, and other memorabilia. The author's grave, off a trail nearby, is marked with a huge lava boulder. NR
House open daily 10–5

HEARST SAN SIMEON STATE HISTORIC PARK, *94 miles south of Monterey via State 1*

On a coastal knoll set against the Santa Lucia Mountains and overlooking the Pacific, publishing magnate William Randolph Hearst created La Cuesta Encantada (The Enchanted Hill), 123 acres of terraced gardens, pools, palatial guesthouses, and the fabled mansion **La Casa Grande**. Hearst built the estate in 1919 to house his immense collection of antiques and art.
For daily tours (8–3) write: Hearst Reservation Office, Box 2390, Sacramento, CA 96811

KING CITY VICINITY
MISSION SAN ANTONIO DE PADUA, *20 miles southwest off U.S. 101*

Situated in the picturesque "Valley of the Oaks," San Antonio de Padua was the third mission begun (July 14, 1771) in California by Father Junípero Serra. The large mission, currently operated as a school for Franciscan brothers, has been restored.

KIT CARSON PASS, *Sierra region, 15 miles west of Woodford on State 88*

Through the Carson Pass, a famous gateway across the Sierras, went U.S. government survey parties, the **California Trail**, and the pony express. In 1844 the famous scout Kit Carson guided the second John Charles Frémont exploring party down from Oregon and over the Sierras into California. A marker now stands at the summit of 8,650-foot Carson Pass where the scout carved his name on a tree during that crossing. The original inscription was cut from the tree and can be seen in Sutter's Fort in Sacramento (*see*).

LAVA BEDS NATIONAL MONUMENT, *about 60 miles northwest of Alturas on State 139*

This craggy, volcano-studded terrain served as the main battlefield of the Modoc War of 1872–73, one of the last major Indian uprisings in the Pacific West. When white settlers began encroaching on the lands of the fiercely independent Modocs, the Indians started attacking wagon trains and ranchers. Although the Modocs had agreed to move north to the Klamath Indian reservation, some of them, because of friction with the Klamaths, soon returned to their homeland north of Tule Lake, where they engaged in open warfare with the settlers. After troops tried to force them back to the reservation, 160 Modocs led by Captain Jack barricaded themselves in a natural fortress in the lava beds that became known as Captain Jack's Stronghold. The government tried to negotiate a truce with the Modocs, but the Indians murdered the leaders of the peace commission. One thousand troops were immediately dispatched to capture the Modocs. Abandoning their fortress, the Indians made one last successful ambush at Hardin Butte and

finally surrendered to the Army.
For further information write: Box 867, Tulelake, CA 96134

LOMPOC
LA PURISIMA MISSION NATIONAL HISTORIC LANDMARK, *4 miles northeast on State 1*
Father Lasuén founded the 11th Franciscan mission in 1787. Missionaries here constructed an elaborate water and drainage system, complete with a filter building. Father Payeras made his permanent home here, and during his 8-year tenure as president of the California missions, La Purisima became headquarters of the mission chain. Today the original buildings have been restored to make La Purisima the most complete extant mission. NR

LOS ANGELES AND VICINITY
CAMPO DE CAHUENGA, *3919 Lankershim Blvd, North Hollywood*
The United States acquired California when Lieutenant Colonel John C. Frémont concluded a treaty of surrender with General Andres Pico, commander of the Mexican forces, at this site on January 13, 1847. Under the lenient terms of the capitulation, the defeated Californios were assured of their rights and were required only to lay down their arms and keep the peace. This treaty was later finalized in the 1848 Treaty of Guadalupe Hidalgo.

EL PUEBLO DE LOS ANGELES STATE HISTORIC PARK, *100 Calle de La Plaza*
In 1781 Governor Felipe de Neve, leading a party of Franciscan priests, 11 families, and a few soldiers, left the Mission San Gabriel to found the new community of El Pueblo de Nuestra Señora la Reina de Los Angeles. By 1800, 30 adobe houses and one church had grown up around a central plaza; a half century later the plaza was the heart of a thriving city. Much of the original Spanish town has been preserved or restored within this park. Today a bronze statue of Governor de Neve stands in the **Old Plaza**. The **Old Mission Church** nearby, the oldest religious edifice in the city, was founded by Franciscans in 1814, funded by proceeds from selling California brandy. On **Olvera Street**, a reconstruction of a typical Mexican village street, stands the **Avila Adobe**, built about 1818 by Don José María Avila, one-time mayor of the town; in 1847, after the Battle of Los Angeles, the house was occupied by Commodore Robert Stockton. Other points of interest include Pico House, an elegant 3-story hotel erected in 1869, and the **Old Plaza Firehouse** of 1884. NR nominee

RIO SAN GABRIEL BATTLEFIELD, *Washington Blvd and Bluff Rd, Montebello*
Early in January, 1847, toward the end of the war with Mexico, American troops under Captain Robert F. Stockton and Brigadier General Stephen W. Kearny routed a force of Californios led by General José María Flores at this site.

MARTINEZ
JOHN MUIR NATIONAL HISTORIC SITE, *4202 Alhambra Avenue*
The great naturalist and conservationist John Muir lived in this late Victorian mansion, built by his father-in-law, from 1890 to 1914—the last 24 years of his life. NR
For further information write: 4202 Alhambra Ave, Martinez, CA 94553

CALIFORNIA

MONTEREY

MONTEREY OLD TOWN NATIONAL HISTORIC LANDMARK, *210 Oliver Street*

Although the sailor Cabrillo first sighted Monterey Bay in 1542, it was Sebastián Vizcaíno who landed here in 1602 and named the site in honor of the Count of Monterey, Viceroy of New Spain. The actual colonization of Monterey, however, did not begin until 1770, when Don Gaspar de Portolá and Father Junípero Serra established a presidio and a mission (*see Carmel Mission*) here. As Monterey expanded, it subsequently became the capital of Alta California under the Spanish, Mexican, and American flags. Aside from the **Vizcaíno-Serra Landing Site**, the 8 buildings within the state monument serve as vivid reminders of Monterey's colorful heritage. The lodging house erected in 1846–47 by a British sailor, Jack Swan, was soon converted into **California's First Theater**. **Casa del Oro**, built about 1850, was a general merchandise store and reputedly a gold depository. In the dwelling known as the **Stevenson House**, Robert Louis Stevenson spent a few months as a boarder in 1879. Begun by the Mexican government about 1827, the **Custom House** (NHL) is the oldest government building in California; when Commodore John Drake Sloat raised the American flag here on July 7, 1846, it signaled the annexation of some 600,000 square miles of land, including California, to the Union. Built in the 1830s, the Thomas Oliver **Larkin House** (NHL) became the prototype of the popular Monterey style, which developed at this time as an amalgam of Spanish colonial and New England influences. **Casa Soberanes** is another example of the Monterey style, and the white-washed adobe **Casa Gutiérrez** represents a typical home during the Mexican period. The **Pacific Building** was constructed in 1847 and rented to the U.S. quartermaster. NR

California's First Theater open: Tues–Sun 9–5. Stevenson House and Larkin House: tours daily except Tues. Custom House and Pacific Building open daily 9–5.

ROYAL PRESIDIO CHAPEL NATIONAL HISTORIC LANDMARK, *550 Church St*

Governor Pedro Fages, military commander of Monterey, founded the Royal Presidio Chapel in 1789 on the site of an earlier mission established by Father Junípero Serra. This unique church is the only extant structure of the original Monterey Presidio, and the only surviving example of 18th-century architecture in Monterey. NR

NOBLE PASS OF NOBLE EMIGRANT TRAIL, *on Park Highway in Lassen Volcanic National Park*

William H. Noble first opened this wagon route across the Sierra Nevada in May of 1852. Emigrants to northern California crossed the desert from the Humboldt River in Nevada, ascended the eastern flank of the Sierra to Noble Pass, and proceeded over the mountains to the town of Shasta. It was from this point that the pioneers first glimpsed the Sacramento Valley.

NORTH BLOOMFIELD

MALAKOFF DIGGINS STATE HISTORIC PARK, *11 miles northeast of Nevada City*

Hydraulic mining, which employed streams of water to erode hill-sides and expose gold-bearing ore, became a popular method of mining during the early 1850s in the rocky reaches of San Juan Ridge. The most colossal hydraulic excavation was undertaken at

Left: the river port of Old Sacramento during the gold rush. Right: the governor's mansion at Sacramento

the Malakoff Mine, in an area characterized by its exquisitely molded pinnacles and minarets. At the nearby Malakoff Mine office in North Bloomfield, gold was reduced to bars.

PACIFIC PALISADES
WILL ROGERS STATE HISTORIC PARK, *14253 Sunset Boulevard*
The famous humorist, film star, and "cracker-barrel philosopher" Will Rogers lived on this 186-acre ranch from 1928 until 1932. Displayed within the ranch house are trophies, works of art, and various Rogers memorabilia. NR
Open daily 10–5

RED BLUFF
WILLIAM B. IDE ADOBE STATE HISTORICAL MONUMENT, *Adobe Road off State 99*
This recently restored adobe house commemorates the pioneer William B. Ide, president of the short-lived Bear Flag Republic. Upon hearing that the Mexican government was planning to expel Americans from California, Ide enlisted a group of settlers to form the Bear Flag Party and marched upon the town of Sonoma (*see Sonoma Pueblo National Historic Landmark*) on June 14, 1846. That November Ide returned to the Sacramento Valley, where he purchased the Rancho de la Barranca Colorada—Red Bluff Ranch—and about 1850 erected an adobe dwelling where the **California-Oregon Trail** crossed the Sacramento River.
Open daily 8–5

SACRAMENTO
GOVERNOR'S MANSION, *16th and H streets*
California's executive mansion was originally constructed in 1877–78 for a local hardware merchant. The Victorian Gothic house was later sold to Joseph Steffens, father of the social reformer Lincoln Steffens. In 1903 the state purchased the residence for $32,500. George Pardee was the first of 13 governors to reside here; Ronald Reagan was the last. NR
Open daily 10–5

CALIFORNIA

OLD SACRAMENTO NATIONAL HISTORIC LANDMARK, *Sacramento Waterfront*

An outgrowth of the settlement established by Captain John A. Sutter in 1839 (*see Sutter's Fort National Historic Landmark*), Sacramento emerged during the gold rush of 1848–49 as a major distribution point, serving the gold fields in the Sierra Nevada to the east and linking them with the coast on the west. Sacramento became the capital of the new state of California in 1854, and in subsequent years the transportation terminus for the first railroad in California (1856), the pony express (1860), river boat, telegraph, and the first transcontinental railroad. The original business district of the river port of Old Sacramento preserves a greater number of buildings—including banks, express buildings, hotels, restaurants, and stores—than any other major city on the Pacific coast. NR

SUTTER'S FORT NATIONAL HISTORIC LANDMARK, *2701 L Street*

Begun by Captain John Augustus Sutter in 1839 in order to protect an extensive land grant of some 72 square miles, this fort on the fork of the American and Sacramento rivers became an important outpost of civilization, providing shelter and supplies for weary travelers making their way west. In 1848 Sutter served as a delegate to the constitutional convention in Monterey that paved the way for California's admission as the 31st state. After the discovery of gold in 1848 at his sawmill in Coloma (*see Coloma National Historic Landmark*), he retired to his farm on the Feather River. During the ensuing stampede for gold, Sutter's property passed out of his hands. Successive attempts to have Congress recognize his land claim proved futile, and Sutter died in poverty back east in 1880. Before reconstruction of the fort began in the 1890s, only the 2-story adobe and oak central building remained standing. NR

SAN DIEGO AND VICINITY

CABRILLO NATIONAL MONUMENT, *south on Point Loma*

This monument, with its dramatic coastal setting, commemorates the Portuguese mariner Juan Rodríguez Cabrillo, who in 1542 discovered the west coast of the United States for Spain. Cabrillo launched his expedition in search of a direct route to the East Indies from Navidad, on the west coast of Mexico, on June 27, 1542. Three months later Cabrillo's 2 ships passed Point Loma, sailed into San Diego Bay, a "closed and very good port," and landed at Ballast Point. Cabrillo claimed this land, which he called San Miguel, for the Spanish king. The expedition later sailed past Monterey Bay and was turned seaward by a storm beyond Point Reyes. Cabrillo then headed south to San Miguel Island, one of the Channel Islands, where in January, 1543, he died of injuries sustained in a fall. The expedition continued under Bartolomé Ferrelo and subsequently sailed as far north as Oregon. Today a statue of Cabrillo, carved by Alvaro De Bree of Portugal, stands on these premises. NR
For further information write: Box 6175, San Diego, CA 92106

MISSION SAN DIEGO DE ALCALA NATIONAL HISTORIC LANDMARK, *7 miles north, in Mission Valley*

Founded on July 16, 1769, by Father Junípero Serra, San Diego de Alcalá was the "mother mission" of the chain of 21 missions. Originally situated on Presidio Hill in what is now Old Town San Diego (*see*), the mission was relocated to its present site in 1774. The first irrigation system in California was developed at the mission, and the first palm and olive trees planted here. NR

OLD MISSION DAM NATIONAL HISTORIC LANDMARK, *north side of Mission Street–Gorge Road*

Constructed between 1800 and 1817 out of native stone and locally produced cement, this dam was the first major irrigation-engineering project to be undertaken on the West Coast. The waters impounded by the dam were used to irrigate the fields of the Mission San Diego de Alcalá 5 miles away. NR

OLD TOWN SAN DIEGO STATE HISTORIC PARK, *4016 Wallace Street*

For the first half century after its founding in 1769, life at San Diego had centered around its presidio (*see*) and the San Diego de Alcalá Mission (*see*). Gradually, however, retired soldiers and their families began to settle on plots of land outside the presidio, and the community of Old Town began to develop. During the Mexican and well into the American period—The Stars and Stripes was raised on the plaza by Marines from the U.S.S. *Cyane* on July 29, 1846—ranches and rancheros flourished here, and Old Town became an international center of the cowhide ("California banknote") and tallow trade. After the droughts of the 1860s and the development of a newer commercial district near the wharf, Old Town began to decline; a disastrous fire in 1872 dealt a death blow to the area as the heart of San Diego. Today 2 of the 4 surviving adobe buildings in Old Town have been restored: **Casa de Estudillo** (NHL), built from 1827 to 1829, the home of José Antonio de Estudillo, who led a distinguished career as a civic leader under both the Mexican and American governments; and the **Machado-Stewart Adobe**, erected in 1830 by José Manuel Machado, a corporal in the San Diego Company. The **San Diego Union Building** has been restored to its appearance in 1868—the date of the first edition of the newspaper. NR
Open: May–Sept 10–6; Oct–Apr 10–5

SAN DIEGO PRESIDIO NATIONAL HISTORIC LANDMARK, *Presidio Park*

Located on a hill in the historic heart of San Diego is the site of the first permanent Spanish settlement on the Pacific coast of California (1769). By 1835 the original structures had fallen into ruin, and in 1838 **Fort Stockton** was built on the site. In 1846 it became a U.S. Army post, and it was here in 1847 that the Mormon Battalion ended its march from Council Bluffs. One may still see fragments of the original fort's ramparts and the commemorative Father Serra Cross and Statue. NR

SAN FERNANDO

MISSION SAN FERNANDO REY DE ESPANA, *15151 San Fernando Road*

Father Lasuén founded this mission on September 8, 1797, and the present church was completed in 1818. Next to the mission is a beautiful "memory garden," said to contain plants from all the other missions. Constructed in 1812, the garden fountain is modeled after one in Córdoba, Spain. NR

SAN FRANCISCO AND VICINITY

ANGEL ISLAND STATE PARK, *San Francisco Bay*

In 1775 the packet *San Carlos*, earliest known Spanish ship to enter San Francisco Bay, dropped anchor beside this island. Commander Juan Manuel de Ayala named it Isla de los Angeles. During the

Left to right in San Francisco: Mission San Francisco de Asís, the Golden Gate Bridge, and an 1890s schooner moored at the Maritime State Park

Mexican period Governor Juan B. Alvarado granted the island to Antonio Mario Osio, who raised cattle and horses here. The United States subsequently employed Angel Island for military purposes. Hostile Indians from Arizona were detained here in the 1870s. After 1892 Angel Island served as San Francisco's Quarantine and Immigration Station. During World War II the island contained an internment camp for German and Italian prisoners of war. NR

FORT POINT NATIONAL HISTORIC SITE

Situated within the presidio of San Francisco (*see*), Fort Point, the most massive brick fortification to be erected on the west coast of North America, guarded the entrance to San Francisco Bay for many decades. Although the fort was never involved in actual fighting, its garrisons supplied forces for campaigns against the Indians in the Far West. An earlier adobe fortification—Castillo de San Joaquin—had been completed by the Spanish in 1794 on Cantil Blanco (White Cliff), the site that Fort Point now occupies. In 1853, after the war with Mexico, U.S. Army engineers began construction of the present fort by blasting away some 85 feet of Cantil Blanco so that the bluff stood about 10 feet above high water. The new fort, bearing resemblance in many of its features to Fort Sumter and boasting a remarkable granite sea wall, was completed in 1861 at a cost of $2.8 million. During the Civil War the well-armed fort discouraged Confederate privateers from entering San Francisco Bay. Fort Point was abandoned for military use in 1905; it was briefly reactivated during World Wars I and II and during the construction of the Golden Gate Bridge in the 1930s. NR

MISSION SAN FRANCISCO DE ASIS, *Dolores Street near 16th Street*

The city of San Francisco grew up around this mission, also known as Mission Dolores, which was started in 1776. Completed in 1784, San Francisco de Asís, with its combination of Moorish, Mission,

and Corinthian styles, is architecturally distinct from its sister missions. Characterized by a massive simplicity, the chapel contains one of the most ornate altars of all the missions, as well as original decorations brought from Mexico and Spain.

OLD UNITED STATES MINT NATIONAL HISTORIC LANDMARK, *5th and Mission streets*

Authorized by Congress in 1852, the first U.S. branch mint outside of Philadelphia opened its doors in 1854 in San Francisco. As a result of the phenomenal production of gold and silver on the western mining frontier at this time, the mint soon functioned on an independent basis, becoming the principal mint of the nation and the chief Federal depository. Completed in 1869, the present Federal-style building was one of the few in San Francisco's financial district to survive the 1906 earthquake. NR

PORTSMOUTH PLAZA, *on Kearny between Washington and Clay Streets*

The scene of many important events in the history of San Francisco, this plaza was named in honor of the sailing sloop U.S.S. *Portsmouth*. When Captain John B. Montgomery came ashore and first raised the American flag here on July 9, 1846, he proclaimed the city a possession of the United States. The city of San Francisco grew up around this Spanish-style plaza.

THE PRESIDIO NATIONAL HISTORIC LANDMARK, *on U.S. 101 and I-480*

One of the oldest and largest military reservations in America, the presidio was founded by the Spanish in 1776 to guard the entrance to San Francisco harbor and has served as a military command post ever since. Currently the presidio is headquarters of the Sixth Army. All that remains of the original Spanish structures is the adobe *commandante's* house, now restored and converted into the officers' club. NR

SAN FRANCISCO BAY DISCOVERY SITE NATIONAL HISTORIC LANDMARK, *4 miles west of San Bruno via Skyline Drive and Sneath Lane*

On November 4, 1769, Gaspar de Portolá and members of his exploring party stood on the summit of Sweeny Ridge and beheld, for the first time, San Francisco Bay. The discovery of this great inland bay encouraged the Spanish government to establish 2 missions in the area, as well as the presidio of San Francisco in 1776. NR

SAN FRANCISCO MARITIME STATE HISTORIC PARK, *Aquatic Park, foot of Polk St.*

Moored along a pier on San Francisco's historic waterfront, these 4 old wooden vessels constitute a fascinating floating display of nautical memorabilia. Carefully restored, each ship represents an important type developed, built, and operated on the Pacific coast. The 453-ton, 3-masted schooner *C. A. Thayer* (NHL), launched in 1895, carried millions of board feet of lumber in her hold; 20 years newer, the steam-powered *Wapama* replaced ships like the *Thayer*. In her heyday the paddle-wheeled *Eureka* of 1890 was the largest passenger ferry in the world. And the flat-bottomed *Alma*, a shallow-draft sailing scow, was especially designed in 1891 to carry bulky cargoes of hay out of the bay into every backwater, tidal flat, and creek.

SAN GABRIEL

MISSION SAN GABRIEL ARCANGEL, *Junipero Street and West Mission Drive*

Fathers Pedro Benito Cambón and Angel Fernández de la Somera established the San Gabriel mission in 1771. For nearly 50 years it served as the only outpost of civilization west of the vast California desert. Partially destroyed in an earthquake, the original church has been restored and boasts massive buttresses and bells. California's first winery was founded behind the mission. Today the largest grapevine in the world—covering more than 12,000 square feet—grows on its grounds. NR

SAN JOSE

NEW ALMADEN NATIONAL HISTORIC LANDMARK, *4 miles south on County G8*

One of the world's 4 great sources of mercury, this mine, since it opened in 1845, has yielded ore of a greater total value than that of any other mine in California. Quicksilver was essential to the processing of gold and silver, so the New Almaden Mine became indispensable during the days of the gold rush. NR

SAN JUAN BAUTISTA AND VICINITY

FREMONT PEAK STATE PARK, *about 10 miles southeast on San Juan Canyon Road*

Captain John C. Frémont and his American soldiers defied the Mexican authorities from March 6 to March 9, 1846, at this site near the crest of Gabilan Peak. Frémont and his men had established a fort and had unfurled The Stars and Stripes from the peak. When the Californios did not attack within 4 days, Frémont broke camp and headed for Oregon.

SAN JUAN BAUTISTA STATE HISTORIC PARK, *3 miles east of U.S. 101*
This picturesque, quaint community remains basically unchanged since the days of the dons; its architecture vividly reflects the Spanish, Mexican, and early American periods of California history. Founded in 1797 by Father Fermín Francisco de Lasuén, the **Mission San Juan Bautista** was one of the largest in the California mission chain. Since it was completed in 1812 the mission church has been in continuous use. A town of adobe buildings gradually grew up around the **Old Central Plaza** (NHL), which over the years was the scene of military parades, bull and bear fights, fandangos, and fiestas. In 1813 a one-story barracks was erected to house Spanish soldiers; in 1858 the restaurateur and hotelkeeper Angelo Zanetta added a second story and converted the building into what became the famous **Plaza Hotel** in the 1870s, when San Juan was one of the main stage stops between San Francisco and Los Angeles. The **Plaza Stable**, built in 1874, stands nearby. José Maria Castro, prefect of the northern district and later commanding general of the Spanish military forces in California, built **Castro House** (NHL) in 1840–41 as his administrative headquarters. Other homes of historic interest include the **Zanetta Cottage**, built in the 1850s.
Open daily 9–5

SAN JUAN CAPISTRANO
MISSION SAN JUAN CAPISTRANO, *Camino Capistrano and Ortega Highway*
This mission has become internationally famous because of the flock of swallows that make their home here; the birds are supposed to arrive punctually every March 19 and depart on October 23. Father Junípero Serra founded California's seventh mission in 1776 and dedicated a small adobe church—now restored—at the site 2 years later. A stone church that was one of the largest and most elaborately decorated of the entire mission chain was constructed from 1797 to 1806, but the earthquake of 1812 caused the tower and heavy roof to come crashing down on the congregation. Today this structure is a picturesque ruin. NR

SAN LUIS OBISPO
MISSION SAN LUIS OBISPO DE TOLOSA, *Chorro and Monteray streets*
Father Junípero Serra founded the fifth in the chain of California missions on September 1, 1772. Erected by the local Chumash Indians, the Prince of Missions, as it became known, contains an unusual combination of belfry and vestibule.

SAN LUIS REY
MISSION SAN LUIS REY NATIONAL HISTORIC LANDMARK, *Mission Road, 4 miles east of Oceanside*
Known as the King of the Missions, San Luis Rey features a composite of Mexican, Moorish, and Spanish architectural styles. Father Lasuén founded the 18th California mission in 1798, and for many years it was the home of more than 3,000 Indians. Although the buildings fell into disuse after secularization in 1834, Abraham Lincoln eventually returned the mission to the church. San Luis Rey is currently a seminary of the Franciscan order. NR

SAN MIGUEL
MISSION SAN MIGUEL ARCANGEL, *on U.S. 101*
The 16th mission in the Franciscan chain was established by Father

Lasuén on July 25, 1797, in an area inhabited by large numbers of Salinan Indians. A parish church today, San Miguel is one of the best-preserved missions, with many of the original decorations still intact. NR

SAN PASQUEL BATTLEFIELD STATE HISTORIC PARK, *8 miles southeast of Escondido*

An important battle in the war between the Californios and Americans occurred at this site on December 6, 1846. Having secured New Mexico for the United States, General Stephen W. Kearny proceeded toward California with a detachment of First U.S. Dragoons. On the way he met Kit Carson, who carried a dispatch affirming American control over California, and Kearny thereupon sent most of his troops back to New Mexico. After making a difficult desert crossing, Kearny's party found themselves opposed by a large force of native California Lancers under the command of General Andres Pico. The Mexican lances and sabers inflicted heavy casualties upon the Americans, and Kearny himself was severely wounded, although he continued to rally his men. Kit Carson and an Indian fled to San Diego for aid, and reinforcements carrying artillery finally returned. Kearny and his men entered San Diego on December 12, claiming victory.

SAN RAFAEL

MISSION SAN RAFAEL ARCANGEL, *5th Avenue and A Street*

The 20th in the chain of 21 California missions was begun on December 14, 1817. The mission proper consisted of a hospital, a chapel, a storeroom, and a monastery. The present mission is a reconstruction on the original site.

SANTA BARBARA

EL PRESIDIO DE SANTA BARBARA STATE HISTORIC PARK

Governor Felipe de Neve, along with Father Junípero Serra and Lieutenant José Francisco Ortega, founded the Santa Barbara presidio on April 21, 1782, to defend and protect the coast of California for Spain. Four years later a mission (*see*) was established and subsequently a village grew up around the barracks. The extensive presidio has long since disappeared, but in **Adobe El Cuartel** (122 East Canon Perdido Street) are preserved two rooms that served as soldiers' barracks in the original garrison.

SANTA BARBARA MISSION NATIONAL HISTORIC LANDMARK, *2201 Laguna Street*

Established by Father Junípero Serra in 1786, Santa Barbara Mission was known as the Queen of the Missions. Completed in 1820, the present mission building, with its beautiful façade, has influenced the development of the mission style of architecture throughout California. As the only mission not secularized by the Mexican decree of 1833, Santa Barbara became important as the Franciscan capital and the see of the first Spanish bishop. NR
Open: Mon–Sat 9:30–5, Sun 1–5

SANTA CLARA

MISSION SANTA CLARA DE ASIS, *University of Santa Clara campus*

Third in the mission chain, Santa Clara de Asís was founded in 1777. In 1851 Santa Clara College was established in the old mission building that was completed in 1822, of which the present structure is a replica.

SANTA CRUZ

SANTA CRUZ MISSION STATE HISTORIC PARK, *Emmet and Mission*
The mission La Exaltatión de la Santa Cruz, 12th in the chain of
California missions, was established in 1791. Earthquakes in 1840
and 1857 completely destroyed the mission. Today a half-size
replica stands near the original site.

SHASTA STATE HISTORIC PARK, *6 miles west of Redding on State 299*
Nestled in the rolling foothills of the Sacramento Valley, this old
ghost town was the metropolis of northern California during the
gold rush. In 1849 prospectors discovered gold in the vicinity:
Major Pierson B. Redding, assisted by Indians, successfully washed
out gold in Clear Creek. Soon hordes of miners poured into the
settlement. During the 1850s virtually all travel and commerce
flowed through this "Queen City of the North"; the wagon road
ended here, and the Oregon pack trail began at this point. After
the 1850s a population of some 3,000 residents, and hundreds of
transients, dwindled to a mere handful of people. On Main Street
are the ruins of a row of brick buildings—once the longest row of its
kind in California. NR

SOLEDAD

MISSION NUESTRA SENORA DE LA SOLEDAD, *west of U.S. 101*
Father Fermín Francisco de Lasuén established this mission in
1791 to serve the Indians of the Salinas Valley. Although the
mission declined after 1825, Father Vincente Francisco Sarriá
stayed on in poverty and ministered to the Indians until his death
in 1835, the year the mission was secularized.

SOLVANG

MISSION SANTA YNEZ, *southern coastal region, off U.S. 101*
Father Estévan Tapis founded this mission in 1804,·primarily to
reach the Indians east of the Coast Range. By 1820 the prosperous
mission owned 12,000 head of livestock; 4 years later Santa Ynez
was almost destroyed in an Indian insurrection. Today the mission
has been restored to its former charm and grace, and it boasts one
of the most beautiful arcades of all the missions.

SONOMA PUEBLO NATIONAL HISTORIC LANDMARK, *on State 12*

The historic structures preserved here evoke not only Sonoma's
dramatic beginnings, but the forceful personálity of the city's
founder, General Mariano Guadelupe Vallejo, as well. Padre José
Altamire established **San Francisco de Solano**, the northernmost of
California's Franciscan missions and the only one begun under
Mexican rule, at the site of the future town in 1823. Ten years later
Vallejo (commander of the northern frontier) came to this fertile
outpost to investigate Russian installations in the area. He secularized the mission in 1834, and in 1835 founded the town of Sonoma,
laying out the 8-acre **Sonoma Plaza** (NR)—the largest in California—
which on June 14, 1846, was the scene of the Bear Flag Revolt. On
that day 33 Americans led by William B. Ide marched upon Sonoma,
imprisoned Vallejo and other Mexican officials, raised the Bear Flag
over the plaza, and proclaimed California an independent republic.
These bold actions of a few induced the U.S. armed forces to enter
and take control of the area. On July 9 the Bear Flag was replaced
by The Stars and Stripes. Erected facing the plaza was the Cuartel,
or **Soldiers Barracks** (1836), which after 1846 housed various con-
tingents of U.S. forces. On the plaza also is a portion of the site of

CALIFORNIA

Vallejo's 2-story adobe town house, **Casa Grande**. On a 20-acre estate near the foothills is the **Vallejo Home**, a redwood frame Victorian house built in 1850.

VENTURA

MISSION SAN BUENAVENTURA, *Main and Figueroa streets*
Founded on March 31, 1782, this was the ninth and last mission personally established by Father Serra. The present mission is a restoration. A great cross atop nearby Mission Hill was raised by Father Serra the year the mission ground was consecrated.

WALKER PASS NATIONAL HISTORIC LANDMARK, *60 miles northeast of Bakersfield on State 178*
On July 24, 1833, Joseph Reddeford Walker, leading about 60 men, set out from Bear Lake in Utah on a fur-trapping expedition. Walker crossed the salt flats of Utah and located the route along the Humboldt River of Nevada that became the **California Trail.** He was the first white man to lead a party westward over the Sierra Nevada at Sonora Pass and finally reached the coast of Monterey. On his return trip in February, 1834, Walker went eastward from the site of modern Bakersfield, discovering the 5,248-foot-high pass through the Sierra that now bears his name. NR

WARNER SPRINGS VICINITY

OAK GROVE BUTTERFIELD STAGE STATION NATIONAL HISTORIC LANDMARK, *13 miles northwest on State 79*
Erected in 1858, this well-preserved adobe building is one of the few surviving original stage stations from the Butterfield Overland Mail Route, which operated from 1858 to 1861 between San Francisco and 2 eastern rail terminals—St. Louis and Memphis. NR

WEAVERVILLE JOSS STATE HISTORIC PARK, *northern inland region, in Weaverville on U.S. 299*
This Taoist temple, known as the Temple of the Forest and Clouds, is the oldest, most authentic Chinese house of worship in California. During the gold rush in the Trinity River region, thousands of Chinese—mainly from Canton—arrived to seek gold. By 1852 some 2,500 Chinese were in the area. Many settled in Weaverville, where they established their own community and about 1853 erected a temple. The original structure burned down in 1873; the following year it was replaced by the present building, which with its fanciful gables and cornices, ornate wooden gate, and bright blue façade recalls its oriental prototypes. The structures on both sides of **Main Street** (NR) preserve an important part of California's Chinese tradition.

WHITTIER

PIO PICO STATE HISTORIC PARK, *6003 Pioneer Boulevard*
Pío Pico, the last Mexican governor of California, made his home in this 2-story, 33-room adobe hacienda. In 1866 the San Gabriel River destroyed half of the house. The remaining 16 rooms of the old adobe have been restored.
Open: Wed–Sun 10–5

YORBA LINDA

RICHARD NIXON BIRTHPLACE, *18061 Yorba Linda Boulevard*
Richard Milhous Nixon, 37th President of the United States, was born in this 5-room house on January 9, 1913. NR

COLORADO

BENT'S OLD FORT NATIONAL HISTORIC SITE, *8 miles east of La Junta on State 194*

In 1830 the brothers Charles, William, Robert, and George Bent and Ceran St. Vrain, having gained experience in the upper Missouri River fur trade, formed a partnership to build a great trading establishment on the Arkansas River. They chose a spot on the north bank of the Arkansas about 12 miles west of the mouth of the Purgatoire River. This strategic location placed them just north of the New Mexico border in the heart of Indian country and on the mountain branch of the **Santa Fe Trail,** a key overland route. By 1833 the massive, impregnable mud fortress, now called Bent's Old Fort, stood completed in the midst of unbroken prairie. The post quickly became the hub of a trading empire that stretched from Texas into Wyoming, from the Rockies to middle Kansas. Bent's Fort was a significant fur-trading post, a rendezvous for trappers and Indians, a way station on the Santa Fe Trail, and the chief point of contact between the southern Plains Indians and the whites. During the Mexican War (1846–48) the fort became a military base for the American conquest of New Mexico. After the war the Indian trade declined, and in 1849 William Bent abandoned the fort. Beginning in 1861 it was rehabilitated as the principal stop of the Barlow & Sanderson stage, mail, and express route between Kansas City and Santa Fe. NR

For further information write: Box 581, La Junta, CO 81050

CENTRAL CITY HISTORIC DISTRICT NATIONAL HISTORIC LANDMARK, *on State 279*

This town, which clings precariously to the steep slopes of Gregory

Top left: mining town of Central City. Right: cliff dwellings at Mesa Verde National Park. Below: Ute Indian Chief Ouray (see monument at Montrose)

Gulch, was the site in 1859 of Colorado's first important gold discovery. News of the gold brought a horde of prospectors, and almost overnight a town of log cabins and tents sprang up; Central City soon became known as the richest square mile on earth. The town is still Victorian in both appearance and atmosphere. The **Teller House** (1872), a hotel for miners, was considered the epitome of frontier elegance. Most of the other buildings in the historic district were built after the fire of 1874: the **Old Armory** (1875), **St. James Methodist Church** (1872), and the **Opera House** (1878), still in use, where Sarah Bernhardt once appeared. NR

CHIMNEY ROCK ARCHAEOLOGICAL SITE, *2 miles east of Piedra River on U.S. 160*

The Indian ruins on the Chimney Rock site, situated in San Juan National Forest on a high mesa, are some 1,000 years old. The only excavation to date has been a pueblo chamber, 200 feet long and 80 feet wide, which is in fair condition. NR

CRIPPLE CREEK HISTORIC DISTRICT NATIONAL HISTORIC LAND-MARK, *State 67*

From the 1891 gold discovery by cowboy Bob Womack until the last mine closed in 1961, gold valued at more than $500 million was dug out of the hills of this district. Among the extant buildings to survive a 1906 blaze in this typical gold camp are the old headquarters of the **Western Federation of Mines,** the former **Midland Railroad Depot,** which now houses the Cripple Creek District Museum, and the 1896 **Imperial Hotel.** NR

Museum open: May 30–Oct 1, daily 9:30–5:15

DENVER

BROWN PALACE HOTEL, *Tremont and Broadway at 17th Street*

The Brown Palace, opened in 1892, was the brainchild of Henry C. Brown, a carpenter who came to Denver in 1860 and within three years was prosperous enough to buy 160 acres on hills east of the town—an area that he called Brown's Bluff and that would one day become the site of many great mansions built by Denver's silver and gold kings. Brown later began making plans to build an elegant Italian Renaissance-style hotel. The Brown Palace, one of the first fireproof buildings in America, took 5 years and $1.6 million to build and $400,000 to furnish. NR

CONSTITUTION HALL, *1507 Blake Street*

On December 20, 1875, a delegation met here to frame Colorado's first state constitution. Today the structure houses the oldest continuous banking firm in the state—the First National Bank of Denver. NR

LARIMER SQUARE, *1400 block of Larimer Street*

This square, part of Denver's Skyline Urban Renewal Project, reproduces the Denver of the 1860s, complete with a flea market, stores, galleries, and flower stalls. The square was the center of Denver's business life in the 19th century.

Shops open: Mon–Sat 11–10, Sun 12–6

THE MOLLY BROWN HOUSE, *1340 Pennsylvania Street*

This Victorian house, situated in Denver's affluent Capitol Hill area, was built about 1890 and purchased in 1894 by Mr. and Mrs. James J. Brown. Mrs. Brown later became famous as the "Unsink-

able Molly Brown" of the Broadway musical. NR
*Open: June 1–Sept 14, Tues–Sun 10–4; Sept 15–May 31, Sun only
12–4. Admission: adults $1.00, children (under 12) 50¢*

STATE CAPITOL, *Capitol Hill, East Colfax and East 14th avenues*
Construction on the 3-story granite capitol was started in 1890 and
completed in 1907 at a cost of almost $3 million. The classical
building is embellished with murals, portraits, statuary, and bronze
doors that depict the history of the state.
Open daily 9–5

UNITED STATES MINT, *300 block of West Colfax*
One of 3 Federal coinage plants in the nation, the Denver mint—
which has been in operation since 1869—is also a gold repository.
NR
Tours available Mon–Fri; closed holidays

**DURANGO-SILVERTON NARROW-GAUGE LINE NATIONAL HISTORIC
LANDMARK,** *between Durango and Silverton, through San Juan National
Forest*
Now part of the Denver and Rio Grande Western Railroad system,
this narrow-gauge railroad is—except for the one in Skagway,
Alaska *(see)*—the sole surviving passenger operation of its kind in
the United States. When it was completed in 1882, the Silverton
train was used to haul ores economically and efficiently from
isolated mountain areas to points where smelters could operate.
The train has been in continuous use since it was built. The typically Victorian coaches and locomotives, all vintage 1880s, now
take tourists through magnificent Rocky Mountain scenery. NR
*Operates daily from last Sat in May to first Sun in Oct. Round trip:
adults $8, children (5–11) $5*

FORT GARLAND STATE HISTORICAL MONUMENT, *25 miles east of
Alamosa via U.S. 160*
This restored adobe fort, at the southern edge of the town of Fort
Garland, was built by the War Department in 1858, when this part
of Colorado was within the territory of New Mexico. The fort was
named in honor of Brigadier General John Garland, commander of
the Department of Mexico. For 25 years Fort Garland was a garrison
for troops protecting settlers from the Ute Indians. In 1866–67 Kit
Carson, the famous Indian scout, commanded the post. Carson's
sympathetic dealings with the Utes averted open warfare and saved
the white settlements in the area. NR
Open: May 1–Oct.15, 9–5

**GEORGETOWN-SILVER PLUME HISTORIC DISTRICT NATIONAL
HISTORIC LANDMARK,** *on I-70*
This region produced more than $90 million in gold, silver, lead,
copper, and zinc between 1859 and 1939. Until the great silver
strike at Leadville *(see)* began in 1878, Georgetown was the most
productive silver camp in Colorado. The still-active communities
of Silver Plume and Georgetown have retained much of their
boom-town atmosphere. The **Georgetown Loop Historic District**
includes early mines and the famous Georgetown Loop, where the
narrow-gauge tracks of the Colorado & Southern Railway formerly
looped back over themselves for easier grade. The only major
mining town never to have been ravaged by fire, Georgetown still
has many 19th-century buildings. The **Hamill House** was the most

luxurious dwelling in Colorado. The **Hotel de Paris** (1875), now a museum, was one of the most celebrated hotels west of the Mississippi. NR

HOVENWEEP NATIONAL MONUMENT, *southwest Colorado and southeast Utah; best approached from U.S. 160 at Pleasant View, CO, then west on graded road 27.2 miles to Square Tower Group, UT*

Hovenweep, situated in the isolated country north of the San Juan River, contains 6 groups of towers, pueblos, and cliff dwellings. Its inhabitants were part of the large group of Pueblo Indians who occupied the Four Corners region of Colorado, Utah, Arizona, and New Mexico from about A.D. 400 until almost 1300. The Pueblos, a farming people, were expert artists and craftsmen. By 1200 they had moved from scattered villages in the open valleys and mesa tops to the heads of the Hovenweep canyons, which contain permanent springs. The Indians built their pueblos and towers here to be near their water sources. However, in 1276, when a 24-year drought started in the San Juan area, the inhabitants of Hovenweep were forced to abandon their homes. NR

For further information write: Mesa Verde National Park, CO 81330

LEADVILLE

LEADVILLE HISTORIC DISTRICT NATIONAL HISTORIC LAND-MARK, on *U.S. 24 and State 91*

Leadville first became famous as a gold-mining area in 1860; later it became the silver capital of Colorado as well. It has been estimated that the district produced about $136 million in silver between 1879 and 1889. After the collapse of silver prices in 1893, Leadville miners once more concentrated on gold production, continuing to do so until the end of the century. Since then lead, zinc, manganese, and molybdenum have been mined in the district. The 9-mile highway of the "Silver Kings" encircles the mining operations that made Leadville a leading ore producer. Many of the early structures have survived. These include the **Tabor House** (1877), built by the famous silver king H. A. W. Tabor and his wife, Augusta; the **Tabor Opera House** (1879); and the Victorian **Healy House** (1878). NR

MATCHLESS MINE AND CABIN, *on East 7th Street extended*

The Matchless Mine was one of the great bonanzas of the Leadville district. After its discovery in 1878 it netted its owner, H. A. W. Tabor, $10 million. Just south of the shaft house is the Matchless Cabin, a one-room wooden shack with a lean-to, where Tabor's second wife, Baby Doe, lived alone until her death in 1935. H. A. W. Tabor's fall was as meteoric as his rise, and when he died virtually penniless in Denver his last instructions to his wife were to hold on to the Matchless. This she did faithfully until she too died impoverished.

Cabin and mine open: May 30–Labor Day, daily 9–5. Admission: 35¢

LOWRY RUINS NATIONAL HISTORIC LANDMARK, *9 miles west of U.S. 160 at Pleasant View*

Named after George Lowry, an early homesteader, Lowry Pueblo was constructed by the Anasazi Indians about A.D. 1075 or slightly earlier. The pueblo once stood 3 stories high and contained about 40 rooms, including 8 kivas, or ceremonial rooms. In addition, one of the largest Great Kivas ever found stands about 60 yards southeast of the pueblo. Archaeologists believe that Lowry Pueblo was occupied intermittently for 100 to 150 years and that it was probably abandoned for the last time before a great drought struck the Southwest in 1276–99. The upper 2 floors of the pueblo were restored in the 1960s. NR

For further information write: Bureau of Land Management, 1211 Main Avenue, Durango, CO 81301

MESA VERDE NATIONAL PARK, *southwest Colorado, southeast of Cortez*
This 52,000-acre park contains hundreds of spectacular cliff dwellings and mesa-top pit houses and pueblos inhabited by Indians from about the first century A.D. until almost 1300. Mesa Verde—the green table—was named by the Spaniards who first saw it in the 1700s. The earliest direct evidence of Indian habitation of what is now Mesa Verde occurred during the Modified Basket Maker Period (A.D. 400–700). During this time people built pit houses, which were shallow holes in the earth covered with sticks, on the mesa top, enabling them to live close to their crops. During the Developmental Pueblo Period (700–1000) the Indians constructed above-ground homes of stone and adobe, arranged in compact groups around open courts. During the Great, or Classic, Pueblo Period (A.D. 1000–1300) the arts and crafts reached their peak. From about 1000 to about 1200 the Indians lived in well-constructed stone pueblos on the mesa top, with some houses reaching a height of four stories. About 1200, possibly because of raids by covetous nomads, the Indians retreated to the greater security of the cliff dwellings, great villages in caves at the heads of canyons, where living conditions were much more difficult than on the mesa top. Then in the 1270s the villages of Mesa Verde were abandoned, probably because of a severe drought that hit the whole region. Among the innumerable attractions here are the **Cliff Palace,** a village of more than 200 rooms and 23 kivas, **Far View House,** a large mesa-top pueblo, **Balcony House,** built into the wall of Soda Canyon, and **Fewkes Canyon Ruins,** a group of cliff dwellings. NR
For further information write: Superintendent, CO 81330

MONTROSE VICINITY
CHIEF OURAY STATE HISTORICAL MONUMENT, *10 miles south on U.S. 550*
The state of Colorado has erected a memorial tribute to the Ute Indians on a site that was the farm of Chief Ouray, who died in 1880, and his wife, Chipeta. The park has a museum devoted to the history and culture of the Utes. NR

PIKES PEAK NATIONAL HISTORIC LANDMARK, *15 miles west of Colorado Springs*
On November 23, 1806, on an expedition to determine the southwest boundary of the Louisiana Purchase, Lieutenant Zebulon M. Pike reached the present site of Pueblo. Pike and a few men then set out to climb the great peak that now bears Pike's name, but they failed to reach the summit. Set forward from the front range of the Rockies, Pikes Peak appears to rise much higher than its actual 14,110 feet. During the gold rush of 1859 it was the landmark that guided thousands of prospectors westward. Many of the Conestoga wagons that crossed the plains bore the inscription "Pikes Peak or Bust!" Pikes Peak was made accessible by the Manitou & Pikes Peak Railway, better known as the cog railway, which has been in operation since 1891. NR

COLORADO

Left: a replica of Pikes Stockade stands in Colorado's San Luis Valley. Right: Pikes Peak National Historic Landmark

PIKES STOCKADE NATIONAL HISTORIC LANDMARK, *about 20 miles south of Alamosa via U.S. 285 and State 136*

This stockade, located on the Conejos River about 5 miles east of Sanford, is a replica of the stockade built in February, 1807, by Lieutenant Zebulon Pike to serve as a winter base for his expedition. Unaware that he had overstepped the vague boundary between the United States and Mexico, Pike raised The Stars and Stripes here. When Spanish officials learned of this they sent an armed force of about 100 men to Pike's fort. Pike and his command were placed under nominal arrest. Pike was taken to Santa Fe and later to Mexico, and was subsequently released on the promise never to return to Mexico. This replica of the stockade closely follows the specifications recorded by Pike. NR

Open: June–Oct, 8:30–7; fall, 9–4

PLATTEVILLE

FORT VASQUEZ STATE HISTORICAL MONUMENT, *one mile south on U.S. 85*

Built about 1835 by Louis Vasquez and Andrew Sublette, both famous mountain men, Fort Vasquez was intended to capture the Indian trade along the South Platte River. According to an early traveler, the fort was about 100 feet square, with 12-foot-high walls pierced at intervals by rifle ports, and towers above 2 of the corners. In 1842 trouble with the Indians forced the abandonment of Fort Vasquez, which gradually fell into ruins. Exhibits in the reconstructed fort and the visitor center tell the story of the Colorado fur trade. NR

Center open: Apr 1–Oct 31, daily 9–5; fort open year round

PUEBLO

EL PUEBLO MUSEUM, *905 South Prairie Avenue*

This museum has exhibits and dioramas illustrating the history of

Pueblo and its neighborhood—an ancient crossroads for Indian trails. On museum grounds is a full-sized reproduction of Fort Pueblo, or El Pueblo, a little walled quadrangle built about 1842 by fur traders to defend themselves against marauding Indians. With the end of beaver hunting, El Pueblo decayed. The mountain men vanished and a few Mexican families occupied the stronghold. At Christmas, 1854, a band of Ute Indians got inside the fort and massacred or carried off its whole population of about 17 Mexicans. The fort fell into ruins, and its adobe bricks were probably used to build the town of Pueblo, which grew up in the wake of the 1859 gold rush.

Open: Tues–Fri 9–5; Sat, Sun, holidays 10–5

SILVERTON HISTORIC DISTRICT NATIONAL HISTORIC LANDMARK, *on U.S. 550*

Situated in one of the principal mining districts in the San Juan basin of southwestern Colorado, Silverton was a boom mining town in the 1880s. Originally named Baker's Park for Captain Charles Baker, the first prospector in the region, this rich silver center played an important role in the mining and economic development of the Rocky Mountain area. A few of the mines still operate. Silverton retains its frontier appearance with the **Grand Imperial Hotel** (1882), the Congregational church (1881), the city hall (1908), and the gold-domed courthouse (1907). A major tourist attraction is a ride on the narrow-gauge railroad (*see Durango*). NR

TELLURIDE HISTORIC DISTRICT NATIONAL HISTORIC LANDMARK, *east of State 145*

Named for tellurium, a nonmetallic element found in the ores of this region, the town of Telluride developed as a result of gold strikes first made in 1875. Several claims were struck, of which the most famous was the Smuggler, where miners uncovered a vein of gold that assayed at $1,200 a ton. The town became one of the busiest gold camps in Colorado after a narrow-gauge railroad— the Rio Grande Southern Railroad—was built to it in 1890. Today, however, only a few mines are in operation. Among the turn-of-the-century buildings that remain are the **City Hall** (1883), the **Sheridan Hotel** (1890s), the **Opera House** (about 1900), and the **Miner's Union Building** (1902). NR

TRINIDAD, *southcentral Colorado, south of Pueblo on I-25*

Trinidad served as a trading post on the Santa Fe Trail until 1880, when the first railroad reached Santa Fe and the great trail passed into history. Two houses of the early period stand on Main Street and Interstate 25. The adobe **Baca House** (NR), dating from 1869, was the home of Don Felipe Baca, one of Trinidad's first settlers. In the rear an old adobe building now houses the **Pioneer Museum**, with exhibits emphasizing the local Spanish heritage. The ornate Victorian **Bloom Mansion** (NR) was built in 1882.

Both houses open: May 15–Oct 15, daily 9–5

UTE MOUNTAIN UTE MANCOS CANYON HISTORIC DISTRICT, *east of State 66 on New Mexico border*

The cliff dwellings and other archaeological ruins of Mancos Canyon are remarkably well preserved remains of the Anasazi culture. Plans are under way to develop this area on the Ute Indian reservation into a recreation park and historical site similar to adjoining Mesa Verde National Park (*see*). NR

CONNECTICUT

COVENTRY

NATHAN HALE HOMESTEAD, *South Street*

In 1776, shortly before Nathan Hale was hanged as a spy by the British, the patriot's father, Deacon Richard Hale, built this house. The elder Hale held court here as a justice of the peace. NR
Open: May 15–Oct 15, daily 1–5

EAST GRANBY

OLD NEW-GATE PRISON, *Newgate Road off Route 20*

From 1775 to 1782 this copper mine—America's first, created in 1707—was converted by the Continental government into a prison to confine Tories and dangerous felons. Prisoners were kept in total darkness in rat-infested caverns at the bottom of the mine shaft. The largest escape occurred in 1781 when 21 prisoners made their way to freedom. After the Revolution the mine served as Connecticut's first state prison until 1827, when the facility was moved to Wethersfield. Today visitors may see the hangman's scaffold in the prison yard, tour the mine tunnels, and see historic exhibits on American penology. NR
Open: Memorial Day–Oct 31, Tues–Sun 10–4:30

EAST HADDAM

GOODSPEED OPERA HOUSE, *Norwich Road, on State 82*

Situated at a river-boat landing on the edge of the Connecticut River, this impressive structure was built in 1876 by William Goodspeed, a civic-minded merchant, shipbuilder, and steamboat and railroad tycoon. The building served as a cultural center as well as Goodspeed's offices, and it still functions as an opera house. NR

Left: Mystic Seaport. Top right: Nathan Hale Homestead in Coventry. Below: Joseph Webb House in Wethersfield

NATHAN HALE SCHOOLHOUSE, *Norwich Road off State 82*
The patriot Nathan Hale taught at this little red one-room schoolhouse in 1773–74, 2 years before the Revolution. Today the structure contains exhibits of historical interest.
Open: summer weekends 1–5

ESSEX
GREAT VALLEY RAILROAD, *Railroad Avenue*
Founded in 1872, the Connecticut Valley Railroad ran from Old
Saybrook to Hartford. Today vintage steam locomotives with
elegant old coaches travel along the old tracks between Essex and
Deep River.
*Excursions: spring, Sat–Sun; June 24–Labor Day, daily; autumn,
Sat–Sun*

FARMINGTON HISTORIC DISTRICT, *main street of the village and surrounding streets*
Dating from 1645, this aristocratic town preserves many old struc-
tures that reflect its wealth and culture. These include the stately
buildings of **Miss Porter's School,** founded in 1843, and the **Stanley-
Whitman House** (NHL), built about 1660, which, with its overhang
and pendants, is one of Connecticut's finest examples of 17th-
century architecture. The latter now houses the Farmington
Museum, containing antique furniture, pottery, china, and silver.
NR
*Open: Apr 1–Nov 30, Tues–Sat 10–12, 2–5; Sun 2–5, Dec 1–Mar 31,
Fri–Sat 10–12, 2–5; Sun 2–5*

GROTON
 FORT GRISWOLD STATE PARK, *Monument and Park Avenue*
This park was the scene of the Battle of Groton Heights on September 6, 1781, when the British, under the command of the traitor
Benedict Arnold, took Fort Griswold, massacred its defenders,
and burned the towns of New London and Groton. The fort, gar-
risoned by some 150 men, was unable to resist its 800 British
besiegers and surrendered. However, the British continued to fire
upon and bayonet the Americans, until 85 patriots were killed.
Today visitors may see the earthen remains of Fort Griswold.
Groton Monument, a giant obelisk, commemorates the massacred
Americans, and a museum contains relics of the battle.
*Monument open: Memorial Day–Labor Day, daily 8:30–11:30;
Labor Day–Columbus Day, Tues, Wed, Fri–Sun 8:30–11:30, 1–4.
Museum open: Memorial Day–Labor Day, Tues–Sun 1–4*

GUILFORD
WHITFIELD HOUSE, *Whitfield Road*
Constructed in 1639 by the Reverend Henry Whitfield, who led a
group of settlers from Surrey, England, and founded Guilford, this
building is the oldest stone house not only in New England, but
quite possibly in the United States. In the community's early days
the house served as parsonage, fort, and meeting hall; it is now a
state historical museum.
Open: Tues–Sun 1–5; closed Dec 15–Jan 15

HARTFORD
BUSHNELL PARK, *along the Park River*
Laid out in 1853 by Frederick Law Olmsted, creator of New York's
Central Park, Bushnell Park was one of the first public parks in

the United States. It was the first park in the world to be voted for and funded by a city. NR

CHARTER OAK MARKER, *Charter Oak Street*
This plaque commemorates the site of the hollow oak tree in which Connecticut's Royal Charter (*see State Library*) was hidden by one Captain Joseph Wadsworth of Hartford in 1687.

NOOK FARM, *Farmington Avenue and Forest Street*
This remarkable neighborhood in the western section of Hartford, once inhabited by a group of interrelated friends and families, became something of a cultural center late in the 19th century, when it boasted such illustrious residents as Harriet Beecher Stowe and Mark Twain. The author of *Uncle Tom's Cabin* lived in a Victorian home (NR) built in 1870 for the last 23 years of her life. Mark Twain had a rambling Victorian-Gothic mansion (NHL) designed on one side in the shape of a river boat, where he lived from 1874 to 1879. The noteworthy interiors, designed by Louis C. Tiffany, have been restored.
Open: Tues–Sat 10–5, Sun 2–5; June 22–Aug 31, also Mon 10–5

OLD STATE HOUSE NATIONAL HISTORIC LANDMARK, *Main and State streets*
Designed by Charles Bulfinch in the Federal style and completed in 1796, this State House has witnessed many important events in the history of Connecticut. The Hartford Convention—a group of delegates promoting Federalist interests—met in the senate chamber in 1814; in 1818 the constitutional convention held its session here; and the Marquis de Lafayette was feted in the building in 1824. It served as Connecticut's capitol until 1879, when the state government moved to its present quarters (*see State Capitol*). NR
Open: Tues–Sat 12–4; closed national holidays

STATE CAPITOL NATIONAL HISTORIC LANDMARK, *on Capitol Hill*
Since 1879 this golden-domed structure has been the official seat of government in Connecticut. The historical mementoes housed here include Israel Putnam's tombstone, the figurehead from Admiral Farragut's flagship *Hartford*, Lafayette's camp bed, and battle flags of Connecticut regiments in the Civil War. NR
Open: Mon–Fri 8:30–4

STATE LIBRARY, *231 Capitol Avenue*
This building contains Connecticut's original Royal Charter, signed by Charles II of England in 1662, which granted the colony virtual self-government. When in 1687 King James II appointed Edmund Andros governor of the Dominion of New England, the honorable magistrates of Connecticut refused to surrender their charter and hid it in a hollow oak (*see Charter Oak Marker*).
Open: Mon–Fri 8:30–5, Sat 9–1

WADSWORTH ATHENAEUM, *600 Main Street*
Designed in the Gothic Revival style by the architect Ithiel Town and erected in 1842 with funds donated by Daniel Wadsworth, this institution was the nation's first free gallery of fine arts open to the public. Today the museum's 65 galleries display art of every period and school. NR
Open: Tues, Thurs, Sat 11–4; Fri 11–9; Sun 1–5; closed holidays

The Tapping Reeve Law School and the Congregational Church in Litchfield

LEBANON

 JONATHAN TRUMBULL HOUSE NATIONAL HISTORIC LAND-MARK, *via State 32 and 87*

Jonathan Trumbull, the only colonial governor to support independence and chairman of the Council of Safety, resided here. During the Revolution the wealthy Trumbull supplied manpower, munitions (*see Revolutionary War Office*), and advice to General Washington, whose phrase "Let us consult Brother Jonathan" became a byword of the day. NR
Open: May 1–Nov 1, Tues–Sat 1–6

REVOLUTIONARY WAR OFFICE, *West Town Street*

Most of the business of the Revolutionary War was conducted at this office, which had originally been a store belonging to John Trumbull, the last colonial governor and first governor of the state of Connecticut. The Council of Safety convened here, and supplies for troops on the front were collected here. Today the war office has been renovated and restored. NR
Open: May 1–Labor Day, Sat 2–5

LITCHFIELD HISTORIC DISTRICT NATIONAL HISTORIC LANDMARK

Serving as a trading center and outpost along Connecticut's northwestern frontier until late in the 18th century, Litchfield today with its central common and Revolutionary houses is one of the best preserved early "New England towns" in the state. Here in 1774 Judge Tapping Reeve founded America's first law school in a one-room building near his home. At classes conducted by Reeve and Judge James Gould in the **Tapping Reeve Law School** (NHL), young men were exposed to American common law in its formative

stages. The school's illustrious alumni include 2 vice presidents—
Aaron Burr and John C. Calhoun—3 members of the U.S. Supreme
Court, 6 cabinet members, and more than 100 U.S. senators and
congressmen. NR
*Reeve House and school open: March 15–Oct 15, Tues–Sat 11–5,
Sun 2–5*

MYSTIC
MYSTIC SEAPORT AND MUSEUM, *along the Mystic River on State 27*
One of the foremost maritime attractions in this country, Mystic
Seaport preserves the authentic flavor of Connecticut's seafaring
past. About 1850 Mystic's shipyards were producing the fastest
clipper ships in the nation. And in 1861 the first regular ironclad
vessel, the *Galena*, was fabricated at Mystic. Today the *Charles W.
Morgan* (NHL), last of the 19th-century wooden whaleships, is
permanently berthed here, as are the square-rigged mariner training ship *Joseph Conrad* and the Gloucester fishing schooner *L. A.
Dunton*. Other features of this coastal village include a planetarium
of celestial navigation and houses of the period.
Open daily 10–4; closed Christmas

NEW CANAAN
JOHN ROGERS STUDIO NATIONAL HISTORIC LANDMARK,
10 Cherry Street
The popular post-Civil War sculptor John Rogers occupied this
frame studio from 1877 until his death in 1914. The self-taught
artist was famous for his so-called Rogers' Groups depicting Civil
War, literary and dramatic, and genre scenes. Today the studio
contains an extensive exhibit of his work. NR
*Open: spring–winter, Tues, Thurs, 10–12, 2–4; Sun, 2–4. July–Aug,
Tues–Sat 2–4*

NEW HAVEN
AGRICULTURAL EXPERIMENT STATION NATIONAL HISTORIC
LANDMARK, *123 Huntington St*
The first agricultural experiment station in the nation was established at this site in 1874. The country's first state food law was
also administered from these premises. Today the station comprises
a vast complex of buildings, laboratories, and greenhouses. NR

FIRST TELEPHONE EXCHANGE NATIONAL HISTORIC LAND-
MARK, *733 Chapel St*
The world's first commercial telephone exchange was established
at this site in 1876. Situated in a room on the ground floor of the
Metropolitan Building, the switchboard could transmit only 2 calls
at once and had to use 6 separate connections to complete each call.
Today a restaurant operates here. NR

FORT NATHAN HALE, *Woodward Avenue*
Overlooking the harbor on the east, the remains of the present fort,
constructed during the Civil War, are on the site of an earlier log
and earthwork fortification that was used during the Revolution and
the War of 1812. NR

JUDGES' CAVE, *West Rock Park off Springside Avenue*
On May 15, 1661, after the Restoration in England, Judges Edward
Whalley and William Goffe, signers of the death warrant of Charles
I, went into hiding from Loyalist troops for several weeks here.

NEW HAVEN GREEN HISTORIC DISTRICT NATIONAL HISTORIC LANDMARK, *bounded by Chapel, Church, Elm, and Temple streets*
This was the site of the original marketplace plotted in 1638 by the Puritan founders of the New Haven colony. Gradually the town of New Haven grew up around the green. The only buildings remaining on the green are 3 churches built about 1815. **Center Church,** the fourth meetinghouse on this site, covers an old burial ground; from its crypt some of the old tombstones may be seen. The congregation of **Trinity Episcopal Church** was formed in 1752. And from the **United Church** Henry Ward Beecher preached to Captain Charles B. Lines's antislavery regiment before it departed for Kansas in 1856. NR

YALE UNIVERSITY, *College Street*
In 1713 the institution that became known as Yale University—named in honor of its patron, the East India trader Elihu Yale—was moved to this site west of New Haven Green. Founded in Branford, the Collegiate School, as it was called, first held classes at Killingworth in 1701 and subsequently at Old Saybrook before moving to the present campus. In 1752 the legislature provided funds for the construction of the Georgian **Connecticut Hall** (NHL), currently the oldest ivy-covered building at Yale. Two other National Historic Landmarks, built for leading American 19th-century scientists, are also on campus: the **James Dwight Dana House** and the **Othniel C. Marsh House.**

NEW LONDON

SHAW MANSION, *11 Blinman Street*
Belonging to Nathaniel Shaw, director of naval affairs for Congress, this house was used as Connecticut's naval headquarters during the Revolutionary War. Many a privateer that sailed from New London in the course of the war was outfitted here. The mansion also served as a hospital for prisoners of war. The British attempted to burn the house in 1781, but kegs of vinegar stored in the attic extinguished the flames. NR
Open: Tues–Sat 1–4

YE ANCIENTIST BURYING GROUND, *Hempstead Street*
Tradition has it that Benedict Arnold sat astride his horse in this cemetery and watched the British burn New London in 1781 (*see also Groton, Fort Griswold*).

NORWALK
LOCKWOOD-MATTHEWS MANSION NATIONAL HISTORIC LANDMARK, *295 West Avenue*
This 60-room mansion was built in 1864 by Detlef Lienau for the financier Le Grand Lockwood, president of the New York Stock Exchange and head of an old and wealthy banking house. The eclectic French Renaissance-Second Empire–style residence contains lavish architectural features and furnishings. NR
Open by appointment

NORWICH AND VICINITY
FORT SHANTOK STATE PARK, *Montville, 4 miles south of Norwich off State 32*
This park contains the site of Fort Shantok, where more battles between Indians occurred than at any other place in New England. The fort was built on a high hill overlooking the Thames River by

the Mohegan Indians under Chief Uncas. As an ally of the Mohegans, the Massachusetts Bay Colony sent some 40 soldiers to Connecticut to help defend the fort against the warring Narraganset Indians of Rhode Island. All that remains of Uncas' stronghold are traces of the original rock wall. Nearby are the **Old Burying Ground,** an ancient Indian cemetery, and the **Mohegan Church,** built by and for the Indians in 1831 and now restored.

LEFFINGWELL INN, 348 *Washington Street*
This inn belonging to Colonel Christopher Leffingwell, an industrialist who founded Connecticut's first paper and knitting mills and was a member of the Committee of Correspondence, served as a local headquarters for patriots during the Revolution. At that time the inn played host to General Washington, who went there to seek Leffingwell's advice on state and military affairs. NR
Open: May 16–Oct 16, Tues–Sun 2–4; June 1–Labor Day, also 10–12:30; Oct 16–May 16, Sat–Sun 2–4

SITE OF THE BATTLE OF THE GREAT PLAINS, 3 *miles north on State 12*
One of the bloodiest encounters in Indian history occurred here in 1743 when the Mohegan Uncas, a friend of the white man, defeated Miantonomoh, the Narraganset sachem.

POMFRET
WOLF DEN STATE PARK, *intersection of U.S. 44 and State 169 and 101*
This park contains the cave where, legend has it, the young Israel Putnam, a future Revolutionary War general, in 1749 singlehandedly slew a dangerous wolf that had been preying on local sheep herds for years. Putnam reputedly lowered himself into the cave at night and shot the wolf by torchlight.

REDDING
PUTNAM MEMORIAL STATE PARK, *State 58*
This park is a memorial to the soldiers of the right wing of the Continental Army under Major General Israel Putnam, who spent the long, bitter winter of 1778–79 encamped here. Putnam chose this site for his winter headquarters so that he could reach West Point within 3 days, watch the British outposts in Westchester, and support the southeast Connecticut coast. The severity of the winter, combined with a lack of food, clothing, and pay, caused the Second Brigade to plan a protest march on the general assembly in Hartford, but Putnam dissuaded the dissidents and imprisoned their ringleader. Today visitors may see the heaps of stones that once served as chimneys for the barracks. A museum contains Revolutionary War relics. NR
Museum open: Memorial Day–Labor Day, daily 12–4

WEST HARTFORD
NOAH WEBSTER HOUSE NATIONAL HISTORIC LANDMARK, 227 *South Main St*
This simple frame house was the birthplace of the lexicographer and orthographer Noah Webster, who has been called the Schoolmaster to America. His spellers, grammars, and dictionaries of the American language have provided the foundation upon which our speech is based. As Webster wrote in 1789, "Let us then seize the present moment, and establish a *national language,* as well as a national government." The modest saltbox contains Webster's

books and manuscripts as well as family mementos. NR
Open: Thurs 10–4 and by appointment

WETHERSFIELD

 JOSEPH WEBB HOUSE NATIONAL HISTORIC LANDMARK, *211 Main St*

On May 22, 1781, George Washington and the Count de Rochambeau met at this elegant colonial mansion and planned the strategy that led to America's decisive victory over Lord Cornwallis and the British at Yorktown and hastened the end of the war. During the days of the Revolution so many officers of the Continental Army stayed here that the house was dubbed "Hospitality Hall." NR
Open: Tues–Sat 10–4; May 15–Nov 1, also Sunday 1–4

 SILAS DEANE HOUSE, *203 Main Street*

This house was erected in 1764 by the wealthy patriot Silas Deane, who during the Revolution was suspected of treason but was eventually exonerated. Referred to as the Father of the American Navy, Deane helped develop the naval strength of the colonies. Acting as the nation's first diplomat, he went to France in 1774 to secure naval supplies and French support. NR
Open: Tues–Sat 10–4; May 15–Nov 1, also Sun 1–4

 OLD WETHERSFIELD HISTORIC DISTRICT, *bounded by the railroad, I-91, and Wethersfield Cove*

One of the most picturesque and historical villages in New England, this district comprises 17th-century houses, Revolutionary War sites, and elegant sea captains' mansions. One of the finest examples of an early colonial house here is the frame **Buttolph-Williams House** (NHL), built in 1692 and restored today. NR
Buttolph-Williams House open: May 15–Oct 15, daily 1–5

WINDSOR

 OLIVER ELLSWORTH HOMESTEAD, *778 Palisado Avenue*

Known as Elmwood, this house commemorates the great statesman Oliver Ellsworth. A signer of the Declaration of Independence, Ellsworth subsequently was one of the original drafters of the Constitution. During the first session of Congress Senator Ellsworth wrote the Judiciary Act, on which our entire Federal judicial system is grounded. In 1796 George Washington appointed Ellsworth third Chief Justice of the U.S. Supreme Court. Three years later he was chosen by President John Adams to be an envoy to France. Upon seeing Ellsworth, Napoleon proclaimed, "We must make a treaty with that man." Today the house contains a Gobelin tapestry presented to Ellsworth by Napoleon. NR
Open: May 1–Nov 1, Tues–Sat 1–6

WOODBURY

GLEBE HOUSE, *Hollow Road*

First used as a rectory, this house was the birthplace of the American Episcopacy. At a secret meeting held here on March 25, 1783, Samuel Seabury was elected the first bishop of the independent American Episcopal church. Although Seabury went to England the following year, the Church of England refused to consecrate him, and he was finally consecrated in Aberdeen, Scotland. Today the house contains a museum of Episcopalianism. NR
Open: April 1–Oct 31, Wed–Sat 11–5, Sun 1–5; Nov 31–April 1, Wed–Sat 11–4

DELAWARE

DELAWARE CITY VICINITY
FORT DELAWARE STATE PARK, *offshore on Pea Patch Island*

Known as the Andersonville of the North, this forbidding island bastion in the Delaware River served as a Federal prison during the Civil War. Begun on the site of an earlier garrison in 1848, the present pentagonal fort, with its bleak granite walls, was completed by 1860 at a cost of $1 million. During the war 300 Union enlisted men and officers were stationed here; 131 guns were put in place at the gun ports to ward off an expected Confederate invasion. Confederate officers were confined in cells on the second story of the main fort, while wooden barracks within a barbed wire stockade elsewhere on the island quartered as many as 12,000 Confederate prisoners of war at one time. A museum at the site houses Civil War memorabilia. NR

Open: Memorial Day–Oct 31, Sat, Sun, and holidays

DOVER AND VICINITY
DELAWARE STATE MUSEUM, *Meetinghouse Square, 316 Governors Avenue*

Housed in 4 separate buildings, this museum contains displays relating to Delaware's history from the early 1600s to the present day. The **Old Presbyterian Church,** built in 1790, and restored today, contains the museum's main collection of furniture, silver, ceramics, and clothing. In this building John Dickinson (*see Dickinson Mansion*) and his committee reportedly drafted the Delaware Constitution of 1792; later, in 1831, the Delaware Constitutional Convention convened at the church. The second museum building, a chapel built in 1880, houses a collection of Indian artifacts. A third edifice contains a log cabin typical of those erected by

Left: Zwaanendael Museum at Lewes. Right: The Strand in New Castle

17th-century Swedish and Finnish settlers. The **Johnson Memorial** building contains the personal memorabilia of Eldridge Reeves Johnson, founder of the Victor Talking Machine Company. NR
Open: Tues–Sat 10–5, Sun 1–5

DICKINSON MANSION NATIONAL HISTORIC LANDMARK, *6 miles south on U.S. 113*

John Dickinson, "Penman of the American Revolution," resided for many years in this Georgian brick mansion, which had been built by his father about 1740. Dickinson drafted the Declaration of Rights adopted by the Stamp Act Congress of 1765 and wrote such famous colonial propaganda tracts as "Letters of a Farmer in Pennsylvania" and "A Song for American Freedom," both of which were published in 1768. He drafted the Articles of Confederation in 1777 and later served as president of Delaware (1781–82) and chief executive of Pennsylvania (1782). He advocated equal representation for all states regardless of size at the Constitutional Convention of 1787. Today the Dickinson Mansion has been restored and contains many fine antiques and Dickinson family memorabilia. NR
Open: Tues–Sat 10–5, Sun 1–5; closed holidays

GOVERNOR'S MANSION, *Kings Highway*

Tradition has it that the home of Delaware's chief executive served as a station on the Underground Railroad in the days preceding the Civil War. The red-brick Georgian house, originally known as Woodburn, was erected about 1790 by Charles Hillyard on land granted to his grandfather by William Penn. Today the mansion contains period antiques and historic artifacts.
Open: Tues afternoons 2–4:30

HALL OF RECORDS, *junction of Legislative Avenue and Court Street*

This repository contains a fascinating collection of historic documents. Highlights of the exhibits include the Royal Charter from Charles II granting the Delaware territory to James, Duke of York; deeds and leases transferring the lands to William Penn; and Penn's 1683 order—executed in 1717—for the laying out of the town of Dover. There are many documents from 1787, explaining how Delaware became the first state to ratify the Constitution.
Open: Mon–Fri 8–4:30; closed holidays

ISLAND FIELD SITE, *about 20 miles from Dover, near South Bowers via U.S. 113*

This archaeological site contains more than 80 graves of Indians who occupied the area from approximately A.D. 600 to 1000. A reconstructed Indian village is located on the premises. NR
Open: July–Aug, daily; spring and fall, 12:30–4:30

OCTAGONAL SCHOOLHOUSE, *northeast of Dover at Cowgill's Corner*

Erected in 1836, this unique octagonal structure, which served as a school for almost a century, stands as a reminder of Delaware's early endeavors in public education. The school is the oldest extant building constructed as a result of the passage of "An Act for the Establishing of Free Schools" by the state legislature in 1829.
Open: Sat–Sun 1–4

OLD STATE HOUSE, *South State Street, east side of the Green*

Erected from 1787 to 1792 on the site of the **Kent County Court House** (built in 1722), and incorporating the bricks and other materials of the earlier structure, the Old State House has been the scene of several important historical events. On December 7, 1787, a convention met at or near this site to ratify the Federal Constitution. During the Civil War, in 1862, troops from Maryland who had invaded Dover to disarm units of the Delaware militia suspected of being Confederate sympathizers occupied the building for 3 days. NR

Open: Mon–Fri 8:30–4:30; closed holidays

FREDERICA

BARRATT'S CHAPEL, *1 mile north on U.S. 113*

Erected in 1780 by Phillip Barratt, a former member of the Church of England who had converted to Methodism, this chapel is known as the Cradle of Methodism. Here in November, 1784, Francis Asbury, who was John Wesley's missionary to America, and Bishop Thomas Coke first administered the sacraments to Methodist communicants and planned the conference to organize the Methodist Episcopal church in this country.

Open: Tues–Sat 9:30–4:30, Sun 1–5

LEWES

1812 MEMORIAL PARK, *on the Canal Basin*

This site, with its naval guns mounted at the water's edge and its granite monument, commemorates the bombardment and defense of Lewes during the War of 1812. The town of Lewes had refused to stock British ships with provisions, despite threats of bombardment. Colonel Samuel B. Davis mustered some 500 men and repeatedly paraded them up and down, so that at a distance the British fleet seemed to see thousands of men instead of a few. The British naval assault occurred on April 6, 1813. That day the townspeople of Lewes collected the cannonballs fired by the enemy and reused them in their own guns. **Cannonball House,** now the Lewes Marine Museum, nearby, still bears scars from the British gunfire.

ZWAANENDAEL MUSEUM, *Savannah Road and King's Highway*

Erected in 1931, this museum commemorates the first Dutch settlement in Delaware, which was named Zwaanendael, meaning Valley of the Swans. Having heard reports of Delaware's fertile shoreline, and of whales sighted in Delaware Bay, Captain David Pieterssen de Vries and 9 other patroons from Hoorn, Holland, organized an expedition to start an agricultural and whaling colony in the area. Early in 1631, 28 men arrived in Delaware on the ship *Walvis* (whale), settled on a tract of land that had been purchased from the Indians in 1629, and began erecting two brick buildings and a surrounding palisade. The captain of the *Walvis* returned to Holland that fall and reported that all was well. In May, 1632, Captain de Vries sailed to Zwaanendael with 50 additional colonists, only to discover that all the settlers had been massacred by the Indians. The settlement was refounded after 1655. Today the museum, modeled after the ancient town hall of Hoorn, contains historical exhibits on Lewes and Lower Delaware.

Open: Tues–Sat 10–5, Sun 1–5; closed holidays

MASON-DIXON MONUMENT, *southwest Delaware, west of Delmar on State 54*

This double crownstone marks the southwestern boundary of Delaware as it was surveyed between 1763 and 1768 by the English astronomer-mathematicians Charles Mason and Jeremiah Dixon.

Ever since overlapping grants of land had been issued to the Penn family of Pennsylvania (in 1682) and the Calverts of Maryland (in 1632), a dispute had raged as to the exact dominions controlled by each colony. Arriving from England in 1763, Mason and Dixon first determined the north-south line between Delaware and Maryland and then measured the east-west border between the 2 states. They subsequently surveyed the Maryland-Pennsylvania boundary. During the Civil War the latter portion of the Mason-Dixon line served to demarcate slave and free states.

NEWARK AND VICINITY

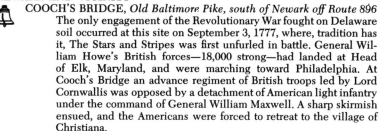

COOCH'S BRIDGE, *Old Baltimore Pike, south of Newark off Route 896*
The only engagement of the Revolutionary War fought on Delaware soil occurred at this site on September 3, 1777, where, tradition has it, The Stars and Stripes was first unfurled in battle. General William Howe's British forces—18,000 strong—had landed at Head of Elk, Maryland, and were marching toward Philadelphia. At Cooch's Bridge an advance regiment of British troops led by Lord Cornwallis was opposed by a detachment of American light infantry under the command of General William Maxwell. A sharp skirmish ensued, and the Americans were forced to retreat to the village of Christiana.

OLD WELSH TRACT BAPTIST CHURCH, *about 6 miles from Newark*
Built in 1746, this one-story brick structure is the oldest extant Baptist church in America and the successor to the first Baptist church erected in Delaware. In 1701 a Baptist congregation emigrated from Wales to Pennsylvania. Two years later they purchased a 30,000-acre tract, part of which fell within Delaware, from William Penn, and constructed a simple log church. Newer brick in the present church indicates where the building was hit by a cannon shot from the nearby engagement at Cooch's Bridge (*see*) during the Revolution.

NEW CASTLE

IMMANUEL CHURCH, *on the Green at Market and Harmony streets*
On the site of the mother church of the Episcopal Diocese of Delaware, William Penn participated in the "Livery of Seizin" ceremony, in which he received "Turf, Twig, Soyle, and Water" to symbolize his ownership of Delaware. Immanuel Parish was founded in 1683 by the Society for the Propagation of the Gospel in America, and its Anglican-style church was completed in 1703.

NEW CASTLE HISTORIC DISTRICT NATIONAL HISTORIC LANDMARK, *bordered by Harmony Street, The Strand, 3rd Street, and Delaware Street*
This unique example of a colonial capital has remained virtually unchanged since the early 19th century. Founded in 1651 as Fort Casimir by the Dutch, New Castle surrendered to the Swedes under Johan Rising in 1654, was retaken by the Dutch under Peter Stuyvesant in 1655 and renamed New Amstel, and was finally captured by the English in 1664, at which time it received its present name. William Penn, who was granted all the land within a 12-mile radius, arrived in New Castle in 1682. The town served as the capital of Delaware from 1704 until the Revolution. Today many fine town houses dating as far back as 1679 are preserved. On the third Saturday in May they are traditionally opened to the public. NR

DELAWARE

THE OLD ARSENAL, *on the Green facing Market Street*
The Federal government erected this arsenal in 1809 when war with England seemed imminent. During the War of 1812 Brigadier General John Stockton was stationed here. In 1831 troops from the recently burned Fort Delaware (*see Delaware City*) were temporarily quartered in the building. The structure currently houses a restaurant.

OLD COURT HOUSE, *Delaware Street between Market and 3rd streets*
Raised on the site of an earlier edifice about 1731, this building served successively as Delaware's colonial capitol, first State House, and county seat. The first structure (which burned down in 1729) was the site of William Penn's reception in America in 1682. In 1750 a surveying commission affixed the spire of the cupola-dome of the present structure as the center point of the 12-mile circle boundary between Pennsylvania and Delaware. In 1776 the legislature met here to approve the Declaration of Independence. After the state capital was moved to Dover in 1777, this building became a courthouse, where state and Federal courts met until 1882.
Open: summer, Tues–Sat 10–5; winter, Tues–Sat 11–4, Sun 1–4

ODESSA HISTORIC DISTRICT, *bounded by Appoquinimink Creek, High Street, 4th Street, and Main Street*
Preserved in this district are distinguished examples of 18th- and 19th-century architecture built by leading citizens of the community who helped make Odessa the commercial hub of a thriving agricultural region. Originally known as Appoquinimink, the village was renamed Cantwell's Bridge in 1731 when Richard Cantwell built a bridge over the creek. Soon farmers were bringing their grain to the granaries and docks by the bridge for shipping to the Delaware River and thence to coastal and foreign ports. By 1855 the town had become an important port from which thousands of bushels of grain were shipped every year, and its name was changed to Odessa in honor of the Russian seaport, which exported Ukrainian grain throughout the world. About this time the emergence of the Midwest as the nation's foremost grain producer caused Odessa to decline. Outstanding among the many fine colonial homes in Odessa today are the Georgian-style **Corbit-Sharp House** (NHL), erected from 1772 to 1774 by William Corbit, a Quaker who operated a tannery; and the **Wilson-Warner House**, whose main Georgian section was built by David Wilson, a prosperous merchant, in 1769. Other landmarks include the **Stable**, erected in 1791 by John Janvier, Sr., a cabinetmaker, and the **Brick Hotel**, built in 1822 by William Polk, which became a popular hostel for teamsters. NR
Buildings open: Tues–Sat 10–5, Sun 2–5; closed holidays

SMYRNA

BELMONT HALL, *1 mile south of Smyrna on U.S. 13*
Begun in 1689 and added to in the 1750s, this Georgian mansion was the home of Thomas Collins, who was the incumbent president of Delaware—as the early governors were called—when the state ratified the Federal Constitution in 1787. During the Revolution the house and grounds were reputedly fortified with a stockade, and a sentry stood guard from the roof. In 1777 the state legislature met at the residence after the Dover State House (*see*) was burned by the British.
Open by appointment

STANTON

HALE-BYRNES HOUSE, *south of Stanton at junction of Routes 4 and 7*

General Washington and his officers, including the Marquis de Lafayette, held a council of war at this house early in September, 1777, shortly before the Battle of Brandywine. Washington had encamped in Stanton on August 28, expecting General William Howe of the British army to pass through the village en route to Philadelphia. Howe, however, went through Newark to the west, and Washington moved his troops toward Brandywine Springs. NR

Open by appointment

WILMINGTON AND VICINITY

BRANDYWINE VILLAGE HISTORIC DISTRICT, *bounded by Tatnall Street, 22nd Street, Vandever Avenue, Mabel Street, and Brandywine Creek*

This village is one of the oldest and quaintest parts of Wilmington. Prior to 1670 the Dutch settler Jacob Van de Vere acquired a tract of land near the creek on which Brandywine Village later grew up. An adjoining parcel of land belonged to a Finn, Andrew Brantwin (also spelled "Brandwine" and "Brainwinde")—whence the origin of the name "Brandywine." The eastern portion of Brandywine Village fell within the Swedish neighborhood of "Bokton." On Sundays a canoe was used for "ferrying the church folk" of this district to Old Swedes Church (*see Holy Trinity*), across the creek. During the Revolution the mill colony operated by Joseph Tatnalls and his son-in-law Thomas Lea near the present Brandywine Bridge provided American soldiers with flour and meal. Subsequently, milling became a major industry of the area. NR

FORT CHRISTINA NATIONAL HISTORIC LANDMARK, *foot of 7th Street*

This monument near "The Rocks" on the Christina River commemorates the site of the first permanent settlement, founded by Swedes in 1638, in the present state of Delaware. Late in 1637 Queen Christina of Sweden and her prime minister, Axel Oxenstierna, sponsored an expedition, led by Peter Minuit, to the New World. On March 29, 1638, the two ships anchored at a natural wharf of rocks on the river, named Christina in honor of the young queen. Minuit then purchased all the land from the river to Bombay Hook from the local Indians for a copper kettle and other trade items, and his soldiers began to erect fortifications. (Earlier, in 1626, Minuit—a French-speaking Walloon in the employ of the Dutch—had been responsible for the famous $24 purchase of Manhattan.) During the next decade colonists, domestic animals, farming implements, and other supplies arrived at Fort Christina, which had been greatly enlarged and served as the principal storehouse of New Sweden and the only port of entry for ships. Under the energetic administration of Governor Johan Printz, the colony expanded to include both banks of the Delaware River and Bay, from Cape May to the Falls of Trenton on the New Jersey side. By 1654 Fort Christina boasted a population of 368; streets and houses had been constructed behind the fort at Christianahamn. The following year, however, Peter Stuyvesant—angered over the Swedish capture of Fort Casimir (*see New Castle Historic District*)—sailed from New Amsterdam, subjugated the Swedish forts, and established Dutch hegemony over the area controlled by New Sweden. Fort Christina was renamed Fort Altena. To celebrate the tricentennial of the Swedish landfall in Delaware, a massive monument of black granite, designed by the noted sculptor Carl Milles and donated by the people of Sweden, was raised at this site. Since Swedes introduced the log cabin to America at Fort Christina, a typical log dwelling erected by early Swedish settlers has been moved to these premises. NR

OLD TOWN HALL, *512 Market Street*
Built in 1798, this edifice served for over a century as the civic center of Wilmington. Ceremonial functions held here include banquets honoring the inaugural of Thomas Jefferson and the 1824 visit of Lafayette. Today the Old Town Hall houses the museum of the Historical Society of Delaware.
Open: Mon 1–9, Tues–Fri 10–5; closed holidays and Aug

THE HAGLEY MUSEUM, *3 miles north on State 52, then 1 mile east*
Occupying a 185-acre tract along the Brandywine River on the site of the original powder works founded by Eleuthère Irénée Du Pont in 1802, this museum contains indoor and outdoor exhibits tracing American industrial development from colonial times to the present. About a mile away stands the stone residence **Eleutherian Mills** (NHL), erected in 1803 by Eleuthère Du Pont near the powder mills, so that labor and management would share the same danger from explosions. As early as 1810 Du Pont's powder mill complex was the largest factory in the nation; it supplied American forces with gunpowder during the War of 1812. After 1860 E. I. Du Pont de Nemours & Company began to diversify its interests. Today the company is primarily a manufacturer of chemicals and is one of the nation's major industries. The main exhibit building is an 1814 textile mill that was converted to the manufacture of powder kegs.
Museum open: Tues–Sat 9:30–4:30, Sun 1–5; house open same hours as museum in mid-April–early June, Oct

HENRY FRANCIS DU PONT WINTERTHUR MUSEUM, *6 miles northwest on State 52*
This museum houses the richest and most extensive collection of early American interior architecture, furniture, and decorative accessories ever assembled. Nearly 200 period rooms provide a vivid record of the American domestic scene between the years 1640 and 1840. Erected in 1839, Winterthur was named after the town in Switzerland whence its owners, Mr. and Mrs. J. A. Biderman, had emigrated. Their grandnephew, Henry Francis Du Pont, developed the 60-acre gardens over a period of about 50 years, and in 1927 began to acquire his famous collection. NR
Write for tour information: Winterthur Reservations Office, Winterthur, DE 19745

HOLY TRINITY (OLD SWEDES) CHURCH NATIONAL HISTORIC LANDMARK, *7th and Church streets*
This church is believed to be the oldest Protestant place of worship still in use in North America. In 1697 the Reverend Eric Bjork emigrated from Sweden, established a pastorate at the village of Christianahamn (*see Fort Christina*), and began, in 1698, to oversee the construction of a Lutheran church on the site of the graveyard near the old fort. Built of stone by English workmen, and rectangular in plan, the structure was consecrated on Trinity Sunday, June 4, 1699. An adjoining Swedish farmhouse, the **Hendrickson House**, contains the church library and museum. NR
Open: Tues–Sun 12–4

DISTRICT OF COLUMBIA

ALVA BELMONT HOUSE (NATIONAL WOMAN'S PARTY), *144 Constitution Ave, NE*

Believed to be one of the oldest buildings on Capitol Hill, this lovely house served from 1801 to 1813 as the home of Albert Gallatin, Secretary of the Treasury under Presidents Jefferson and Madison. It was partially burned in 1814 when patriots under Commodore Joshua Barney fired from here on the British as they advanced toward the Capitol. After years of abuse, the house was restored in 1921. Eight years later it was purchased as headquarters of the National Woman's Party and named for its president, Alva Smith Vanderbilt Belmont.
Open daily 2–4

ARTS CLUB OF WASHINGTON, *2017 I Street, NW*

For the first 6 months of his Presidency, James Monroe lived in this Federal town house while the White House (*see*) was being restored following its burning by British forces during the War of 1812. Monroe had previously lived here during his years as Secretary of War in James Madison's cabinet. Later it was the home of such distinguished Americans as Charles Francis Adams, congressman and diplomat son of John Quincy Adams, and Union general Silas Casey; the house has been the headquarters of the Arts Club since 1916. NR
Open: Mon–Sat 9–5; closed holidays

BATTLEGROUND NATIONAL CEMETERY, *6625 Georgia Avenue, NW*

Union soldiers who fell during the Battle of Fort Stevens (*see Fort Stevens*), July 11–12, 1864, lie buried in the small cemetery

Left: the White House from Lafayette Square. Right: west front of the Capitol.
Below: the Jefferson Memorial framed by cherry blossoms

half a mile south of the battlefield. Monuments near the circle of graves pay tribute to the Pennsylvania, Ohio, and New York units that successfully repelled the attack of General Jubal A. Early's Confederate troops. NR

CHESAPEAKE & OHIO CANAL NATIONAL MONUMENT

On July 4, 1828, President John Quincy Adams turned the first spadeful of earth marking the beginning of construction on the Chesapeake & Ohio Canal. Running 185 miles from Georgetown in the Capital to Cumberland, Maryland, the canal cost $11 million. By the time it was completed in 1850 railroads had outstripped water routes to the west, and the unprofitable canal was eventually abandoned. Today 2½-hour trips down the canal on mule-drawn barges are available. Trips leave from 30th Street south of M Street, NW, and from Great Falls, Maryland. (*See also Maryland.*)

Trips: May–Oct, Sat, Sun, holidays; departures, 10:30, 12:30, 3

CITY HALL (DISTRICT COURTHOUSE) NATIONAL HISTORIC LANDMARK, *4th and E streets, NW*

Begun in 1820 by George Hadfield, one of the architects of the Capitol (*see*), this Greek Revival building was originally a city hall and then a courthouse where many famous trials were held. John Surratt, one of the conspirators in the assassination of President Lincoln, was tried here in 1867; he was later released. NR

CONGRESSIONAL CEMETERY, *1801 E Street, SE*

Since 1817, when 100 burial sites were set aside for use by the Federal government, many legislators and executive officials who died in the Capital have been buried here. To date 14 senators and 43 representatives are interred in this cemetery, along with such other notables as Vice President Elbridge Gerry, John Philip Sousa, Mathew Brady, and Sioux chief Scarlet Crow. NR

DECATUR HOUSE NATIONAL HISTORIC LANDMARK, *748 Jackson Place, NW*

Commodore Stephen Decatur, naval hero of the Tripolitan war and the War of 1812, lived in this house designed for him by Benjamin Latrobe for the last 14 months of his life. Famous for having said, "Our country . . . may she always be in the right; but our country, right or wrong," Decatur was killed in a duel by Captain James Barron, an old and bitter enemy. Subsequent residents of this lovely brick mansion include Henry Clay, Martin Van Buren, and Judah Benjamin. The restored house displays Decatur memorabilia. NR

Open daily 10–5; closed Christmas

DUMBARTON OAKS, *1703 32nd Street, NW*

In 1944 representatives of the United States, Great Britain, the Soviet Union, and China met in this stately Georgian mansion to discuss a permanent postwar international organization. The agreements reached here, known as the Dumbarton Oaks Plan, served as the basis of the United Nations Charter. Today the mansion houses Harvard University's Center for Byzantine Studies, featuring formal gardens, an extensive library, and a pre-Columbian art collection.

House open: Tues–Sun 2–4:45; gardens: daily 2–4:45

FORD'S THEATRE, *511 10th Street, NW*

With the stage set for the second scene of the third act of *Our American Cousin*, Ford's Theatre looks almost exactly as it did on

April 14, 1865, when shortly after 10 P.M. John Wilkes Booth crept into the presidential box and shot Abraham Lincoln. Built by John T. Ford in 1863, the theatre was closed following the assassination. Attempts to reopen it in June met with such public outrage that the government took over the building. Not until 1968, when the present restoration was completed, was the building again open to the public as a theatre. An outstanding museum of Lincolniana is housed in the basement. NR

Museum open daily 9–5; closed Christmas

FORT DE RUSSY, *Rock Creek Park near Oregon Ave and Military Rd*
This fort was one of the many defenses established during the Civil War to protect Washington from a Confederate advance. The fort is located in the 1,754-acre natural woodland park that follows Rock Creek through the Capital.

FORT DUPONT, *Fort Dupont Park, Alabama Avenue, southeast entrance*
In 1861 this site was selected as part of the defenses of the nation's Capital. Located within the 393-acre park, the fort is to be restored.

FORT LESLEY J. McNAIR, *4th and P streets, SW*
Since 1791 there have been military operations at this site overlooking the Potomac and Anacostia rivers. Named for a World War II general killed at Normandy, the fort now houses the National War College, the Industrial College of the Armed Forces, and the Inter-American Defense College.

FORT STEVENS, *13th Street between Piney Branch Road and Rittenhouse Street, NW*
On July 11–12, 1864, Union soldiers held back an attack by General Jubal A. Early's Confederate troops while President Lincoln watched from a nearby parapet. Federal soldiers who fell during the battle are buried at Battleground National Cemetery (*see*).

FREDERICK DOUGLASS HOME, *1411 W Street, SE*
"Do not judge me by the heights to which I have risen," said slave-born Frederick Douglass, "but by the depths from which I have come." The self-educated son of a slave mother and an unknown white father, Douglass fled north in 1838 and rose to become, in Lincoln's words, "one of the most meritorious men . . . in the United States." As lecturer, author, and editor-publisher of the *North Star*, Douglass was one of the nation's leading abolitionist spokesmen. After the Civil War, for which he raised Negro troops, he served in a variety of government posts including marshal for the District of Columbia and minister to Haiti. Douglass lived here at Cedar Hill from 1879 until his death in 1895; today the restored house and museum are preserved as a memorial to him. NR

Open: Mon–Fri 9–3:30, Sat–Sun 10–3:30

GEORGETOWN HISTORIC DISTRICT NATIONAL HISTORIC LANDMARK
Laid out in 1751 and incorporated as an independent town in the District of Columbia in 1789, this quaint area was the hub of social and diplomatic life in the early days of the Republic. It was annexed to the city of Washington in 1878 and today still retains its early-19th-century charm. Although many of the beautiful town houses and public buildings predate the Revolution (among them the **Old Stone House,** built in 1765), most were constructed after 1800. NR

DISTRICT OF COLUMBIA

HOUSE WHERE LINCOLN DIED, *516 10th Street, NW*
After Abraham Lincoln was shot by John Wilkes Booth at Ford's Theatre (*see*) on the night of April 14, 1865, the President was moved across the street to William Petersen's home. Here in the small back bedroom on the first floor Lincoln died at 7:22 A.M., April 15. The modest house was purchased by the government in 1896 and was subsequently restored to its appearance on that fateful day. NR
Open daily 9–5; closed Christmas

JEFFERSON MEMORIAL, *south bank of the Tidal Basin*
Built of limestone and marble and dedicated in 1943, this Classical monument to the third President of the United States houses a 19-foot bronze statue by Rudolph Evans and inscriptions from Jefferson's writings. Although he chose to be remembered as the "author of the Declaration of American Independence, of the Statute of Virginia for Religious Freedom, and father of the University of Virginia," Thomas Jefferson also served his country as minister to France, governor of Virginia, Secretary of State, Vice President, and President. NR
Open daily 8 A.M.–midnight; closed Christmas

LAFAYETTE SQUARE HISTORIC DISTRICT NATIONAL HISTORIC LANDMARK
This site, across Pennsylvania Avenue from the White House, was selected by George Washington as a public park and was later named in honor of the Marquis de Lafayette, America's first ally and Revolutionary War hero. In the park is a noted equestrian statue of Andrew Jackson. Many of the buildings surrounding the square are considered the most beautiful in the Capitol. Among them is the **Presidential Guest House** (formerly the **Blair House**), which served as the executive mansion for President Truman and his family while the White House was being restored.

LIBRARY OF CONGRESS NATIONAL HISTORIC LANDMARK, *1st Street and Independence Avenue, SE*
Founded in 1800 to serve congressmen and government officials, the original Library of Congress was destroyed when the British burned the Capital in 1814. Today's library of more than 43 million items began with the purchase of 6,487 volumes from Thomas Jefferson's extensive personal library. Among the many items of historical importance on display are the private papers of 23 Presidents, including Jefferson's rough draft of the Declaration of Independence and the first and second drafts of Lincoln's Gettysburg Address. NR
Exhibit halls open: Mon–Sat 8:30 A.M.–9:30 P.M., Sun and holidays 11–9:30

LINCOLN MEMORIAL, *foot of 23rd Street at Arlington Memorial Bridge*
Built as a monument to one man, this memorial has become a rallying place and symbol of equality for all Americans. Surrounding the awesome seated statue of Lincoln, designed by Daniel Chester French, are the 16th President's most famous speeches—the Gettysburg Address and the Second Inaugural. But the true monuments to Lincoln have been the demonstrations for racial equality held here, such as Marian Anderson's 1939 concert and Martin Luther King's March on Washington in 1963. NR

NATIONAL ARCHIVES, *Constitution Avenue between 7th and 9th streets*
> The chief national repository for government records, documents, and publications, the National Archives features many outstanding displays in the Exhibition Hall. Here, along with many other historical items, are the original copies of the Declaration of Independence, the Constitution, and the Bill of Rights.
> *Open: Mar–Sept, Mon–Sat and holidays 9 A.M.–10 P.M., Sun 1–10; Oct–Feb, Mon–Sat and holidays 9–6, Sun 1–6*

NATIONAL COLLECTION OF FINE ARTS AND NATIONAL PORTRAIT GALLERY (OLD PATENT OFFICE), *F and G streets between 7th and 9th streets, NW*
> Begun in 1840 and completed in 1867, this beautifully restored Greek Revival building, a National Historic Landmark, once served as a Civil War hospital and as the site of President Lincoln's second inaugural ball. It was built as the headquarters of the United States Patent Office and now houses the outstanding collections of the National Portrait Gallery and the National Collection of Fine Arts, a part of the Smithsonian Institution (*see*). NR
> *Open daily 10–5:30; closed Christmas*

THE OCTAGON HOUSE NATIONAL HISTORIC LANDMARK, *1741 New York Ave, NW*
> James Madison made this unusual house the temporary executive mansion after the British burned the White House during the War of 1812. Here in 1815 he signed the Treaty of Ghent, officially ending the war. Misnamed, the Octagon House has only six sides. It was built by Colonel John Tayloe at the suggestion of George Washington and is now the headquarters and museum of the American Institute of Architects. NR
> *Open: Mon–Fri 8:30–5*

PAN AMERICAN UNION, *17th Street between C Street and Constitution Avenue, NW*
> Founded in 1889 at the first meeting of the International Union of American Republics (forerunner of the Organization of American States), the Pan American Union was originally a commercial bureau. Now the permanent secretariat of the OAS, the world's oldest international organization, the union building was completed in 1910 and has long been considered one of the most beautiful in the Capital. NR
> *Open: Mon–Sat 8:30–4; closed holidays*

PENNSYLVANIA AVENUE NATIONAL HISTORICAL SITE
> Pierre L'Enfant, designer of Washington, D.C., planned Pennsylvania Avenue as the shortest distance between the White House and the Capitol (*see both*). Since 1791, when it was laid out, the avenue has been a ceremonial route for presidential inaugurations, 6 presidential funeral processions (including Lincoln's and Kennedy's), wartime victory celebrations, and various public and official demonstrations. Included in the historical site are the **Federal Triangle, Judiciary Square,** and sections of the commercial district of Washington. NR

PENSION BUILDING, *4th and 5th streets between F and G streets, NW*
> Built to commemorate Civil War veterans and to house the newly established Pension Office, this red-brick building is still occupied

by governmental agencies. Because of its spacious 4-story interior court, the building was used for 7 inaugural balls from Grover Cleveland's first in 1885, when the building was completed, to William Howard Taft's in 1909. Noteworthy on the façade is a 3-foot-high terra cotta frieze depicting the military forces of the Civil War. NR

PHILADELPHIA NATIONAL HISTORIC LANDMARK, *Smithsonian Institution, 14th Street and Constitution Avenue, NW*
The only surviving gunboat built and manned by Americans during the Revolutionary War, the *Philadelphia* was raised from the bottom of Valcour Bay, a channel in Lake Champlain, in 1935. She had gone down there on October 11, 1776, during a 7-hour battle in which Benedict Arnold's fleet of 16 small boats was severely defeated by a superior British force under Sir Guy Carleton. Preserved by the cold waters of the bay, the *Philadelphia* is now on display in the Smithsonian Museum of History and Technology. NR
Open: June 14–Labor Day, daily 10–9; Sept–June 13, daily 10–5:30

RHODES'S TAVERN, *601–603 15th Street and 1431 F Street, NW*
Built in 1800, this Federal-style structure is the oldest extant commercial building in Washington. In its long history Rhodes's Tavern has served as a polling place (in the 1802 municipal election), as a store, a boardinghouse, a bookstore, and as a bank. (The Bank of the Metropolis, with Andrew Jackson as one of its original stockholders, opened here in 1814.) Also that year the British command directed the burning of the White House (*see*) and the Treasury from here. NR

ST. JOHN'S EPISCOPAL CHURCH NATIONAL HISTORIC LANDMARK, *16th and H streets, NW*
Famous as the "Church of Presidents," St. John's is considered an outstanding example of early-19th-century architecture. Since 1816, when the church was completed and James Madison came here to worship, every presidential family has occupied Pew 54. NR
Open daily 9–5

SMITHSONIAN INSTITUTION
Established in 1846 with money willed by James Smithson, the illegitimate son of the first Duke of Northumberland, the Smithsonian has grown to include a vast complex of museums, art galleries, and research facilities constituting one of the most extensive collections in the world. Among the components of the Institution are the Museum of History and Technology, the Arts and Industries Building, the National Gallery of Art, the Museum of Natural History, and the National Collection of Fine Arts and the National Portrait Gallery (*see*). Within this complex one can see the original "Star-Spangled Banner," the Revolutionary War gunboat *Philadelphia* (*see*), an outstanding collection of gowns belonging to the nation's First Ladies, Charles Lindbergh's *Spirit of St. Louis*, and John Glenn's *Friendship 7*. The famous original reddish-brown building, a National Historic Landmark, now houses administration offices and Smithson's tomb. NR
Open daily 10–5:30; closed Christmas

UNITED STATES CAPITOL NATIONAL HISTORIC LANDMARK
Symbol of the nation and seat of the Congress, the Capitol was officially begun when George Washington laid the cornerstone on

September 18, 1793. The building was based on Dr. William Thornton's design, revised by Benjamin Latrobe. Construction continued under a number of architects, and the famous domed structure topped by the bronze statue *Freedom* was not completed until 1906. Another addition was begun in 1958. The Senate occupies the north wing of the Capitol, and the House of Representatives the south. Until 1935 the Supreme Court also held sessions here. From the Court's old basement office Samuel F. B. Morse sent out the world's first telegraph message in 1844. Since 1817, when James Monroe became Chief Executive, official presidential inaugurations have been held outside the east front of the Capitol, where a temporary platform is constructed for the swearing-in. NR
Open daily 9–4:30; closed holidays

WASHINGTON CATHEDRAL, *on Mount St. Alban at Massachusetts Avenue and Wisconsin Avenue, NW*
This Gothic cathedral will be one of the largest in the world when it is completed in 1985. Among the distinguished Americans buried here are President Woodrow Wilson, Admiral George Dewey, and Secretaries of State Frank Kellogg and Cordell Hull.

WASHINGTON MONUMENT, *The Mall between 14th and 16th streets*
The tallest masonry structure in the world, this 556-foot-tall monument to George Washington was designed in the 1830s, begun on July 4, 1848, and not finished until December, 1884. From an observation platform near the top of the monument (accessible by elevator), there is a beautiful view of the city the first President selected as the nation's Capital. NR
Open daily 9–5; closed Christmas

THE WHITE HOUSE, *1600 Pennsylvania Avenue*
In 1792 George Washington laid the cornerstone at the mansion that has been the home of every American President except him. Designed by James Hoban on a site selected by Washington himself, the 132-room White House is today much larger than it was in 1800 when John Adams moved in. Burned by the British in 1814, the "President's Palace" was not occupied again until 1817, when new white paint applied to the exterior walls gave it its present name. From 1948 to 1952 the White House underwent extensive renovation. (During this time President Truman and his family lived in the historic **Blair House** across the street.) Under Mrs. John F. Kennedy the Executive Mansion was redecorated with authentic furnishings of historical importance. Among the rooms open to the public are the **State Dining Room,** which can accommodate 140 guests; the **Blue Room,** furnished in the period of James Monroe's administration; and the **East Room,** where Nellie Grant, Alice Roosevelt, and Lynda Bird Johnson were married. On display in the East Room is Gilbert Stuart's famous portrait of George Washington, which Dolley Madison saved from the British. NR
Open: summer, Tues–Fri 10–12, Sat 10–2; winter, Tues–Sat 10–12

WOODROW WILSON HOUSE NATIONAL HISTORIC LANDMARK, *2340 S Street, NW*
When President Wilson left the White House in 1921, he moved to this red-brick mansion. Here he lived as a semi-invalid until his death 3 years later. Now a museum, the house contains its original furnishings and Wilson memorabilia. NR
Open daily 10–4; closed Christmas

FLORIDA

BRADENTON AND VICINITY
DE SOTO NATIONAL MEMORIAL, *5 miles west and 2 miles north on 75th Street W*

This 25-acre memorial is situated on a site visited by the Spanish adventurer Hernando de Soto and his lieutenant Luís de Moscoso on the first leg of their epochal 4,000-mile expedition through the Southeast. On May 30, 1539, De Soto and an expedition comprising some 600 men and 220 horses landed somewhere on the southwest coast of Florida, probably between Tampa Bay and Fort Myers. Hoping to discover cities of gold, the Spaniards instead found discomfort, disappointment, and despair. The journey soon deteriorated into a succession of skirmishes between the conquistadors and hostile Indians. In May, 1841, at Chickasaw Bluff, near Memphis, De Soto and his band became the first white men to see and to cross the Mississippi, which they called the Great River. The following year, having wandered as far as eastern Oklahoma, they again reached the banks of the Mississippi. By this time De Soto's forces had been decimated by hunger, exposure, and Indian attacks. Ill with fever, De Soto himself died on May 21, 1542, and was buried in the Great River. Under the leadership of Moscoso, 300 surviving explorers finally made their way to Mexico.

For further information write: Box 1377, Bradenton, FL 33505

GAMBLE MANSION CONFEDERATE MUSEUM, *at Ellenton on U.S. 301, on the Manatee River*

Built between 1845 and 1850 as the plantation house for Major Robert Gamble's 3,500-acre sugar plantation, the lavish Greek Revival Gamble mansion is the oldest building on the west coast

Left: St. Paul's Episcopal Church in Key West. Top right: Gamble Mansion in Bradenton. Below: a 1673 engraving of St. Augustine

of Florida. The mansion is also designated the Judah P. Benjamin Memorial, for at the close of the Civil War Confederate Secretary of State Benjamin hid from Federal troops there. NR

Open: Mon–Sat 9–5, Sun 1–5. Admission: adults 25¢, children free

BUNNELL VICINITY

BULOW PLANTATION RUINS HISTORIC MEMORIAL, 9 *miles southeast off State S-5A*

In the 1820s and 1830s this plantation was one of the finest in Florida, producing thousands of acres of sugar cane, cotton, and indigo. Today all that remains are the ruins of its sugar mill and slave quarters, several well-preserved wells, a springhouse, and the foundations of Bulowville, the plantation's splendid mansion. In December, 1836, during the Second Seminole War, Federal forces under Major Benjamin Putnam set up headquarters at Bulowville. Late in January he retreated to St. Augustine, and the Seminoles laid waste to the entire region. NR

BUSHNELL VICINITY

DADE BATTLEFIELD HISTORIC MEMORIAL, *on State 476, just west of U.S. 301*

On December 28, 1835, this battlefield was the scene of the Dade Massacre, in which the Seminoles, unwilling to allow white men to drive them from their homeland to reservations west of the Mississippi, ambushed and massacred more than 100 Federal troops. The site contains a museum with interpretive exhibits. NR

CAPE KENNEDY AIR FORCE STATION AND JOHN F. KENNEDY SPACE CENTER, *across Indian River from U.S. 1 between Titusville and Cocoa*

The Cape Kennedy Air Force Station has been the launching site of U.S. manned flights since May 5, 1961, when Navy Commander Alan B. Shepard, Jr., was hurled about 115 miles into outer space in *Freedom VII,* his Project Mercury capsule. Since then over 2,000 missiles have been blasted into space from Cape Kennedy. The Cape Kennedy Air Force Station, which is east of the space center across the Banana River, serves both as the actual launching site and as a development and testing center for military and NASA missile systems. NASA offers daily (except Christmas and major launching days) escorted 2-hour bus tours of the space center and Air Force station. Visitors see the **Moon Launch Pad,** the 525-foot-high **Vehicle Assembly Building,** the **Mission Control Center** for some of the early manned flights, and the **Air Force Museum.** On Sundays visitors may follow a marked route in their own cars. The Visitor Information Center, on State 405, 6 miles east of U.S. 1 at a point just south of Titusville, offers displays and exhibits that explain the U.S. space program.

NASA bus tours: daily 8–2 hours before sunset. Fee: adults $2.50, servicemen and children (12–18) $1.25, children (3–11) 50¢

CEDAR KEY HISTORIC MEMORIAL, *on west coast in town of Cedar Key, on State 24*

This memorial covers 19 acres in the town of Cedar Key, once a bustling Gulf Coast port. During the Civil War blockade-runners carried cotton, lumber, and naval supplies out of Cedar Key to obtain foreign exchange for the Confederacy and brought in vital supplies. Union forces raided the port in 1862, and it remained in Federal hands for the rest of the war. In the post-bellum period Cedar Key was the site of a timber industry boom as well as a shipbuilding, fishing, and oystering center. In the **St. Clair Whitman Museum** there are exhibits relating to regional history and a famous shell collection. NR nominee

CRYSTAL RIVER AND VICINITY

CRYSTAL RIVER STATE ARCHAEOLOGICAL SITE, *2 miles northwest on U.S. 19–98*

This archaeological site, covering about 30 acres on the north bank of the scenic Crystal River, was used as a ceremonial center by Indians, who were probably most active here from about 200 B.C. until A.D. 1400. In addition to the various mounds scattered over the area, the site contains a museum whose unique design permits visitors to look through large plate-glass windows at adjacent Indian temple, burial, and kitchen midden (refuse) mounds. The site also contains 2 steles (stone slabs used for commemorative purposes) that are the only known stone steles in the U.S. NR

YULEE SUGAR MILL HISTORIC MEMORIAL, *at Old Homosassa on State 490, west of U.S. 19*

This 6-acre state memorial contains the ruins of what was once U.S. Senator David Levy Yulee's thriving sugar plantation, which began productive operation in 1851. During the Civil War Federal vessels blockaded the mouth of the Homosassa River, but the Yulee plantation still managed to supply the Confederate forces with sugar, syrup, and fruit, which were smuggled out through canals near the river's mouth. On May 28, 1864, Federal troops burned the Yulee mansion on Tigertail Island, but the sugar mill, much further inland, was spared. Today the mill and parts of the grinding machinery have been restored. NR

FLORIDA KEYS AND VICINITY

FORT JEFFERSON NATIONAL MEMORIAL, *Dry Tortugas Islands, 68 miles west of Key West in Gulf of Mexico*

Fort Jefferson was the largest of the chain of seacoast defenses built from Maine to Texas in the first half of the 19th century. The fort, once the key to control of the Gulf of Mexico, is the main attraction of the 7 Dry Tortugas Islands and the surrounding shoals and waters of the Gulf of Mexico, all of which are included in this 90-square-mile national monument. The Dry Tortugas are a cluster of coral keys that form the southwest tip of Florida Reef. In 1513 explorer Ponce de León named them *las Tortugas*—the Turtles—because of the large number of turtles breeding in the area. The U.S. Army began constructing Fort Jefferson in 1846, and although work continued for almost 30 years, the fort was never actually completed. Surrounded by a moat, this 6-sided brick fort covers most of 16-acre Garden Key. Its 8-foot-thick walls are 50 feet high, and its massive foundations rest on coral rock and sand 10 feet below sea level. The fort, built to garrison 1,500 men, has 3 gun tiers designed to hold 450 cannon. In January, 1861, unarmed, half-completed Fort Jefferson was occupied by Federal troops to keep it from falling into the hands of Florida secessionists. After 1865, by which time it was militarily obsolete, the fort was used as a prison. Its inmates included several of the men accused of plotting Lincoln's assassination. In the 20th century fires and hurricanes turned the fort into a ruin. The monument may be reached by boat or seaplane from Key West (*see*). NR

For further information write: Superintendent, Everglades National Park, Box 279, Homestead FL 33030

KEY WEST, *about 130 miles south southwest of Miami via U.S. 1*
Key West, the southernmost city of the continental United States,
is a tiny island city about 3 miles wide and 5 miles long. It lies at
the end of the treacherous Florida Reef and is strategically situated
between the Gulf of Mexico and the Atlantic Ocean. Key West was
sighted in 1513 by Ponce de León when he sailed along the Florida
Keys. The island's first owner was a Spanish cavalry officer who in
1821 sold it to John Simonton, an Alabama businessman. Key West
began its rise to prominence as an international harbor and wreck-
ing depot in the 1820s, when a U.S. naval base was established
there. In 1831 Army barracks were built at Key West, and in 1845
construction began on **Fort Zachary Taylor** (recently designated a
national monument), built as part of the United States coastal
defense system. Key West was the only southern town to remain in
Union hands throughout the Civil War. In 1912 Key West became
the terminus for the railroad linking Miami and Key West. Built
by Henry Flagler (*see Palm Beach*), this railroad was destroyed by
the hurricane that devastated Key West in 1935. The town remained
isolated until 1938, when the 122-mile-long Overseas Highway (a
section of U.S. 1) was completed between Florida City and Key
West. Key West was a vital military and naval base in both world
wars. The **Key West Historic District** (NR) includes the **Audubon
House,** where John James Audubon lived in 1832 while painting
Florida wildlife, and the **Ernest Hemingway House and Museum**
(NHL), where the Pulitzer Prize-winning author lived from 1931
until his death in 1961. The **East and West Martello Towers,** both
open to the public, are old Civil War forts built in 1861.

JACKSONVILLE VICINITY
FORT CAROLINE NATIONAL MEMORIAL, *10 miles east, on the St.
Johns River*
This national memorial contains a reconstruction of Fort Caroline,
a fortified settlement established in 1564 by a group of French
Huguenots commanded by René de Laudonnière. On August 28,
1565, just as the Fort Caroline settlers—suffering from hunger and
Indian attacks—were about to give up and sail home, Jan Ribault
arrived at the fort with fresh supplies from France. That same
day a Spanish armada under Pedro Menéndez de Avilés encountered the French ships, tried unsuccessfully to board them, and
then sailed down the coast to a site where on September 8, 1565,
they established St. Augustine. The French quickly sailed south
to attack the Spaniards, and Menéndez, realizing that Fort Caroline would probably be lightly guarded, marched north and attacked
and captured the French fort, killing most of its garrison. The
Spaniards renamed the fortification **Fort San Mateo** and established a garrison there. They later slaughtered most of the remaining
Frenchmen (*see St. Augustine, Fort Matanzas National Monument*).
In April, 1568, a group of angry Frenchmen and their Indian allies
attacked San Mateo in revenge, killing most of the Spanish troops
and burning the fort. The original site of Fort Caroline was washed
away in 1880 when the St. Johns River was deepened. NR
*For further information: 12713 Fort Caroline Rd, Jacksonville FL
32225*

FORT CLINCH STATE PARK, *on north end of Amelia Island, 3 miles
north of Fernandina Beach on State A1A*
A pentagonal structure of brick and concrete, Fort Clinch was begun
in 1847 as part of a series of coastal defenses. The fort occupied a

strategic site commanding the entrance to the St. Marys River and guarding the passage through Cumberland Sound into the deep-water harbor of Fernandina. In 1850 it was named in honor of General Duncan Lamont Clinch, who played an important role in the Second Seminole War. Fort Clinch was far from completed when the Confederates seized it in 1861. Its location was important to the South because Fernandina Harbor was a convenient haven for blockade-runners. In February, 1862, the fort was abandoned to a Federal force, restoring Union control of the Georgia coast. NR

FORT GEORGE ISLAND STATE HISTORICAL SITES, *about 25 miles east on Fort George Island*

This island encompasses the **Huguenot Memorial** and the **Kingsley Plantation State Historic Site** (NR), each of which relates to a different period in Florida's history. The Huguenot Memorial honors the group of French Huguenots who, under the leadership of Jan Ribault, probably disembarked on or near the east shore of Fort George Island on May 1, 1562, before establishing a short-lived colony at present-day Port Royal Sound, South Carolina. In the 1580s the Spanish established the mission of **San Juan del Puerto** on the island, which they called San Juan. The mission was destroyed in 1702 during Queen Anne's War by James Moore, the British governor of South Carolina, while he was en route to attack St. Augustine. In 1736 James Oglethorpe, British governor of Georgia, renamed the island St. George in honor of King George II and built **Fort St. George** there. In 1740, during the War of Jenkins' Ear, Fort St. George served as his base in his unsuccessful attack on St. Augustine (*see*). Oglethorpe was subsequently obliged to destroy Fort St. George and to withdraw from the island, which was clearly within Spanish territory. Not until Florida became a British province (1763–83) was there peace in the Fort George Island area. After 1767 the island was owned by a succession of planters. In 1817 Fort George was bought by Zephaniah Kingsley, Jr., who used the island as headquarters for his extensive slave operations. The Kingsley Plantation Historic Site occupies 14 acres on the northern end of the island. It includes the original site of Fort St. George, a 2-story white frame house that is the oldest plantation in Florida, and the plantation slave quarters.

YELLOW BLUFF FORT STATE HISTORIC SITE, *1 mile south of State 105 on New Berlin Road*

Yellow Bluff Fort, which once stood on elevated terrain above the shoreline of the St. Johns River, consisted of triangular earthworks erected by Confederate troops in the summer of 1862 to protect their guns. Another battery was erected on the opposite side. For

Coastal defenses from left to right: an engraving of the French Huguenot settlement at Fort Caroline, 1565; U.S. Fort Clinch, 1847, both near Jacksonville;

20 days in September, 1862, these batteries prevented a Federal squadron of 6 vessels from coming upriver to Jacksonville.

NAPLES VICINITY
COLLIER-SEMINOLE STATE PARK, *17 miles south via U.S. 41*
This 6,432-acre tract occupies a portion of Big Cypress Swamp, an area between the west coast of Florida and the western edge of the Everglades. In the park are bronze monuments honoring the U.S. troops and the Seminoles who fought and died during the Second Seminole War. In 1836, after the U.S. government ordered the Seminoles to reservations west of the Mississippi, many fled to the Everglades and Big Cypress Swamp. By 1842, however, most of the Indians had been killed or deported. Today most of Florida's Seminoles—about 1,000 in all—live on reservations in Big Cypress Swamp and the Everglades.

OKEECHOBEE BATTLEFIELD NATIONAL HISTORIC LANDMARK, *4 miles southeast of Okeechobee on U.S. 441*
A key battle of the Second Seminole War (1835–42) occurred at this site on Christmas Day, 1837. Here on the swampy north shore of Lake Okeechobee, Zachary Taylor soundly defeated a band of Seminole and Mikasuki warriors. NR

OLUSTEE BATTLEFIELD HISTORIC MEMORIAL, *2 miles east of Olustee via U.S. 90*
On February 20, 1865, this battlefield was the site of the major Civil War engagement on Florida soil. The campaign began when a Federal expedition landed at Jacksonville on February 7, 1865. The Federals began marching westward, but they met little opposition and got within 3 miles of Lake City. However, a sharp skirmish with the enemy on February 11 forced the invaders to retreat to Sanderson. On February 20 the 2 armies met at Olustee. By late afternoon the Confederates were almost out of ammunition. Staff officers, couriers, and orderlies worked feverishly to bring fresh supplies to the front lines from an ammunition car in the rear. The arrival of additional Confederate troops at about the same time that the ammunition reached the front enabled the Southerners to advance. The Union forces were forced to withdraw. For the rest of the war, Federal forces in Florida were confined to Jacksonville, Fernandina, and St. Augustine. NR

PALM BEACH, *at north end of island between Lake Worth and Atlantic Ocean*
In the 1890s Henry Morrison Flagler (1830–1913), one of the original partners of the Standard Oil Company and a pioneer developer of Florida, supervised the laying out and construction of

and Castillo de San Marcos National Monument, built by the Spanish at St. Augustine between 1672 and 1692

Palm Beach township, which was soon recognized as a fashionable winter resort. In 1902 Flagler completed **Whitehall**, his own mansion on Whitehall Way, which now houses the **Henry Morrison Flagler Museum**. Built at a cost of $4 million, Whitehall is typical of the Palm Beach showplaces built early in the 1900s. Flagler's restored private railroad car is on the grounds.

Museum open: Tues–Sun 10–5. Admission: $1, children 50¢

PENSACOLA AND VICINITY

FORT PICKENS STATE PARK, *17 miles south of Pensacola on State 399*
The main historical attraction of this 1,659-acre park, situated on the western tip of Santa Rosa Island, is pentagonal Fort Pickens, built between 1829 and 1834 to defend the deepwater harbor of Pensacola. Its walls were 12 feet thick, 40 feet high, and they had casements for some 250 guns. In 1693, when the Spanish explored and surveyed the Gulf of Mexico coast, they named the point where Fort Pickens now stands Siguenza Point; in August, 1718, they built the first fortification there. This battery was destroyed by the French in 1719. The Spanish returned to Siguenza Point in 1723 and constructed a new fort and settlement there, which survived until 1752, when Santa Rosa Island was devastated by a hurricane. Fort Pickens was named in honor of General Andrew Pickens, a Revolutionary War hero from South Carolina. It remained in Union hands throughout the Civil War, and when fighting waned toward the end of the war, Fort Pickens was used as a prison. From 1886 to 1888 the Apache chief Geronimo and some of his band were incarcerated at the fort. NR

FORT SAN CARLOS DE BARRANCAS NATIONAL HISTORIC LANDMARK, *U.S. Naval Air Station, 6 miles southwest of Pensacola beyond Bayou Grande, via Palafox Street and State 294 and 295*
Fort San Carlos de Barrancas is a semicircular brick structure that was built by the Spanish in 1787, during the last period of Spanish occupation of West Florida. It was constructed on the site of the earlier **Fort San Carlos de Austria**, built by the Spanish in 1698 (*see Pensacola Historic District*) and destroyed by the French when they invaded the Pensacola area in 1719. In 1818, when Andrew Jackson invaded Pensacola for the second time, he accepted the surrender of the Spanish governor at Fort San Carlos and in effect seized control of Spanish West Florida for the United States. San Carlos de Barrancas was enlarged by U.S. troops in the 1830s and 1840s, and during the Civil War it was occupied first by Florida state troops and then by Union forces. NR

PENSACOLA HISTORIC DISTRICT, *bounded by Chase Street, 9th Avenue, Pensacola Bay, and Palafox Street*
Pensacola's historic district preserves this city's long history through both museum exhibits and restorations. The initial Spanish settlement at Pensacola under the explorer Don Tristán de Luna y Arellano lasted only from 1559 to 1561. In 1698 the Spanish made a second, strictly military, occupation in the Pensacola area, where they built **Fort San Carlos de Austria**, later replaced by Fort San Carlos de Barrancas (*see*). In 1752 the successful settlement of the Pensacola area finally began. During the War of 1812 the British based troops in Pensacola even though the city was still Spanish territory; they withdrew in 1814 when Andrew Jackson seized the town. In 1818, during the First Seminole War, Jackson took Pensacola again and held it until the following year, when Spain sent

troops to control local Indians who were allegedly raiding U.S. territory. During the Civil War Pensacola changed hands several times. Of major historical interest in this district is the **Site of Old Fort George**—on the northwest corner of Palafox and La Rua streets—built by the British in the 1770s. The fort was the site in 1781 of a Revolutionary War battle in which the Spanish retook Pensacola. **Plaza Ferdinand VII** (NHL), at the western boundary of the historic district, was the center of Spanish community life. Here on July 17, 1821, Jackson, the new governor of Florida Territory, accepted West Florida from Spain. The **Hispanic Museum**, on Tarragon and Zarragossa streets, houses historical exhibits. **Seville Square** was the social center of Pensacola in the prosperous 1870s, and most of the homes facing the square date from this period. NR

PORT ST. JOE
CONSTITUTION CONVENTION STATE MUSEUM, *1½ miles east on U.S. 98*

This museum stands on a 13-acre tract that allegedly preserves the site where the historic Florida constitutional convention met in 1838. There are interpretive exhibits relating to the convention and to the now-vanished town of St. Joseph.
Museum open daily 9–12, 1–5. Admission: adults 25¢, children free

FORT GADSDEN HISTORIC SITE, *6 miles southwest of Sumatra*

This 78-acre tract preserves the earthworks and trenches of 2 forts, both of which were situated at Prospect Bluff on the east bank of the Apalachicola River—a strategic position that afforded control of the river traffic into the interior. The first fort (known as **British** or **Negro Fort**) was erected by the British during the War of 1812, even though Prospect Bluff was well within Spanish territory. When the British abandoned Florida in 1815, they left the fort and its munitions to their Indian and black allies, who subsequently made a practice of hijacking Apalachicola River traffic and of helping runaway slaves from upriver plantations. These activities angered the Americans, who gave orders to destroy the fort. On July 27, 1816, an American force moved upriver to the fort and was fired upon. The Americans returned the fire, causing an explosion that killed all but 30 of the fort's 300 inhabitants. In 1818, when Prospect Bluff was still within Spanish territory, Andrew Jackson ordered an American fort built on the site of the ruined British fort. It was named for Lieutenant James Gadsden, who supervised its construction and who in 1835 would make the famous Gadsden Purchase. Despite protests from Spain the United States garrisoned the fort until Florida became a U.S. territory in 1821. NR

ST. AUGUSTINE AND VICINITY
CASTILLO DE SAN MARCOS NATIONAL MONUMENT, *1 Castillo Drive; access via U.S. 1 and State A1A*

The northernmost outpost of Spain's New World empire, this great fortress was built between 1672 and 1696 to protect St. Augustine. The impregnable *castillo* is a symmetrical 4-sided building surrounded by a 40-foot-wide moat. It is the oldest masonry fortification in the United States; its 30-foot-high sloping walls, which are 16 feet wide at the base, are made of native shellstone called coquina, with mortar made from shell limestone. The *castillo's* baptism by fire occurred in 1702, during Queen Anne's War, when the British colonists of South Carolina burned St. Augustine and unsuccessfully besieged the fort. In 1740, during the War of Jen-

FLORIDA

kins' Ear, General James Oglethorpe of Georgia captured and burned St. Augustine, but failed to take the *castillo* after a long siege. The fortress was also the target of raids by pirates and Indians, and the base from which the Spanish made several forays (1686, 1706, 1742) into the Carolinas and Georgia. The *castillo* was garrisoned by the British when they controlled Florida (1763–83). After Florida passed to the United States in 1821, the U.S. Army renamed the *castillo* Fort Marion in honor of the Revolutionary War hero Francis Marion. It was used as a prison, notably for Indians during the Second Seminole War, and during the Civil War Confederate forces occupied the fort briefly until Federal troops took it in 1862. During the Spanish-American War (1898), ironically, it served as a prison for Spanish soldiers. NR

For further information: 1 Castillo Dr, St. Augustine, FL 32084

FORT MANTANZAS NATIONAL MONUMENT, *about 14 miles south*

Here, in 1565, the Spaniards under Admiral Pedro Menéndez de Avilés massacred the French who had sailed south to attack newly established St. Augustine. The French fleet, commanded by Jan Ribault, was shipwrecked far south of St. Augustine, and some 300 survivors began marching north toward Fort Caroline (*see Jacksonville*). At Matanzas Inlet, at the mouth of the Matanzas River, the French castaways were met by Menéndez and his band, who slaughtered nearly all of them, including Ribault. Since then the area has been known as Matanzas, Spanish for "slaughters." Beginning in 1569 the Spanish fortified the area. During the War of Jenkins' Ear, the Spanish in 1740–42 constructed Fort Matanzas. This coquina structure, still impressive though now partially destroyed, stands on tiny Rattlesnake Island, near the mouth of the Matanzas River. This fort was subsequently occupied by the British, the Spanish for a second time, and then the Americans. NR

For further information write: 1 Castillo Dr, St. Augustine FL 32084

ST. AUGUSTINE TOWN PLAN HISTORIC DISTRICT NATIONAL HISTORIC LANDMARK, *bounded by Orange Street and Castillo de San Marcos, the Matanzas River, King Street, and Cordoba Street*

The first permanent European settlement in the United States and the long-time seat of Spanish power in East Florida, St. Augustine was established in 1565 by Don Pedro Menéndez de Avilés. Menéndez was successful in his purpose—to drive the French out of the region (*see Jacksonville, Fort Caroline National Memorial; St. Augustine, Castillo de San Marcos and Fort Matanzas National Monuments*). The Spanish subsequently controlled St. Augustine during 2 periods: from 1565 to 1763, when their power in the New World was at its height, and from 1783 to 1821, when their strength was crumbling. Strategically located on the edge of the Gulf Stream—the route the Spanish treasure fleets followed on their return trips to Spain—St. Augustine served the Spanish as a military base from which to combat British and French influence in the region. The town was also the headquarters of Spain's missionary effort to Christianize the Indians. St. Augustine's street system was laid out in 1598, and even though the British held the town from 1763 to 1783, its physical layout is still that of a typical 16th-century Spanish colonial walled town. The **Plaza de la Constitución,** containing a public market and lined with important civic buildings, dates from 1598 and is the oldest public square in the U.S. Many other extant or reconstructed buildings in St. Augustine reflect the Spanish influence, including 3 National Historic Landmarks: the

Llambias House, at 31 St. Francis Street, the **Gonzales-Alvarez House** ("Oldest House"), at 14 St. Francis Street, and the **Cathedral of St. Augustine**, on Cathedral Street. NR

ST. MARKS

FORT SAN MARCOS DE APALACHE NATIONAL HISTORIC LAND-MARK, *30 miles south on U.S. 319 and State 363*

This museum is built on the foundation of an old Federal hospital begun in 1857 on the site of several previous fortifications dating back to the early Spanish colonial period. In 1679 the Spanish governor of Florida built the wooden Fort San Marcos here at the junction of the St. Marks and Wakulla rivers. In subsequent years two more Spanish forts and a British trading post occupied the site. A curious episode occurred in 1800 when Fort San Marcos was held by William Augustus Bowles, a disgraced British officer who captured the fort with a band of Indians and proclaimed himself king of Florida. Five weeks later the Spanish returned with a flotilla of 9 vessels and retook the fort. Indian raids on the U.S. provoked Andrew Jackson to invade Florida in 1818 and take Fort San Marcos. Two British subjects were tried at the fort and convicted of inciting the Indian raids, and their execution set off a diplomatic crisis between the United States and Great Britain; Jackson withdrew a few months later, leaving Fort San Marcos once more under Spanish control. After Florida passed to the U.S. in 1821, Fort San Marcos was occupied and abandoned several times, and in 1857 the U.S. government built a marine hospital on the site. In 1861 the Confederates seized the complex, renamed it **Fort Ward,** and superimposed entrenchments and fortifications on the various existing ruins. The Confederates held the fort until May, 1865, and the earthworks they built can still be seen. NR

SEBASTIAN INLET STATE PARK, *between Sebastian Inlet and town of Sebastian on State A1A*

This 8-acre park is located on the western edge of the narrow barrier island south of Sebastian Inlet. It occupies the site used by the survivors and later the salvagers of a dozen Spanish treasure ships that were destroyed off this part of Florida's Atlantic coast by a hurricane in July, 1715. About 700 people perished in this wreck, but some 1,500 survivors made it to shore. By April, 1716, at least $6 million in gold and silver coinage had been recovered from the sunken ships. Additional millions remained on the ocean bottom until recently, when treasure salvors working for the Real Eight Company made substantial finds. The state of Florida has retained a portion of this treasure, which is exhibited in the **McLarty State Museum** within the park. NR

TALLAHASSEE AND VICINITY

NATURAL BRIDGE HISTORIC MEMORIAL, *6 miles east of Woodville off U.S. 319*

At the Battle of Natural Bridge, on March 6, 1865, a Confederate force commanded by General William Miller held off Union troops under General John Newton, who withdrew to Key West. This victory kept Tallahassee from falling into Union hands. NR

STATE CAPITOL, *South Monroe Street*

The central portion of this present-day capitol building dates back to 1839 and was the meeting place of Florida's secession convention in 1861. Tallahassee has been the capital since 1824.

GEORGIA

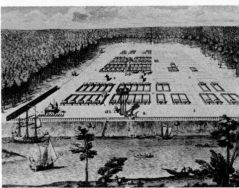

ANDERSONVILLE NATIONAL HISTORIC SITE, *1 mile east of Andersonville on State 49*

This historic site contains **Andersonville Prison** (formerly named Camp Sumter), where nearly 13,000 Union soldiers died between February, 1864, and April, 1865. In August of 1864 nearly 33,000 Federals were imprisoned in the 26-acre stockade; heat, crowding, and disease took their grim toll. The prison superintendent, Captain Henry Wirz, was the only Confederate official to be executed by the Federal government for war crimes. However, witnesses had testified that Wirz was not personally responsible, and he was posthumously exonerated from charges of cruelty. Visitors can see unfinished escape tunnels made by the inmates as well as the site of the stockade and the surrounding fortifications. This national historic site also contains **Andersonville National Cemetery,** the burial place of the Union soldiers who died while imprisoned at Andersonville. NR

For further information write: Superintendent, Andersonville, GA 31711

ATLANTA AND VICINITY

CYCLORAMA OF THE BATTLE OF ATLANTA, *at Park Avenue and the Boulevard*

The Cyclorama Building in Grant Park contains a huge painting—50 feet high and 400 feet long—that depicts the famous Battle of Atlanta, on July 22, 1864. The battle, the culmination of the Atlanta campaign (*see also Marietta*), came 2 days after the Battle of Peachtree Creek, in which General William Tecumseh Sherman's Federals had successfully moved closer to Atlanta, rail hub and

Left: the state capitol dome in Atlanta. Top right: the equestrian sculpture on Stone Mountain in progress. Below: a 1734 view of Savannah

manufacturing center of the Confederacy. Although the city was protected by 12 miles of earthworks, entrenchments, and gun emplacements, it could not hold out against the Union army. At the Battle of Atlanta some 4,000 Federals and 8,000 Confederates lost their lives. Atlanta subsequently remained under siege while Sherman captured the vital railroad lines in and out of the city, cutting Atlanta off from supplies and reinforcements. On September 2 Atlanta surrendered to Sherman, who evacuated the city and set fire to it on November 14, just before he began his destructive March to the Sea. Grant Park also contains **Old Fort Walker**, a Confederate battery built in 1864, and some Civil War breastworks. NR

Open daily 9–5:30

HARRIS HOUSE NATIONAL HISTORIC LANDMARK, *1050 Gordon Street, SW*

Joel Chandler Harris, creator of *Uncle Remus and Brer Rabbit* and other folk tales, resided in this gray frame house, known as Wren's Nest, from 1881 until his death in 1908. NR

Open: Mon–Sat 9:30–5, Sun 2–5. Admission: adults $1, children 30¢

STATE CAPITOL, *Capitol Square*

Atlanta became Georgia's capital in 1868. The present capitol, surmounted by a dome plated in gold leaf, was patterned after the National Capitol and was completed in 1889. A state museum of science and industry is inside. NR

Museum and capitol open: Mon–Fri 8:30–4, Sat 9–3

STONE MOUNTAIN PARK, *just east of I-285*

This historical park is noted for the colossal equestrian sculpture of Generals Robert E. Lee and Stonewall Jackson and Jefferson Davis carved into the granite wall of massive Stone Mountain. An ante-bellum plantation, a main house with period furnishings and dependencies, has been reassembled here from other Georgia locations.

Open daily: summer 10–9, rest of year 10–5. Admission: $1.60, children 60¢

AUGUSTA

FORT AUGUSTA SITE, *in churchyard of St. Paul's Episcopal Church, 605 Reynolds Street*

The city of Augusta (named in honor of King George III's mother) was marked off in 1735 by James Oglethorpe, who was attracted to the area by the possibility of lucrative trade with the Indians. Although relations between the Indians and the colonists were fairly peaceful, Oglethorpe ordered the construction of Fort Augusta in 1736 to protect his new trading post. During the 1750s and 1760s the village of Augusta developed as a military outpost. In 1780 the British gained control of the town, renaming Fort Augusta **Fort Cornwallis**. Patriot Colonel Elijah Clarke tried in vain to capture the fort in September, 1780; the next year Light-Horse Harry Lee successfully stormed Fort Cornwallis, forcing the British to surrender in June, 1781. After the Revolution, when tobacco was first introduced from Virginia, Augusta became the state's main tobacco market. In 1788, while Augusta was the state capital (1786–95), Georgia ratified the Federal Constitution there. During the Civil War, by which time Augusta had become Georgia's main cotton market, the town was selected as the site of the **Confederate Powder**

Mill. Augusta escaped destruction by Sherman in 1864 and was not taken by Union forces until after Lee's surrender in April, 1865.

MACKAY HOUSE, *1822 Broad Street*
This restored colonial frame house, built about 1760, was the scene of an important Revolutionary War battle in September, 1780. Revolutionary forces under Colonel Elijah Clarke attempted to wrest the house from a group of British troops and Cherokees who were holding it. After a 4-day siege British reinforcements arrived, forcing the Americans to retreat. The British captured 29 wounded patriots and hanged 13 of them from the staircase of the house. NR
Open: Tues–Sat 9–5, Sun 2–5

BLAKELY VICINITY

KOLOMOKI MOUNDS NATIONAL HISTORIC LANDMARK, *6 miles north off U.S. 27*
This 1,293-acre state park preserves 7 mounds that were built by Kolomoki Indians in the 12th and 13th centuries. At that time the complex, one of the most important population centers in North America, included burial mounds, a huge temple mound, a ceremonial plaza, a main village, and several surrounding villages. Kolomoki was a true city, small by modern standards but large for its day, with the main village alone probably supporting a population of some 2,000 Indians. NR

CALHOUN VICINITY

NEW ECHOTA RESTORATION, *3 miles north of Calhoun on State 225*
This restoration is a reconstruction of New Echota, the last capital (1825–38) of the Cherokee nation in the East. The small, independent Cherokee nation—whose homeland stretched across northern Georgia into North Carolina, Tennessee, and Alabama—had discarded the traditional Indian system of tribal rule and had patterned its government after that of the United States. At New Echota in 1821 the Cherokees adopted the written form of their language invented by Sequoya. The restoration includes the **Print Shop,** where the newspaper called the *Cherokee Phoenix* was printed in both Cherokee and English from 1828 to 1834; the **Court House,** meeting place of the Cherokee supreme court; **Vann's Tavern;** and the **Worcester House,** the home and mission of Rev. Samuel Worcester, who arrived at New Echota in 1827. After the removal of the Cherokee to the West in 1838, New Echota fell into ruins and most of the buildings were torn down.
Open: Mon–Sat 9–5, Sun 2–5; closed holidays

CARTERSVILLE

ETOWAH MOUNDS NATIONAL HISTORIC LANDMARK, *3 miles south off State 113*
Indians occupied this area between A.D. 1000 and 1500—during the Mississippian period of Indian culture. Etowah was a fortified town that at one time supported a population of several thousand Indians, who lived in windowless houses within the palisade. The village contained 7 pyramids that were grouped around 2 public squares. The largest of the pyramids, 53-foot-high **Mound A,** covered several acres and dominated the scene. Clay ramps with log steps led to the tops of these mounds, where funeral temples and chiefs' residences were located. A museum exhibits artifacts taken from the mounds. NR
Open daily 9–5; closed holidays

CHICKAMAUGA AND CHATTANOOGA NATIONAL MILITARY PARK.
See TENNESSEE

COLUMBUS HISTORIC DISTRICT, *roughly bounded by 9th, 4th, and 2nd streets and Broadway*
Laid out in 1828 as a trading post on Georgia's western border, Columbus was one of the last frontier towns of the 13 original colonies. The historic district contains the **Oglethorpe Marker,** commemorating General James Oglethorpe's 1739 treaty with the Upper Creek Indians, which confirmed Georgia colony's title to the land lying between the Savannah and Altamaha rivers. In the historic district there are about 612 original structures. NR

CRAWFORDVILLE
ALEXANDER H. STEPHENS MEMORIAL STATE PARK, *off U.S. 278*
This park contains **Liberty Hall,** the ante-bellum residence of Alexander H. Stephens, vice president of the Confederacy. Near the house, which has been restored, is a Confederate museum.
House and museum open: Tues–Sun 9–5

DAHLONEGA
DAHLONEGA COURTHOUSE GOLD MUSEUM, *in Old Lumpkin County Courthouse, Public Square*
This museum commemorates the nation's first gold rush, which occurred in 1829 in northeast Georgia. The region was then Cherokee Territory, and the Indians regarded the hordes of prospectors who streamed across their land as intruders. The Cherokees had refused to sell their land in north Georgia to the United States; however, in 1830 the state of Georgia assumed ownership of gold-yielding Cherokee Territory, calling it Cherokee County. When Cherokee County was later divided into 10 smaller counties, the gold-discovery area became Lumpkin County. Dahlonega, from a Cherokee phrase meaning "place of yellow metal," was made the seat of Lumpkin County in 1833. A branch of the U.S. mint that operated at Dahlonega from 1838 to 1861 coined more than $6 million worth of Georgia gold. The dome of the state capitol in Atlanta (*see*) is gilded with Lumpkin County gold. NR
Museum open: Tues–Sat 9–5:30, Sun 2–5:30

DARIEN
FORT KING GEORGE HISTORICAL SITE, *1 mile east of U.S. 17 on Fort King George Drive*
This 12-acre site contains the moat and earthen parapet of Fort King George (NR), built in 1721 by the British as part of a chain of frontier defenses. A 3-story wooden blockhouse, this fort was the southernmost British outpost in America and the first British settlement in what is now Georgia. It was abandoned in 1733, and 3 years later the area was settled by Scottish Highlanders, who built a stockade nearby called **Fort Darien.** An interpretive museum is in nearby Darien.
Open: Tues–Sat 9–5, Sun 2–5

LOUISVILLE
JEFFERSON COUNTY COURTHOUSE, *East Broad Street*
Louisville, which succeeded Savannah and Augusta (*see both*) as Georgia's capital, was laid out in 1786. The last session of the state legislature was held in Louisville's State House in 1805 before the capital was moved to Milledgeville (*see*). Today the Jefferson

County Courthouse, built from material of the old state capitol, occupies the site of that building. Louisville also contains the **Old Market House**, also known as the Old Slave Market, one of the few extant slave markets in the South.

MACON

CITY HALL, *Poplar St at intersection of Cotton Ave and 1st St*
Built in 1836 as a bank, this structure was purchased for the Macon city hall in 1860. It was the temporary capitol of Georgia from November 18, 1864, until March 11, 1865, when Sherman's troops were threatening the capitol at Milledgeville (*see*). On March 11, 1865, city hall was the site of the last meeting of the Georgia general assembly under the Confederate States of America. Having resisted 2 Union attacks, Macon surrendered to the forces of Union General James H. Wilson on April 20, 1865 (after Lee's surrender), thus ending Wilson's Raid through Alabama into Georgia.

OCMULGEE NATIONAL MONUMENT, *on east edge of Macon on U.S. 80E and 129*
The Indian temple mounds in this national monument are in 2 locations: the Macon Plateau section and the detached Lamar area, about 3 miles south of Macon (the latter is not presently open to the public). About A.D. 900 groups of Mississippian-culture Indians moved into the Macon area, dispossessing Woodland-culture Indians, who continued their agricultural way of life at a safe distance from the newcomers. The Mississippians built extensively at Ocmulgee, notably a fortified town of some 500 to 1,000 people, huge temple mounds that supported ceremonial temples on their flat tops, earth lodges (circular ceremonial buildings heavily framed and covered with earth), and burial mounds. The Mississippian civilization of the Macon Plateau disappeared from Ocmulgee about A.D. 1100. The surrounding people, descendants of the Woodland-culture group, then assumed the dominant role in central Georgia. Some of these Indians were the direct ancestors of the Creek Indians. The monument contains a visitor center with an archaeological museum. From the museum visitors may take tours of the **Earthlodge,** a restored ceremonial building with a 1,000-year-old floor. The **Temple Mound Drive** leads to the 3 largest mounds and the site of a 1690 British colonial post. NR
For further information write: Box 4186, Macon, GA 31208

MARIETTA AND VICINITY

KENNESAW MOUNTAIN NATIONAL BATTLEFIELD PARK, *2 miles north, off U.S. 41*
This park preserves the sites of several battles and skirmishes that occurred in June, 1864, during Sherman's Atlanta campaign, when the Union general was pushing his armies southward from Chattanooga toward Atlanta. He intended to pit his force of nearly 100,000 men against Confederate General Joseph E. Johnston's army of 60,000 and to crush the Confederates or disrupt their communications. By June Sherman had forced Johnston back to Kennesaw Mountain. On June 22 the 2 armies met at Kolb's Farm, 6 miles south of Big Kennesaw Mountain; the Southern forces withdrew after suffering heavy losses. On June 27 Sherman launched 2 major offensives, both of which failed, resulting in heavy Union losses. Finally on July 2 Johnston abandoned Kennesaw and retreated to Atlanta, which would soon be devastated by Sherman. NR
For further information write: Box 1167, Marietta, GA 30060

NEW HOPE CHURCH MONUMENT, *on State 92, 4 miles northeast of Dallas*

This monument commemorates the campaign of New Hope Church, from May 25 to 28, 1864. Sherman's Federal army made a series of unsuccessful assaults on General Joseph Johnston's Confederate troops, who were protecting the Atlanta roads. Casualties were high—the Confederacy lost 3,000 men, the Union 2,400—but Sherman's relentless drive toward Atlanta was temporarily halted.

MIDWAY AND VICINITY

FORT MORRIS, *about 10 miles east of U.S. 17 off State 38*

The remains of Fort Morris, one of the nation's few surviving Revolutionary earthworks, stand on a low bluff just south of the old town of **Sunbury**, a Midway River port rivaling Savannah in the 1770s. Constructed about 1776, Fort Morris was the largest fortification of its kind in Georgia at that time, enclosing about an acre within its ramparts. In January, 1779, Fort Morris, the last post to fly colonial colors after the fall of Savannah, surrendered to the British. NR

MIDWAY CONGREGATIONAL CHURCH, *on U.S. 17*

The town of Midway, Georgia's "Cradle of Liberty," was established as the Midway Society on August 28, 1754, by a group of settlers from Dorchester, South Carolina. The group, which included Puritans, French Huguenots, Scots, and Carolinians, went to Georgia in search of better land. On a grant of 32,000 acres in the Midway District of Georgia, they organized the Midway Society along the lines of a New England town. Selectmen, elected at annual town meetings, governed the community as well as the church (which was served by Presbyterian ministers). When Georgia failed to send delegates to the Second Continental Congress in 1775, Midway asked to be annexed to South Carolina. Denied its request, the Midway parish sent its own delegate, Lyman Hall, to Congress. The following year 2 Midway citizens, Lyman Hall and Button Gwinnett, helped draft and then signed the Declaration of Independence. In 1778 the British burned the Midway Church and all other buildings in the town, forcing the colonists to flee. The church, rebuilt in 1792, still stands, having been spared when Midway was again ravaged in 1864; adjacent to it is the **Midway Museum,** which honors the settlement's founders. *Museum open: Tues–Sat 9–5, Sun 2–5; closed holidays*

MILLEDGEVILLE, *central Georgia, on U.S. 441*

Laid out in 1803, Milledgeville served as the state capital from 1807 to 1868. The town—which largely escaped Sherman's wrath—retains much of its original plan. The **Old State Capitol,** now part of Georgia Military College, was the meeting place of the Georgia secession convention from January 16 to 19, 1861. The **Old Governor's Mansion** (1838), a fine example of Greek Revival architecture, was the residence of 8 successive Georgia governors until the capital was moved to Atlanta in 1868. NR

SAVANNAH AND VICINITY

FORT JACKSON MARITIME MUSEUM, *3 miles east via Islands Expressway*

The site of Fort Jackson has been used for military defense of Savannah since 1734, when a battery was built in this vicinity. By 1798 a mud fort stood here, and in 1809 the U.S. government com-

pleted a new fortification, named Fort Jackson in honor of James Jackson, Revolutionary soldier, governor of Georgia, and United States senator. Rebuilt in brick and enlarged in 1842, Fort Jackson was occupied by Confederate troops from 1861 until Savannah fell to General Sherman in December, 1864. Today the fort houses a maritime museum. NR
Open: Mon–Sat 9–5, Sun 1–5

FORT McALLISTER, *10 miles east of Richmond Hill on State 67*
This massive Confederate earthwork was begun in 1861 and named for the McAllister family, who owned a plantation nearby. In 1863 the fort successfully resisted bombardments from monitor-type Union vessels, thereby demonstrating that earthen fortifications could withstand contemporary naval ordnance. Fort McAllister was finally captured by General Sherman's army on December 13, 1864, thus ending the famous March to the Sea. Savannah, defenseless without Fort McAllister, was evacuated and occupied by the Federals on December 21, 1864—in time for Sherman to present the city to Lincoln as a Christmas gift. NR
Open: Tues–Sat 9–5, Sun 1–5

FORT PULASKI NATIONAL MONUMENT, *17 miles east via U.S. 80*
Built between 1829 and 1847 on Cockspur Island as part of the chain of coastal defenses constructed in the first half of the 19th century, supposedly impregnable Fort Pulaski was the pride of Savannah. The fort was named after Casimir Pulaski, a hero of the Revolution *(see Savannah Historic District).* After Georgia's secession it was occupied by Confederate forces. On April 11, 1862, Union rifled cannon forced the surrender of the fort, demonstrating for the first time that old-style masonry fortifications were ineffectual against modern weapons. The capture of Fort Pulaski, strategically located at the mouth of the Savannah River, cut Savannah's access to foreign trade and tightened the hold of the Union naval blockade on the South's economic life. The **John Wesley Memorial** honors a missionary to the Indians who arrived at the island on February 5, 1736. NR
For further information write: Box 98, Savannah Beach, GA 31328

LOW BIRTHPLACE NATIONAL HISTORIC LANDMARK, *10 Oglethorpe Ave, East*
Juliette Gordon Low, founder of the Girl Scouts of America, was born and reared in this Regency-style house. Patterning her organization after the British Boy Scouts and Girl Guides, in 1912 she formed 2 troops of Savannah area girls, which in 1915 became incorporated as the Girl Scouts. NR
Open: Mon–Sat 10–4, Sun 2–4:30; closed Wed. Admission: $1.00, children 60¢

SAVANNAH HISTORIC DISTRICT NATIONAL HISTORIC LANDMARK, *bounded by Bay, East Broad, Gwinnett, and West Broad streets*
This significant area of Georgia's colonial capital reflects much of the original plan devised by Savannah's founder, James Oglethorpe. Here he established the first settlement in Georgia, in February, 1733, as a debtors' colony. Laid out on a grand scale, with broad avenues and many open squares, Savannah was one of the first planned cities in North America. Of the 24 squares in the original plan, 5 are on Bull Street, within the historic district. During the Revolutionary War Savannah, with its strategic harbor, was an im-

portant target. The city was garrisoned by some 1,000 men under Patriot General Robert Howe when a superior British force captured it in 1778. In October, 1779, an unsuccessful Franco-American attempt to retake Savannah resulted in the loss of about 800 men, including the Polish-born Revolutionary War hero Casimir Pulaski. In 1782, after their defeat at Yorktown, Virginia, the British evacuated Savannah and the war was over in Georgia. Few of Savannah's colonial structures survived the fire of 1796. The district preserves many Regency buildings of merit, notably those built between 1816 and 1825 by the English architect William Jay. NR

SEA ISLANDS
FORT FREDERICA NATIONAL MONUMENT, *on St. Simons Island, 12 miles north of Brunswick*
Fort Frederica was established in 1736 by General James Oglethorpe to strengthen Great Britain's hold on the coastal area claimed also by Spain and France. At first it was a small defense bastion and fortified town of 116 settlers. During the War of Jenkins' Ear (1739–42), Frederica served as Oglethorpe's headquarters for his operations against Spain. After the British unsuccessfully attempted to seize the Castillo de San Marcos (*see*) in St. Augustine, Florida, the Spanish retaliated by attacking Fort Frederica. On July 7, 1742, at the Battle of Bloody Marsh, Oglethorpe beat back a superior force of 3,000 men under Governor Manuel de Montiano of Florida. Never again would Spain be a major threat to Georgia. In 1748, after King George's War, Fort Frederica declined in strategic importance. In 1763, with the end of Anglo-Spanish contention for the coastal area, the few remaining troops were withdrawn from Frederica, and the town and fort gradually fell into ruins. Visitors may tour the monument, which includes the ruins of the fort, the barracks, and the town moat and wall, as well as the foundations of several dwellings. The **Bloody Marsh Battle Site** is 6 miles south of Frederica. NR
For further information write: Box 816, St. Simons Island, GA 31522

SAINT CATHERINES ISLAND NATIONAL HISTORIC LANDMARK, *between Saint Catherines Sound and Sapelo Sound*
During the 17th century this island was the site of the Spanish Franciscan **Mission of Santa Catalina de Gualé,** one of the most important on the Georgia coast at that time. The mission was abandoned in 1686 in the face of English raids from the Carolinas. NR

WARM SPRINGS
LITTLE WHITE HOUSE, *off U.S. 27A*
Built by President Franklin Delano Roosevelt in 1932 and used as his presidential retreat, the Little White House remains substantially as it was when he died there on April 12, 1945.
Open daily 9–5. Admission: adults $1.25, children 75¢

WASHINGTON VICINITY
KETTLE CREEK BATTLEFIELD, *8 miles southwest, north of State 44*
This Revolutionary War battlefield was the site of an engagement on February 14, 1779, between Georgia and South Carolina militia (under Elijah Clarke, John Dooly, and Andrew Pickens) and a Tory force under Colonel John Boyd. The Tories were driven across Kettle Creek and dispersed after Boyd was killed. The Battle of Kettle Creek boosted patriot morale and helped check the strong Loyalist cause in Georgia and South Carolina.

HAWAII

ISLAND OF HAWAII

CAPTAIN COOK MEMORIAL, *across Kealakekua Bay from Napoopoo Village*

This monument was built on the spot where the British navigator Captain James Cook was slain in a fight with the Hawaiians in January, 1779. Tensions had arisen as a result of the Englishmen's inhumane treatment of the natives.

CITY OF REFUGE NATIONAL HISTORICAL PARK, *at Honaunau*

Situated on a shelf of lava overlooking the Pacific Ocean, this square sanctuary is set off by a great stone wall laid without mortar about A.D. 1550 by the ruling chief of Kona. It was the most important of old Hawaii's sacred places of refuge (a pu, uhonau) established by a king and operated by priests from a temple (heiau). Vanquished warriors, tabu breakers, and all other fugitives were admitted here and assured protection. Fierce wood-sculptured representations (Hi, i) of the old Hawaiian gods were set on poles above the palisades of the compound to warn intruders off the sacred grounds. In times of war, refugees would remain at the sanctuary until the conflict ended. Lawbreakers escaped the death penalty or other punishment by undergoing purification by the resident priests at the refuge; they would then be free to return to their homes in safety. Temples, palace grounds, royal fishponds, and stone platforms—where chiefs' houses stood—can be seen along the foot trails. NR

For further information write: Honaunau, Kona, HI 96726

Left: wood carvings at City of Refuge on Hawaii. Top right: a mission church on Hawaii. Below: the Arizona Memorial at Pearl Harbor on Oahu

KAMAKAHONU NATIONAL HISTORIC LANDMARK, *on the northwest edge of Kailua Bay*

While residing at this site from 1812 until his death in 1819, King Kamehameha I met with his council and instituted some of his most important agricultural and economic policies. His son and successor, the reformer King Kamehameha II, who also lived here, abolished the tabu system and the native Hawaiian religion in 1819. Today only the remains of the Kamehameha home and the king's personal heiau (temple) still stand. NR

PUUKOHOLA HEIAU NATIONAL HISTORIC LANDMARK, *southwest of Kawaihae off State 26*

Heeding a prophecy that whoever erected a heiau at this site would rule the Hawaiian Islands, Kamehameha the Great built a stone temple here and dedicated it in 1791 with 11 human sacrifices. Among those put to death was Kamehameha's principal rival, Keoua. Thereafter Kamehameha consolidated his power and founded the kingdom of Hawaii. NR

ISLAND OF KAUAI

COOK LANDING SITE NATIONAL HISTORIC LANDMARK, *southwest section, Waimea Bay, 2 miles southwest of State 50*

At this spot on Waimea beach the English explorer Captain James Cook, in 1778, became the first European to set foot on Hawaiian soil. While sailing across the Pacific Ocean from the Society Islands to North America, Cook was the first westerner to sight the Hawaiian archipelago, which he named the Sandwich Islands in honor of his patron, the Earl of Sandwich. NR

OLD RUSSIAN FORT NATIONAL HISTORIC LANDMARK, *southwest section, on State 50, 200 yards southwest of Waimea Bridge*

The ruins of this hexagonal stone fort recall the period of international rivalry for influence in the Hawaiian Islands. In 1817 Dr. Georg Anton Scheffer, a German surgeon in the employ of the Russians, was refused trading rights on Oahu. He subsequently came over to Kauai, where he allied himself with King Kaumaulii and erected this fort, which flew the Russian flag. Scheffer briefly succeeded in making Kauai a Russian protectorate before other nations applied pressure; he was finally expelled by King Kaumaulii. NR

WAILUA COMPLEX OF HEIAUS NATIONAL HISTORIC LANDMARK, *east coast at mouth of the Wailua River*

These ruins illuminate important aspects of Polynesian culture. The archaeological complex consists of 4 temples, a city of refuge, royal birthstones (where royal children had to be born in order to be certified royal), a rock where human sacrifices were made, and a restored priest's home. NR

ISLAND OF MAUI

IWAO STREAM, *in Iao Valley, 3 miles west of Wailuku on State 32*

The battle of Kepaniwai ("the damming of the waters") took place beside this stream in 1790. After invading the island, the Hawaiian army under Kamehameha the Great slaughtered most of the Maui warriors, whose bodies dammed up the stream and reddened its waters with blood.

HAWAII

LAHAINA HISTORIC DISTRICT NATIONAL HISTORIC LANDMARK, *State 30*

The royal capital of the islands until 1845, Lahaina is primarily known as the center of the American whaling industry that flourished in the Pacific from 1840 until 1865 and greatly influenced the Americanization and subsequent annexation of Hawaii by the United States in 1898. The **Hale Paahao Prison,** constructed of massive coral blocks in 1851, housed many a disorderly whaler in the mid-19th century. Lahaina was also a center of missionary activity, and many Hawaiian and missionary children attended the **Lahainaluna School,** which was founded in 1831. The **Hale Pa'i Printing House** contains the press on which Hawaii's first newspaper, *Ka Lama,* was printed in 1834. NR

PIILANIHAIE HEIAU NATIONAL HISTORIC LANDMARK, *4 miles north of Hana at the mouth of Honomaele Gulch*

Constructed in the 16th century, this heiau—measuring 340 by 425 feet—is the largest temple in the Hawaiian Islands. Its builder, Piilani, was a great ruling chief of Maui. NR

ISLAND OF MOLOKAI

FATHER DAMIEN'S STATUE, *on north shore of the Kalaupapa Peninsula*

This statue is a memorial to the Belgian Roman Catholic priest Father Damien de Veuster, who devoted his life to caring for the victims of Hansen's disease. Arriving in Hawaii in 1864, Father Damien was so appalled by conditions at the isolated leper colony of Kalaupapa that he made his home there, caught the disease in 1873, and died of it in 1889.

ISLAND OF OAHU

HONOLULU AND VICINITY

IOLANI PALACE NATIONAL HISTORIC LANDMARK, *364 S King St*

The only royal palace in the United States, this structure housed Hawaii's last 2 monarchs and also served as the seat of authority for the provisional government, the republic, the territory, and the state of Hawaii. Legislative sessions were held at the palace from 1895 until 1968, the house meeting in the throne room, and the senate convening in the dining room. Replacing an earlier palace built in 1845, the current Iolani Palace was constructed from 1879 to 1882 as a residence for King Kalakaua. After his death in 1891, Queen Liliuokalani occupied the premises. The ceremony formally transferring the sovereignty of the Hawaiian Islands to the United States took place on the palace steps on August 12, 1898. NR
Throne Room open: Mon–Fri 8–12, 1–4; Sat 8–12

MISSION HOUSES AND KAWAIAHAO CHURCH NATIONAL HISTORIC LANDMARK, *King and Kawaiahao streets*

These buildings commemorate the first contingent of Protestant missionaries who arrived from New England in 1820 and in subsequent years strongly influenced the religion, education, medical practices, and economics of the Hawaiians. Built in 1821 of timbers from New England, the **Frame House** is the oldest structure of its kind on the islands. A **Printing House** was erected in 1823 to house the Ramage press—a replica of which operates today—which struck off the first printing on Hawaii. The **Levi Chamberlain House** of

1831 was a home and also a depository for mission supplies. The Reverend Hiram Bingham dedicated his Congregational **Kawaiahao Church** in 1842. In Honolulu's oldest house of worship, King Kamehameha III is believed to have uttered, "The life of the land is perpetuated in righteousness," which has since become Hawaii's motto. NR
Houses open: Tues–Sun 10–5. Church open: Mon–Sat 8:30–4

NATIONAL MEMORIAL CEMETERY OF THE PACIFIC, *at the top of Puowaina Drive*
Situated in Punchbowl Crater, this cemetery is the final resting place of 17,000 veterans of World War II, the Korean War, and Vietnam.
Open daily 8–5

NUUANU-PALI, *7 miles from Honolulu via Pali Highway*
This towering cliff was the scene of a bloody battle of 1795 in which Kamehameha the Great defeated the Oahuans and consolidated his control over the Hawaiian Islands. Kamehameha and his warriors had landed at Waikiki and crossed the plain to the Nuuanu Valley, where they encountered Oahuan forces. Defeated, the Oahuans either escaped over the surrounding mountain ridges or were forced over the Pali precipice to their death.

PEARL HARBOR NATIONAL HISTORIC LANDMARK, *3 miles south of Pearl City on State 73*
Here at a great U.S. naval bastion, Japan, on December 7, 1941, conducted the surprise air attack that precipitated the United States' entry into World War II. The battleship U.S.S. *Arizona* was sunk that day with 1,102 sailors trapped within, and the U.S.S. *Utah* went down with 58 men on board. Today the remains of the *Arizona* serve as a memorial to those who lost their lives. NR

ROYAL MAUSOLEUM, *2261 Nuuanu Avenue*
Begun immediately after the death of Kamehameha IV in 1863 and completed in 1865, this Gothic-style mausoleum of coral block became the necropolis of the Kamehameha dynasty. On October 30, 1865, 18 coffins of kings and ancient chiefs were removed from the grounds of the royal palace and interred here. A chapel on the premises was consecrated in 1922.
Open: Mon–Fri 8–4; Sat 8–noon

WASHINGTON PLACE, *320 South Beretania Street*
Constructed in 1846 by an American sea captain, John Dominis, this house has served as the official governor's residence since 1922. The dwelling received its name in 1848 from Anthony Ten Eyck, the American commissioner, who rented rooms here for the U.S. legation. Dominis' son married the future Queen Liliuokalani, who resided in the house after her retirement from public life.

HALEIWA VICINITY
PUU O MAHUKA HEIAU NATIONAL HISTORIC LANDMARK, *4 miles northeast of Haleiwa on State 83*
The largest heiau (temple) in Oahu is believed to be the site where 2 of Captain George Vancouver's officers were sacrificed by the natives in 1792. The sailors were captured while in search of water for their ship, the *Daedalus*. Twelve years earlier a priest at this heiau had predicted the conquest of Hawaii by foreigners. NR

IDAHO

ALMO

CITY OF ROCKS NATIONAL HISTORIC LANDMARK, *on State 77*
While making their way across the continent on the **California Trail,**
pioneers stopped and camped near these fantastic rock formations.
For posterity they scratched names, dates, and even messages on
the rocks. This natural landmark was probably first discovered by
the Joseph B. Chiles party in 1842. NR

BOISE

ASSAY OFFICE NATIONAL HISTORIC LANDMARK, *210 Main Street*
Erected in 1870–71, this public building stands as a reminder of
the importance of mining in the Pacific Northwest. Gold, silver, and
other ores were evaluated here so that they could be priced and sold
by their producers. NR

COEUR D'ALENE VICINITY

CATALDO MISSION NATIONAL HISTORIC LANDMARK, *20 miles*
east on U.S. 10
A symbol of the Jesuit contribution in the settling of the West,
Cataldo Mission is the oldest building in Idaho. Originally known
as Sacred Heart, the mission was erected about 1848 by a priest
aided by Indians. Over the next 25 years, missionaries here converted nomadic tribesmen to Christians and farmers. NR

IDAHO CITY, *40 miles northeast of Boise via State 21*
After the discovery of gold in the Boise Basin in 1862, Idaho City
became a boom town with a population of 40,000. The metropolis
served as capital of the Idaho Territory and was the site of the state's
first newspaper. It is now a ghost town.

Left: the Lolo Trail over the Bitterroots. Top right: Sacred Heart Mission at
Cataldo. Below: a painting of Old Fort Hall by Bethel Morris Farley

LEMHI PASS NATIONAL HISTORIC LANDMARK, *12 miles east of Tendoy off State 28*

In 1805 the Lewis and Clark expedition crossed the Continental Divide at this point in the Lemhi Mountains. The Shoshone Indians who lived in this range supplied the party with horses, food, and guides to the navigable waters of the Columbia River. NR

NEZ PERCE NATIONAL HISTORICAL PARK, *northern Idaho, within an area 10–50 miles east of Lewiston via U.S. 12*

This vast stretch of country, encompassing 12,000 square miles, preserves and interprets the history and culture of the Nez Perce Indians and that of the white men—fur traders, missionaries, miners, and soldiers—who eventually engulfed and defeated them. In 1805 Meriwether Lewis and William Clark, on their expedition to the Pacific, became the first explorers to encounter the Nez Perce, whom they found to be "among the most amiable men we have seen." For the next half century the Nez Perce maintained friendly relations with white settlers in the region. With the discovery of gold in Idaho in 1860, the U.S. government negotiated a treaty with the Indians, appropriating many of their lands and establishing reservations. A rebellious branch of the Nez Perce refused to honor the terms of the treaty and subsequently instigated the Nez Perce War of 1877, which raged until their leader, Chief Joseph, who was retreating with his followers toward Canada, finally surrendered. Today 23 widely scattered and dissimilar sites within the park commemorate this significant chapter in the annals of the Northwest. Important sites include (in order of their accessibility driving eastward from Lewiston on U.S. 95, and returning via State 13 and U.S. 12) **Fort Lapwai,** erected by Army volunteers in 1862 to promote harmonious relations between settlers and Indians on the newly created reservations. At **White Bird Battlefield,** on June 17, 1877, the Nez Perce routed a contingent of U.S. soldiers in the opening engagement of the Nez Perce War. A month later **Clearwater Battlefield** was the scene of a clash between the Indians and the Army, which ended in a draw. Lewis and Clark were introduced to the Nez Perce tribe at **Weippe Prairie** (NHL) on the western side of the Bitterroot Range. Idaho's first major gold discovery occurred at the town of **Pierce** in 1860. And the **Lolo Trail** (NHL) **and Pass,** originally an Indian path leading over the Bitterroot Mountains to buffalo country in Montana, were used by Lewis and Clark on their westward journey. During the Nez Perce War the trail provided an escape route for some 700 Indians who were being pursued by U.S. troops. NR

For further information write: Box 93, Spalding, ID 83551

POCATELLO VICINITY

FORT HALL NATIONAL HISTORIC LANDMARK, *11 miles north*

Strategically situated at "the Bottoms" of the Snake River near the division of the Oregon and California trails, this fort was associated with the fur trade, the westward migration, and the transportation-supply route to gold mines in Idaho and Montana. Erected in 1834 by the fur trader Nathaniel Wyeth, the fort was sold to the British Hudson's Bay Company two years later. The Stars and Stripes was again unfurled at Fort Hall when the United States gained possession of the Oregon Country in 1846. The original Fort Hall was destroyed during a flood in 1863, and the present replica was built about 11 miles from the former site. NR

Open: Apr 1–May 31, 11–3; June 1–Sept 15, 9–8

ILLINOIS

CHICAGO HISTORICAL SOC

BEMENT

BRYANT COTTAGE STATE MEMORIAL, *on State 105*

Tradition has it that on the eve of July 29, 1858, Abraham Lincoln and Stephen A. Douglas, rival candidates for the U.S. Senate, met at this cottage in the heart of the Illinois Corn Belt and discussed arrangements for the now-famous series of 7 debates that were held that fall.

Open daily 8–5

BISHOP HILL

BISHOP HILL STATE MEMORIAL, *2 miles north of U.S. 34*

A colony of Swedish religious dissenters, established by Eric Jansson and Jonas Olson, thrived at Bishop Hill from 1846 until 1862. The inhabitants of this "prairie Utopia" excelled at every type of business, and Bishop Hill soon became a major center of commerce between Rock Island and Peoria. Religious and social differences finally caused the dissolution of the settlement in 1862. The **Colony Church,** which originally served as an apartment-church, now houses a collection of primitive paintings by Olof, Krans, a former resident of the village. NR

Open daily 9–5; closed holidays

BLOOMINGTON

DAVID DAVIS MANSION, *Monroe and Davis streets*

Situated on the estate known as Clover Lawn, this mansion was completed in 1872 for David Davis, an independent politician who was instrumental in securing the presidential nomination for his close friend Abraham Lincoln at the Chicago Republican Conven-

Left: the Old Water Tower in Chicago. Top right: the Cahokia Court House.
Below: a view of Galena in its heyday in the mid-1800s

tion of 1860. In 1862 Lincoln appointed Davis to the U.S. Supreme Court, where he made a landmark decision for civil liberty in the Milligan Case by restricting the right of military courts to try civilians. Davis was elected U.S. senator in 1877.

Open: Tues–Sun 1–5; closed holidays

CAHOKIA

CAHOKIA COURT HOUSE STATE MEMORIAL

Raised about 1737 by Captain Jean Baptiste Saucier, builder of Fort de Chartres (*see Prairie du Rocher*), this log structure, now reconstructed, is not only the oldest private dwelling in Illinois, but the oldest of all courthouses west of the Allegheny Mountains. The building was purchased in 1793 for use as a courthouse. The first court sessions and the first elections in Illinois were held here.

Open daily 9–5; closed holidays

CHURCH OF THE HOLY FAMILY NATIONAL HISTORIC LANDMARK, *just off State 3*

Completed in 1799 and still in use, the Church of the Holy Family is believed to be the oldest church in Illinois. NR

CHARLESTON VICINITY

LINCOLN LOG CABIN STATE PARK, *9 miles south between State 16 and 121*

This park contains the reconstructed 2-room log cabin where Abraham Lincoln's father, Thomas Lincoln, and his stepmother, Sarah Bush Lincoln, lived from 1837 until their death. Both are buried in nearby **Shiloh Cemetery.** One mile north of the park is the **Moore House,** where Mrs. Lincoln's daughter, Mrs. Reuben Moore, lived. It was here that Lincoln paid his last visit to Coles County on January 31, 1861, before leaving for his inauguration.

Cabin open daily 9–5; Moore House open: summer, daily 9–5

CHESTER VICINITY

 FORT KASKASKIA STATE PARK AND MEMORIAL, *10 miles north off State 3*

This park on the Mississippi River is the site of Fort Kaskaskia, which was originally erected by the French in 1736. During the French and Indian War in 1761, the French rebuilt the fort with heavy palisades; they destroyed it in 1766 to prevent its occupation by the victorious British. A memorial on nearby Kaskaskia Island houses a 650-pound bell, given "For the Church of Illinois" by King Louis XV of France in 1641. The bell rang the night of July 4, 1778, when George Rogers Clark seized Kaskaskia from the British, and was thereafter known as the Liberty Bell of the West. At the foot of the hill where Fort Kaskaskia once stood is the French colonial **Pierre Menard Home** (NHL), begun in 1802 and sometimes referred to as the Mount Vernon of the West. Menard was the presiding officer of the first territorial legislature, and in 1818 was the first lieutenant governor of Illinois.

House open daily 9–5; closed holidays

CHICAGO AND VICINITY

CHICAGO PORTAGE NATIONAL HISTORIC SITE, *at the Chicago Sanitary and Ship Canal*

From the time of its discovery in 1673 by Father Jacques Marquette and Louis Joliet, until 1836, this portage, or "carrying place," has served as a strategic link between the waters of the Great

Lakes (Lake Michigan) and those of the Mississippi River system (the Des Plaines River). In later years the portage was used by Robert Cavalier, pioneers of New France, and fur traders, and had an important role in the American settlement of the old Northwest. As one of the 5 great "keys of the continent," the portage provided an economic basis for Chicago, today one of the nation's largest cities. A bronze tablet affixed to a huge boulder marks the western terminus of the portage. NR

DOUGLAS TOMB STATE MEMORIAL, *east end of 35th Street*
This shrine is dedicated to the memory of Stephen A. Douglas, who served as justice of the Illinois supreme court, member of the U.S. House of Representatives, and U.S. senator; he was best known as a political rival of Abraham Lincoln.

HULL HOUSE NATIONAL HISTORIC LANDMARK, *800 South Halsted Street*
Jane Addams, pioneer social worker, founded this settlement house in 1889 in the slums of Chicago. Here she provided the poor with a variety of social services. She later became the first American woman to receive the Nobel Peace Prize. NR
Open: Mon–Fri 9–5, Sat 10–3, Sun and holidays 12–4

OLD WATER TOWER, *Michigan and Chicago avenues*
This landmark is one of the few survivors of the Great Chicago Fire of 1871, which almost destroyed the entire city.

PULLMAN HISTORIC DISTRICT NATIONAL HISTORIC LAND-MARK, *east of Cottage Grove Avenue between 103rd and 115th streets*
During the 1880s George M. Pullman, inventor and manufacturer of the Pullman sleeping car, had this model settlement built for his employees. In 1894 the Illinois supreme court declared the company-sponsored housing project illegal, and the dwellings were sold to private owners. Many of the old structures stand today. NR

RIVERSIDE HISTORIC DISTRICT NATIONAL HISTORIC LAND-MARK, *Riverside*
In 1866 Frederick Law Olmsted and Calvert Vaux, landscape architects of New York's Central Park, were commissioned to design this Chicago suburb, one of the earliest preplanned communities in the country. NR

ROBIE HOUSE NATIONAL HISTORIC LANDMARK, *5757 South Woodlawn Avenue*
Designed by Frank Lloyd Wright and completed in 1909, this Prairie-style house won international renown for its innovative features. It is a precursor of the modern split-level residence. Today the house is headquarters of the Adlai E. Stevenson Institute of International Affairs of the University of Chicago. NR
Open by appointment

SITE OF FIRST SELF-SUSTAINING NUCLEAR REACTION NATIONAL HISTORIC LANDMARK, *South Ellis Avenue between East 56th and 57th streets*
On December 2, 1942, scientists, headed by the Italian-born physicist Enrico Fermi, produced the world's first self-sustaining nuclear chain reaction here in a converted squash-rackets court beneath the west stands of Stagg Field. NR

DIXON
>LINCOLN MONUMENT STATE PARK, *Lincoln Statue Drive between Calena and Hennepin avenues*
>>During the Black Hawk War of 1832 (*see Rock Island*) Abraham Lincoln, captain of a company of Illinois Volunteers, first met Army officers Zachary Taylor and Jefferson Davis while encamped at the Dixon Blockhouse, one mile west of the present monument.

EAST ST. LOUIS
>CAHOKIA MOUNDS NATIONAL HISTORIC LANDMARK, *east on U.S. 40*
>>The remains of the largest prehistoric Indian town—representing the fountainhead of Mississippian culture—in the United States have been uncovered at this site. From 50,000 to 60,000 dwellings were built here between A.D. 600 and A.D. 1400. Nearly 100 earthen mounds, used as platforms for rulers' houses or as mortuary temples, were constructed at Cahokia. **Monks' Mound,** a burial mound 1,037 feet long, 790 feet wide, and 100 feet high, is the largest in the nation. NR

>EADS BRIDGE. *See* ST. LOUIS, MISSOURI

GALENA HISTORIC DISTRICT
>This once-important river-boat town on the Galena River preserves many fine examples of architecture built when Galena was the wealthiest city of Illinois in the mid-1800s. Historic structures include the **Market House,** formerly the hub of agricultural activities; the **John Dowling House,** erected in 1825 and the oldest residence in Galena; and a replica of the **J. R. Grant Leather Store,** where Ulysses S. Grant clerked for his father in 1860. Galena gave 9 generals, including Grant, to the Union army during the Civil War. Afterward the citizens of Galena presented Grant with a house as a token of their gratitude. Today the restored **Grant House** (NHL) contains family memorabilia. NR
>*Grant House and Market House State Memorials open daily 9–5. Grant Leather Store and Dowling House open: May 1–Nov 1, daily 9–5*

GALESBURG
>CARL SANDBURG BIRTHPLACE, *331 East 3rd Street*
>>The eminent poet, biographer, novelist, journalist, and folk singer Carl Sandburg was born in this house to uneducated Swedish immigrants on January 6, 1878. Sandburg published his first book of verse in 1904. Ten years later he published the poem "Chicago," which made him famous. In subsequent years Sandburg wrote a complete biography of Abraham Lincoln.
>>*Open: Tues–Sat 9–12, 1–5; Sun 1–5*

>OLD MAIN NATIONAL HISTORIC LANDMARK, *Knox College campus*
>>In 1858 one of the famous Lincoln-Douglas debates, highlighting the issues of the sectional controversy that was propelling the nation toward war, took place in this building. NR

GRAND DETOUR
>DEERE HOME AND SHOP NATIONAL HISTORIC LANDMARK, *just off State 2*
>>Here in 1837 John Deere invented and manufactured the steel plow that revolutionized agriculture in the old Northwest. This

implement, which enabled farmers to make clean furrows, led to the cultivation of vast stretches of Illinois, Indiana, and Ohio. NR

Open: May 1–Nov 1, daily 9–5

KICKAPOO

JUBILEE COLLEGE, *14 miles west off U.S. 150*

One of the pioneer educational institutions in Illinois, this college was founded in 1839 as an Episcopal seminary by Bishop Philander Chase. Operating until 1862, Jubilee's curriculum was considered to be excellent for its day. Alumni included Adlai E. Stevenson, who served as Vice President during Grover Cleveland's second term. It is now operated as a state park. NR

LAWRENCEVILLE VICINITY

LINCOLN TRAIL STATE MEMORIAL, *9 miles east at Lincoln Memorial Bridge*

In the spring of 1830 the Lincoln family migrated from Indiana, crossed the Wabash River, and entered Illinois at the site of this monument. Following essentially the same route as the National Memorial Highway today, the family journeyed on to the Sangamon River, southwest of Decatur, where they erected a crude cabin. There they suffered so many hardships during the winter of 1830–31 that they started back for Indiana in the spring.

LEWISTON AND VICINITY

DICKSON MOUNDS STATE MEMORIAL, *5 miles from Lewiston off State 78*

The largest known prehistoric Indian cemetery, consisting of exposed burials and burial offerings, is preserved at this site. More than 2,500 men, women, and children were interred in a crescent-shaped mound; 200 skeletons can be seen as they were placed centuries ago. The mound is representative of the Mississippian culture, which flourished in the area from about A.D. 900 to A.D. 1300. Other excavated structures include the **Cross Shaped House,** the **Circular House,** and a **Mississippian Lodge.** NR

LINCOLN

POSTVILLE COURTHOUSE STATE MEMORIAL, *east of U.S. 66*

Abraham Lincoln visited this courthouse, the seat of Logan County, twice a year between 1839 and 1848 while traveling the eighth judicial circuit as an itinerant attorney. In 1848 the county seat was moved to Mount Pulaski (*see*). The present courthouse is a reconstruction.

Open daily 9–5; closed holidays

METAMORA

METAMORA COURTHOUSE, *on State 116 and 89*

During the years before the Civil War, Abraham Lincoln practiced law in this courthouse, which was erected in 1845 and has been restored. Lincoln's close friend Judge David Davis (*see Bloomington, David Davis Mansion*) presided here.

Open daily 9–5

METROPOLIS VICINITY

FORT MASSAC STATE PARK, *east of Metropolis on U.S. 45*

Fort Massac, which stood on this site bordering the Ohio River, served as an important link between Fort de Chartres (*see Prairie du Rocher*) and the north and east. Built in 1757, Fort Massac was the last Ohio fort erected under French rule. After the English take-over, Fort Massac fell into neglect, thus making it easier for George Rogers Clark, in June, 1778, to enter Illinois and pass unnoticed through the area with his Kentucky "Long Knives" on their way to Fort Kaskaskia (*see Chester*). NR

MOUNT PULASKI
MOUNT PULASKI COURTHOUSE STATE MEMORIAL, *on the town square*

The seat of Logan County from 1848 to 1853, this Greek Revival courthouse was the scene of many cases tried by Abraham Lincoln, who spent more than half of his legal career away from Springfield riding the eighth judicial circuit as an itinerant barrister. Today the courthouse has been restored.

Open daily 9–12, 1–5; closed holidays

NAUVOO HISTORIC DISTRICT NATIONAL HISTORIC LANDMARK
From 1839 until 1846 Nauvoo flourished as headquarters for the Church of the Latter Day Saints and principal settlement of the Mormons. Having fled religious persecution in Missouri, the Mormons, led by the church's founder, Joseph Smith, came to Illinois, where they established the community of Nauvoo. The town grew rapidly and within a few years boasted a population of 20,000. In 1841 Smith laid the foundation of a great temple, which was never completed because of his assassination, in 1844, by an angry mob in nearby Carthage. This structure was later destroyed. Illinois authorities became increasingly hostile toward the Mormons, whom they suspected of harboring criminals in their town. In 1846 the Mormons were expelled from the state. Led by Brigham Young, Smith's successor and the church's greatest colonizer, the Mormons began the trek tha took them to the Valley of the Great Salt Lake in Utah. Nauvoo, from 1849 until 1858, was occupied by the Icarians, a communistic sect comprised of Frenchmen and Germans. Today only such fragments as the sunstone in Nauvoo State Park remain of the temple. Among the original Mormon buildings that still stand are the **Joseph Smith Homestead**, the **Mansion House** (Smith's second Illinois residence), the **Brigham Young House**, the **Old Arsenal**, and the **Time and Seasons Buildings**, which housed the church printing office. NR

Houses open: June 1–Sept 15, daily 8–6; Sept 16–May 31, daily 8:30–5

OTTAWA VICINITY
STARVED ROCK NATIONAL HISTORIC LANDMARK, *6 miles west on State 71*

Stategically situated on the lower rapids of the Illinois River, Starved Rock was the first major center of French influence in Illinois, the site of the Illini Indians' principal village and the scene of savage warfare. Father Jacques Marquette and Louis Joliet became the first white explorers to visit the area in 1673. Two years later Marquette established a mission at the Great Indian Village near the rock. Robert Cavalier, Sieur de La Salle, built **Fort St. Louis** atop the rock in 1683 in order to control the waterway connecting Canada with the Mississippi Valley. During the late 1680s, forays by the Iroquois Indians drove the friendly Illini away from the rock and made the fortress untenable. Fort St. Louis was abandoned in 1691, and it subsequently decayed and disappeared. Legend has it that Starved Rock earned its name in 1769, when the

Lincoln's Tomb at Springfield and the Onstot cabin at Lincoln's New Salem

Illini, trapped on the rock by the Ottawas and Pottawatomies, were starved into submission and annihilated. NR

PRAIRIE DU ROCHER VICINITY
FORT DE CHARTRES NATIONAL HISTORIC LANDMARK, *4 miles west at terminus of State 155*

Constructed between 1753 and 1758, Fort de Chartres served as the seat of French civil and military government in the Illinois Country and was reputed to be the strongest fort in North America. The British never attacked the imposing stone bastion during the French and Indian War. Afterward Fort de Chartres was the last French stronghold to surrender to the British (1765). Fort de Chartres subsequently became a British outpost in the Illinois Country until it was abandoned and destroyed in 1772. NR

ROCK ISLAND
BLACK HAWK STATE PARK, *off U.S. 67 and on State 2*

This park commemorates the Black Hawk War of 1832, which cleared the way for white settlement of northwestern Illinois. The land on which the capital villages of the Sauk and Fox nations had stood for nearly a century was ceded to the United States in 1804. The chief, Black Hawk, refused to recognize the cession, and he led his warriors to several victories over the Americans during the War of 1812. However, white settlers continued to encroach on Black Hawk's land, and in 1832 a full-scale conflict resulted. Although the Indians terrorized much of northwestern Illinois, and there were a number of sharp skirmishes, Black Hawk finally fled to Wisconsin, where he surrendered.

SPRINGFIELD AND VICINITY
LINCOLN HOME STATE MEMORIAL, *8th and Jackson streets*

Abraham Lincoln resided in this simple frame house—the only

home he ever owned—during the crucial years from 1844 to 1861, when he rose from a small-town lawyer to the Presidency of the United States. It was in the north parlor that Lincoln, on May 17, 1860, received the committee informing him of his nomination as the Republican presidential candidate. Lincoln also held a grand public levee here to bid good-by to well-wishers before departing for Washington, D.C., in February, 1861. NR
Open daily 9-5; closed holidays

LINCOLN TOMB STATE MEMORIAL, *Oak Ridge Cemetery*
This monument contains the tombs of Abraham Lincoln, Mary Todd Lincoln, and 3 of their 4 sons. Soon after Lincoln's assassination on April 14, 1865, the citizens of Springfield raised funds for a memorial to the martyred President. Larkin G. Mead, Jr., designed the monument, which was dedicated in 1874. NR
Open daily 9-5; closed holidays

LINCOLN'S NEW SALEM STATE PARK, *about 20 miles northwest off State 97*
While living in this village from 1831 to 1837, Abraham Lincoln embarked on his career of law and statesmanship. During his residence here, Lincoln enlisted in the Black Hawk War (*see Rock Island*) and was elected to the Illinois general assembly in 1834. Today New Salem has been authentically reconstructed; the only old structure remaining is the **Onstot Cooper Shop,** where young Lincoln studied by firelight. NR
Buildings open: April 15-Oct 15, daily 8:30-5

OLD STATE CAPITOL NATIONAL HISTORIC LANDMARK, *Adams Street*
The political careers of Abraham Lincoln, Stephen A. Douglas, and Ulysses S. Grant are linked to the Sangamon County Courthouse, which was begun in 1837 and served as Illinois' fifth State House until 1869. Lincoln sat in the state legislature here from 1840 to 1841; in 1858 he accepted the Republican nomination for the U.S. Senate and made his famous "House Divided" speech in the structure. Lincoln's political rival Douglas debated here during the 1858 Senate campaign and in 1861 made his famous address urging citizens to rally behind the Union. Grant served in the State House in 1861 as Illinois adjutant general. NR
Open daily 9-5; closed holidays

VACHEL LINDSAY HOME, *603 South 5th Street*
Built in 1830, this house was the residence of the poet Vachel Lindsay. It presently contains displays of his original manuscripts and drawings. NR
Open: June 1-early Sept, daily 9-5

VANDALIA
VANDALIA STATE HOUSE, *at 4th and Gallatin on State 140*
Abraham Lincoln served as leader of the "Long Nine"—a group of representatives whose total height measured 54 feet—during the 3 sessions of the state legislature held at this capitol building between 1836 and 1839. Lincoln and his colleagues convinced the general assembly that the government of Illinois should be moved from Vandalia, which had served as state capital for 19 years, to Springfield.
Open daily 8-5; closed holidays

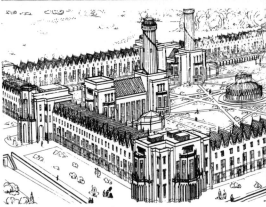

CORYDON

CORYDON CAPITOL STATE MEMORIAL, *Old Capitol Avenue*

Constructed in 1812 for use as the Harrison County Courthouse, this square blue limestone structure became territorial capitol in 1813, when the seat of the Indiana territorial government was moved from Vincennes to Corydon, a more central location. In June, 1816, elected delegates to a constitutional convention met here to frame a state constitution. After Indiana was formally admitted to the union in December, 1816, the territorial capitol became state capitol until 1824, when the seat of government was again moved, this time to Indianapolis.

Open: Thurs–Tues 9–11:30, 12:30–5

EVANSVILLE VICINITY

ANGEL MOUNDS NATIONAL HISTORIC LANDMARK, *about 5 miles east off State 662*

This 421-acre archaeological site contains the largest group of prehistoric Indian mounds in Indiana. A city of about 1,000 people flourished here late in the 15th century. The largest mound, the chief's mound, is at the center of the city. Built in 3 levels, the mound covers nearly 5 acres at its base and at its highest point rises to 44 feet. A visitor center offers exhibits and information. NR

Open: Apr 30–Labor Day, daily 9–12, 1–5; closed Sun in winter

FOUNTAIN CITY

LEVI COFFIN HOUSE NATIONAL HISTORIC LANDMARK, *115 North Main Street*

This house was a major stopping place on the Underground Railroad, the route by which runaway slaves made their way to Canada

Left: George Rogers Clark statue in Vincennes. Top right: Fort Ouiatenon near Lafayette. Below: plan of Robert Owen colony at New Harmony

and freedom. After crossing the Ohio River at one of 3 points—Cincinnati, Ohio, and Madison and Jeffersonville, Indiana—fugitives were taken to Fountain City (then called Newport). From there they journeyed to Canada by one of 3 routes. Between 1827 and 1847 Quakers Levi and Catherine Coffin provided shelter and assistance for some 2,000 runaway slaves. According to tradition, one of those Coffin sheltered was Eliza Harris, heroine of *Uncle Tom's Cabin*. The Coffin house has been restored, with period furnishings. NR
Open: Feb 15–Dec 15, Tues–Sun 1–5

INDIANAPOLIS

BENJAMIN HARRISON HOME NATIONAL HISTORIC LANDMARK, 1230 N Delaware St

Benjamin Harrison, 23rd President of the U.S. and grandson of William Henry Harrison, 9th President, built this house in 1874. At that time he was a prominent Indianapolis lawyer, a career he had resumed after having served as an officer in the Civil War. Harrison lived here until his death in 1901, except for the years he served as U.S. senator (1881–87) and President (1889–93). In 1888 he accepted his party's nomination for President in the back parlor of the house. The home has been restored as a national shrine with many of the original furnishings. NR
Open: Mon–Sat 10–4, Sun 12:30–4

JAMES WHITCOMB RILEY HOUSE NATIONAL HISTORIC LANDMARK, 528 Lockerbie St

The famous Hoosier poet lived here the last 23 years of his life, continuing to produce a steady stream of the humorous, simple poems that made him so popular. The home is preserved as it was when Riley lived here and includes displays of memorabilia. NR
Open: Tues–Sat 10–4, Sun 12–4

LAFAYETTE AND VICINITY

FORT OUIATENON, 4 miles southwest on South River Road

A replica of an 18th-century blockhouse marks the site of probably the earliest French military post in Indiana. Eager to protect French traders from the English and to promote fur trade with the Indians, the French in about 1720 erected a fortified trading post—several cabins surrounded by a stockade—at the Indian village of Ouiatenon. Forts Miami and Vincennes were established in the region at about the same time. Only Vincennes became a permanent settlement. NR

TIPPECANOE BATTLEFIELD NATIONAL HISTORIC LANDMARK, 7 miles northeast on State 225

Here on November 7, 1811, William Henry Harrison scattered an Indian army led by the Prophet, brother of Tecumseh. As governor of Indiana Territory, one of Harrison's tasks was to persuade the Indian tribes to cede their land to whites. Although initially successful—by 1810 the Indians had given up the lower third of Indiana—Harrison met with growing Indian resistance. Two Shawnee brothers, Tecumseh and the Prophet, organized a confederacy committed to the principle that the land was held by all tribes in common and therefore could not be sold by any one tribe. After negotiations in 1810 between Tecumseh and Harrison failed to resolve the land dispute, Harrison in 1811 led an expedition against Prophet's Town, headquarters of Tecumseh's confederacy, where discontented Indians from every Indiana tribe had gathered. Because his orders from President Madison had been to give the Indians one last chance to relinquish their lands, Harrison did not launch an immediate attack. Instead he arranged to meet with the Prophet on the morning of November 7. The Prophet, however, attacked before dawn. In the bloody battle that followed, the Indians first routed the colonial troops, then were themselves forced to flee, abandoning Prophet's Town, which the Americans burned before returning to Vincennes. The battle was not conclusive, for Indians continued to attack white settlements. But it marked the end of united Indian military power and destroyed the work of Tecumseh. A monument marks the site of the battle. Relics are on display in the **Tippecanoe County Historical Museum** in Lafayette. NR

LINCOLN CITY
LINCOLN BOYHOOD NATIONAL MEMORIAL, *just south on State 162*

This memorial preserves part of the farm where Abraham Lincoln spent most of his boyhood. In 1816, when Abe was 7, Thomas Lincoln moved his family here from Kentucky. Life was hard as the family struggled to bring forest land under cultivation, and Abe, a tall, strong boy, did his share of plowing, planting, and harvesting. He also became an expert axman. In 1818, when he was 9, his mother, Nancy Hanks Lincoln, died. The following year Thomas married Sarah Bush Johnston, a widow with 3 children. She gave Abe and his sister, Sarah, love; to Abe she also gave encouragement and support. Young Lincoln was amiable and talkative, but he was also a loner and a thinker. He became a prodigious reader, reading whenever he could snatch a moment, even when his plowhorse rested in the field. In 1830, when he was 21, his family moved again, this time to Illinois. Today the memorial includes the Lincoln homesite and Nancy Hanks Lincoln's grave. Around the homesite is a "living historical farm," with reconstructed log buildings and fields restored and worked as they would have been in Lincoln's day. There is also a visitor center that features a museum and a film on Lincoln's Indiana boyhood. NR
Open: summer, daily 7–6; Nov 1–Apr 1, Wed–Sun 8–5

METAMORA
WHITEWATER CANAL STATE MEMORIAL, *south on U.S. 52*

The memorial is a restored 10-mile section of the old canal, a 76-mile waterway constructed between 1836 and 1845. Built to provide cheaper transportation up the Whitewater Valley into the interior, the canal extended along the banks of the Whitewater River from Laurenceburg to Hagerstown. Boats were towed by teams of 6 to 8 mules walking single file along the bank. The canal's usefulness was first impaired by severe floods and washouts, and finally destroyed when in 1866 the Whitewater Valley Railroad was built parallel to it. The restored section includes a feeder dam (one of 7 in the original canal), an operating canal lock (one of 56), a covered wooden aqueduct, and an old gristmill now used as a museum. Weekend visitors can also take a boat trip through one of the locks.

NEW HARMONY HISTORIC DISTRICT NATIONAL HISTORIC LAND-MARK

New Harmony was the home of two ambitious but short-lived 19th-century experiments in communal living. In 1815 Father George Rapp, a Lutheran Church dissenter, led his followers from Pennsylvania to Indiana, where he founded the village of Harmonie. The Rappites believed in community ownership, anticipated the second coming of Christ, and practiced celibacy in preparation. Urged on by their demanding leader, the hard-working, rigidly disciplined colonists in 10 years turned a wilderness into a thriving, self-sufficient community. Despite the community's success, in 1825 Rapp decided to return to Pennsylvania. Harmonie was purchased by Welsh philanthropist Robert Owen, who was eager to establish a utopian community. Scottish philanthropist William Maclure, who joined Owen, was particularly interested in education, and soon a distinguished group of educators and scientists gathered there. The colony established the first kindergarten in the U.S., the first trade school, and the first free public school system. However, by 1827 the experiment had failed, probably because the colony lacked competent farmers and businessmen. Today about 35 of the old Rappite buildings remain, several of which are in the New Harmony State Memorial. NR

TERRE HAUTE

EUGENE V. DEBS HOME NATIONAL HISTORIC LANDMARK, *451 N Eighth St*

Eugene V. Debs, the noted labor leader and Socialist, was an early advocate of industrial unionism, the organization of workers by industry rather than by craft. In 1893 he organized the first industrial union, the American Railway Union, and in 1894 he was a leader of the Pullman strike in Chicago. Arrested and jailed for 6 months for his part in that strike, he thereafter formed first the Social Democratic party, a liberal workers' party, and then, in 1900, the Socialist party of the U.S. He remained the Socialist leader and spokesman until his death in 1926, running for President 5 times during that period. His home has been preserved as a public memorial. NR

Open: Sun 2–4 and by appointment

UNDERWOOD

PIGEON ROOST STATE MEMORIAL, *south on U.S. 31*

Here, on September 3, 1812, 24 inhabitants of the 3-year-old settlement of Pigeon Roost were massacred and their village was burned by marauding Shawnees. The massacre was the last of whites by Indians in Indiana Territory. A limestone monument marks the mass grave in which the victims were buried.

VINCENNES

 GEORGE ROGERS CLARK NATIONAL HISTORICAL PARK

Located on the site of old **Fort Sackville**, this park commemorates the George Rogers Clark expedition of 1778–79, which was instrumental in wresting control of the old Northwest from the British. Vincennes was originally an important French trading post. After the French and Indian War it came under British control. By the time of the Revolution, the British dominated the old Northwest and were encouraging devastating Indian raids on frontier settlements. Clark, a Virginian, realized that the best way to end the Indian attacks would be to overcome the British. He persuaded the Virginia legislature to finance an expedition to capture the Northwest, and in June, 1778, set out with 175 men to take **Kaskaskia, Cahokia,** and **Vincennes.** The 3 lightly held towns surrendered

without struggle. But Colonel Henry Hamilton, the angry British governor, led a British contingent from Detroit that easily retook Vincennes in December, 1778. Clark then decided on a daring move. Knowing that Hamilton thought himself safe from attack until spring, he set out in February from Kaskaskia with 127 men. Hungry and cold, they marched for 18 days across icy swamps and flooded rivers. Arriving at Vincennes, they so surprised the British garrison at Fort Sackville that the latter held out only one night. On February 24 the British surrendered. Clark's victory marked the failure of British efforts to keep Americans out of the Northwest. The George Rogers Clark Memorial, located in the park, contains a bronze statue of Clark and several large murals. NR
Open: Apr–Oct, daily 9–5; Nov–Mar, closed Mon and Tues

GROUSELAND NATIONAL HISTORIC LANDMARK, *3 W Scott St*
William Henry Harrison built this mansion in 1804 and lived here until 1812, while he served as first governor of Indiana Territory. Originally on a 300-acre estate, the house served both as a home and as military headquarters. In 1810 Harrison met with the Shawnee chief Tecumseh under the trees in front of the house. Their inability to agree on a peaceful land settlement led to war the following year (*see Lafayette, Tippecanoe Battlefield*). Harrison served in Congress for several years and in 1840 became ninth President of the U.S. Grouseland contains period furnishings, including many of Harrison's belongings. NR
Open: Mon–Sat 9–5, Sun 12:30–5; closed holidays

INDIANA TERRITORY STATE MEMORIAL, *Harrison Street*
The main building of the memorial is a small frame house that served as the first capitol of Indiana Territory after its creation in 1800. The first territorial assembly met here until the capital was transferred from Vincennes to Corydon (*see Corydon Capitol*) in 1813. In 1804–5 the building also reputedly served as capitol of part of the Louisiana Territory. The house has been restored and furnished with several pieces of original furniture. Next to the territorial capitol is a reconstruction of the **Elihu Stout Print Shop**, the first newspaper printing shop in Indiana. Stout put out his paper—first called the *Indiana Gazette* and then the *Western Sun*—from 1804 until 1845. In 1830 Abraham Lincoln supposedly saw his first printing press here.
Open: Mar 1–Dec 4, daily 9–5; Dec 5–Feb, closed Sun and Mon

ST. FRANCIS XAVIER CHURCH (OLD CATHEDRAL), *2nd and Church streets*
Built between 1825 and 1841, this brick Romanesque structure occupies the site of the log chapel erected by French Canadian settlers about the time Vincennes was founded, sometime before 1727. During the 1740s a bell was brought from France for the chapel. Known as the Liberty Bell of the Old Northwest, on July 20, 1778, it called the inhabitants of Vincennes to the church, where Father Pierre Gibault administered the oath of allegiance to the U.S. The next year it rang at the capture of Fort Sackville (*see George Rogers Clark National Historical Park*). The bell is now in the steeple of the present church. The **Simon Brute Library**, behind the cathedral, contains an extensive rare-book collection, the oldest of which dates from 1476. Nearby is the **Old French Cemetery**, where Indians, missionaries, and early settlers are buried.
Open daily 9–5

IOWA

ADAIR

SITE OF JESSE JAMES TRAIN ROBBERY, *along U.S. 6 west of Adair*
Perpetrated by Jesse James and his gang, the first robbery of a
moving train in the West occurred at this site (marked by a locomotive wheel) on July 21, 1873. A Chicago, Rock Island, and Pacific
train was derailed here, and its passengers were divested of their
money and valuables. As a result, Jesse James and his brother
Frank were catapulted into national notoriety.

AMANA VILLAGES NATIONAL HISTORIC LANDMARK, *20 miles west of Iowa City and 20 miles southwest of Cedar Rapids*

This was the most successful of the utopian communities that
flourished in the United States in the middle years of the 19th
century. An outgrowth of a German religious group who called
themselves the Inspirationists, the sect immigrated to America
after 1842, settled first in Ebenezer, New York, and then moved to
Iowa in 1855, where they founded the village of Amana (the biblical
term for "remain faithful"). The Amana Society subsequently established 5 other villages "one hour by oxen" apart and purchased the
town of Homestead in 1861, where such houses as the **Amana Heim,**
with its original furnishings, provide an authentic view of life in the
Amana colony. NR
House open: April 15–Nov 1, daily 10–4:30; Sun 12–4:30

ARNOLDS PARK

GARDNER CABIN, *off U.S. 71*
The Rowland Gardner family, first victims of the Spirit Lake
Massacre of 1857, lived in this log cabin. Renegade Sioux Indians

*Top left: the Herbert Hoover birthplace near Iowa City. Below: Sunday in
Amana Village early in the 1900s. Right: Floyd Monument near Sioux City*

led by Inkpaduta, after demanding and receiving food from the
Gardners, killed them. Fourteen-year-old Abigail Gardner was
taken captive, but lived to reach civilization again. The Indians
continued their rampage for 6 days, murdering 43 settlers in the
Iowa Great Lakes region. Today the restored cabin contains relics
of the tragic event.

Open: Memorial Day–Labor Day, daily 11–5

BRIDGEWATER

MORMON TRAIL PARK, *about 2 miles southeast off State 189*
A segment of the old wagon route used by the Mormons on their
journey to Utah passes through this park. Led by Brigham Young,
the Mormons began their trek west in 1846 after being expelled
from Nauvoo, Illinois. While traversing southern Iowa they crossed
11 counties and established 8 camps or stations. Many of the migrants settled in western Iowa.

CHEROKEE

PILOT ROCK, *south of Cherokee off U.S. 59*
This giant glacial boulder, known to the Sioux Indians as Woven
Stone, was used as a landmark by pioneers and Indians, whose
trails led to this site.

COUNCIL BLUFFS

DODGE HOUSE NATIONAL HISTORIC LANDMARK, *605 3rd Street*
This palatial residence was completed in 1869 for General Gren-
ville M. Dodge, who earned worldwide renown as chief engineer
for the construction of the Union Pacific Railroad. The eastern
part of the nation's first transcontinental railroad extended from
Omaha to Promontory Point, Utah. Dodge won the rank of major
general during the Civil War and in later years was active as a
builder, financier, statesman, and counselor of Presidents. NR

Open: Feb–Dec, Tues–Sat 10–5; Sun 2–5

CROTON

CROTON CIVIL WAR MEMORIAL PARK
A skirmish fought on August 5, 1861, at Athens, Missouri, across
the Des Moines River from Croton, was the only occasion in which
enemy cannon fire fell upon Iowa soil during the Civil War.

ESTHERVILLE

FORT DEFIANCE STATE PARK, *1 mile southwest on State 245*
This park is the site of a former fort, which was built in 1862–63
to protect settlers in the area from the warlike Sioux Indians. A
cavalry unit was stationed at the fort until it was abandoned after
15 months.

FOREST CITY VICINITY

PILOT KNOB STATE PARK, *4 miles east and 1 mile south on State 332*
Rising to one of the highest elevations in Iowa, this 300-foot-high
glacial formation was a landmark used to guide pioneers.

FORT ATKINSON, *just north of town on State 24*

This fort was founded in 1840 by Brigadier General Henry Atkinson
in order to keep the Winnebago Indians under surveillance and
prevent the tribe from returning to their homelands in Wisconsin.
In 1832 the Indians, in a treaty with the Federal government, ceded
their lands east of the Mississippi and agreed to move to a 40-mile-

wide "neutral ground" in Iowa. However, the Sioux, who liked to hunt in this ground, were hostile to the Winnebagos, who settled there only in small bands. Finally in 1840 U.S. troops oversaw the Winnebago move. Fort Atkinson was heavily armed, but it was never attacked. When the Winnebagos moved to a reservation in Minnesota in 1848, Fort Atkinson was no longer needed and its buildings fell into ruin. The present fort is a reconstruction.
Open: May–Oct, Tues–Fri 1–5; Sat–Sun 10–5

FORT DODGE HISTORICAL MUSEUM, STOCKADE, AND FORT, *near junction of U.S. 20 and 169*

Built in 1850 as a garrison for the Sixth U.S. Infantry Dragoons, Fort Dodge was established to protect settlers in the area from the hostile Sioux Indians. Major William Williams, who later became the first mayor of the city of Fort Dodge, founded the fort. The post, the most northerly in Iowa, was abandoned prematurely in 1853; Indian hostilities continued for several years. The present fort is a replica, built about one mile from the original site.
Open: summer, daily 9–8

GREENFIELD VICINITY

HENRY A. WALLACE BIRTHPLACE, *9 miles southeast off State 25*
This farmhouse is the birthplace of Henry Agard Wallace (1888–1965), Iowa's only Vice President of the United States.

IOWA CITY AND VICINITY

HERBERT HOOVER NATIONAL HISTORIC SITE, *West Branch, 5 miles east via U.S. 80*
Herbert Hoover, the nation's 31st President, was born on August 10, 1874, in a 2-room frame cottage, which has now been restored, at this site. The son of a Quaker blacksmith, Hoover graduated from Stanford in 1895, worked as a mining engineer, and later became Food Administrator for the U.S. during World War I. He served as Secretary of Commerce from 1921 to 1928, the year he was elected President. After the stock market crash in 1929, Hoover's popularity waned, and he was defeated by Franklin D. Roosevelt in 1932. President and Mrs. Hoover's graves, a Quaker meetinghouse, a restored blacksmith shop, and the **Herbert Hoover Presidential Library** are also on the premises. NR
For further information write: Box B, West Branch, IA 52358

OLD CAPITOL, *University of Iowa campus*
Erected between 1840 and 1842, this Greek Revival structure served as Iowa's first state capitol. Four territorial legislatures convened in the building prior to Iowa's admission to the Union in 1846. The final version of the state constitution, which still remains the fundamental law of Iowa, was drafted here. In 1857 the seat of government was moved to Des Moines, and the Old Capitol subsequently became the first building owned by the University of Iowa.

PLUM GROVE STATE HISTORIC MONUMENT, *727 Switzer Avenue*
Known as the Mount Vernon of Iowa, this red-brick residence was built in 1844 for Robert Lucas, the first governor of the territory of Iowa. In 1838 President Martin Van Buren appointed Lucas, former governor of Ohio, to the Iowa post. While serving his 3-year term in office, Lucas won the so-called Honey War, a dispute with Missouri involving Iowa's southern boundary.
Open: April 15–Nov 15, Wed–Mon 1–5

IOWA

McGREGOR

PIKES PEAK STATE PARK, *2 miles south of McGregor on State 30*

On June 17, 1683, Louis Joliet and Father Jacques Marquette became the first Europeans to discover Iowa when they floated from the Wisconsin River on to the Mississippi opposite Pikes Peak. In 1805 the U.S. government sent 26-year-old Zebulon Pike—later discoverer of Pikes Peak in Colorado—to the area to select sites suitable for fortifications. He chose this hill overlooking the confluence of the Wisconsin and Mississippi rivers as a strategic point, although a fort was never erected here.

MARQUETTE

EFFIGY MOUNDS NATIONAL MONUMENT, *3 miles north on State 76*

This monument in the Upper Mississippi River valley provides information on the burial customs of the prehistoric Indians who lived in this region about A.D. 1000. The numerous burial mounds preserved here are unique to this part of the country in that they were built in the shapes of animals. Twenty-nine of the 191 known mounds at the monument are in the form of bear and bird effigies; the largest is the 137-foot-long **Great Bear Mound**. The **Marching Bear Mound Group** includes an alignment of 10 bears and 3 bird effigies. NR

For further information write: Box K, McGregor, IA 52157

MOUNT PLEASANT ·

HARLAN HOUSE, *122 North Jefferson*

James A. Harlan, U.S. senator, Secretary of the Interior, and close personal friend of Abraham Lincoln, resided in this house (built in 1857) during his career in the national government. Harlan also served as president of nearby **Iowa Wesleyan College**, which was founded in 1842, the first college west of the Mississippi River. The Harlan House is currently a hotel and restaurant and contains Harlan memorabilia and town documents.

Iowa Wesleyan College open: Mon–Fri 8–5

ONAWA

LEWIS AND CLARK STATE PARK, *2 miles west on State 175*

Meriwether Lewis and William Clark camped in this area for several days in August, 1804, during their expedition to the Northwest via the Missouri River.

PETERSON

FORT PETERSON, *on the farm of Mr. and Mrs. Duane Johnson*

A plaque here marks the original site of Fort Peterson—one of a string of forts in Iowa—which was built and manned by the Northern Border Brigade after the Spirit Lake Massacre (*see Arnolds Park*) of 1857.

SIOUX CITY

SERGEANT FLOYD MONUMENT NATIONAL HISTORIC LANDMARK, *Glenn Ave and Lewis Rd*

Situated on Floyd's Bluff overlooking the Missouri River, this 100-foot-high stone obelisk marks the grave of William Floyd, the only person to die on the Lewis and Clark expedition of 1804–6. Passing away on August 19–20, 1804, from a "stomach disorder," Floyd was also the first U.S. soldier to die west of the Mississippi on land included in the Louisiana Purchase of 1803. This site was the first to be designated a National Historic Landmark. NR

KANSAS

ABILENE

DWIGHT D. EISENHOWER HOME, *201 South East 4th Street*
The late President Dwight D. Eisenhower spent his boyhood at
this house, residing here from 1898 until he left for West Point in
1911. An adjacent museum contains Eisenhower memorabilia. NR
Open daily 9–4:45; closed holidays

COUNCIL GROVE NATIONAL HISTORIC LANDMARK, *near U.S. 56 and
State 177*
Incorporated as a town in 1858, Council Grove was the most important way station on the Santa Fe Trail. Beneath the giant **Council
Oak** (the remains of which are preserved) U.S. commissioners
negotiated a treaty with the Osage Indians in 1825 for a passage
across their land. This right of way became the **Santa Fe Trail.** Later
travelers held councils here to plan for their mutual safety on the
long journey across lands inhabited by hostile tribes. A treaty concluded with the U.S. government in 1846 gave this region to the
Kaw Indians, for whom the Methodist Episcopal Church erected in
1850–51 a 2-story **Mission School,** which still stands. NR
Old Kaw Mission open: Mon–Sat 10–12, 1:30–5; Sun 2–5

COURTLAND

PIKE-PAWNEE STATE MONUMENT, *2 miles east and 8 miles north
on State 266*
In 1806 Lieutenant Zebulon Pike visited the Pawnee village that
stood within this park, lowered the Spanish flag from the chief's
lodge, and raised The Stars and Stripes for the first time in Kansas.
The Pawnees, a farming, hunting people, lived in this section of the

*Top left: Hollenberg Pony Express Station near Hanover. Below: Medicine
Lodge, drawn in the 1880s. Right: cowboy statue on Boot Hill in Dodge City*

Central Plains in round earth lodges until the pressures of white settlement drove them from Kansas in 1875. Twenty-two former lodge sites may be seen at the **Pawnee Indian Village** (NR), and a museum displays Pawnee artifacts.

Museum open: Tues–Sat 10–5, Sun 1–5; closed holidays

DODGE CITY AND VICINITY

Known in the 1870s and 1880s as the wickedest little city in America, this frontier town was a rendezvous for buffalo hunters, cowboys, cattlemen, railroad builders, saloonkeepers, Indians, dance-hall girls, thugs, and gamblers. Founded with the coming of the Santa Fe Railroad in 1872, Dodge City soon became a major shipping center for cattle as well as a market for buffalo hides and meat. Although the town was notorious for vice and violence, lawless elements were eventually kept in check by such "2-gun marshals" as Bat Masterson and Wyatt Earp. Today **Boot Hill**, where outlaws were buried without ceremony with their boots on, **Old Fort Dodge Jail**, now a museum, and a replica of **Old Front Street**, replete with saloons, serve as reminders of Dodge City's colorful past.

Jail open: winter, daily 8–6; summer, daily 7:30–10

SANTA FE TRAIL REMAINS NATIONAL HISTORIC LANDMARK, *9 miles west of Dodge City on U.S. 50*

Created between 1820 and 1850, these rut remains from the Santa Fe Trail are preserved in rangeland overlooking the Arkansas River. Ten to 20 miles upstream at the Cimarron Crossing the trail divided; one branch followed the river, while the other formed the shorter Cimarron Cutoff route. NR

FORT LARNED NATIONAL HISTORIC SITE, *west of Larned on U.S. 156*

During the 1860s and early 1870s Fort Larned was the principal guardian of the Kansas segment of the **Santa Fe Trail.** Soldiers stationed here escorted the mails and patrolled a region infested with hostile Indians. In 1867 the fort was the base for Major General Winfield S. Hancock's abortive campaign against the Plains Indians. Fort Larned was a key post during the Indian War of 1868–69, which violated the Treaties of Medicine Lodge (*see Medicine Lodge Peace Treaty Site*) and was finally suppressed by Lieutenant Colonel George A. Custer. Troops were withdrawn from the fort—well preserved today—in 1878. NR

For further information write: Box 69, Larned, KS 67550

FORT RILEY

FIRST TERRITORIAL CAPITOL, *on State 18, 2 miles west of fort*

On July 2, 1855, Kansas' first territorial legislature met at this stone warehouse—now restored—in the boom town of Pawnee. Anti-slavery Kansans called the predominantly proslavery representatives the Bogus Legislature because they had been elected with the aid of Missourians who had crossed the border to vote. This legislature relocated the capitol at the Shawnee Methodist Mission (*see Kansas City*) and met there on July 16. NR

Open: Mon–Sat 10–12, 2–5; Sun and holidays 1:30–5

FORT SCOTT NATIONAL HISTORIC AREA, *on U.S. 54*

This western outpost was prominent in 3 distinct periods of Kansas history. Fort Scott was founded in 1842 by the U.S. Dragoons to preserve peace among the Cherokee, Osage, and other tribes in the territory: By 1853 the Indian frontier had moved farther west and troops were withdrawn. At the time of the Civil War, the struggles of Bleeding Kansas, in which proslavery factions fought free-soil forces, centered in this region, and Fort Scott was reactivated. The fort saw service for the last time between 1869 and 1873, when it maintained order in settler-railroad troubles. Many buildings from the 1840s are preserved. NR

HANOVER

HOLLENBERG (COTTONWOOD) PONY EXPRESS STATION NATIONAL HISTORIC LANDMARK, *6 miles north of U.S. 36*
Erected in 1857 by Gerat H. Hollenberg, this structure served from 1860 to 1861 as the westernmost pony express station in Kansas. Situated on the heavily traveled **Oregon-California Trail**, this building was also a relay station for the Overland Mail (1858–69) and a way station for travelers. Today the edifice is perhaps the nation's only unmoved, unaltered pony express station. NR
Open: Tues–Sat 10–5, Sun 1–5; closed holidays

HAYS

FORT HAYS FRONTIER HISTORICAL PARK, *south on old U.S. 40*
Established in 1865, this fort provided protection to travelers, settlers, and construction gangs on the Union Pacific against hostile Indians. Buffalo Bill Cody was made chief scout for the Fifth Cavalry here, and George A. Custer led his famous Seventh Cavalry from the post against marauding Indians. Fort Hays was abandoned in 1889. The stone blockhouses remain virtually unchanged. NR

HIGHLAND

IOWA, SAC, AND FOX MISSION, *12 miles east on State 136 off U.S. 36*
This mission was founded in 1837 by the Presbyterian missionaries Samuel and Elizabeth Irvin to serve the Iowa, Sac, and Fox Indians, who were removed by treaty from lands in northwestern Missouri to the present Doniphan County, Kansas. Kansas' second printing press was set up here in 1843, and in 1846 a 3-story building was erected, serving as an Indian school until 1863. NR
Open: Tues–Sat 10–5, Sun 1:30–5

KANSAS CITY AND VICINITY

SHAWNEE METHODIST MISSION NATIONAL HISTORIC LANDMARK, *Fairway, 53rd Street and Mission Road*
Founded in 1830 by Rev. Thomas Johnson, this mission became one of the largest and most important Indian missions in the pre-Civil War trans-Mississippi West. In 1838 the mission was located at its present site on the **Santa Fe and Oregon trails**, near their points of origin, and extended to include an Indian manual labor school. In 1855 the first territorial legislature met here after it left the First Territorial Capitol (*see Fort Riley*) in Pawnee. NR
Open: Mon–Sat 10–5, Sun 1–5; closed holidays

LEAVENWORTH

FORT LEAVENWORTH NATIONAL HISTORIC LANDMARK
Established in 1827 to protect traffic on the **Santa Fe Trail** from Indians, this Army post served for 30 years as the chief base of operations on the Indian frontier. From the fort in 1839, Colonel S. W. Kearny mounted a campaign against the Cherokees with the largest U.S. cavalry force yet assembled. During the war with Mexico in 1846, Fort Leavenworth was the outfitting post for the Army of the West. And in 1881 General William Tecumseh Sher-

man founded the Command and General Staff College, the world's largest tactical school for military training, at the post. NR

LYONS VICINITY

CORONADO AND QUIVIRA HISTORICAL MARKER, *4 miles west*
This marker is situated near the site of one of the largest villages of the "Kingdom of Quivira," visited by Francisco Vásquez de Coronado in the summer of 1541 in his quest for wealth.

MANHATTAN

BEECHER BIBLE AND RIFLE CHURCH, *to the east at Wabaunsee on State 18*
This stone church was built by a colony of Connecticut emigrants to Kansas in 1862, during the proslavery-free state controversy. Henry Ward Beecher's congregation in Brooklyn, New York, sent money to these antislavery sympathizers to buy rifles, which arrived in crates marked "Bibles." NR

MEDICINE LODGE

MEDICINE LODGE PEACE TREATY SITE NATIONAL HISTORIC LANDMARK, *southeast of town*
At this site in October, 1867, U.S. commissioners negotiated with the Kiowa, Comanche, Arapaho, Apache, and Cheyenne Indians treaties that paved the way for the construction of railroads and the eventual settlement of the area. NR

OSAWATOMIE

JOHN BROWN MEMORIAL PARK AND JOHN BROWN CABIN, *10th and Main streets*
This park commemorates the militant abolitionist John Brown, who spent 20 months in Kansas Territory at the height of the strife between free-soil and proslavery factions. Brown arrived at Osawatomie, a free-soil village where 5 of his sons had settled, in October, 1855. The following May Brown and his sons attacked a proslavery camp, killing 5 people. The retaliatory Battle of Osawatomie ensued on August 30, 1856; a proslavery force of 400 raided Osawatomie, drove out the defenders—40 men led by Brown—killed Brown's son, and burned the town. Preserved today is the log cabin belonging to Brown's brother-in-law, Rev. Samuel Adair. NR
Cabin open: Tues–Sat 10–12, 1–5; Sun and holidays 1:30–5

PAWNEE ROCK

PAWNEE ROCK MEMORIAL PARK, *near U.S. 56*
This bold, projecting cliff of red sandstone was the most distinctive landmark on the Kansas segment of the **Santa Fe Trail.** One of the most dangerous points on the central plains, the rock was used by Indians as a hiding place to ambush passing wagon trains. NR

TRADING POST

MARAIS DES CYGNES MASSACRE SITE, *4 miles northeast*
This was the scene of the infamous massacre of May 19, 1855, when Charles A. Hamelton, a border ruffian, and his gang of 30 proslavery sympathizers crossed into Kansas from Missouri, took 11 unarmed free-state men prisoner, and shot them. Five of the free-state men were killed, and these victims subsequently became martyrs to the cause of freedom. In 1858 John Greenleaf Whittier commemorated the killings in a poem, "Le Marais du Cygne," and John Brown built a fort at the murder site. NR

ABRAHAM LINCOLN BIRTHPLACE NATIONAL HISTORIC SITE, *central Kentucky, about 3 miles south of Hodgenville on U.S. 31E*

This 116-acre site contains nearly 100 acres of Sinking Springs Farm, which President Lincoln's parents purchased in 1808. The Lincolns lived in a one-room log cabin near a large limestone spring, and here Abraham Lincoln was born on February 12, 1809. The family remained on this farm for about 2½ years before losing it because of a defective land title; they then moved to Knob Creek, about 10 miles to the northeast, and subsequently relocated to Indiana. Landmarks from the Lincoln period are **Sinking Spring** and **Boundary Oak,** a giant white oak that was a survey marker at the time of Lincoln's birth. A granite and marble memorial building houses the Lincoln birthplace cabin. NR

For further information write: Route 1, Hodgenville, KY 42748

BARBOURVILLE VICINITY

DR. THOMAS WALKER STATE SHRINE, *5 miles southwest on State 459, off U.S. 25E*

This shrine honors Dr. Thomas Walker, physician and surveyor, who was employed by the Loyal Land Company of Charlottesville, Virginia, to explore its grant of 800,000 acres in "Kentucky." On March 6, 1750, Walker and 5 Virginians left Charlottesville, and on April 13 the group discovered Cumberland Gap (*see*), a natural notch through the Cumberland Mountains. The party followed Warrior's Path, an ancient Indian trail through the gap, into southeastern Kentucky for about 10 miles until they came to a river that Walker named the Cumberland. Near the river the explorers built a one-room pioneer cabin—the first dwelling built by white men

Top left: Ashland, Henry Clay's home in Lexington. Below: Cumberland Gap National Historical Park. Right: an engraving of Fort Boonesborough

in Kentucky. The shrine contains a replica of **Walker's Cabin.** The Walker party spent the next 2 months exploring eastern Kentucky. *Open daily all year*

BARDSTOWN AND VICINITY

CAMP CHARITY SITE, *about 10 miles east of Bardstown on U.S. 62*
A marker on this location identifies the site of Camp Charity, where in September, 1861, after Kentucky's neutrality had been breached by both sides, Confederate General John Hunt Morgan recruited and trained the troops for his Second Kentucky Confederate Cavalry. Known as Morgan's Raiders, these famed and feared cavalrymen sacked numerous towns in Kentucky before July 7, 1863, when they crossed the Ohio River to start their famous raid into Indiana and Ohio.

MY OLD KENTUCKY HOME STATE PARK, *about 1 mile east of Bardstown on U.S. 150*
This park contains the Federal mansion, originally called Federal Hill, immortalized through Stephen Collins Foster's ballad "My Old Kentucky Home," which he wrote while visiting his cousins here in 1853. Foster's song is now Kentucky's state song. NR
Open: June 18–Labor Day, daily 9–7:30. Rest of year, daily 9–5. Dec–Feb, closed Mon. Admission: adults $1, children 25¢

BLUE LICK SPRINGS

BLUE LICKS BATTLEFIELD STATE PARK, *on Licking River on U.S. 68*
This 100-acre park encompasses most of the Blue Licks Battlefield, where on August 19, 1782, Indians and British soldiers ambushed and defeated a force of Kentucky pioneers. Often called the last battle of the Revolution, this engagement ended in the worst defeat suffered by Americans in Kentucky during the Revolution. It was also the last significant battle against Indians in Kentucky. Daniel Boone was one of the commanders; his son Israel was among those killed. There is a battlefield museum.
Museum open: Apr 1–Oct 31, daily 9–5. Admission: adults 75¢, children 50¢

COLUMBUS

COLUMBUS-BELMONT BATTLEFIELD STATE PARK, *on State 80 just outside Columbus*
This 177-acre park on the bluffs of the Mississippi River was the site of a strongly fortified Civil War position known as the Confederacy's Gibraltar of the West. In September, 1861, Confederates under General Leonidas Polk fortified the bluff with 140 cannon and stretched a massive, mile-long chain across the Mississippi to prevent Union gunboats from going south. However, the fall of Confederate defense positions elsewhere forced evacuation starting late in February, 1862. There is a museum, and visitors may also see trenches, a section of the chain, and its 6-ton anchor.
Museum open: May 30–Labor Day, daily. May 1–30, weekends only

COVINGTON VICINITY

BIG BONE LICK STATE PARK, *on State 338, 26 miles southwest of Covington via I-75 and U.S. 42*
This 175-acre park is the site of extensive remains of prehistoric mastodons, mammoths, Arctic elephants, and other mammals that came to Big Bone Lick during the Ice Age in search of its salt springs. As the mammals died their carcasses mired into the bogs

around the springs. Scientists are still finding their bones in the bogs. NR

CUMBERLAND GAP NATIONAL HISTORICAL PARK, *southeast Kentucky, west Virginia, and north Tennessee; access via U.S. 25E*

Cumberland Gap, a natural passage through the Cumberland Mountains, was known to the Indians long before Dr. Thomas Walker discovered it in 1750 (*see Barbourville, Dr. Walker Shrine*). In the mid-1760s, after the French and Indian War, small hunting parties began to cross through Cumberland Gap. Daniel Boone traversed the gap as early as 1769, and after he blazed the **Wilderness Road** through the gap in 1775 (*see Fort Boonesborough*) settlers poured westward. Boone's Wilderness Road became the main artery of the trans-Allegheny migration that helped extend the United States' boundaries into the Northwest and westward to the Mississippi. By 1783 some 12,000 settlers had entered Kentucky, mostly through Cumberland Gap. In 1796 the Wilderness Road was widened and improved for wagon traffic. During the Civil War both Union and Confederate forces sought control of the gap, and it changed hands several times until the Federals captured it in September, 1863. This national park covers almost 32 square miles. Besides the gap itself, the park includes 2 miles of the **Wilderness Road**, Civil War fortifications, and **Tri-State Peak**, where Kentucky, Tennessee, and Virginia meet. NR
For further information write: Box 840, Middlesboro, KY 40965

DANVILLE AND VICINITY

CONSTITUTION SQUARE STATE SHRINE, *Main Street, Danville*

Founded in 1775, Danville was the seat of government of the Kentucky District of Virginia from 1785 until 1792. This shrine contains an authentic reproduction of Kentucky's first courthouse square, with a replica of the log courthouse where Kentuckians first met in 1784 to propose withdrawing from Virginia and becoming a separate state. The 10 meetings prior to statehood and the framing and adopting of the first state constitution took place at the Danville courthouse. Constitution Square also includes replicas of the old jail, pillory, and Meeting House—the first Presbyterian church in Kentucky. The post office building, constructed in 1792 and the first west of the Alleghenies, is original.
Buildings open daily 9–5

ISAAC SHELBY STATE SHRINE, *6 miles south, ½ mile off U.S. 127*

This shrine contains the burial place of Isaac Shelby (1750–1826), a soldier and statesman who served as Kentucky's first governor (1792–96). During a second term as governor (1812–16), Shelby and General Andrew Jackson negotiated the Jackson Purchase (1818). The United States paid the Chickasaw Indians $300,000 for 8,500 square miles that now comprise Kentucky's 8 counties west of the Tennessee River and the 20 westernmost counties of Tennessee.

McDOWELL HOUSE NATIONAL HISTORIC LANDMARK, *125-S 2nd Street*

Dr. Ephraim McDowell was a famous pioneer surgeon, the "father of abdominal surgery." Here on Christmas Day, 1809, he performed the first recorded abdominal operation. His **Apothecary Shop**, next door, was the first drugstore west of the Alleghenies. NR
Open: Mon–Sat 10–4, Sun 2–5. Admission: adults $1, children 25¢

KENTUCKY

FAIRVIEW

JEFFERSON DAVIS MONUMENT STATE SHRINE, *just east on U.S. 68 and State 80*

This 22-acre park is situated on the site where Jefferson Davis, president of the Confederacy, was born in 1808. There is a replica of the actual birthplace, a log cabin built by Davis' father, Captain Samuel Davis, a Revolutionary War officer. The **Jefferson Davis Monument**, a 351-foot-high concrete-cast obelisk, is one of the highest monuments in the United States.

Monument elevator open: June 1–Sept 13, daily 9–5. Sept 13–Dec 1 and March 1–May 31, closed Mon. Dec–Feb, weekends only

FORT BOONESBOROUGH STATE PARK, *13 miles north of Richmond on State 388*

This park preserves the site of Boonesborough, one of the first permanent fortified settlements in Kentucky. It was founded in April, 1775, by Daniel Boone and a group of 30 frontiersmen. In March, 1775, Richard Henderson, a North Carolina judge, and associates purchased the Cherokee claim to 20 million acres south of the Kentucky River, where they planned to establish a private colony called Transylvania. Boone was engaged to lay out the capital of this vast new territory. Starting from Long Island of the Holston (now Kingsport, Tennessee) on March 10, Boone and his axmen hacked their way through "turrabel cainbrakes" to cut the Wilderness Road through Cumberland Gap (*see*). On April 1, 1775, after a 208-mile journey, the party reached the Kentucky River and laid the first logs of Fort Boonesborough. The next month Boonesborough was the scene of the Transylvania Convention, the first legislative assembly west of the Appalachians. This convention organized a provisional democratic government for the Transylvania colony, but the Continental Congress ignored Transylvania's plea to be recognized as a 14th colony. The fort was attacked several times during the Revolutionary War, when the British encouraged Indian raids. During a 2-week siege in September, 1778, Daniel Boone and the fort's 60 defenders managed to drive off some 400 Indians and 40 French-Canadians. Even though western settlement resumed following frontier hero George Rogers Clark's brilliant campaign against the British in 1778–79, Boonesborough, because of its isolated position on the frontier, soon became a ghost town.

FRANKFORT

OLD STATE HOUSE, *Broadway and St. Clair streets*

On June 1, 1792, when Kentucky entered the Union as the 15th state, the legislature convened at Lexington and later that year chose Frankfort (laid out in 1786) as the site for the state capital. The Greek Revival edifice known today as the Old State House or Old Capitol served as capitol from 1830 until 1910. It contains the state historical society museum, whose collection includes the pistol with which Aaron Burr killed Alexander Hamilton. During the Civil War Frankfort was the only capital of a state remaining loyal to the Union to be captured by Confederates. This event, the high point of the Southern effort in Kentucky, occurred when General Edmund Kirby-Smith seized and held the town from September 3 to October 4, 1862. On October 4, while Richard Hawes was being installed as provisional Confederate governor, Union troops appeared on the edge of town. The Confederates and their new governor hastily retreated. NR

HARRODSBURG

OLD FORT HARROD STATE PARK, *on U.S. 68 and U.S. 127*

This 28-acre park contains a reconstruction of Fort Harrod, built in 1774 soon after the town of Harrodsburg was laid out by Captain James Harrod and a band of frontiersmen as the first permanent English settlement west of the Alleghenies. The fort contains a blockhouse, cabins, and a log schoolhouse, just as it did when it was the stockaded refuge for the early settlers who poured into Kentucky through the Cumberland Gap (*see*). In 1776 the Virginia legislature formed Kentucky County (the area that would become the present state of Kentucky in 1792), with Harrodsburg as its seat of government. This state park also includes the **Lincoln Marriage Temple**, a brick structure that shelters the log cabin in which Abraham Lincoln's parents were married on June 12, 1806; the **Mansion Museum**, devoted to Kentucky history; and the **Pioneer Cemetery**, the oldest burial ground west of the Alleghenies.

Open: Mar–Nov, Tues–Fri 9–5; weekends all year. Admission: adults 50¢, children 25¢

LEXINGTON

ASHLAND NATIONAL HISTORIC LANDMARK, *on U.S. 25*

Henry Clay, famous American statesman known as the Great Pacificator, lived at Ashland from 1811 until his death in 1852. During a long period of service to the nation, he was a U.S. senator, Secretary of State, and a presidential candidate. He is best known for the Compromise of 1850, by which he sought to avoid civil war. This reconstruction of the mansion is now a museum housing the Clay family memorabilia. The **Henry Clay Law Office** (NR) is preserved at 176 North Mill Street, and he is buried in the **Lexington Cemetery**.

Open daily 9:30–4:30. Admission: adults $1, children 30¢

OLD MORRISON NATIONAL HISTORIC LANDMARK, *Transylvania College*

Transylvania College, chartered in 1780, is the oldest college west of the Appalachian Mountains. The Greek Revival Morrison College, built early in the 1800s, is the oldest building on the campus.

WEST HIGH STREET HISTORIC DISTRICT

This district preserves some of the first structures built in Lexington. Founded in 1779 and named for the Revolutionary Battle of Lexington, this city is also rich in Civil War tradition. Occupied by Union troops in September, 1861, the city fell to General E. Kirby-Smith and his Confederates the following year; it changed hands 3 times after that. The **Mary Todd Lincoln House** (NR), where President Lincoln's wife spent her girlhood, is nearby at 574 West Main Street, but is not open to the public at the present time. NR

LOUISVILLE

FORT NELSON SITE, *7th and Main streets*

A granite monument on this spot commemorates the founding of Louisville in 1779 and the building of Fort Nelson on this site in 1781–82. The town site was first surveyed in 1773. In 1778 Colonel George Rogers Clark and 20 families came down the Ohio River and established themselves on Corn Island (now flooded), opposite present-day Louisville. The next year Clark built a fort opposite Corn Island and established the first permanent settlement at Louisville. This fort served as a supply base for his famous Revolutionary War expeditions against the British and Indians at Kaskaskia, Cahokia, and Vincennes. The news of Clark's victories in the Northwest brought many settlers to Louisville.

LOCUST GROVE, 561 *Blankenbaker Lane*
An excellent example of frontier Georgian architecture, Locust Grove was built about 1790 by William Groghan and his wife, Lucy Clark Groghan, sister of Revolutionary hero George Rogers Clark. In 1809 Clark retired here; he is buried at **Cave Hill Cemetery.** NR
Open: Tues–Sat 10–4:30, Sun 1–4:30. Admission: adults $1

ZACHARY TAYLOR NATIONAL CEMETERY, 7½ *miles east on U.S. 42*
This cemetery contains the tomb of Zachary Taylor, Mexican War hero and 12th President of the United States. His home, Springfield (NR), is not open to the public at the present time.
Cemetery open daily 8–5

PERRYVILLE BATTLEFIELD NATIONAL HISTORIC LANDMARK, 2 *miles north of Perryville, just off U.S. 68 and U.S. 150*
The Battle of Perryville, fought on October 8, 1862, was one of the bloodiest clashes of the Civil War; it marked the end of any serious attempt on the part of the Confederates to gain possession of Kentucky. A Confederate army of 16,000 under General Braxton Bragg had been sweeping through Kentucky in an effort to obtain supplies and enlist troops. At Perryville the Southerners were met by Union General Don Carlos Buell and his 60,000-man army. Buell ordered 28,000 of his men into battle, and by nightfall over 7,500 Blues and Grays were dead, wounded, or missing. Bragg's forces retreated to Harrodsburg and then into Tennessee. This shrine, which preserves only 30 acres of the actual battle site, contains the burial grounds of both Union and Confederate soldiers. NR
Open: Apr 1–Oct 31, daily 9–5; closed Mon except June–Aug

RICHMOND BATTLEFIELD SITE, *just south of town on U.S. 25*
In 1862 Confederate General E. Kirby-Smith led some 12,000 troops into Kentucky through Cumberland Gap and began marching toward Lexington with the intention of invading north of the Ohio River. Smith met no resistance until he reached Richmond, where on August 29–30, 1862, his troops attacked some 7,000 Federals. The Confederates drove the Union forces back to the Kentucky River, and Smith's army continued northward to Lexington (*see*).

SPRINGFIELD
LINCOLN HOMESTEAD STATE PARK, 5 *miles north of U.S. 150 on State 528*
This park is located on a portion of the farm that belonged to Bathsheba Lincoln, the President's grandmother. It includes the **Lincoln Cabin,** a replica of the log cabin where Bathesheba lived and where Thomas Lincoln, the President's father, spent his boyhood. The replica, made of 100-year-old logs, stands on the same spot as the original cabin; it contains several pieces of pioneer furniture made by Thomas Lincoln. The **Berry House,** which has been moved here from nearby Beechland, is the actual house where Lincoln's mother, Nancy Hanks, lived prior to her marriage to Thomas Lincoln in 1806. The **Blacksmith Shop** is a reproduction of the combined blacksmith and carpentry shop in which Thomas Lincoln learned his woodworking craft.
Houses open: May–Sept, daily 9–5. Admission: adults 50¢

LOUISIANA

BATON ROUGE

    BATTLE OF BATON ROUGE STATE MONUMENT, *330 South 19th Street*

        This monument marks the site of the Battle of Baton Rouge, a bloody 2-hour conflict fought on August 5, 1862. After the fall of New Orleans and Baton Rouge to the Federals in the early summer of 1862 (*see Triumph, Fort Jackson*), Baton Rouge was almost continually held by the North without resistance. An exception was the engagement of August 5, in which Confederates unsuccessfully tried to regain control of the city.

    OLD STATE CAPITOL, *North Boulevard and Lafayette Street*

        The capital of Louisiana since 1849, Baton Rouge has existed under 7 governments since its beginning as a French military outpost in 1719. The town subsequently passed to Britain, Spain, West Florida, the Republic of Louisiana, and the Confederacy before rejoining the Union. The Old State Capitol, a castellated Gothic-style structure, was built in 1847–50; it was gutted by fire in 1862 and was not rebuilt until 1880–82, when the seat of Louisiana government returned to Baton Rouge from Shreveport (*see*), where it had been throughout much of the Civil War. The Old State Capitol was abandoned as the seat of government in 1932, when the present **Louisiana State Capitol** was built. The Louisiana Art Commission now maintains an art gallery in the Old Capitol.
        Open: Mon–Fri 8–4:30, Sat 1–5

CHALMETTE NATIONAL HISTORICAL PARK, *on east bank of Mississippi River, southeast of New Orleans via State 39*

        This park preserves the site of the **Battle of New Orleans,** General Andrew Jackson's stunning victory over the British at Chalmette

Top left: the French Quarter in New Orleans. Below: Acadian House Museum in St. Martinville. Right: Louisiana State Capitol at Baton Rouge

Plantation on January 8, 1815. The British planned to capture New Orleans, gain control of the mouth of the Mississippi, and hamper the westward expansion of the United States. A preliminary encounter occurred within 7 miles of New Orleans on December 23, 1814, when Jackson and his 5,000-man army (composed mostly of militia) halted the advance of 7,500 seasoned British regulars under General Sir Edward Pakenham. The Americans withdrew to Chalmette, where Jackson ordered his men to fortify a dry canal running from the Mississippi to an impassable swamp with fence rails, posts, wooden kegs, and mud. After 2 unsuccessful attacks on the American position at Chalmette, on December 23 and January 1, 1815, Pakenham launched a final strike at the American line on January 8. He made 3 head-on assaults and within 30 minutes the British had lost some 2,000 men; the Americans, 71. A visitor center is located in the **Beauregard House,** an ante-bellum plantation mansion; the park also includes a portion of the American defense line and the now-inactive **Chalmette National Cemetery.** NR
For further information write: Box 429, Arabi, LA 70032

CHEF MENTEUR

FORT MaCOMB STATE MONUMENT, *22 miles east of New Orleans via U.S. 90*

Fort MaComb was one of 2 forts, the other being Fort Pike (*see*), built after the War of 1812 to protect the water approaches to New Orleans. MaComb was garrisoned by both Confederates and Federals during the Civil War.

GRAND ISLE, *at southwest entrance to Barataria Bay, access via State 1*

For several years early in the 19th century Grand Isle was the headquarters of Jean and Pierre Lafitte, swashbuckling pirates who sold slaves and smuggled goods in New Orleans. However, during the Battle of New Orleans (*see Chalmette National Historical Park*) the Lafittes and their band, known as the Baratarians, fought bravely for the Americans; they were subsequently pardoned by President Madison. Directly opposite Grand Isle, about 1 mile across Barataria Pass on the southern end of Grand Terre Isle, are the ruins of **Fort Livingston,** occupied by both Confederates and Federals during the Civil War.

MANSFIELD VICINITY

MANSFIELD BATTLE PARK STATE MONUMENT, *4 miles southeast of Mansfield via U.S. 84 and State 175*

This park covers 44 acres on the site of the last Southern victory of the Civil War. In the Battle of Mansfield, on April 8, 1864, some 15,000 Confederate soldiers commanded by General Dick Taylor attacked and stopped 40,000 Union troops under General Nathaniel P. Banks. This decisive battle terminated the 1864 Red River campaign, in which 2 Union forces unsuccessfully tried to take Shreveport and conquer the Red River territory. Banks retreated to Pleasant Hill, where he was defeated on April 9. The Federals then retired to Alexandria There is a battlefield museum.
Open: Tues–Sat 9–5, Sun 1–5. Admission: adults 50¢

MANY VICINITY

FORT JESUP NATIONAL HISTORIC LANDMARK, *6 miles northeast on State 6*

Fort Jesup, established in 1822 by Zachary Taylor, was the most southwesterly military outpost in the United States until 1846.

In 1845 the American Army concentrated at Fort Jesup for the invasion of Mexico and the liberation of Texas under General Taylor. In 1846 the American frontier was moved to the Rio Grande, and Fort Jesup was abandoned as a military post. This 22-acre state monument contains only one original building—a log kitchen. NR
Museum open: Tues–Sat 9–5, Sun 1–5

MARKSVILLE

MARKSVILLE PREHISTORIC INDIAN SITE NATIONAL HISTORIC LANDMARK, *State 1*

Situated on a bluff overlooking the Old River, this monument occupies the site of an ancient fortified Indian village enclosed by low earthen embankments that still stand. The park includes 6 burial mounds probably built between A.D. 300 and 600; most have been restored to their original condition. There is an on-site museum. NR
Open: Mon–Sat 10–4, Sun 10–6. Admission: adults 50¢

NATCHITOCHES

BURIAL SITE OF ST. DENIS, *corner of Front and Church streets, beneath McClung's Drugstore*

This is the burial site of Louis Juchereau de St. Denis (1676–1744), a Canadian-born Frenchman who in 1714 founded the French settlement of Natchitoches on the site of an old Indian village. Natchitoches is the oldest town in Louisiana.

FORT ST. JEAN BAPTISTE DE NATCHITOCHES SITES, *Jefferson and New Second streets and vicinity*

In 1714 Louis Juchereau de St. Denis began building Fort St. Jean Baptiste on the banks of the Red River (now Cane River) to protect fledgling Natchitoches from marauding Indians and Spaniards. It was the first fortified outpost on the frontier between French Louisiana and Spanish territory. In 1735–37, because of floods and Indian attacks, the French abandoned the original fort and constructed a second fort on higher ground, 200 yards to the west on a site now occupied by the **American Cemetery.** The French used this second fort until 1749, and it was still in existence in 1769. Today, however, there are no above-ground traces of either fort.

NEW ORLEANS

CABILDO NATIONAL HISTORIC LANDMARK, *709 Chartres Street*

This structure, also known as the Casa Capitular, was built in 1795 as the seat of the Cabildo, or administrative and legislative council for Spanish Louisiana. The ceremony in which Louisiana Territory, after having been under Spanish control since 1763, was receded to the French, occurred at the Cabildo on November 30, 1803. On December 20, 1803, another ceremony, representing the transfer of sovereignty of Louisiana Territory from France to the United States, took place there. The building, which was used for public offices until 1911, now contains part of the **Louisiana State Museum.** NR
Open: Wed–Sun 9–5. Admission: adults 50¢, children 25¢

JACKSON SQUARE NATIONAL HISTORIC LANDMARK

Originally called the Place d'Armes, this square in the heart of the Vieux Carré (*see*) has been the center of the city since it was first laid out. In Jackson Square on December 20, 1803, the United States flag was raised for the first time over the newly purchased Louisiana

Left: the Beauregard House Museum at Chalmette National Park displays memorabilia of the Battle of New Orleans. Right: an engraving of the 1815 battle

Territory. Andrew Jackson was received in this square by the citizens of New Orleans after his encounter with the British at Chalmette (*see*). Jackson Square, now a tree-shaded public park, contains an equestrian statue of Jackson and a flagpole symbolizing the transfer of the Louisiana Territory to the United States. The square offers a fine view of the **Basilica of St. Louis,** dating from 1794. NR

URSULINE CONVENT NATIONAL HISTORIC LANDMARK, *114 Chartres St*

Built between 1748 and 1752 on the site of a 1734 convent, this structure is one of the few remaining links to New Orleans as the French capital of Louisiana. The original convent was founded by Ursuline nuns who arrived from France in 1728. The present structure, which was extensively remodeled in 1924, is now part of the rectory of St. Mary's Italian Church. NR

Open: Sept 1–June 1, Tues, Thurs, Sat 11–2; rest of year, 10–2. Admission: adults $1, students 50¢

VIEUX CARRE HISTORIC DISTRICT NATIONAL HISTORIC LANDMARK

The French Quarter, or Vieux Carré, which covers some 85 blocks, is the nucleus of the original city of New Orleans. The district, famous for its narrow streets, flower-filled courtyards, and old Creole homes with wrought-iron balconies, retains much of the flavor of early New Orleans. The city was founded in 1718 by the French governor of Louisiana, Jean Baptiste le Moyne, Sieur de Bienville, who 3 years later plotted the city into 80 rectilinear blocks. In 1722 New Orleans, named in honor of the Duc d'Orleans, Regent of France, replaced Biloxi as the capital of French Louisiana. In 1763, when France ceded Louisiana to Spain, New Orleans became the capital of Spanish Louisiana. The metropolis grew rapidly, and new buildings replaced the many structures destroyed by the fires of 1788 and 1794. After the War of 1812 New Orleans became a major port for the growing steamboat traffic on the Mississippi. Most of the structures in the Vieux Carré were built between 1794 and 1850. Many of them represent unique fusions of architectural styles, notably French, Spanish, and Greek Revival. Some of the landmarks that date back to the French and Spanish periods include the **Cabildo**, the **Ursuline Convent**, and **Jackson Square** (*see all*). Other notable sites in the French Quarter include the **Presbytère** (NHL), used as a courthouse after its completion in 1813; **Lafitte's Blacksmith Shop** (NHL), reputed to be the shop operated by the pirate brothers Jean and Pierre Lafitte (*see Grand Isle*); the **Bank of the United States**, noted for its fine wrought-iron balconies; and **Maspero's Exchange**, a popular coffee house dating from 1788. NR

PHOENIX

FORT DE LA BOULAYE NATIONAL HISTORIC LANDMARK, *about 1 mile north on State 39*

This fort, also known as Fort Iberville, was founded in January, 1700, by the brothers Pierre le Moyne, Sieur d'Iberville, and Jean Baptiste le Moyne, Sieur de Bienville, to proclaim possession of the mouth of the Mississippi River for France. The fort, a 28-foot-square wooden blockhouse equipped with 6 cannon, was situated on a low ridge along the east bank of the Mississippi. Indian threats probably forced the French to abandon the post by 1704, although Louis Juchereau de St. Denis, the founder of Natchitoches (*see*), remained at Fort Boulaye for several years. NR

RIGOLETS

FORT PIKE STATE MONUMENT, *30 miles east of downtown New Orleans via U.S. 90*

Built between 1819 and 1828, Fort Pike was constructed to guard Rigolets Pass, one of the channels leading into New Orleans. The Confederates temporarily took possession of Fort Pike in 1861. There is a museum in one of the old barracks buildings. NR
Open: summer, Mon–Fri 1–4:30, Sat 12–5, Sun 1–6; winter, Tues–Fri 1–4:30, weekends 12–5.

ROBELINE VICINITY

PRESIDIO OF LOS ADAES SITE, *about 2 miles northeast off State 6*

In 1717, threatened by French encroachment from Fort St. Jean Baptiste at Natchitoches (*see*), the Spanish established the mission of **San Miguel de Los Adaes**—the only Spanish mission to be founded in Louisiana—about 14 miles southwest of Natchitoches. In 1721, after the French had attacked and destroyed this mission, the Spanish returned and rebuilt, on an adjoining hill, the palisaded Presidio of Nuestra Señora del Pilar de los Adaes. This presidio, or fort, was an important Spanish outpost and the capital of the frontier province of Texas until 1773. Originally the presidio, mission, and village of Los Adaes—of which few traces remain today—covered about 40 acres; more than 9 acres are maintained as a historical park.

SAINT FRANCISVILLE VICINITY

AUDUBON MEMORIAL STATE PARK, *3 miles east of Saint Francisville on State 965, off U.S. 61*

This 100-acre tract is carved out of the famous ante-bellum plantation **Oakley**, where John James Audubon, ornithologist and artist, painted 32 of the plates for his *Birds of America*. The house has been restored and furnished as it was when Audubon stayed there as a tutor in the 1820s.

House open: Mon–Sat 9–4:45, Sun 1–4:45. Admission: adults $1.03

SAINT MARTINVILLE

LONGFELLOW-EVANGELINE MEMORIAL STATE PARK, *1 mile north of Saint Martinville via State 31*

This memorial occupies 157 acres in the heart of the region settled by the French Acadians after the British expelled them from Nova Scotia in 1755. The park also honors Henry Wadsworth Longfellow, who in his poem "Evangeline" described the hardships suffered by the Acadians. The **Acadian House Museum** occupies a plantation house built about 1765 by an early French commandant at Poste des Atakapas, later St. Martinville.

Museum open: Mon–Sat and holidays 8:30–4:30, Sun 12:30–4:30

SHREVEPORT, *northwest corner of Louisiana, traversed by U.S. 20*

Built on land formerly occupied by the Caddo Indians, Shreveport developed during the early 1830s, when settlers began to drift into Caddo country and build log cabins along the Red River. This Indian territory was traversed by the military road that the U.S. Army used to haul supplies between Alexandria and Natchitoches (*see*) and then northwest to Fort Towson, Oklahoma. Because of the difficulty of this overland haul, the War Department requested that the Red River be cleared of the Great Raft, an almost solid accumulation of driftwood that blocked navigation on the river for some 160 miles. north of present-day Campti. This formidable task was accomplished by Henry Miller Shreve (1785–1851), a trader and steamboat builder, who began clearing the river at Campti in 1833. By 1839 the river was cleared as far as Fort Towson. Shreveport developed between 1835 and 1839, when it was incorporated as a town, and the city prospered greatly during the period of the steamboat and King Cotton. Shreveport, which saw no military action during the Civil War, became the Confederate capital of Louisiana in 1863. When Federal gunboats were attempting to ascend the Red River during General Nathaniel P. Banks's Red River campaign of 1864, the Shreveport Confederates had few cannon. Charred logs, cut to resemble artillery pieces, were placed along the ramparts of river-front fortifications. The remnants of one of these forts, known as **Fort Humbug**, still stands in Fort Humbug Memorial Park at the foot of Stoner Avenue. Fortunately for the city, Banks and his Federals were turned back at Mansfield (*see*).

TRIUMPH VICINITY

FORT JACKSON NATIONAL HISTORIC LANDMARK, *2½ miles southeast via State 23*

Situated on the west bank of the Mississippi River, Fort Jackson, begun in 1792 and enlarged in 1815 and 1861, is a bastioned, star-shaped embattlement with huge brick casements, heavy bombproofs, and a surrounding moat. During the Civil War the defense of New Orleans was entrusted to Fort Jackson and to Fort St. Philip (NHL), on the east bank of the Mississippi 5 miles north of Fort Jackson. On April 18, 1862, Union Admiral David Farragut and a fleet of 24 wooden gunboats and 19 mortar schooners arrived in striking distance of both forts. Forts Jackson and St. Philip held out under heavy fire until April 24, when Farragut steamed past them toward New Orleans. The city surrendered without bloodshed and was occupied by Union troops on May 1, 1862. Fort Jackson is open to the public; Fort St. Philip, privately owned, is not. NR

ARNOLD TRAIL TO QUEBEC, *along Kennebec River through Wyman and Flagstaff lakes, along Dead River and Chain of Ponds*

In the fall of 1775, Colonel Benedict Arnold and 1,100 troops took this 194-mile route, extending from Fort Popham (*see Popham Beach*) north and west to the Canadian border at Coburn Gore, on their historic march to attack Canada. On the way, the expedition passed **Fort Western** (NR) at Augusta, **Fort Halifax** (NHL) (*see*) at Winslow, and the old **Pownalborough Court House** (NR) in Dresden. Only 600 men survived the crossing of the Maine wilderness. Today 33 interpretative panels are displayed along the trail. NR *Panels available for viewing: June 15–Oct 15*

AUGUSTA

BLAINE HOUSE NATIONAL HISTORIC LANDMARK, *Capitol and State streets*

This Classical Revival-style home belonged to James G. Blaine, the prominent politician who was Speaker of the House of Representatives (1869–75), ran unsuccessfully for the Presidency (1884), and became Secretary of State (1889–92); Blaine's lasting achievement was his founding of the Pan American Union in 1890. Since 1919 the house has been used as Maine's executive mansion. NR *Open: Mon–Fri 2–4*

BRUNSWICK AND VICINITY

MERE POINT MEMORIAL

This marker commemorates the offshore landing made in Casco Bay by U.S. Army pilots on September 6, 1924, during the first circumnavigation of the world by air. The round-the-world flight

Top left: Portland lighthouse. Below: Roosevelt Home in Roosevelt-Campobello International Park near Lubec. Right: Fort Edgecomb at Edgecomb

originated 5 months earlier in Seattle, Washington, when the pilots headed west across Canada and Alaska. Although planning to land in Boston on the return lap, the aviators, because of bad weather, were forced to land in Maine off Mere Point.

STOWE HOUSE NATIONAL HISTORIC LANDMARK, *63 Federal Street*

In this white frame house in 1851–52, Harriet Beecher Stowe wrote *Uncle Tom's Cabin*. This indictment of slavery prompted President Lincoln to remark upon meeting Mrs. Stowe that she was "the little lady who started this great war." The study contains Mrs. Stowe's original furnishings. The house is currently an inn. NR

CASTINE

 FORT GEORGE STATE MEMORIAL, *off State 166*

Erected by the British in 1779 at the strategic approach to the Penobscot River, this fort played a prominent role in the Revolution and in the War of 1812. When it was built, the fort cut off Boston merchants from one of their best sources of lumber. Although the largest amphibious expedition of the Revolution, under Commodore Saltonstall and General Lovell, was sent to capture Fort George, the American fleet was annihilated instead, and the clash virtually marked the end of the Continental Navy. At the end of the War Fort George was the last British post to be evacuated. In 1812 the British took possession of this area and rebuilt and garrisoned Fort George, which they held until April 25, 1815, when they blew up the post and left. NR
Open: May 30–Labor Day, daily 10–6

EDGECOMB

FORT EDGECOMB STATE MEMORIAL, *off U.S. 1, on Davis Island in the Sheepscot River*

This fort was built in 1808 to protect the seaport of Wiscasset, which boasted one of the deepest harbors in Maine and was at that time the most important shipping port north of Boston. Henry Dearborn, then Secretary of War, supervised the fort's construction. Fort Edgecomb never saw any military activity; the only time its 18-pound guns were fired was on March 4, 1809, to salute the inauguration of President James Madison. The original blockhouse stands today, and the stockade has been reconstructed. NR
Open: May 30–Labor Day, daily 10–6

FORT KENT VICINITY

FORT KENT STATE MEMORIAL, *¾ mile southwest, off State 11 or 161 and U.S. 1*

This fort was constructed in 1839 for the undeclared and bloodless Aroostook Border War, which concerned a boundary dispute between Maine and New Brunswick. A misunderstanding about the northeastern boundary had existed between the United States and Canada since 1783. The controversy flared up in the 1830s, when Maine lumberjacks along the Aroostook River tried to oust rival "trespassing" Canadians. Finally, in 1839, the aroused citizens of Maine and the province of New Brunswick called out their respective militias to protect their public lands. President Martin Van Buren thereupon dispatched General Winfield Scott to the area to maintain the peace and negotiate a truce with New Brunswick, which he accomplished. The dispute was finally resolved and the boundary fixed in the Webster-Ashburton Treaty of 1842. Today

the original blockhouse contains a museum. NR
Open: May 30–Labor Day, daily 10–6

HARPSWELL AND VICINITY
EAGLE ISLAND, *2½ miles south of Bailey Island in Casco Bay*
This island was the summer retreat where Admiral Robert E. Peary planned the expedition that resulted in his discovery of the North Pole on April 6, 1909. Known as Sawungun to ancient coastal Maine Indians, the island was renamed by Peary in honor of the whaler *Eagle*, which carried him on his first trip to the Arctic in 1893. Peary's residence and guest cottage still stand. NR
Open: June 20–Labor Day, daily 10–6

HARPSWELL MEETING HOUSE NATIONAL HISTORIC LAND-MARK, *on State 123*
This little-altered example of an early New England church was built from 1757 to 1759 by Elisha Eaton, a carpenter and son of the first pastor. This structure served as church and town meeting hall until 1844, when the property was sold to the town. The building, in Harpswell Center, is currently a town meeting place. NR

KITTERY AND VICINITY
FORT McCLARY STATE MEMORIAL, *south on Kittery Point Road off State 103*
Built in 1809 and enlarged in 1844–45 following hostilities with Great Britain over the northeastern boundary (*see Fort Kent State Memorial*), Fort McClary has long been associated with the defense of Portsmouth Harbor. A fortification known as **Fort William** was erected on the site as early as 1715 to protect the Massachusetts Bay Colony—of which Maine was a part—from "unreasonable duties" imposed by the colony of New Hampshire. During the Revolution, defenses at this post prevented the British from attacking Kittery or Portsmouth. The original fort had completely disappeared by 1803. Today the hexagonal blockhouse has been restored. NR
Open: May 30–Oct 10, daily 10–6

JOHN PAUL JONES MEMORIAL, *on U.S. 1 just east of the Badger Island Bridge*
The U.S.S. *Ranger*, the first man-of-war to hoist The Stars and Stripes, was built and launched near this site in 1777. Under the command of John Paul Jones, the warship received the first European salute accorded the U.S. flag in the Bay of Quiberon, France, on February 14, 1778. Two monuments and a flagpole are at the site.

PEPPERELL HOUSE NATIONAL HISTORIC LANDMARK, *State 103*
This late Georgian mansion was erected about 1760 by Lady Mary Pepperell, widow of Sir William Pepperell, who during King George's War in 1745 successfully laid siege to the French fortress of Louisbourg on Cape Breton Island, Nova Scotia. For this exploit, George II made Pepperell a baronet, the first title of its kind conferred upon a native American. NR
Open: June 15–Sept 15, Tues–Sat 11–4

LUBEC VICINITY
ROOSEVELT-CAMPOBELLO INTERNATIONAL PARK, *Campobello Island, Passamaquoddy Bay, New Brunswick, via F.D.R. Memorial Bridge*
A resort of wealthy American businessmen since 1879, rocky, rugged Campobello Island was the summer home of Franklin D.

Roosevelt from the time he was one in 1883 until he was stricken with polio in 1921. During his Presidency, Roosevelt returned to his "beloved island" 4 times. Today this 3,000-acre memorial to international friendship between the United States and Canada includes the 34-room Dutch colonial "cottage" where Roosevelt and his family lived after 1910; the house has been restored to its original appearance.

Open: May 18–Oct, daily 10–6

MACHIAS VICINITY

FORT O'BRIEN, *5 miles south on State 92*

Also known as **Fort Machias**, this fort was the scene of the first naval engagement of the Revolutionary War, which took place near the mouth of the Machias River on June 12, 1775. A few weeks earlier the Machias townspeople, led by Jeremiah O'Brien, had captured a British ship, the *Margaretta*, which was going to supply Boston with lumber. In retaliation the British sent a fleet under Sir George Collier to punish the rebels. The fortifications built here were not strong enough to resist the British, who routed the colonists. Subsequently, General Washington garrisoned Fort O'Brien, which became part of the national defense in 1781. During the War of 1812 the British took the fort and burned the barracks. Today only the breastworks remain. NR

Open: May 30–Labor Day, daily 10–6

PEMAQUID BEACH VICINITY

ANCIENT PEMAQUID RESTORATION SITE, *Pemaquid Point near the mouth of the Pemaquid River*

Occupying a strategic position as the last outpost between the French and the English, Pemaquid—Maine's first permanent settlement—was the site of 4 forts that played an important role in the history of the area during the 17th and 18th centuries. Although English fishermen had visited the area since early in the 1500s, a stable settlement was not made until 1625, when the Indian chief Samoset sold the Pemaquid Peninsula to one John Brown for 50 beaver skins. **Fort Pemaquid** was erected in 1630 for defense against pirates and was burned in 1676 by Indians during King Philip's War. **Fort Charles** replaced it in 1677, but this new fort was destroyed during the Penobscot Indian massacre of 1689. New England's earliest stone fort, **Fort William Henry** (NR)—now reconstructed adjacent to this site—was built in 1692 and leveled by the French 4 years later. **Fort Frederick**, the last fort, was constructed in 1729 and survived until the citizens of Bristol tore it down in 1776 to prevent the British from occupying it. Dwelling foundations and artifacts from the 16th and 17th centuries have been unearthed at the site. A museum is also on the premises. NR

Open: May 30–Labor Day, daily 10–6

POLAND SPRING VICINITY

SHAKER VILLAGE, *Sabbathday Lake, off State 26*

This religious community was established in 1793 in accordance with the principles of faith expounded by Mother Ann Lee, a founder of the Shaker sect, who brought the first Shaker colony to America in 1774. Standing today in one of the last remaining Shaker villages in the country are the old **Shaker Meeting-House** (1794), which now contains a museum, and the **Stone Building**, a community residence. NR

Open: May 30–Sept 30, Tues–Sat 10–4:30

POPHAM BEACH VICINITY

FORT POPHAM STATE MEMORIAL, *north of Popham Beach on Hunnewell Point*

The site of this semicircular granite fort, begun in 1861 to guard the Kennebec River during the Civil War and never completed, is closely associated with England's first attempt to colonize New England, as well as with earlier Viking explorations. In 1607—the year of the landing at Jamestown, Virginia—100 colonists under the leadership of Raleigh Gilbert and George Popham attempted to establish a settlement on nearby Sabino Head. The **Popham Colony** (NR) lasted less than a year (during which time the *Virginia*, the first vessel built in America, was constructed), and most of its members returned to England. Markings on a boulder in the vicinity indicate that Vikings had landed here as early as the 11th century. NR
Open: May 30–Labor Day, daily 10–6

PORTLAND

SPRING STREET HISTORIC DISTRICT

Preserved in this district are many fine examples of architecture that reflect Portland's prosperity as a shipbuilding, steamboat, and rail center in the 19th century. Notable structures include the Federal-style **McLellan-Wingate-Sweat Mansion** (NHL), built in 1800, and the Victorian **Morse-Libby House** (NHL) of 1859. NR
McLellan-Wingate-Sweat Mansion open: Tues–Sat 10–5, Sun 2–5.
Morse-Libby House open: June 15–Oct 15, Tues–Sat 10:30–4:30

WADSWORTH-LONGFELLOW HOUSE NATIONAL HISTORIC LANDMARK, *487 Congress Street*

The famous poet Henry Wadsworth Longfellow resided in this house—built by his grandfather in 1785 and the oldest brick home in Portland—from his birth in 1807 until his second marriage in 1843. It was here that Longfellow composed "The Rainy Day" after his first wife's death in 1835. NR
Open: June 15–Oct 15, Mon–Sat 9:30–4:30

PROSPECT VICINITY

FORT KNOX NATIONAL HISTORIC LANDMARK, *on State 174 off U.S. 1*

The site for this granite fort was chosen during the Aroostook War (*see Fort Kent State Memorial*) to defend Maine from a British invasion by way of the Penobscot River. The fort itself was begun somewhat later, in 1844, and was completed in 1864. Volunteers were garrisoned at the post during the Civil and Spanish American wars. NR
Open: May 1–Nov 1, daily 10–6

ST. CROIX ISLAND NATIONAL MONUMENT, *on the Canadian border on the St. Croix River*

In 1604 the French explorers Sieur du Monts and Samuel de Champlain founded the first European settlement on the Atlantic coast north of Florida. Although one third of the 120-man expedition died during the winter of 1604–5 and the party moved to Port Royal, Nova Scotia, this venture led to the founding of New France. In later years St. Croix Island played a significant role in establishing the permanent boundary between the United States and Canada. There are no federal facilities at St. Croix Island, and it is not open to the public at the present time. NR

MAINE

SOUTH BERWICK VICINITY
VAUGHAN WOODS MEMORIAL, *off State 96 or 236*
In 1634 a ship named *The Pied Cow* sailed up the Salmon Falls River, anchored at what was subsequently called Cow Cove within this stretch of forest, and brought Maine its first cows and America its first sawmill, which was erected nearby. On a bluff high above the river is the **Hamilton House** (NHL), which was raised in 1785 by Colonel Jonathan Hamilton, a wealthy West India trader, and later became the setting of Sarah Orne Jewett's novel *The Tory Lover*. Miss Jewett's childhood home is also in South Berwick.
Woods open: Memorial Day–Sept 30, daily 10–6. Hamilton House open: June–Sept, Wed–Sat 1–5; closed holidays

STOCKTON SPRINGS VICINITY

FORT POWNALL MEMORIAL, *southeast on Fort Point*
Situated to protect the Penobscot River, this fort was constructed in 1759 during the French and Indian War by Royal Governor Thomas Pownall. Garrisoned by General Jedediah Preble and 84 soldiers, the fort never saw action because General James Wolfe captured Quebec in September, 1759, thus ending hostilities. During the Revolution in 1775, Captain Mowatt of the British forces stripped the fort of guns and ammunition, while later that year Colonel Cargill of the patriots burned the fort and filled in the ditches to keep it from falling to the British. Today only the stone foundations and earthworks remain. NR

THOMASTON VICINITY
MONTPELIER (HENRY KNOX HOME) REPLICA, *1 mile east on U.S. 1*
General Henry Knox, commander of the artillery during the Revolution and the nation's first Secretary of War in George Washington's cabinet, erected the original mansion on this site in 1794. The youngest major general in the Revolution at the age of 31, Knox is credited with planning all the battles won by Washington. NR
Open: May 30–Oct 31, daily 10–5

WINSLOW

FORT HALIFAX NATIONAL HISTORIC LANDMARK, *on U.S. 201*
The oldest extant blockhouse in the United States was part of a larger defensive complex built in 1754, during the French and Indian War. Governor William Shirley of Massachusetts (of which Maine was a part until 1820) had the fort constructed to protect settlers in the area from Indians. During the Revolution Colonel Benedict Arnold and 1,100 of his men stopped at this wilderness outpost on their expedition to Quebec in 1775. NR
Open: May 30–Labor Day, daily 10–6

YORK
OLD YORK GAOL NATIONAL HISTORIC LANDMARK, *4 Lindsay Road, facing U.S. 1A*
The oldest English public building in the United States was begun in 1653 in accordance with the colonial laws of Massachusetts (of which Maine was a part), which stipulated that each county have a "house of correction." At that time a single stone cell—now the dungeon—with walls 2½ feet thick was constructed. Enlarged considerably in 1720, the structure served as a prison for the whole province of Maine until 1760 and was used as the York County jail until 1860. The building now contains a museum. NR
Open: June–Oct 1, Mon–Sat 9:30–5, Sun 1:30–5

MARYLAND

ANNAPOLIS

CHASE-LLOYD HOUSE NATIONAL HISTORIC LANDMARK, *22 Maryland Avenue*

Built from 1769 to 1774, this Georgian town house belonged to Samuel Chase, a signer of the Declaration of Independence. In 1802 Francis Scott Key (*see Baltimore, Fort McHenry*) married Mary Tayloe here. NR

Open: Mon–Sat 10–12, 2–4; closed Dec 25

 MARYLAND STATE HOUSE NATIONAL HISTORIC LANDMARK, *on State Circle*

Completed in 1779, this building was the scene of several historic events, the most significant of which occurred on January 14, 1784, when the Continental Congress ratified the Treaty of Paris, thereby bringing the Revolution to its official end. This structure served as our National Capitol from November 26, 1783, to August 13, 1784. On December 23, 1783, George Washington resigned his commission as commander-in-chief in the **Old Senate Chamber.** And in May, 1784, Thomas Jefferson was appointed minister plenipotentiary here to represent American interests abroad. Today the edifice is the oldest state capitol still in use. Its **Flag Room** contains the only American flag known to have been carried in battle during the Revolution. Out in front is one of the old iron cannon used to arm the *Ark* and the *Dove*, the two ships that brought the first settlers to Maryland in 1634. NR

Open: Mon–Fri 9–5; closed Thanksgiving and Dec 25

OLD TREASURY BUILDING, *State Circle*

Maryland's oldest public building, this one-story brick structure was built in 1735 to serve as the colony's financial headquarters.

Top left: U.S. Naval Academy at Annapolis. Below: Hampton National Historic Site at Towson. Right: aerial view of Fort McHenry in Baltimore

The monetary policies instituted here enabled Maryland to remain solvent during the Revolution.
Open: Mon–Fri 9–5, Sat–Sun 10–4

ST. JOHNS COLLEGE, *College Avenue*
Chartered in 1784–85, St. Johns College succeeded King William's School, which was founded in 1696 as the first free school in the colonies. Notable alumni of St. Johns include Francis Scott Key (*see Baltimore, Fort McHenry*) and the nephews of George Washington. On campus is the **Birthplace of Charles Carroll**, a barrister, signer of the Declaration of Independence, and one of the drafters of the Maryland Declaration of Rights in 1776. The library houses part of the Thomas Bray Collection, which was brought to Annapolis in 1697 and was the earliest public library in the colonies. Under a tulip poplar known as the **Liberty Tree**, the Sons of Liberty congregated during the Revolution.

U.S. NAVAL ACADEMY NATIONAL HISTORIC LANDMARK, *Maryland Ave and Hanover St*
Since its founding in 1845 by George Bancroft, then Secretary of the Navy, the Naval Academy has produced career officers and has wielded considerable influence in naval affairs. The chapel here contains the tomb of John Paul Jones, naval hero of the Revolution. A museum displays flags, weapons, and other historical relics. NR
Grounds open daily 9–5. Museum open: Mon–Sat 9–5, Sun 12–5. Tours of the academy available

ANTIETAM NATIONAL CEMETERY. *See* SHARPSBURG

BALTIMORE
BALTIMORE & OHIO TRANSPORTATION MUSEUM AND MOUNT CLARE STATION NATIONAL HISTORIC LANDMARK, *Pratt and Poppleton streets*
Mount Clare Station initiated regular passenger train service in the United States in 1830 and in 1844 received the world's first official telegraph message, "What God hath wrought," sent by Robert Morse from Washington, D.C. A **Passenger Car Roundhouse** and an **Annex** house a historical collection of locomotives and railroad cars. NR
Open: Wed–Sun 10–4

BASILICA OF THE ASSUMPTION OF THE VIRGIN MARY, *Mulberry and Cathedral streets*
Designed in the Classical Revival style by the famous architect of the young Republic Benjamin Latrobe, and built between 1806 and 1831, this church is the oldest Catholic cathedral in the United States. Six of the prelates who have presided at the basilica, including Father John Carroll, the country's first archbishop, and James Cardinal Gibbons, are buried in the crypt. NR

EDGAR ALLAN POE HOUSE, *203 North Amity Street*
While residing here from 1832 to 1835, the poet Edgar Allan Poe wrote his first short stories. NR
Open Sat 1–4

FLAG HOUSE NATIONAL HISTORIC LANDMARK, *844 East Pratt at Albemarle*
It was here that Mary Young Pickersgill fabricated the 36- by

42-foot flag, with 15 stars and 15 stripes, that flew over Fort Mc-Henry (*see*) during the British bombardment in 1814 and inspired Francis Scott Key to compose "The Star-Spangled Banner." NR
Open: Tues–Sat 10–4, Sun and holidays 2–4:30

FORT McHENRY NATIONAL MONUMENT AND HISTORIC SHRINE, *3 miles from Baltimore center via East Fort Avenue*
Strategically situated at the entrance to Baltimore's inner harbor, Fort McHenry bravely resisted a 25-hour bombardment by the British during the War of 1812, preventing Baltimore's occupation by the enemy and inspiring our national anthem. This star-shaped military defense, replete with bastions, batteries, magazines, and barricades, was built between 1798 and 1803 on the site of an earlier fort and was named after James McHenry of Baltimore, sometime secretary to George Washington during the Revolution and U.S. Secretary of War from 1796 to 1800. After the burning of Washington in 1814, the British planned a joint naval and land attack on Baltimore, "the great repository of the hostile spirit of the United States against England." On September 12, 1814, the British land forces encamped on the outskirts of the city. The following morning the British fleet anchored about 2 miles below Fort McHenry and began its siege. Over the next 25 hours nearly 1,800 bombs, rockets, and shells were fired by the British, but Fort McHenry suffered only moderate damage with few casualties. Francis Scott Key, a young lawyer, witnessed the event from an American truce ship on the Patapsco River. At night, when the flag was obscured, Key knew that the fort was in American hands as long as the gunfire continued. By the dawn's early light The Stars and Stripes was still flying, and Key was prompted to write "The Star-Spangled Banner." Fort McHenry functioned as an active military post, serving in every subsequent American war through World War II. Today the fort has been restored to its pre-Civil War appearance. NR
For further information write: Supt, Baltimore, MD 21230

PEALE'S (MUNICIPAL) MUSEUM NATIONAL HISTORIC LAND-MARK, *225 N Holliday St*
Established in 1814 by the portraitist and scientist Rembrandt Peale, this structure is the first of its kind in this country to be created exclusively for museum use. Purporting to provide "an elegant rendezvous of taste, curiosity and leisure," the museum operated until 1830, when it was converted into Baltimore City Hall and remained thus for the next 45 years. NR
Open: Tues–Fri 10:30–4:30, Sat–Sun 1–5; closed holidays

U.S.S. *CONSTELLATION* NATIONAL HISTORIC LANDMARK, *Pier 1, Pratt St*
Launched in 1797, this 36-gun frigate, nicknamed the Yankee Racehorse, is the nation's oldest warship. The first commissioned ship in the U.S. Navy, it saw action against the pirates in Tripoli in 1802, the British in 1812, and in the Civil War. NR
Open: Labor Day–June 20, Mon–Sat 10–6, Sun 12–6; June 20–Labor Day, Mon–Sat 10–4, Sun 12–5

WASHINGTON MONUMENT, *Mount Vernon Place*
Executed between 1815 and 1829, this 178-foot-tall column was the first formal monument, with the exception of the tower at Washington Monument State Park (*see Hagerstown*), to be raised in honor of George Washington.

Two scenes along the Chesapeake & Ohio Canal

CHESAPEAKE & OHIO CANAL NATIONAL MONUMENT, *extending from Georgetown in Washington, D.C., to Cumberland, Maryland*

Begun on July 4, 1828, and following the Potomac River and trans-Allegheny trade route to the Ohio River, this waterway was planned to provide a much-needed transportation link between the commercial establishments of the eastern seaboard and the rich raw materials of the West. Seeing the need for developing our natural resources, Thomas Jefferson in 1806 allocated Federal funds for the construction of a national highway across the Alleghenies. The resulting National Road, completed in 1817, bore such heavy traffic that an even more economical means of transportation was sought. Water transportation, it was believed at the time, via canals and improved riverbeds would solve the problem. Ironically, the Chesapeake & Ohio Canal was begun the same day that work started on the Baltimore & Ohio Railroad at Baltimore. Among the difficulties encountered in the construction of this canal were shortages of building supplies, difficult negotiations to secure land for right of way, inadequate skilled labor (workers from Europe were eventually hired), disease, labor riots, and a bitter struggle with the B & O Railroad for property rights. The canal opened as the individual sections were completed. By 1850 the canal extended 184½ miles to Cumberland. Plans to continue it westward to Pittsburgh were abandoned because the B & O Railroad, finished 8 years earlier, had made the canal obsolete. An economic failure, the canal was seriously damaged in 2 floods and finally closed in 1924. NR (*See also District of Columbia.*)

CHURCH CREEK

OLD TRINITY PROTESTANT EPISCOPAL CHURCH, *via State 335*
Built in 1674, Old Trinity is the oldest Protestant church still in use in this country. The restored church contains a silver chalice and red velvet cushion donated by Queen Anne.

EASTON
THIRD HAVEN QUAKER MEETING HOUSE, *south end of Washington Street*
> Erected in 1684, this building is the oldest frame house of worship in the United States. When visiting Quakers on the Eastern Shore, William Penn occasionally attended services here.
> *Open daily 9–5*

EMMITSBURG
TOMB AND SHRINE OF THE BLESSED MOTHER SETON, *St. Joseph's College, on U.S. 15*
> This shrine commemorates the Venerable Elizabeth Ann Seton, a widow and Catholic convert, who was beatified in 1963 and is currently a candidate for becoming the first American-born saint. In 1808 she founded an order of nuns, the Sisters of Charity; the following year she was named Mother Superior of the order by Bishop John Carroll of Baltimore. She also established a Catholic girls' boarding school, which became St. Joseph's College.

FREDERICK
BARBARA FRITCHIE HOME, *156 West Patrick Street*
> This house is a replica of the one that belonged to Barbara Fritchie, heroine of John Greenleaf Whittier's poem, who reputedly defied Stonewall Jackson and his "rebel hordes" during the Civil War.
> *Open daily 8–5*

HAGERSTOWN VICINITY
FORT FREDERICK STATE PARK, *west of Hagerstown at Big Pool via I-70 and State 56*
> Named after Frederick Calvert, the sixth Lord Baltimore, this huge stone fort was erected in 1756, during the French and Indian War, to defend outlying settlements. Garrisoned by Maryland militia companies, the fort was kept in a constant state of readiness until the capture of Fort Duquesne in November, 1758. Subsequently Fort Frederick provided refuge to settlers during Chief Pontiac's Indian uprising, quartered British and German prisoners during the Revolution, and was reactivated to protect the B & O Railroad and the Chesapeake & Ohio Canal (*see*) at the time of the Civil War.

GREENBRIER STATE PARK, *10 miles east of Hagerstown on U.S. 40*
> The Battle of South Mountain, in which Federal and Confederate soldiers fought for control of 3 strategic passages through the mountain—Turner's, Fox's, and Crampton's gaps—occurred near this park on September 14, 1862. General Robert E. Lee, with 20,000 men, successfully prevented General George B. McClellan, with 25,000 Union troops, from seizing the gaps. In all, 5,780 men were killed or wounded. Shortly thereafter Lee was forced to abandon the gaps and retreated to Antietam (*see*).

WASHINGTON MONUMENT STATE PARK, *4 miles east of Boonsboro*
> The world's first monument dedicated to the memory of George Washington was erected on the summit of South Mountain by the citizens of Boonsboro on July 4, 1827. During the Antietam (*see*) and Gettysburg campaigns of the Civil War, the rough stone tower, which had already fallen into ruin, was repaired and used as a Union signal station. A replica of the original monument stands.

HARPERS FERRY NATIONAL HISTORICAL PARK. *See* WEST VIRGINIA

MARYLAND

MOUNT VERNON VICINITY

 GENERAL SMALLWOOD'S RETREAT, *Smallwood State Park*

George Washington, George Mason, and other founding fathers gathered at this house, belonging to William Smallwood, to discuss launching the new Republic. During the Revolution Smallwood distinguished himself by saving Washington's retreating army from a British land and naval attack at White Plains, New York, and for his bravery at the Battle of Camden, South Carolina.

Open: March–Nov, daily 10–7, or by appointment

PISCATAWAY NATIONAL PARK, *across the Potomac River from Mount Vernon*

Known mainly for providing visitors to Mount Vernon with a scenic view across the Potomac, Piscataway Park is also the site of **Fort Washington** and an ancient Indian burial ground. The site was inhabited by Archaic Indians as early as 3000 B.C., and later the Piscataway Indians lived here from the 14th to the late 18th century. George Washington purchased this land in 1752. In 1809 Fort Washington was erected on a promontory overlooking the Potomac River as the first fortification to defend the Nation's Capital. During the War of 1812 the original fort was destroyed by the British. Immediately after the war Major Pierre L'Enfant, who laid out the District of Columbia, designed a second fort for the site, which was completed in 1824 and still stands today. The enclosed masonry fortification, with its drawbridge, moat, bastions, and batteries, is an excellent example of a 19th-century coastal defense. NR

For further information write: c/o National Capital Parks-East, 5210 Indian Head Highway, Oxon Hill, MD 20021

NEW WINDSOR

JOHN EVANS MEETING HOUSE, *on Sams Creek, Carroll County*

Constructed about 1765, this small log chapel was the first Methodist meeting house in America.

REHOBETH

REHOBETH PRESBYTERIAN CHURCH

Constructed in 1706, this small brick church is the oldest Presbyterian church in America. It was founded by the Reverend Francis Makemie, who immigrated to the lower Eastern Shore in 1683 and established the Presbyterian sect in this country.

SAINT MARYS CITY AND VICINITY

FREEDOM OF CONSCIENCE MONUMENT

This massive limestone figure with its face lifted heavenward commemorates the 1649 Act Concerning Religion, which guaranteed religious freedom to all inhabitants of the province of Maryland.

LEONARD CALVERT MONUMENT

This column, honoring Maryland's first colonial governor, Leonard Calvert, stands on the site where Calvert purchased a village for the colony from the Indian King Yaocomico in 1634.

OLD STATE HOUSE

Completed in 1676, this building served for 18 years as the seat of the first colonial government to practice religious toleration. The governor's council and the general assembly convened here annually. A replica of the original structure stands today.

Open: Tues–Sun 10–5; closed Jan 1 and Dec 25

POINT LOOKOUT STATE PARK, *where the Potomac River empties into Chesapeake Bay, via Route 5*

> This is the site of the former **Camp Hoffman**—named for Colonel William Hoffman, Commissioner of Prisons—where more than 20,000 Confederate prisoners were detained between 1863 and 1865. Sanitary and medical facilities were grossly inadequate at Camp Hoffman: 3,384 lives were lost during the course of the war.

SHARPSBURG VICINITY

ANTIETAM NATIONAL BATTLEFIELD SITE, *north and east of Sharpsburg on State 34 and 65*

> Also known as the Battle of Sharpsburg, the engagement that occurred at this site near the Virginia border on September 17, 1862, was the bloodiest battle of the Civil War; it also marked the turning point in the conflict between the North and South. Robert E. Lee's effort to move the war to the North was frustrated, and thenceforth the Confederate armies were placed entirely on the defensive. And the unexpected Union victory gave President Abraham Lincoln the opportunity to issue the preliminary Emancipation Proclamation 5 days later. After his victory at Manassas (the Second Battle of Bull Run) in Virginia, General Lee advanced into Maryland and moved westward, with the Federal forces under George B. McClellan, commander of the Army of the Potomac, in pursuit. Lee, with 41,000 Confederate soldiers, took up battle position at Sharpsburg near Antietam Creek. McClellan had most of his 87,000 troops in the vicinity. The fighting began at dawn on September 17 when the Union division commander Joseph Hooker launched an artillery attack on Stonewall Jackson's Confederate troops at a cornfield on the **Joseph Poffenberger Farm.** The battle raged all day over a widespread area of 12 square miles. Scenes of heavy clashes included the **Dunkard Church,** "**Bloody Lane,**" which produced 4,000 casualties, and **Burnside Bridge,** where a few Confederates successfully held off Union forces. The timely arrival of another Confederate division prevented a Union rout, and the battle ended at dusk at a site now marked by the **Hawkins Zouaves Monument.** During the battle 12,410 Federal troops and 10,700 Confederates were killed or wounded. Today the battlefield is marked with 200 tablets and monuments. Vertical cannon barrels indicate where 6 generals were killed. At nearby **Antietam National Cemetery,** founded in 1865, 4,773 Federal soldiers, as well as a number of men killed in action in later wars, are buried. NR
> *For further information write: Box 158, Sharpsburg, MD 21782*

TOWSON

 HAMPTON NATIONAL HISTORIC SITE, *535 Hampton Lane, just off State 146*

> Constructed between 1783 and 1790, this lovely Georgian mansion—symbolizing the height of post-Revolutionary opulence—belonged to the Ridgely family, long prominent in Maryland. In 1745 Charles "the Merchant" Ridgely acquired the 1,500-acre tract that formed the basis of Hampton, the family estate. Iron deposits found on the land supplied military stores to patriot forces during the Revolution. Charles Ridgely, builder of this home, was a member of the Maryland House of Burgesses and served on the committee to draft a state constitution. His heir, a nephew, Charles Carnan Ridgely, was governor of Maryland from 1815 to 1818. The mansion has been restored with original furnishings. NR
> *Open: Tues–Sat 11–5, Sun 1–5; closed Jan 15–Feb 15 and holidays*

MASSACHUSETTS

AMESBURY

WHITTIER HOME NATIONAL HISTORIC LANDMARK, *86 Friend St*
The author of "Snow-Bound" and "The Barefoot Boy," John Green-leaf Whittier, lived in this white frame house from 1836 to 1892. NR
Open: Tues–Sat 10–5

ARLINGTON

JASON RUSSELL HOUSE, *7 Jason Street*
Built about 1680, this frame dwelling was the site on April 19, 1775, of the massacre of Jason Russell and 11 other minutemen who took cover there. Holes made that day by British bullets may still be seen.
Open: Apr–Nov, daily 2–5

AUBURN

GODDARD ROCKET LAUNCHING SITE NATIONAL HISTORIC LANDMARK, *Pakachoag Golf Course, off Upland Street*
Granite markers show where Robert H. Goddard, the brilliant physicist, launched the world's first liquid-fuel rocket on March 16, 1926. NR

BOSTON

BEACON HILL HISTORIC DISTRICT NATIONAL HISTORIC LANDMARK
After the erection of the new Massachusetts State House (*see*) in the 1790s, Beacon Hill became the city's most elegant residential district, home of the old "Brahmin" families. Red-brick houses—individualized by hidden gardens, wrought-iron balconies, gas-lights, foot scrapers, and carriage houses—still delight the eye,

Left: an engraving of Faneuil Hall in Boston. Right: Menemsha Harbor on Martha's Vineyard. Below: Hancock Shaker village

although many have been converted into apartments. The **Harrison Gray Otis House** (a state historic landmark), at 85 Mt. Vernon Street, was designed by Charles Bulfinch and has been described as the handsomest house in Boston. **Louisburg Square** (pronounced "Lewisburg") is a private cul-de-sac maintained by the owners of the beautiful houses around the park; William Dean Howells, Louisa May Alcott, and Jenny Lind each lived on the square. **Chestnut Street** is famous for its lovely recessed doorways. Historian Francis Parkman lived at Number 50 (NR), and Edwin Booth resided at 29A; Julia Ward Howe and later John Singer Sargent lived at 13. NR

BOSTON COMMON

    Purchased by the town of Boston from settler William Blaxton (or Blackstone) in 1634 for about $150, this historic 5-sided tract served as a training field for the military and as a grazing area for Boston's cattle. In 1638 gallows were built on one of the 4 hills on the 50-acre common; there Indians, Quakers, and other condemned individuals were executed. A ducking stool at the Frog Pond was used for "scolds and raillers," and a whipping post and stocks were built for those who profaned the Sabbath. British redcoats mustered here prior to the Battle of Bunker Hill. Various monuments and tablets on the common commemorate some of the many historic events that took place here.

BUNKER HILL NATIONAL HISTORIC LANDMARK, *Monument Square, Charlestown*

    Besieged on the Boston peninsula since the battles at Lexington and Concord, the British attempted to break the siege on June 17, 1775, by storming Breed's Hill in Charlestown, which had been occupied by colonial militia under Colonel William Prescott. The ensuing battle, referred to as the Battle of Bunker Hill (which the Americans had considered occupying but had rejected in favor of nearby Breed's Hill), ended in an American retreat; but the rebels inflicted heavy casualties on the enemy, and their valiant defense of the hill heightened the colonial determination to resist. A granite obelisk, 221 feet high, marks the site of the battle. NR
Open daily 9–4

DORCHESTER HEIGHTS NATIONAL HISTORIC SITE, *Telegraph Hill, South Boston*

    In March, 1776, cannon captured months earlier by Ethan Allen at Fort Ticonderoga and hauled to Boston on sleds by Henry Knox finally reached their destination, Dorchester Heights, which had been occupied by George Washington's troops. When the cannon began barraging the redcoats, General Howe, the British commander, realized that his situation was hopeless. On March 17 the British evacuated the city, giving the Americans their first major victory of the war. A white marble monument, 118 feet high, commemorates the site. NR

FANEUIL HALL NATIONAL HISTORIC LANDMARK, *Dock Square*

    Known as the Cradle of Liberty because of the many protest meetings held here during the Revolutionary period, Faneuil Hall was built in 1742 and given to the city by Peter Faneuil, a local merchant. At street level was a public market; above was a town hall. Destroyed by fire in 1761, the structure was rebuilt, and in 1805 Charles Bulfinch enlarged it and added a third story. During the

British occupation of Boston, the redcoats used the hall as a theater. Today the building, its famous grasshopper weathervane intact, houses historical paintings, a library, and a military museum. NR
Hall open: Mon–Fri 9–5, Sat 9–12, Sun 1–5

KING'S CHAPEL NATIONAL HISTORIC LANDMARK, *Tremont and School streets*
King's Chapel was erected in 1754 on the site of the first Anglican church in New England, which had been built in 1686 by the royal governor of Massachusetts. After the Revolution the chapel became America's first Unitarian church. In the adjoining burial ground are the graves of John Winthrop and other early settlers. NR
Open daily 10–4

MASSACHUSETTS STATE HOUSE NATIONAL HISTORIC LANDMARK, *Beacon Hill*
On July 4, 1795, Sam Adams and Paul Revere laid the cornerstone for a new State House: a red-brick domed structure designed by Charles Bulfinch. The Massachusetts General Court first met in the new building in January, 1798. Today additions on both sides surround the original Bulfinch building. Historic documents, battle flags, and paintings depicting scenes in Massachusetts history are on display, as is the famous "sacred codfish," which hangs in the house of representatives. NR
Open: Mon–Fri 9–5

"OLD GRANARY" BURIAL GROUND, *Tremont St at Bromfield St*
So named because the town granary once stood on the site of nearby **Park Street Church** (where William Lloyd Garrison gave his first antislavery address in 1829), this historic burial ground contains the graves of 3 signers of the Declaration of Independence—John Hancock, Samuel Adams, and Robert Treat Paine—as well as those of Paul Revere, James Otis, and Benjamin Franklin's parents.
Open daily 8–4

OLD NORTH CHURCH NATIONAL HISTORIC LANDMARK, *193 Salem Street*
Built in 1723 by William Price, a Boston print-seller and draftsman who had made a study of Christopher Wren's London churches, Old North (Christ Church Episcopal) is the oldest extant church in Boston. From its 190-foot-high steeple were hung the signal lanterns alerting colonial patriots that British troops were on their way to Lexington and Concord. In 1954 a hurricane blew the steeple down and it was replaced, but the original window from which the lanterns burned in 1775 was saved and built into the new steeple. General Thomas Gage, royal governor of the colony, is said to have watched the Battle of Bunker Hill from the steeple, and in 1817 President James Monroe received Communion here. NR
Open daily 9–4

OLD SOUTH MEETINGHOUSE NATIONAL HISTORIC LANDMARK, *Washington and Milk streets*
Like Faneuil Hall, Old South (NR) was the scene of angry public protests during the Revolutionary period. James Otis, Sam Adams, and John Hancock all spoke from the pulpit, and it was here that the signal to begin the Boston Tea Party was given. During the war General Burgoyne removed the pews and pulpit and established a riding school for his troops in the meetinghouse. Directly across

the street, at 17 Milk Street, is the site of **Benjamin Franklin's Birthplace.** NR

Open: June–Sept, Mon–Fri 9–5, Sat 9–4; Oct–May, Mon–Sat 9–4

OLD STATE HOUSE NATIONAL HISTORIC LANDMARK, *Washington Street at State*

> It was in front of the Old State House, built in 1713 as headquarters for the royal governors, that the famous Boston Massacre took place in March, 1770. Six years later the Declaration of Independence was read to excited Bostonians from the east balcony. In 1789 George Washington viewed a parade in his honor from another balcony. NR
>
> *Open: Mon–Sat 9–4*

REVERE HOUSE NATIONAL HISTORIC LANDMARK, *19–21 North Sq*

> The oldest frame house in Boston, built about 1670, was purchased in 1770 by Paul Revere. From here on April 18, 1775, the silversmith began his famous "midnight ride." The house has been restored and furnished in the style of the period when the patriot lived here (1770–1800). NR
>
> *Open: Mon–Sat 9–3:45*

U.S.S. *CONSTITUTION* NATIONAL HISTORIC LANDMARK, *Boston Naval Shipyard, Charlestown*

> Launched in 1797, the *Constitution* won fame during the War of 1812 when she was victorious in several battles against British vessels. The 44-gun frigate, called Old Ironsides because of the copper sheathing made for her by Paul Revere, was due to be dismantled in 1830, but Oliver Wendell Holmes's poem "Old Ironsides" aroused a public outcry. NR
>
> *Open daily 9:30–4*

BROOKLINE

JOHN FITZGERALD KENNEDY NATIONAL HISTORIC SITE, *88 Beals Street*

> The 35th President of the United States was born in this 9-room house on May 29, 1917. His father, Joseph P. Kennedy, a young bank president, had purchased the house 3 years earlier, just prior to his marriage to Rose Fitzgerald, daughter of John F. Fitzgerald, a Boston politician. John, the couple's second son, was born upstairs in the master bedroom. The Kennedys moved to a larger home in 1921, but the family repurchased the house in 1966. Rose Kennedy has supervised the restoration and refurnishing of the house, which now looks as it did in 1917. NR
>
> *Open: Apr–Nov, daily 9–5; Dec–Mar, Tues–Sun 9–4:30*

CAMBRIDGE

CAMBRIDGE COMMON, *between Garden and Waterhouse streets and Massachusetts Avenue*

> The common pasture for the cows of Cambridge was the scene of several public executions during the pre-Revolutionary period. Here, under a large elm tree, George Washington took command of the Continental Army on July 3, 1775.

CHRIST CHURCH NATIONAL HISTORIC LANDMARK, *Garden Street*

> Built in 1761, Christ Church (NR) is the oldest church in Cambridge; it was used as a barracks for colonial soldiers during the Revolution, when the metal pipes of the organ were melted down

to make bullets. Adjacent to the church is the **Old Town Burying Ground,** where many early settlers were buried.

HARVARD UNIVERSITY, *Harvard Square and environs*
The nation's oldest college was founded in 1636 on the northwest bank of the Charles River. Funded by a grant from the General Court of Massachusetts Bay, the school also received £780 and 320 books from the estate of a minister, John Harvard, for whom the college was subsequently named. Originally founded as a school for Puritan ministers, Harvard developed into one of the world's great universities. The center of the university is still **Harvard Yard,** where the freshmen live and many classes are held. **Massachusetts Hall** (NHL) is the oldest building at Harvard; it was constructed in 1720. **University Hall** (NHL), in the center of the yard, was designed by Charles Bulfinch and built of Chelmsford granite in 1813–15; a statue of John Harvard by Daniel Chester French stands in front of the hall. A huge Victorian Gothic structure, **Memorial Hall** (NR), was built as a memorial to Harvard men killed in the Civil War. An information center is situated at 1350 Massachusetts Avenue.

VASSALL-CRAIGIE-LONGFELLOW HOUSE NATIONAL HISTORIC LANDMARK, *105 Brattle St*
Major John Vassall, a young Royalist, built this Georgian mansion in 1759; he fled to England during the Revolution, when his Tory sympathies made his presence unwelcome. From July, 1775, to April, 1776, General George Washington made the house his head-quarters as he commanded the Continental Army during the siege of Boston. The 3-story clapboard mansion was later purchased by Dr. Andrew Craigie, whose widow rented rooms after his death. One boarder was the poet Henry Wadsworth Longfellow, whose rooms were on the second floor and whose study had once been Washington's bedroom. When Longfellow married Frances Appleton, her father gave them the house as a present. Longfellow lived there until his death in 1882. Today the house is furnished as it was during the poet's lifetime. NR
Open: May–Oct, Mon–Fri 10–5, Sat 12–5, Sun 1–5; Nov–Apr, Mon–Fri 10–4, Sat–Sun 2–4

CONCORD AND VICINITY
ANTIQUARIAN HOUSE, ½ *mile southeast on State 2A*
This brick building contains 17 period rooms, furnished authentically with antiques dating as far back as 1685. Other attractions include a replica of Ralph Waldo Emerson's study with the original furnishings; the lantern that hung on the Old North Church on the night of Paul Revere's ride, a diorama of the Concord battle, and a room displaying Thoreau's books, flute, and some of the equipment he used at Walden.
Open: Feb–Nov, Mon–Sat 10–4:30, Sun 2–4:30

EMERSON HOUSE NATIONAL HISTORIC LANDMARK, *Cambridge Turnpike and State 2A*
Ralph Waldo Emerson built this square white house in 1820 and lived in it from 1835 until he died in 1882. When the philosopher traveled to Europe, his friend Thoreau occupied the dwelling. The Victorian interior has been preserved, with Emerson's furniture and possessions on view. NR
Open: Apr 19–Nov 30, Tues–Sat and holidays 10–11:30, 1:30–5:30; Sun 2:30–5:30

MINUTEMAN NATIONAL HISTORICAL PARK

After the bloody encounter at Lexington (*see*) on April 19, 1775, the British troops marched on to Concord and began to search for and destroy the rebels' military supplies. Massed on a hillside above the **Old North Bridge,** some 400 militia and minutemen saw smoke rising from the center of town and assumed erroneously that the British were burning Concord. Advancing under orders not to shoot unless fired upon, the Americans encountered at the bridge 3 British companies, which volleyed, killing 2 minutemen. In the ensuing fight Americans killed 2 redcoats, fatally wounded another, and hit 9 more; the astonished British retreated, regrouped with their other units, and then began marching back to Lexington. At **Meriam's Corner,** however, Americans began firing on them from behind stone walls, trees, and fences; their numbers swelled by newcomers who had heard of the encounters at Lexington and the Old North Bridge, the local patriots cut across fields and maintained a steady harassment of the retreating troops. By firing upon the king's soldiers on that momentous day, Americans marked the end of a long political battle and the beginning of the shooting war that was to lead to independence. Minuteman National Historical Park is composed of 750 acres in 3 units. **Battle Road Unit,** between Meriam's Corner in Concord and Fiske Hill in Lexington, preserves 4 miles of the historic battle route. The park headquarters, on Route 2A in Lincoln, is included in this unit, as is the Fiske Hill Information Station; both have interpretive facilities. In the **North Bridge Unit** stands Daniel Chester French's Minuteman Statue, and a visitor center on Liberty Street has a sound-and-slide program and other exhibits. **The Wayside Unit,** on Route 2A, features the home of Samuel Whitney, Concord's muster master, built in 1775; Nathaniel Hawthorne, the Alcotts, and Margaret Sidney lived there in later years. Throughout the park, modern buildings are being removed and the historic houses and landscape are being restored to their 1775 appearance. NR

Park headquarters open: Mon–Fri 8–5; July–Aug, weekends 9–6. Fiske Hill Information Station open daily 8–sunset. North Bridge Visitor Center open: June–Sept, daily 8–6; Sept–May, 8–5; Sept–mid-Oct, weekends 8–6. Wayside Unit open: Apr–May, Sept–Oct, Thurs–Mon 9–4:30; June–Aug, daily 9–4:30

OLD MANSE NATIONAL HISTORIC LANDMARK, *Monument Street*

Built in 1769 on the banks of the Concord River, this clapboard, gambrel-roofed house was the home of the Reverend William Emerson, who stood in his yard on April 19, 1775, and watched the minutemen fight the redcoats at the Old North Bridge. His grandson, philosopher Ralph Waldo Emerson, spent much of his boyhood in the house, and Nathaniel Hawthorne was a tenant there from 1842 to 1846. NR

Open: June 1–Oct 15, Mon–Sat 10–4:30, Sun 1–5; Apr 19–Memorial Day, Oct 16–Nov 11, Sat 10–5, Sun and holidays 1–4:30

ORCHARD HOUSE NATIONAL HISTORIC LANDMARK, *399 Lexington Road*

Louisa May Alcott wrote the first part of *Little Women* in this house, which she called Apple Slump because it stood in an orchard. Actually 2 old houses were joined together and refurbished by the Alcott family; the 2½-story dwelling was the writer's home from 1858 to 1868. NR

Open: Apr–Nov, Mon–Sat 10–5, Sun 2–6

WALDEN POND NATIONAL HISTORIC LANDMARK, 1½ *miles south on State 126*

A cairn and tablet on the north shore of this 64-acre pond mark the site of Henry David Thoreau's famous cabin, erected in 1845. The naturalist-poet remained there for more than 2 years, "living deep and sucking out all the marrow of life." His book *Walden* is an account of his experience. The area is now a state reservation, where vacationers can camp, swim, and fish. NR

WRIGHT TAVERN NATIONAL HISTORIC LANDMARK, 2 *Lexington Road*

Built in 1747, this tavern was a gathering place for minutemen on April 19, 1775, and a resting place for the British officers who later that day sent their men to Concord. NR
Open: Mon–Sat, 9:30–5:30; Apr 19–mid-Oct, Sun 1:30–5

CUMMINGTON

BRYANT HOMESTEAD NATIONAL HISTORIC LANDMARK, *Route 112*

This beautiful Dutch Colonial white clapboard house was the childhood home and later the summer residence of William Cullen Bryant, the famous poet and newspaper editor. NR
Open: June 15–Sept 15, Tues–Sun 10–5

DEERFIELD

OLD DEERFIELD VILLAGE NATIONAL HISTORIC LANDMARK, *Route 5*

First settled in 1669, Deerfield was the northwest frontier of New England and the target of French and Indian attacks. In 1675, during King Philip's War, the Bloody Brook Massacre resulted in the evacuation of the town, which was deserted for 7 years. The great Deerfield Massacre of 1704, during Queen Anne's War, saw half the town burned, 49 residents killed, and 111 others taken to Canada as prisoners. Among the many historic houses open to visitors today are the **Frary House,** parts of which were built before the 1704 massacre but which was rebuilt during the mid-18th century as a tavern (Benedict Arnold is believed to have stopped there); the **John Sheldon Indian House,** a reproduction of the house that was the focal point of the 1704 massacre—its original door, split by a tomahawk, is on view in **Memorial Hall,** a museum of Indian and early American artifacts; the **Hall Tavern,** an 18th-century inn moved here from its original site at Charlemont on the Mohawk Trail; the **Asa Stebbins House,** built in the 1790s for the son of the county's richest landowner; and the **Wilson Printing House,** an 1816 printing shop with a working hand press. NR
Houses open: Mon–Sat 9:30–12, 1–4:30; Sun 1:30–4:30

DUXBURY

JOHN ALDEN HOUSE, 105 *Alden Street*

Jonathan Alden, third son of Pilgrims John Alden and Priscilla Mullens, built this home in 1653; his parents also lived here.
Open: June 20–Labor Day, daily 9–5

STANDISH MONUMENT RESERVATION, *Crescent Street, South Duxbury*

A 130-foot tower with a statue of Myles Standish on top commemorates the Pilgrims' military leader, who lived near here from 1632 to 1656.

EAST WEYMOUTH

ABIGAIL ADAMS BIRTHPLACE, *North and Norton streets*

The wife of John Adams and the mother of John Quincy Adams, Abigail Smith Adams, was born here in 1744. The original house was built in 1685; only a portion of that first dwelling remains.
Open: July–Aug, Tues–Fri 1–4

FALL RIVER

U.S.S. *MASSACHUSETTS, Battleship Cove*

The state's official war memorial, the *Massachusetts* ("Big Mamie"), was commissioned in 1942 and saw action in both the Atlantic and Pacific during World War II. Visitors may tour the main deck, gun turrets, bridge, and other areas.
Open: June 1–Sept 30, daily 9–7:30; Oct 1–May 31, daily 9–4

HANCOCK

HANCOCK SHAKER VILLAGE NATIONAL HISTORIC LANDMARK, *U.S. 20*

Exemplifying Mother Anne Lee's injunction to "put your hands to work and your hearts to God," this restored community of 1790 is marked by functional simplicity. There are 18 buildings, including a unique round stone barn, and some 65 rooms furnished with authentic Shaker items. NR
Open: June–Oct 15, daily 9:30–5

HARVARD

FRUITLANDS MUSEUMS STATE HISTORIC LANDMARK, *Prospect Hill Road*

Fruitlands is the 18th-century farmhouse in which Bronson Alcott, father of Louisa May Alcott, lived from June, 1843, to January, 1844, while attempting to establish a transcendental community. On the same grounds are an **American Indian Museum,** the **Old Shaker House,** and a gallery featuring artists of the Hudson River school.
Open: Memorial Day—Sept 30, Tues–Sun 1–5

HINGHAM

OLD SHIP CHURCH NATIONAL HISTORIC LANDMARK, *Main St*

Built in 1686 and altered in 1731 and 1755, the Old Ship Church is believed to be the oldest surviving church in the original 13 colonies and the only 17th-century church surviving in New England. The roof is reminiscent of the inverted hull of a ship. NR
Open: July–Aug, Tues–Sun, 12–5

LEXINGTON

BUCKMAN TAVERN NATIONAL HISTORIC LANDMARK, *Bedford Street*

Built in 1703, this tavern was the rallying place of the minutemen on the morning of April 19, 1775. Warned by Paul Revere and others that a British force was approaching, local rebels gathered here to await the redcoats' arrival. NR
Open: Apr 19–Oct 31, Mon–Sat 10–5, Sun 1–5

HANCOCK-CLARKE HOUSE NATIONAL HISTORIC LANDMARK, *35 Hancock St*

Samuel Adams and John Hancock, Revolutionary leaders, were guests in this 1698 parsonage on the night of April 18, 1775, when Paul Revere warned them of the British approach. NR
Open: Apr 19–Oct 31, Mon–Sat 10–5, Sun 1–5

MASSACHUSETTS

Left: the famous Minuteman Statue at Old North Bridge in Concord. Right: a detail from an engraving of the Battle of Lexington

LEXINGTON GREEN NATIONAL HISTORIC LANDMARK

Under orders to confiscate military supplies stored by the rebels at Concord, Lieutenant Colonel Francis Smith and 700 British regulars arrived at Lexington Green at dawn on April 19, 1775. They were met there by 50 or 60 minutemen, who had been told by Captain John Parker, "Stand your ground; don't fire unless fired upon, but if they mean to have a war, let it begin here." No one knows who fired the first shot, but it was followed by a British barrage and bayonet attack. Eight Americans were killed and 10 wounded. The cheering British regrouped and marched on to Concord. NR

MINUTEMAN NATIONAL HISTORICAL PARK. *See* CONCORD

MUNROE TAVERN, *1332 Massachusetts Avenue*

Built in 1695 and subsequently altered, this building was used as headquarters by British troops on April 19, 1775. In 1789 George Washington was entertained at a dinner here.
Open: Apr 19–Oct 31, Mon–Sat 10–5, Sun 1–5

LOWELL
WHISTLER BIRTHPLACE, *243 Worthen Street*

James McNeill Whistler, the famous painter, was born here in 1823. Etchings by Whistler are displayed in the Parker Art Gallery.
Open: Tues–Sun, 2–4:30

MARBLEHEAD

LEE HOUSE NATIONAL HISTORIC LANDMARK, *161 Washington St*
Built in 1768 by Colonel Jeremiah Lee, who entertained Washington and Lafayette here, this Georgian-style town house is now the home of the Marblehead Historical Society. NR
Open: mid-May–Oct 12, Mon–Sat 9:30–4

MARTHA'S VINEYARD

Permanently settled in 1642, this island became a whaling center in the 18th century. Between West Tisbury and Edgartown is the **Mayhew Memorial**, erected by Indians 300 years ago in memory of Rev. Thomas Mayhew, Jr., the first missionary to the Indians.

NANTUCKET HISTORIC DISTRICT NATIONAL HISTORIC LANDMARK

Settled by men and women fleeing the religious intolerance of mainland communities, Nantucket developed into one of the world's great whaling ports. By 1768, 125 whaling ships were based here. Among the buildings open to visitors are the **Jethro Coffin House** (NHL), which was built in 1686 and is the oldest house on the island; the **1800 House,** a typical Nantucket dwelling of that period; and the **Hadwen House-Satler Memorial,** an elegant mansion built for a wealthy whale-oil merchant. The **Whaling Museum** has one of the nation's outstanding exhibits on that bygone activity, and the **Maria Mitchell Memorial House** preserves the birthplace of America's first woman astronomer. Other sites of interest are the **Old Gaol, Old Mill,** and **Quaker Meeting House.** NR

NEW BEDFORD DISTRICT NATIONAL HISTORIC LANDMARK

From 1820 until the Civil War, New Bedford was the country's greatest whaling port; in 1845 alone, some 158,000 barrels of sperm oil, 272,000 barrels of whale oil, and 3 million pounds of whalebone were brought in by the 10,000 seamen who sailed on New Bedford ships. In recent years historic buildings in the now-decayed waterfront area have been restored. Among the leading sites are the **Seamen's Bethel,** the historic church that Herman Melville used as a setting in *Moby Dick;* the **Third District Court** (NR), an Italianate Revival structure built in 1853; the **Whaling Museum,** containing superb exhibits including a half-size model of the whaling bark *Lagoda* with all her equipment; the **Rotch Counting House** (NR); and the **U.S. Customhouse** (NHL).

NORTHAMPTON

CALVIN COOLIDGE MEMORIAL ROOM, *Forbes Library, 20 West St*
This memorial contains papers and memorabilia of Calvin Coolidge, the 30th President of the United States, who practiced law in Northampton and served there as mayor (1910–11).
Open: Mon–Sat 9–8:30, Sun and holidays 2–6

PELHAM

PELHAM TOWN HALL STATE HISTORIC LANDMARK, *Amherst Road*
Built in 1743, Pelham Town Hall is the oldest meetinghouse in continuous use in Massachusetts; town meetings have been held here since the hall was erected, making the building a symbol of the New England tradition of direct democracy. Nearby is a monument to Daniel Shays, the Pelham farmer who led Shays's Rebellion in 1786. NR
Open by application to town of Pelham

MASSACHUSETTS

PITTSFIELD

BERKSHIRE ATHENAEUM

The city's public library contains a room devoted to the works and personal effects of Herman Melville, the author of *Moby Dick*. Melville lived and worked at **Arrowhead** (NHL), on Holmes Road in Pittsfield, near **Holmesdale**, summer home of Oliver Wendell Holmes.

Open: Sept 15–June 15, Mon–Fri 9–9, Sat 9–6; June 16–Sept 14, Mon, Wed, Fri 9–9; Tues, Thurs, Sat 9–6

PLYMOUTH AND VICINITY

COLE'S HILL NATIONAL HISTORIC LANDMARK, *Carver Street*

Of the 102 persons who landed at Plymouth Rock in December, 1620, more than half died during that first winter. Many were buried on Cole's Hill, a site now marked by a statue of the Indian chief Massasoit. NR

MAYFLOWER II, *State Pier, Water Street*

This is a full-size replica of the ship that brought the Pilgrims to America. The original vessel carried 102 passengers and 25 crewmen to the New World on a voyage that took 66 days.

Open: Apr 1–June 16, Sept 5–Oct 21, weekdays 9–5, weekends 9–6:30; June 17–Labor Day, daily 9–8:30; Oct 22–Nov 30, daily 9–5

PLIMOUTH PLANTATION, *2 miles south off State 3A*

This is a full-scale replica of the Pilgrim colony as it appeared in 1627. The fort-meetinghouse overlooks houses and gardens, workshops, and an Indian campsite. There are demonstrations of 17th-century crafts by costumed guides.

Open: Apr–May, weekdays 10–4, weekends 10–5; June 1–June 16, Sept 5–Oct 21, weekdays 9–4, weekends 9–5; June 17–Labor Day, 9–6; Oct 22–31, 9–4; Nov 10–4

PLYMOUTH ROCK, *Water Street*

A granite portico now shelters the rock that according to tradition was the Pilgrims' steppingstone to the New World. The date 1620 has been carved on the rock. NR

PROVINCETOWN

On November 11, 1620, the Pilgrims came ashore at the tip of Cape Cod, the site of present-day Provincetown, and "fell upon their knees & blessed God of Heaven, who had brought them over ye vast & furious ocean." The *Mayflower* lay at anchor for 5 weeks offshore here before the settlers decided to sail across the bay to the site of Plymouth. Today Provincetown is a summer resort and artists' colony.

QUINCY

ADAMS NATIONAL HISTORIC SITE, *135 Adams Street*

Four generations of one of America's most distinguished families lived in this Georgian clapboard house, which John Adams called Peacefield but which subsequent generations referred to as the Old House. The oldest section was built in 1731 by Major Leonard Vassall, a West Indian sugar planter. John Adams was minister to Great Britain when he bought the house in 1787; the next year he added several new rooms and moved in. Adams and his wife retired to Peacefield when his Presidency ended in 1801 and lived there until his death in 1826. His son, President John Quincy

Adams, made the Old House his summer home, as did his son, diplomat-historian Charles Francis Adams, who erected the stone library adjoining the garden. Brooks and Henry Adams, members of the fourth generation, also spent many summers there. Brooks, who died in 1927, was the last Adams to occupy the house, which is not a "period piece" but clearly shows the changing tastes of its various occupants over 140 years. NR
Open: Apr 19–Nov 10, daily 9–5

JOHN ADAMS BIRTHPLACE NATIONAL HISTORIC LANDMARK, *133 Franklin St*

John Adams, second President of the United States, was born here in 1735. The saltbox house was erected in 1681. NR
Open: Apr 19–Sept 30, Tues–Sun 10–5

JOHN QUINCY ADAMS BIRTHPLACE NATIONAL HISTORIC LANDMARK, *141 Franklin Street*

After his marriage to Abigail Smith in 1764, John Adams moved into this house, which had been left to him by his father; Adams used the kitchen as his law office. John Quincy Adams, the sixth President, was born here in 1767. NR
Open: Apr 19–Sept 30, Tues–Sun 10–5

SALEM

CHESTNUT STREET AREA STATE HISTORIC LANDMARK

Laid out in 1796 and enlarged in 1804, Chestnut Street is a monument to Salem's prosperity in the 18th century, when ships owned by local men traded all over the world. The affluent shipowners, merchants, and other distinguished townsmen built elegant mansions, many of them designed by the brilliant architect Samuel McIntire. Most of the homes were completed about 1830 and are superb examples of the Federal style. **Hamilton Hall** (NR), a McIntire building on the corner of Chestnut and Cambridge, is regarded as a link between the simple houses of the turn of the century and the more ornate homes built in the following decades.

ESSEX INSTITUTE, *132 Essex Street*

In addition to a large museum containing art and historical objects from the colonial and Federal periods, the institute maintains several excellent examples of Salem homes from different periods; all have been restored and furnished authentically. The **John Ward House** (NHL), dating from 1684, is the oldest. The **Crowninshield-Bentley House** was built in 1727, and the **Peirce-Nichols House** (NHL) was erected in 1782. Samuel McIntire designed it and also the magnificent **Gardner-Pingree House** (NHL), built in 1804 for a sea captain and considered McIntire's finest work.

HOUSE OF SEVEN GABLES STATE HISTORIC LANDMARK, *54 Turner Street*

Built about 1668 by Captain John Turner, this house was visited several times by Nathaniel Hawthorne, who made it famous when he used its name for his novel. Six other old buildings are now preserved as part of the House of Seven Gables complex. Among them are **Hawthorne's Birthplace,** a simple gambrel-roofed house built about 1750 and moved here later, and the **Retire Beckett House,** built in 1655 by the founder of a shipbuilding family.
Open: July 1–Labor Day, daily 9:30–4:45; Labor Day–June 30, daily 10–4:45

MASSACHUSETTS

SALEM MARITIME NATIONAL HISTORIC SITE, *Derby Street*

Founded in 1626, Salem was the first town in the Massachusetts Bay Colony. Fishing and shipping were the primary industries, and by 1643 fish, lumber, and provisions were being sent to the West Indies, where they were exchanged for sugar and molasses; those items were brought home and made into rum. Later Portugal and Spain became prime markets for dried fish. Restrictive measures passed by the English Parliament after 1763 brought this thriving trade to a standstill, and during the Revolution the captains of Salem aided the colonial cause by becoming privateers and preying on English ships. In the prosperous years after the war, Salem ships voyaged all over the world, and after the discovery of gold in California, local shipowners reaped large profits by sailing around Cape Horn to San Francisco. However, Salem's harbor was too shallow to accommodate the larger ships of the latter half of the 19th century, and Boston and New York replaced her as leading seaports. Visitors to the National Historic Site may see **Derby Wharf,** which extends 2,000 feet into the harbor and was one of the great mercantile centers of the young United States; the **Custom House,** directly opposite the wharf, which was built in 1819 (Nathaniel Hawthorne worked there as surveyor of the port of Salem from 1846 to 1849); **Derby House,** erected by merchant Elias Haskett Derby in 1761–62; the **West India Goods Store;** the **Scale House,** where various weighing devices were kept; the **Bonded Warehouse,** where cargoes were stored; and the **Hawkes House,** a merchant's mansion designed about 1780 by Samuel McIntire. NR
Open daily 8:30–5; closed holidays

THE WITCH HOUSE, *310½ Essex Street*

Built in 1642, this was the home of Jonathan Corwin, one of the judges who presided during the witchcraft trials that resulted in 20 executions in 1692. Some preliminary witchcraft examinations took place in the house, although the actual trials were conducted in the **Courthouse,** at Washington and Federal streets.
Open: May 1–Oct 31, daily 10–6; rest of year by appointment

SANDWICH

Settled in 1637, Sandwich became famous in the 19th century for the colored glass made here from a secret formula that has since been lost. Examples of Sandwich glass may be seen at the **Sandwich Glass Museum,** on State 130. On the same road are **Hoxie House,** a saltbox built about 1637 and furnished with late-17th-century antiques, and **Dexter's Grist Mill,** a restored 17th-century mill.
House and mill open: June 15–Oct 1, daily 10–5. Admission: 75¢

SAUGUS

SAUGUS IRONWORKS NATIONAL HISTORIC SITE, *east of U.S. 1*

Early New England's most sophisticated ironworks was opened at Saugus (then known as Hammersmith) in 1648 and was soon turning out 8 tons of iron a week. Built with English capital and operated by brawny Scottish and English workers, the blast furnace produced crude pig iron and cast ware, which was then converted at a forge into bars of wrought iron, from which tools and other hardware could be made. At the rolling and slitting mill some of the bar iron was rolled and made into rods from which nails could be cut. Shortage of capital and lack of effective labor and management resulted in the ironworks' demise in 1670. Today's ironworks is a careful reconstruction based on archaeologically excavated founda-

tions and other remains. A museum displays artifacts uncovered during the excavations. The **Old Ironmaster's House** was built in 1636 by one of the first proprietors, Timothy Dexter, and is a fine example of a 17th-century frame dwelling with peaked gables. NR
Open: April–Oct, daily 9–5; Nov–Mar, daily 9–4

SOUTH SUDBURY
WAYSIDE INN STATE HISTORIC LANDMARK, *Wayside Inn Road*
Built by Samuel Howe sometime between 1686 and 1702, this is believed to be the oldest operating inn in the United States. Known first as Howe Tavern and later as the Red Horse, the inn was visited by Henry Wadsworth Longfellow, who immortalized it in 1862 in "Tales of a Wayside Inn." Henry Ford acquired the inn in 1923.
Open daily 7:30–9

STOCKBRIDGE
MISSION HOUSE STATE HISTORIC LANDMARK, *Main Street*
Erected in 1739, this building was the home of John Sergeant, who was the first missionary to the Housatonic Indians. The house is now a museum of American frontier life. NR
Open: Memorial Day–Labor Day, Tues–Sat 10–5, Sun and holidays 11–4; Labor Day–Oct 15, Sat and Sun only

STURBRIDGE
OLD STURBRIDGE VILLAGE, *junction of Massachusetts Turnpike, I-86, U.S. 20, and State 131*
Eighteenth-century New England comes back to life in Old Sturbridge, an authentic re-creation of an old farming community. More than 40 buildings are open to visitors. Clustered around the village green are the meetinghouse, general store, and various shops and private homes. Elsewhere on the grounds are a working farm, a gristmill, a sawmill, and numerous buildings where men and women in authentic costumes demonstrate various crafts and skills just as they were performed a century ago.
Open: Apr–Oct, daily 9:30–5:30; Dec–Feb, daily 10–4; Mar, Nov, 9:30–4:30; closed holidays

SWAMPSCOTT
MARY BAKER EDDY HISTORICAL HOUSE, *23 Paradise Road*
Mrs. Eddy was living here in 1866 when she first formulated the Christian Science religion.
Open: May 15–Oct 15, Mon–Sat 10–2, Sun 2–5; Oct 16–May 14, Mon–Fri 10–3

WEST BARNSTABLE
WEST PARISH MEETINGHOUSE, *1 mile south on State 149*
Believed to be the country's oldest Congregational church, this meetinghouse was erected in 1717. The church bell was cast by Paul Revere in 1806; the steeple cock came from England in 1723.
Open daily 8–5

WILLIAMSTOWN
WILLIAMS COLLEGE
Opened as a free school in 1791, Williams became a men's college 2 years later. Among the fine old buildings on the grounds are **West College,** a brick edifice erected in 1790, and the **Van Rensselaer Manor House,** a late Georgian residence moved here from Albany, New York, after it was marked for demolition.

MICHIGAN

BAY FURNACE, *northwest Upper Peninsula between Munising and Au Train, off State 28*

For 7 years, until fire swept through the town in 1877, Bay Furnace was a busy ironmaking center, drawing on a nearby hardwood forest as a source of charcoal. Remains of the old-time furnace used in the production of pig iron are still visible here. NR

BEAVER ISLAND, *upper Lake Michigan, about 35 miles west of the Straits of Mackinac*

Originally settled by the French about 1600, and now a hunting and fishing area with a predominantly Irish population, this largest isle of the Beaver archipelago had a memorable intermediate history as a thriving Mormon colony. In 1847 a small band of Mormons from Wisconsin, led by James Jesse Strang, settled here and set up a capital at **St. James.** Before he was slain by rebellious followers in 1856, Strang was made king, established an authoritarian rule, and represented the district in the state legislature. Shortly after his death, the resentment of non-Mormons of the mainland led to forceful dissolution of the colony and deportation of its more than 2,000 members. The **Mormon Print Shop** (NR), Main and Forest streets, St. James, built in 1850, houses the collection of the Beaver Island Historical Society.

CAMBRIDGE JUNCTION

WALKER TAVERN, *Cambridge State Historical Park on U.S. 12 at State 50*

This reconstructed stagecoach tavern, originally built about 1833, offers an authentic view of travelers' accommodations in an era when the site was a key point on the journey from Chicago to

Top: view of Fort Mackinac on Mackinac Island. Left: the Soo Locks at Sault Sainte Marie. Right: Noah Webster Home at Greenfield Village in Dearborn

Detroit. Daniel Webster and James Fenimore Cooper stayed here.
Across the road is the original location of **Walker Brick Tavern,**
constructed in 1854. NR

COPPER HARBOR VICINITY
FORT WILKINS, *Fort Wilkins State Park, 3 miles east on U.S. 41*
Built in 1844 and occupied intermittently until 1870, the restored
fort in the copper country of the Upper Peninsula recalls a time
when mining operations required protection from Indians. It is
now a historical museum. NR
Open: May 15–Oct 15, 8–7; June to Labor Day, 7–10

DEARBORN
COMMANDANT'S QUARTERS, *21950 Michigan Avenue*
This most important remaining building of the old **Detroit Arsenal**
dates from 1833 and is now restored as a military museum. NR

FORD (FAIR LANE) ESTATE NATIONAL HISTORIC LANDMARK,
4901 Evergreen Road
Henry Ford's 56-room residence, constructed of Indiana limestone,
was completed in 1915. It and the surrounding grounds (1,346 acres
on the River Rouge) are now part of the Dearborn campus of the
University of Michigan, and the grounds are open to the public
without charge. NR

GREENFIELD VILLAGE, *Village Road and Oakwood Boulevard*
The physical layout of this community is that of a typical American
village of the 19th century, but the idea behind it is completely
novel. In effect, this is a collective historical site with more than
90 structures representing famous homes or places of work; some
are reconstructions, but many are authentic buildings moved from
their original locations. Included are the homes of Noah Webster,
Luther Burbank, Stephen Foster, and Henry Ford; the courthouse
where Lincoln practiced law; the Dayton cycle shop of the Wright
brothers; and the Menlo Park laboratory of Thomas Edison. There
is also a Mississippi River paddle-wheel steamboat, which floats
on a pond. NR
*Open: June 15–Labor Day, daily 9–6; rest of year, Mon–Fri 9–5,
Sat–Sun 9–5:30*

HENRY FORD MUSEUM, *Village Road and Oakwood Boulevard*
Built by Ford and dedicated to Edison, this 14–acre museum has
replicas of Independence Hall, Congress Hall, and the old city
hall of Philadelphia. Exhibits trace the development of American
industry, agriculture, transportation, communications, science,
education, home furnishings, and interior design. There is a
separate exhibit of Ford's personal belongings, together with a
street of early American shops that display and demonstrate pre-
industrial crafts of the gunsmith, locksmith, and others.
*Open: June 15–Labor Day, daily 9–6; rest of year, Mon–Fri 9–5,
Sat–Sun 9–6*

DETROIT
FORT STREET PRESBYTERIAN CHURCH, *631 West Fort Street*
Built between 1855 and 1870, the church was partially destroyed
by fire in 1876; it was then restored carefully according to the
original gothic specifications, which include a 265-foot spire. A
guided tour is conducted each Sunday after the 11 A.M. service. NR

MICHIGAN

FORT WAYNE, *6053 West Jefferson Avenue*
Now a military museum housing also exhibits of Indian lore, the original structure was finished in 1848 at a strategic bend in the Detroit River. The museum is open without fee. NR

MARINERS' CHURCH, *170 East Jefferson Avenue*
This gothic structure, with an interior that is nautical in design, was completed in 1849 on a site 800 feet from its present location. It was moved, stone by stone, in 1956, and stands amid the modern Detroit Civic Center. It is open to people of all denominations. NR

DRUMMOND ISLAND, *eastern tip of Upper Peninsula, between North Channel and the main body of Lake Huron*
On the western end of this island, now a haven for sportsmen, is the site of **Fort Drummond** (NR), built by the British and occupied by them from 1815 to 1828. In 1822 it was established that title to the property belonged to the United States. Traces of fort buildings remain, together with parade grounds and a cemetery.

FRANKLIN VILLAGE HISTORIC DISTRICT, *bounded by the Franklin River, Bowden Street, Romany Way, Scenic Highway, and Franklin Road*
The village dates from 1825; the boundaries of the historic district represent, approximately, the limits of the village as it existed in 1870. This well-preserved community includes some 25 structures that are important historically or architecturally, including the **Broughton Wagon Shop** and **Van Every Mill**. For the most part the buildings here are intact and only slightly modified. NR

GRAND RAPIDS VICINITY
NORTON MOUND GROUP NATIONAL HISTORIC LANDMARK, *2 miles south on Indian Mound Drive*
The burial grounds of the Hopewell Indians date from approximately 4 B.C. to A.D. 400. Of about 40 original mounds in the area, a center of Hopewell culture, 17 remain. Excavations have produced stone artifacts, copper implements and beads, deer antlers, and containers of conch shell. A number of these relics are on display at the Grand Rapids Public Museum. NR

JACKSON, *70 miles west of Detroit*
On July 6, 1854, the Republican Party was founded and named at a convention here, after preliminary meetings of component groups held earlier. A tablet marks the site of the historic convention held "under the oaks."

LANSING
MICHIGAN STATE CAPITOL, *Capitol Avenue at Michigan Avenue*
This structure, designed by Elijah Myers and opened in 1878, is one of the oldest unaltered capitols in the United States. Exhibits in the rotunda trace the state's history. NR

MACKINAW CITY AND VICINITY
FORT MICHILIMACKINAC NATIONAL HISTORIC LANDMARK, *near Mackinac Bridge at the terminus of U.S. 31*
This was the predecessor of Fort Mackinac (*see Mackinac Island*), but its history dates from 1715, when the French built an outpost in an area marked by busy trade with the Indians. The fort passed into British hands in 1761, when the conclusion of the French and Indian War marked the end of France's North American empire. For

some 20 years Fort Michilimackinac was the most important British outpost on the Great Lakes, though in 1763 the garrison suffered heavily during Pontiac's Indian uprising. Between 1779 and 1781, fearing that this mainland fort could not be defended against American raids, the British abandoned it and erected a new fort on Mackinac Island. The site of old Fort Michilimackinac was determined by archaeological investigation; in 1959 restoration of the stockade was begun, and it also contains a museum. NR

MACKINAC ISLAND NATIONAL HISTORIC LANDMARK, *across the Straits of Mackinac*

Historic **Fort Mackinac** is the principal attraction here, though by no means the only one. One of the oldest existing forts in the United States, it was begun by the British in 1780 and remained in active service until 1895. It first came into American hands in 1796. The British again gained possession during the War of 1812, but after 1815 the outpost was under American control again. The stone ramparts, the three blockhouses, the officers' quarters, and the sally ports are all from the original fort; the other structures that are part of the overall design date from the late 1820s to the late 1870s. Nearby **Fort Holmes** is a reconstructed log building erected by the British during the War of 1812. There are also many points of interest connected with the thriving fur trade of the period from 1815 to about 1840, and with early community life following the cessation of hostilities. Among these are **Astor House**, which served as the headquarters of the American Fur Company; **Robert Stuart House** (NR), agency house of the company; **Beaumont Memorial**, a reconstruction of the company store; **Biddle House**, which probably was built before 1800 and is believed to be the oldest surviving residential structure on the island; **Mathew Geary House** (NR); the **Indian Dormitory** (NR), built in 1838 to house visiting Indians who had business with the Indian Agency on the island; and **Mission House** (NR) and **Mission Church** (NR).

ST. IGNACE

ST. IGNACE MISSION NATIONAL HISTORIC LANDMARK, *State and Marquette streets, Marquette Park*

In 1671 Jacques Marquette was instrumental in founding a mission on the northern shore of the Straits of Mackinac. It was named in honor of St. Ignatius Loyola, founder of the Jesuit order. In 1677, 2 years after his death, Marquette's body was moved from Ludington and reburied near the mission chapel. NR

SAULT SAINTE MARIE

ST. MARYS FALLS CANAL NATIONAL HISTORIC LANDMARK, *St. Marys River*

A man-made wonder has harnessed a natural wonder here. Lake Superior and Lake Huron are connected by the St. Marys River, but because of their difference in elevation (Lake Superior is 23 feet higher), the river would not be navigable without locks. The first **Soo Locks** were constructed in 1855; additions and modernization continued through 1943. The locks are operated jointly by the governments of the United States and Canada from April to December. **Fort Brady** in Sault Sainte Marie was constructed in 1893 to protect the Soo Locks and was garrisoned until 1944. The site has been preserved, but many of the fort's structures have become administrative and classroom buildings of Lake Superior State College, whose campus is open to the public. NR

MINNESOTA

ELK RIVER VICINITY

KELLEY HOMESTEAD NATIONAL HISTORIC LANDMARK, *2 miles southeast on U.S. 10, 52, and 169*

From 1868 until 1870 this farmhouse served as the first headquarters of the National Grange of the Patrons of Husbandry, an organization founded in 1867 by Oliver H. Kelley to educate and otherwise benefit farmers. Today the house has been restored. NR
Open: May 1–Nov 1, daily 10–4

FAIRFAX

FORT RIDGELY STATE MEMORIAL PARK, *7 miles south off State 4*

Built in 1853 adjacent to the Dakota (Sioux) Reservation, which had been established by treaty in 1851, Fort Ridgely played a major role in the Dakota War of 1862. Crop failure and the late arrival of their annuity for their ceded land provoked the Indians to declare war, and they laid siege to Fort Ridgely on August 20, 1862. Although outnumbered by twice as many warriors, the fort's defenders, using cannon fire as a deterrent, held out until reinforcements arrived on August 27 and forced the Indians to retreat up the Minnesota Valley, where they fought until the war finally ended on September 23. Today the commissary and magazine have been restored, and the foundations of other buildings excavated. NR
Open: May 1–Sept 30, daily 10–6; Oct, Sat 10–4, Sun 1–4

GRAND PORTAGE NATIONAL MONUMENT, *38 miles from Grand Marais on U.S. 61*

This portage, or "great carrying place," linked the Great Lakes to the interior network of waterways of western Canada and was a principal route of explorers, fur traders, missionaries, and military

Left: the capitol dome in St. Paul. Top right: Grand Portage National Monument. Below: Mayowood estate in Rochester

expeditions of the late 1700s. Before the advent of white men, Indians used this strategic 9-mile-long trail, which extended from the western shore of Lake Superior to the navigable waters of the Pigeon River, now the Canadian boundary line. In 1732 Sieur de la Vérendrye was the first European to cross the Grand Portage in his search for the "western sea." He was followed by French voyageurs transporting furs from the Canadian northwest to eastern markets. From 1778 until 1803 the British-run North West Company of Montreal, the renowned fur traders, made the eastern end of the portage their "grand depot," or inland headquarters. The shipping and distributing center that grew up here was called Grand Portage and was the earliest settlement (subsequently abandoned) in Minnesota. Today on the excavated site of the North West Company is a reconstructed stockade with a gatehouse, blockhouses, and dining hall. NR
For further information write: Box 666, Grand Marais, MN 55604

GRANITE FALLS VICINITY
UPPER SIOUX AGENCY HISTORIC DISTRICT, 9 *miles south via State 67*
Situated at the confluence of the Minnesota and Yellow Medicine rivers, this agency was founded about 1853 on a newly created Dakota Indian Reservation. The agency served as administrative center for the Wahpeton and Sisseton bands of the Sioux Tribe. A similar center (*see Redwood Falls Vicinity*) was built 30 miles downstream. NR
Open: May 1–Oct 30, daily 10–sunset

HIBBING VICINITY
HULL-RUST-MAHONING OPEN PIT IRON MINE NATIONAL HISTORIC LANDMARK, *3rd Avenue East*
Opened in 1895, the 9 Mesabi Range mines on this site were among the earliest to be worked by open-pit or strip-mining techniques. The mine has yielded more than a billion tons of iron ore. NR
Mine viewing stand open: June 1–Labor Day, daily 9–9

LITTLE FALLS
CHARLES A. LINDBERGH MEMORIAL PARK, 2 *miles southwest on County 52*
This house on the banks of the Mississippi River was built by Charles Lindbergh, Sr., a Republican congressman from 1906 until 1916 and father of the famous aviator. Charles, Jr., spent some of his happiest childhood moments at this farm. An interpretive center displays Lindbergh family memorabilia. NR
Open: April 17–Oct 31, daily 10–5

MENDOTA
OLD MENDOTA, *at the confluence of the Minnesota and Mississippi rivers*
The oldest permanent settlement in Minnesota, Mendota was a trading-post village for the American Fur Company in the 1820s and 1830s. On **Pilot Knob**, a bluff above the town, the Sioux Indians in 1851 signed the Treaty of Mendota, ceding large tracts of land to the U.S. government. Historic structures that stand today include the **Henry H. Sibley House**, Minnesota's first stone house, built in 1835 by the man who became the state's first governor; the **Jean Baptiste Faribault House**, erected in 1836 by a pioneer fur trader; and the home of Hypolite du Puis, secretary to General Sibley,

which is presently run as the **Sibley Tea House.** NR
Houses open: May 1–Oct 31, Mon–Sat 10–5, Sun and holidays 1–6;
June 15–Sept 1, closed Mon

MINNEAPOLIS AND VICINITY

AMERICAN SWEDISH INSTITUTE, *2600 Park Avenue*

Swedish farmers were among the waves of immigrants who settled
in the Minneapolis-St. Paul area between 1840 and 1870. Today
their artifacts—glass, textiles, and furniture—are preserved here. NR
Open: Tues–Sun 2–5

FORT SNELLING NATIONAL HISTORIC LANDMARK, *confluence of the Mississippi and Minnesota rivers off State 5 and 55*

Established in 1819 on land obtained from the Sioux Indians in 1805
by Captain Zebulon Pike, this post was the northwestern link in a
chain of forts extending from Lake Michigan to the Missouri River.
For the next 30 years, garrisons at Fort Snelling oversaw affairs
with the Sioux and Chippewa Indians, controlled traffic on both
rivers, operated a local fur-trade depot, and acted as the only police
and government for an area of 90,000 square miles. After the
Minnesota Territory was created in 1848 and the capital situated at
St. Paul, the post's frontier duty was over. Fort Snelling was reactivated during the Sioux uprising of 1862, and it played a supporting role when the site of conflict between Indians and settlers
shifted west. From the Civil War until World War II, Fort Snelling
served as a training center for troops. Of the original structures,
the **Round Tower** is believed to be the oldest building in Minnesota.
NR
Open: June–Aug, daily 11–8, May, Sept, Oct, Mon–Fri 9–5; Sat–Sun
11–8

MOUNTAIN IRON VICINITY

MOUNTAIN IRON MINE NATIONAL HISTORIC LANDMARK, *north of the village*

Production from this open-pit mine made Minnesota the leading
supplier of iron ore in the country and enabled the United States to
become the world's leading steel manufacturer. With the opening of
the mine in 1892 came the discovery that Minnesota's Mesabi
Range contained the world's largest deposits of iron ore. NR

PINE CITY VICINITY

CONNOR'S FUR POST, *Pine City exit of I-35, then 1½ miles west off County 7*

Erected in 1804 by Thomas Connor, an employee of the British
North West Company, this reconstructed log building on the Snake
River was a backwoods wintering post, where Indians traded furs
for manufactured goods. In 1816, after the U.S. government pro-
hibited foreigners from trading, Connor affiliated himself with
the American Fur Company and relocated his post. NR
Open: May–Oct, Tues–Sun 10–6; Oct, Sat–Sun 1–6

PIPESTONE NATIONAL MONUMENT, *1 mile north of Pipestone via U.S. 75 and State 23 and 30*

Preserved on this tract are the renowned quarries of soft red stone
from which the Plains Indians and other tribes produced a great
proportion of their calumets, or ceremonial pipes. All tribal ceremonies involving treaties or other agreements were solemnized by
the ritual smoking of pipes. The quarrying itself was accompanied

by an extended ritual because the stone was believed to be a gift from the gods. Although white men were not permitted to visit the quarries, the eminent artist George Catlin camped at the sacred site in 1836, and his description of the quarries was the first to be published. Today 3 of the quarries are still in use. NR

For further information write: Superintendent, Pipestone, MN 56164

REDWOOD FALLS VICINITY

LOWER SIOUX AGENCY HISTORIC DISTRICT, *9 miles east, off County 2*

This was one of the 2 administrative centers established about 1853 by the U.S. government on the newly created Dakota Indian Reservations (*see St. Peter, Traverse des Sioux State Park*). Members of the Mdewakanton and Wahpekute bands of the Dakota or Sioux tribe came here to receive payments for their land from the Federal government. During the Dakota War in 1862, the Lower Agency was the first place attacked. Thirteen persons were killed here on August 18, and the buildings were burned and plundered. A 2-story stone warehouse is the sole extant survivor of the massacre. A modern interpretive center contains historical displays on the Dakotas. NR

Open: June 1–Sept 30, daily 10–6. Oct 1–May 31, Mon–Sat 10–4; Sun 1–4

ROCHESTER

MAYO CLINIC BUILDINGS NATIONAL HISTORIC LANDMARK

In 1889 Dr. William Worrall Mayo and his two sons, Dr. William James Mayo and Dr. Charles Horace Mayo, opened a family clinic that subsequently made Rochester world-famous. The Mayo Clinic Complex currently includes the 19-story **Mayo Building** of diagnostic facilities, the **Plummer Building** of laboratories and libraries, and other buildings for patient care and research. Also in Rochester are the **Mayo Museum,** with medical exhibits, **Mayo Park,** with statues of the clinic's founders, and **Mayowood** (NR), the former estate of Dr. Charles H. Mayo, whose 40-room mansion is now filled with antiques. NR

Clinic Complex tours: Mon–Fri 12 and 2. Museum open: Mon–Fri 9–9, Sat 9–5, Sun 1–5. Mayowood tours: April through November

ST. PAUL

ALEXANDER RAMSEY HOUSE, *265 South Exchange Street*

Completed in 1862, this mansion belonged to Alexander Ramsey, who held more high offices than any other man in Minnesota's history. Appointed first territorial governor in 1849, Ramsey was elected governor in 1859. At the outbreak of the Civil War he was the first governor to offer troops to Abraham Lincoln. Ramsey was later a U.S. senator and Secretary of War under President Rutherford B. Hayes. NR

Open: Tues–Fri 10–4, Sat–Sun 1–4; closed holidays

MINNESOTA STATE CAPITOL BUILDING, *University Avenue between Wabash and Cedar streets*

Designed by Cass Gilbert and completed in 1905, this State House, with its massive unsupported dome, is one of the most magnificent capitols in the country. The cornerstone was laid on July 27, 1898, by Alexander Ramsey, first territorial governor of Minnesota, and second governor of the state (*see Alexander Ramsey House*). NR

Tours: Mon–Fri hourly 9–4; Sat hourly 10, 11, 1–3; Sun hourly 1–3

MINNESOTA

ST. PETER
TRAVERSE DES SIOUX STATE PARK, *north along west side of U.S. 169*
The largest single Indian treaty in the nation's history was concluded at this site in 1851 between the U.S. government and the Dakota or Sioux Indians. By the terms of this and the Treaty of Mendota (*see Old Mendota*), 24 million acres of southern Minnesota were opened to white settlement, and the Indians agreed to move to reservations along the upper Minnesota River.

SAUK CENTRE
LEWIS BOYHOOD HOME NATIONAL HISTORIC LANDMARK, *812 Sinclair Lewis Avenue*
Sinclair Lewis, a leading novelist of the 1920s and 1930s, resided in this frame house until he was 18. Lewis' 1920 novel *Main Street* paints a realistic picture of small-town America and derives from his early experiences in Sauk Centre. NR

STILLWATER
ST. CROIX BOOM SITE NATIONAL HISTORIC LANDMARK, *3 miles north via State 95*
Operating from 1856 until 1914, this site was one of the earliest and longest-lived major log storage areas in Minnesota. Over $15\frac{1}{2}$ billion feet of logs floated from the upper St. Croix River and its tributaries to this spot, where they were sorted, measured, and made into rafts for shipment downstream. The **W. H. C. Folsom House,** built in the 1850s by a founder of the St. Croix Boom, stands in the nearby town of Taylors Falls. Nothing of the boom remains. NR
Folsom House open: June 1–Oct 1, Tues–Sun 1–4

TOWER VICINITY
SOUDAN IRON MINE NATIONAL HISTORIC LANDMARK, $\frac{1}{2}$ *mile north of State 169*
Minnesota's oldest and deepest underground mine opened in 1884 on one of the richest iron deposits in the country, an event that signaled the state's emergence as the nation's leading iron producer. At its peak in 1892, the mine produced more than 568,000 long tons of high-grade ore. The mine closed in 1962. Extant today are the engine house, drill shop, crusher house, and dry house. NR
Open: May 20–Sept 4, daily 9–4. Sept 5–30, daily 11–4

TWO HARBORS VICINITY
SPLIT ROCK LIGHTHOUSE, *about 20 miles northeast on U.S. 61*
This lighthouse was built in 1909 as a navigational aid to ships on Lake Superior, whose cargoes of iron ore caused their compass needles to deflect from the true north, throwing them off course.

VINELAND
KATHIO SITE NATIONAL HISTORIC LANDMARK, *off U.S. 169*
From prehistoric times until the 1740s this site, as well as other villages on the southwestern shore of Mille Lacs Lake, was the ancestral homeland of the Dakota or Sioux Indians. In 1679 the French explorer and trader Daniel Greysolon, Sieur Du Luth, visited the area and observed a flourishing Sioux community. Early in the 1700s the Chippewa tribe began encroaching on this region. A decisive 3-day battle was fought in 1745 in which the Sioux were routed by the Chippewas and forced to relocate to the south and west. The Mille Lacs Indian Museum is nearby. NR
Museum open: May 1–Sept 1, daily 10–4

MISSISSIPPI

BILOXI VICINITY

BEAUVOIR, *200 West Beach Boulevard, 5½ miles west on U.S. 90*
In the wake of the Civil War, the former president of the Confederacy, Jefferson Davis, settled at Beauvoir, where he resided as a symbol of the "lost cause" until his death in 1889. In the **East Cottage** he wrote his apologia, *The Rise and Fall of the Confederate Government*. The house, filled with Davis' original furnishings, and cottages are currently maintained as a Confederate shrine. NR
Open daily 8:30–5

BOLTON VICINITY

CHAMPION HILL BATTLEFIELD, *about 4 miles southwest*
A hotly contested battle that marked the approaching climax of General Ulysses S. Grant's western campaign occurred on May 16, 1863, when Union forces were advancing west toward Vicksburg (*see Vicksburg National Military Park*) after taking the state capital at Jackson. At Champion Hill some 29,000 Federals under the command of John A. McClernand and James B. McPherson clashed with fewer than 20,000 Confederates under Lieutenant General John C. Pemberton. The hill changed hands 3 times in the course of the fighting, and Pemberton was finally forced to withdraw toward Vicksburg and the Big Black River (*see Smith's Station, Big Black River Battlefield*). NR

BRICES CROSS ROADS NATIONAL BATTLEFIELD SITE, *6 miles west of Baldwyn off State 370*
On June 10, 1864, Confederate General Nathan Bedford Forrest, with 3,500 soldiers, won a brilliant tactical victory at this site over 8,100 Union troops under the command of General S. D. Sturgis. The Union commander of the western armies, General William T.

Top: the Union fleet running the blockade at Vicksburg. Below: Connelly's Tavern at Natchez. Right: Fort Massachusetts on Ship Island near Gulfport

Sherman, during his invasion of Georgia, had left a particularly vulnerable line of communications extending through the middle of Tennessee, and General Forrest was planning to lead his cavalry against this line. A Federal force under Sturgis had been sent from Memphis by Sherman to attack Forrest and hold him in Mississippi. The armies clashed at Brices Cross Roads, and after a fierce daylong engagement, the defeated Union troops retreated to Memphis. Although the Confederates had checked the Union advance and captured Federal supplies and artillery, the victory did not bring relief to the South, because Sherman had prevented any attack on the Nashville-Chattanooga Railroad, the vital Union communications link. NR

For further information write: Box 948, Tupelo, MS 38802

CLARKSDALE

SUNFLOWER LANDING, *14 miles west*
The Spanish conquistador Hernando de Soto first sighted the Mississippi River at this spot in May, 1541.

COLUMBUS, *east Mississippi near Alabama state line*

Situated at the point on the Tombigbee River where the Spanish explorer Hernando de Soto crossed on his westward expedition of 1540, Columbus is the home of **Franklin Academy** (1821), the state's first public school, and **Mississippi State College for Women** (1884), the nation's oldest state-supported women's college.

GREENVILLE

WINTERVILLE MOUNDS STATE HISTORIC SITE, *5 miles north on State 1*
Constructed between A.D. 1000 and 1300 by Indians known as the Temple Mound Builders—predecessors of the Choctaw, Chickasaw, and Tunica tribes—this mound group, now restored, was probably used for ceremonial purposes. When these mounds were built, the lower Mississippi Valley Indians were undergoing a change from a hunting-fishing existence to an agricultural system permitting the growth of large villages. In 1540 the Spanish explorer Hernando de Soto observed the Temple Mound culture at its height.

Open: Tues–Sun 9–6

GULFPORT VICINITY

FORT MASSACHUSETTS, *south on Ship Island*
Strategically situated at the entrance to Biloxi Bay, Fort Massachusetts provided a vital link in the naval blockade of the South during the Civil War by serving as a base of Union operations along the Gulf Coast. The fort and other installations on Ship Island were taken from the secessionists by Federal forces on September 17, 1861. Many Confederate prisoners were confined in the fort's dungeons during the course of the war. NR

Boat trips from Biloxi and Gulfport: Apr–Sept, daily 10, 2

JACKSON

GOVERNOR'S MANSION, *316 East Capitol Street*
During the Civil War, when Jackson was occupied by Federal troops, Generals Ulysses S. Grant and William T. Sherman made this Greek Revival mansion their headquarters. Since its completion in 1842, the building has housed 35 consecutive Mississippi governors. NR

Open: Mon–Fri by appointment

OLD CAPITOL, *100 North State Street*

Erected in 1833, 16 years after Mississippi entered the Union as the 20th state, this State House served as the seat of government in Mississippi until 1903. The building currently houses the State Historical Museum. NR

Open: June–Aug, Mon–Sat 9:30–4:30, Sun 1–5

HOLLY SPRINGS

In November, 1862, General Ulysses S. Grant's Federal troops seized this rail center, where they established a supply depot for their advance on Vicksburg. On December 20, 1862, the town was retaken by Confederates under General Earl Van Dorn, who took at least 1,500 Union prisoners and destroyed $1.5 million in supplies.

LOUISVILLE

NANIH WAIYA HISTORICAL MEMORIAL, *Route 3*

Begun about the fifth century A.D. by ancestors of the Choctaw Indians, this pyramidal mound was used by these early people as a fort, burial site, and place of worship. Modern descendants of the Choctaws consider this sacred spot to be the birthplace of their race. Other sites in the vicinity include the **Nanih Waiya Cave,** and near present-day Philadelphia, the **Site of the 1830 Signing of the Dancing Rabbit Treaty,** in which a major portion of the Choctaws ceded their lands to the Federal government and agreed to move to Oklahoma.

MERIDIAN

MERREHOPE, *905 31st Avenue*

This house was one of the 4 dwellings left standing in Meridian after General William T. Sherman's troops destroyed the town in 1864. Marching from Vicksburg, Union forces under Sherman entered Meridian on February 14. As Sherman recorded it, "For five days 10,000 men worked hard and with a will in that work of destruction. . . . Meridian, with its depots, store-houses, arsenals, hospitals, offices, hotels and cantonment, no longer exists." NR

Open: Mar–Dec 15, Tues–Sat 10–12, 2–4:30; Sun 2–4:30

NATCHEZ AND VICINITY

CONNELLY'S TAVERN ON ELLICOTT'S HILL, *Jefferson and Canal streets*

In defiance of the Spanish, who had governed Natchez since 1779, The Stars and Stripes was first raised at this tavern in 1797. The following year Mississippi became a U.S. territory.

Open daily 9–5

LONGWOOD (NUTT'S FOLLY) NATIONAL HISTORIC LANDMARK, *1½ miles southeast*

Designed in 1860 by the architect Samuel Sloan for Dr. Haller Nutt, this 5-story mansion, with its glass-enclosed "Moorish" tower, was the largest and most ornate octagonal house in the nation. The outbreak of the Civil War prevented the structure's completion. NR

Open daily 9–5

NATCHEZ TRACE PARKWAY, *crossing Mississippi diagonally from Natchez in the southwest to Tupelo in the northeast*

During the early decades of the 19th century, the Natchez Trace contributed to the nation's growth by serving as the highway binding the Union with the old Southwest. Originally an Indian trail, the Natchez Trace evolved into a pioneer road that ran 500 miles from Natchez to Nashville. In 1801 and 1807 the road received Federal improvements. Today a national parkway, extending also into Alabama and Tennessee, with exhibits and markers along the way, is being built along the route of the old Natchez Trace. **Mt. Locust,** a frontier farmhouse that served as an inn, has been restored at Washington, 20 miles northeast of Natchez.

For further information write: Box 948, Tupelo, MS 38801

OCEAN SPRINGS, *on U.S. 90 on the Gulf Coast*

In 1699 Pierre le Moyne, Sieur d'Iberville, founded **Fort Maurepas,** the first permanent European settlement on the Mississippi Delta, at the site of the present town of Ocean Springs, on the eastern side of Biloxi Bay. The community became known as Biloxi, "first people," and in 1719 was moved across the bay to its present site.

OXFORD

FAULKNER HOME (ROWAN OAK) NATIONAL HISTORIC LAND-MARK, *Old Taylor Road*

William Faulkner, chronicler of the Deep South and one of America's major 20th-century fiction writers, resided in this Greek Revival house from 1929 until his death in 1963. Drawing upon experiences and memories of his home town of Oxford, Faulkner created the mythical Yoknapatawpha County as the locale for such family sagas as *Sartoris* and *The Sound and the Fury.* Faulkner received the Nobel Prize for his cumulative work in 1949. NR

Open by Appointment

PORT GIBSON VICINITY

GRAND GULF STATE HISTORICAL PARK, *7 miles northwest*

Situated on the Mississippi River, just below Vicksburg, this military park was the site of Confederate-held forts, which were fired upon by Union gunboats on April 29, 1863, in an unsuccessful attempt to clear the way for General Grant's army to secure a bridgehead on the eastern shore of the river before marching upon Vicksburg. The next day the Federals crossed the river at Bruinsburg.

Open: Tues–Sat 9–6, Sun 9–12

RAYMOND

RAYMOND BATTLEFIELD, *2½ miles southwest on State 18*

On May 12, 1863, a Union division under Major General John A. Logan met stiff resistance from a Confederate brigade under Brigadier General John Gregg at this village, situated about 15 miles from the state capital at Jackson. The fighting at Raymond lasted several hours until the outnumbered Confederates retired to Jackson. The close outcome of the engagement convinced General Ulysses S. Grant that it was necessary to reduce Confederate forces at Jackson before advancing on to Vicksburg (*see Vicksburg National Military Park*). NR

SMITH'S STATION VICINITY

BIG BLACK RIVER BATTLEFIELD, *between Smith's Station and Bovina*

A Civil War engagement took place here on May 17, 1863, the day before the siege of Vicksburg (*see Vicksburg National Military Park*) began. Confederate troops under General John C. Pemberton had withdrawn from the Champion Hill Battlefield (*see*) and entrenched themselves in the swampy lowlands along the Big Black

River between Jackson and Vicksburg to await reinforcements. When the expected division failed to arrive, the Confederates, in danger of being prevented from crossing the river, retired in disorder, burned the bridges, and pulled back toward Vicksburg's defensive works. Although the Federals were temporarily halted, they crossed the river triumphantly the next day and took 1,700 Confederate prisoners. NR

TUPELO NATIONAL BATTLEFIELD, *on State 6, about 1 mile west of intersection with U.S. 45*

The last major Civil War battle in Mississippi was fought here on July 14–15, 1864, between 9,400 Confederate cavalrymen led by Generals Nathan Bedford Forrest and Stephen D. Lee, and more than 14,000 Union troops under Generals Andrew J. Smith and Joseph A. Mower. After the Union defeat at the Battle of Brices Cross Roads (*see*), General William T. Sherman had dispatched Smith and Mower to follow Forrest "to the death if it costs 10,000 lives and breaks the Treasury." The Federals' purpose in this engagement was to protect Sherman's supply line—the Nashville-Chattanooga Railroad—in central Tennessee, which was needed to carry food and ammunition to Sherman's army during his drive into Georgia. Although the fighting was gallant, neither side could claim complete victory. Forrest's men were repulsed, and the safety of the railroad was assured for the Union, but Forrest remained at large. NR

For further information write: Box 948, Tupelo, MS 38801

VICKSBURG

VICKSBURG NATIONAL MILITARY PARK, *adjoining Vicksburg*

This park was the scene of the siege of Vicksburg in 1863, the decisive Civil War campaign in the West that gave the Union control of the Mississippi River and divided the Confederacy in two. Strategically situated on high bluffs overlooking the Mississippi, Vicksburg, with its almost impregnable defenses, was known as the Gibraltar of the Confederacy and was the key link in a chain of Confederate fortifications extending from Louisville, Kentucky, to New Orleans, Louisiana. Its capture was considered essential to the Union. After Federal attempts to seize Vicksburg by land and amphibious assaults failed in 1862, General Ulysses S. Grant, on May 18, 1863, launched a campaign to take the stronghold by siege. After 47 days the beleaguered city, defended by Confederates under General John C. Pemberton, surrendered on July 4. Today the remains of 9 major Confederate forts, 13 Union approaches, miles of breastworks, gun emplacements, and rifle pits, as well as 1,600 monuments marking the positions of the armies, are preserved. About 2 miles north of town is the **Vicksburg National Cemetery,** where 17,912 soldiers are buried. NR

For further information write: Box 349, Vicksburg, MS 39180

WARREN COUNTY COURTHOUSE NATIONAL HISTORIC LANDMARK, *Court Square*

As Vicksburg's most prominent landmark, this courthouse became a symbol of Confederate resistance to General Ulysses S. Grant during his siege of Vicksburg in 1863. After the Confederate surrender, Union Colonel William F. Strong raised his garrison flag from the cupola. Today the Greek Revival structure contains a museum with Confederate relics. NR

Open: Mon–Sat 8–5; Sun 2–5

MISSOURI

ARROW ROCK NATIONAL HISTORIC LANDMARK, *Arrow Rock State Park*
Founded in 1829, this frontier town on the Missouri River gained
prominence as one of the starting points of the **Santa Fe Trail.**
Traffic was so heavy in the area by 1817 that a ferry across the
Missouri began operating that year, and in 1821 the first of many
expeditions to the Southwest originated here. Three early governors of Missouri—Meredith M. Marmaduke, Claiborne F. Jackson,
and John S. Marmaduke—also came from Arrow Rock. Preserved
today are such historic structures as the **Arrow Rock Tavern,**
begun by Judge Joseph Huston in 1834, the **Old Court House,** the
Dr. Matthew Walton Hall House, and the **Old Seminary,** which
was used as a dormitory by students in the 1830s. The 2-room brick
cottage known as the **George Caleb Bingham House** (NHL) was
occupied intermittently by the nation's foremost painter of the
frontier scene from 1837 to 1845. NR
*Tavern open: Tues–Sun 10–7; closed January. Hall and Bingham
houses open: June–Aug, tours daily, 9, 11, 1, 3*

BOONESBORO
BOONE'S LICK STATE HISTORIC SITE, *19 miles northwest of Boonville via State 87*
In 1805 two of Daniel Boone's sons, Nathan and Daniel Morgan
Boone, manufactured salt at this spring, one of the earliest centers
of white penetration in Missouri. The salt was shipped to St. Louis
and other settlements. NR

*Left: the Gateway Arch and Old Courthouse at Jefferson National Expansion
Memorial in St. Louis. Right: Harry S Truman Birthplace in Lamar and an
engraving of the 33rd President*

BOONVILLE, *northeast of I-70 on State 5*

On June 17, 1861, this town was the scene of the first land battle of the Civil War. Here General Nathaniel Lyon with Federal troops defeated state troops led by the pro-Confederate governor, Claiborne F. Jackson. This victory gave the Union control of the Missouri River. During the war the **Lyric Theater** (NR), originally called Thespian Hall, served as a hospital and troop barracks. Completed in 1857, this Greek Revival edifice is the oldest surviving continuously used theater west of the Alleghenies.

CAPE GIRARDEAU

TRAIL OF TEARS STATE PARK, *10 miles north on State 177*

This park contains a segment of the route known as the Trail of Tears, which was taken by the Cherokees in 1838 on their forced march from Georgia to Indian Territory (Oklahoma). Among the many who perished along the way was Princess Otahki, whose grave is now marked with a memorial. NR

DIAMOND VICINITY

GEORGE WASHINGTON CARVER NATIONAL MONUMENT, *about 3 miles southwest on County V*

This small farm was the birthplace and boyhood home of the Negro scientist George Washington Carver, who, born into slavery in 1860, rose to become a world-renowned teacher, botanist, agronomist, and pioneer conservationist. Carver's education culminated in a master of science degree awarded by Iowa State in 1894. From 1896 until his death in 1943, Carver was on the staff of Alabama's Tuskegee Institute. NR

For further information write: Box 38, Diamond, MO 64840

FLORIDA VICINITY

MARK TWAIN BIRTHPLACE SHRINE STATE HISTORIC SITE, *south on State 107*

On November 30, 1835, Missouri's most famous literary son, the author and humorist Mark Twain, was born as Samuel Clemens in the 2-room cabin enshrined here. NR

Open: Tues–Sun 10–5

FULTON

WESTMINSTER COLLEGE GYMNASIUM NATIONAL HISTORIC LANDMARK

On March 5, 1946, in this brick gymnasium on the Westminster College campus, Sir Winston Churchill delivered the momentous speech in which he coined the lasting phrase "Iron Curtain" and admitted for the first time in public that the Soviet Union posed a serious threat to the security of the West. Although general reaction was at first incredulous, the speech paved the way for the promulgation of the Truman Doctrine of containment in 1947, and for the formation of NATO. NR

HANNIBAL

MARK TWAIN BOYHOOD HOME NATIONAL HISTORIC LANDMARK, *208 Hill Street*

Samuel Clemens spent his boyhood in this house from the time he was 4 in 1839 until 1853. Using the pen name Mark Twain, he later wrote *Adventures of Huckleberry Finn* and *The Adventures of Tom Sawyer*, both of which reflect his boyhood experiences here. NR

Open: June–Sept, daily 8–8; Sept–June, daily 8–5; closed holidays

MISSOURI

INDEPENDENCE

TRUMAN HOME NATIONAL HISTORIC LANDMARK, *Delaware Street and Truman Road*

Harry S Truman, 33rd President of the United States, occupied this Victorian house from his retirement from office in 1953 until his death in 1972. He lies buried in the courtyard of the nearby **Harry S Truman Memorial Library and Museum.**

Library open: Mon–Sat 9–5; Sun 2–5; closed holidays

LEXINGTON

ANDERSON HOUSE AND BATTLE OF LEXINGTON STATE HISTORIC SITE, *via U.S. 24*

This bloody Civil War engagement—which took place from September 18 to September 20, 1861, between James A. Mulligan, commander of Federal troops, and Major General Sterling Price of the Missouri State Guard—ended in a victory for the South. Overlooking the battlefield, where hillside trenches are still visible, is the mansion, built in 1853 by Colonel Oliver Anderson, a Confederate sympathizer who was imprisoned at the outbreak of the war. During the fighting the house changed hands 3 times and was used by both sides as a field hospital. Today stains on the floors bear testimony to the bloodshed that occurred. Battle scars are also apparent in the **Lafayette County Courthouse** (NR), whose east column contains a cannonball. NR

Anderson House open: Tues–Sat 10–4; Sun 1–5; closed holidays

LACLEDE

PERSHING BOYHOOD HOME STATE HISTORIC SITE, *State and Worlow streets*

This restored rural Gothic structure was the boyhood home of John J. Pershing, Commander in Chief of the American Expeditionary Forces in Europe during World War I. In 1919 Congress named Pershing General of the Armies, a title held by only one other person, George Washington. NR

Open: Tues–Sat 10–4; Sun 12–5; closed holidays

LAMAR

TRUMAN BIRTHPLACE STATE HISTORIC SITE, *11th Street and Truman Avenue*

Harry S Truman, the 33rd President of the United States and the only Missourian to hold that office, was born here May 8, 1884. NR

Open: Tues–Sat 10–4; Sun 12–5; closed holidays

MARSHALL VICINITY

UTZ SITE NATIONAL HISTORIC LANDMARK, *12 miles north, adjoining Van Meter State Park*

From the 1600s until 1728 this site was the principal village of the Missouri Indians. When Père Marquette explored the Mississippi River in 1673, he wrote of the "Messouri" Indians at this approximate location. The arrival of the French early in the 1700s introduced white men's diseases and alcohol, to which the Indians succumbed. The tribe was nearly decimated by 1728. NR

PILOT KNOB

FORT DAVIDSON STATE HISTORIC SITE, *Business Loop of State 21*

The Civil War Battle of Pilot Knob, fought here on September 27, 1864, between the troops of Union Commander Thomas Ewing and Confederate Major General Sterling Price, resulted in an important

Union victory and shattered Confederate morale in the state. NR

ST. CHARLES

FIRST MISSOURI STATE CAPITOL STATE HISTORIC DISTRICT, *208-14 S Main St*

Erected in 1820, these buildings, now restored, served as Missouri's seat of government from the time the state joined the Union in 1821 until 1826. While in session here, the territorial legislature passed the Second Missouri Compromise, which reversed an earlier provision in the state constitution forbidding the immigration of free Negroes into Missouri. This second compromise received congressional approval and enabled President James Monroe to sign the act admitting Missouri to statehood. NR
Open: Tues–Sat 10–4; Sun 12–5

STE. GENEVIEVE

STE. GENEVIEVE HISTORIC DISTRICT NATIONAL HISTORIC LANDMARK

Founded in 1832 on the west bank of the Mississippi River, Ste. Genevieve was originally part of the vast French Territory of Louisiana and was the first permanent settlement within the present boundaries of Missouri. In 1785 floods forced the town to relocate 3 miles upstream. Preserved at Ste. Genevieve are such structures as the **Louis Bolduc House** (NHL), built about 1785 and exemplifying the *poteaux-sur-solle* (vertical post on sill) construction that was common to the French settlements of the Mississippi Valley. NR
Louis Bolduc House open: April 1–Nov 1, daily 10–4

ST. JOSEPH

JOHN PATEE HOUSE NATIONAL HISTORIC LANDMARK, *12th and Penn streets*

One of the best-known hotels west of the Mississippi, the Patee House, erected in 1858, served as headquarters for Russell, Majors, and Waddell, the overland freighting firm that operated the pony express from 1860 to 1861. On April 3, 1860, a shot fired in front of the hotel sent the first relay rider galloping toward Sacramento. NR
Open: May 30–Labor Day, Mon–Sat 10–5; Sun 1–5. Labor Day–late Oct, Sat–Sun 1–5

ST. LOUIS

ANHEUSER-BUSCH BREWERY NATIONAL HISTORIC LANDMARK, *721 Pestalozzi Street*

In 1873, while running the brewery founded by his father-in-law, Eberhard Anheuser, Adolphus Busch perfected a method of pasteurizing beer that enabled the product to be shipped great distances. This German immigrant was also an early advocate of refrigerated cars and icehouses for storing beer. Many of the original buildings, with their elaborate ornamentation, still stand. NR
Tours: Mon–Fri 9:30, 10:15, 10:45, 1, 1:45, 2:30, 3:30

EADS BRIDGE NATIONAL HISTORIC LANDMARK, *spanning the Mississippi at Washington Street*

Designed by James B. Eads and completed in 1874, this cantilevered arch bridge of iron and steel contained structural innovations that established a precedent for bridge building throughout the world. Carrying a railroad on its lower deck and a road at its upper level, the bridge was an important factor in the development of St. Louis and the trans-Mississippi West. NR

MISSOURI

GOLDENROD SHOWBOAT NATIONAL HISTORIC LANDMARK, *400 North Wharf Street*

Launched in 1909 and known in its day as the World's Greatest Showboat, the *Goldenrod* is the last extant example from the second great era of showboating that ended in the 1920s. Performances of melodrama typical of the period are given on board. NR

JEFFERSON NATIONAL EXPANSION MEMORIAL NATIONAL HISTORIC SITE, *between Washington and Poplar streets*

Situated on the site of the original village of St. Louis, which was founded by Pierre Laclède in 1764, this memorial commemorates the vast expansion of the United States following Thomas Jefferson's Louisiana Purchase of 1803. This historic acquisition doubled the area of the young republic, and assured this nation a major role in the settlement of North America. Soaring 630 feet high, a **catenary arch** of stainless steel, designed by Eero Saarinen, is symbolic of St. Louis' gateway location; the city was the hub of mid-continental commerce, transportation, and culture, and the meeting place for pioneers starting west. Within this park stand the **Old Courthouse**, where Dred Scott made his legal appeal for freedom and focused national attention on the slavery issue, and the **Old Cathedral**, completed in 1834 on land designated earlier by Pierre Laclède for religious purposes. NR

For further information write: 11 N 4th St, St. Louis, MO 63102

SIBLEY

FORT OSAGE NATIONAL HISTORIC LANDMARK, *north edge of town on the Missouri River*

The first U.S. Army post west of the Mississippi and the first in the Louisiana Purchase was founded in 1808 by General William Clark of the Lewis and Clark expedition. Fort Osage was the most successful of the 28 "factories" (Indian trading posts) established by the Federal government between 1795 and 1822 to assure the Indians fair prices for their furs. Today the fort has been restored. NR

Open daily 9–5; closed holidays

SPRINGFIELD VICINITY

WILSON'S CREEK NATIONAL BATTLEFIELD PARK, *about 12 miles southwest off U.S. 60*

Fought here on August 10, 1861, the Battle of Wilson's Creek was a bitter engagement between Confederate and Union troops for control of Missouri in the first year of the Civil War. Because of its strategic position on the Missouri and Mississippi rivers, Missouri's allegiance to the Union was of utmost concern to the Federal government. However, many Missourians, including Governor Claiborne F. Jackson, aided the secessionists. This encounter between the Federal forces of Brigadier General Nathaniel Lyon and the army of the Missouri State Guard under General Sterling Price, which was joined by Confederate troops and the Arkansas State Guard, occurred in the fields and bluffs overlooking Wilson's Creek outside the town of Springfield. Most of the 4-hour battle took place on a ridge now known as **Bloody Hill**, where General Lyon was killed and his outnumbered soldiers forced to flee. Although victorious, the Confederates were unable to pursue the Federals beyond Springfield or to take control of Missouri. The North lost 1,319 men, and the Confederates 1,230—the heaviest casualties in any trans-Mississippi Civil War battle. NR

For further information write: Box 38, Diamond, MO 64840

MONTANA

BANNACK HISTORIC DISTRICT NATIONAL HISTORIC LANDMARK,
22 miles west of Dillon on secondary road off State 278

In July, 1862, discovery of gold in this area caused Bannack, Montana's oldest town, to spring up overnight. Two years later Bannack became the first capital of Montana Territory. Among the surviving structures of this ghost town is **Montana's First Jail,** symbol of an early attempt to control a lawless frontier. NR

BEARPAW MOUNTAINS, *16 miles south of Chinook off U.S. 2*

One of the last major battles of the Indian wars was fought on this site in northern Montana in 1877. Several bands of Nez Perce, including that of Chief Joseph, seeking to escape confinement on a reservation in Idaho, had fled to Montana that year. After an engagement at Big Hole (*see*), the Indians had tried to reach safety in Canada. Intercepted near the Bearpaw Mountains by U.S. forces under General Nelson Miles, the Indians surrendered on October 5 after a 4-day battle. NR

BIG HOLE NATIONAL BATTLEFIELD, *12 miles west of Wisdom, 18 miles east of U.S. 93*

On August 9–10, 1877, a group of some 700 Nez Perce Indians, including the band of Chief Joseph, was surprised by a U.S. force led by Colonel John Gibbon. The Indians nevertheless recovered sufficiently to put the attackers themselves under siege before withdrawing and continuing their flight from Idaho, where the Nez Perce had been consigned to a reservation. The national monument to this battle covers 666 acres; bullet-scarred trees are still in evidence. At a visitor center the battle is described in an audio-visual program, and exhibits of firearms include the howitzer

Left: photograph of Lt. Col. George A. Custer. Right: Sioux Chief Red Horse's interpretation of the Battle of the Little Big Horn

captured by the Nez Perce. There is a self-guiding trail through the siege area. NR

For further information write: Yellowstone National Park, WY 82190

BILLINGS VICINITY
PICTOGRAPH CAVE NATIONAL HISTORIC LANDMARK, 7 *miles southeast via U.S. 87, in Indian Caves Park*
Archaeological findings dating from about 2000 B.C. have been recorded at this site, whose walls display a variety of Indian pictographs. The findings are important in reconstructing the prehistoric occupation of the northwestern plains. NR

BROWNING VICINITY
CAMP DISAPPOINTMENT NATIONAL HISTORIC LANDMARK, *12 miles northeast on the Blackfoot reservation*
On July 23, 1806, Meriwether Lewis and 9 other members of the Lewis and Clark expedition reached this site, the northernmost point on the route of the historic expedition. They were making a side trip on the way back from the Pacific; on instructions from President Jefferson they were exploring the Marias River and the possibility of an overland route between its headwaters and those of the Saskatchewan. NR

BUTTE HISTORIC DISTRICT NATIONAL HISTORIC LANDMARK
The first settlement here dates from 1864, when prospectors came looking for gold. In the following decade there was a silver boom, but the importance—and wealth—of Butte rests on copper. Since the original settlement, an area of less than 5 miles square has accounted for more than $2 billion in mineral wealth and has earned for Butte the name "copper metropolis." NR

CUSTER BATTLEFIELD NATIONAL MONUMENT, 15 *miles south of Hardin on the Crow reservation*
On June 25–26, 1876, one of the most famous battles in American history took place on this site, the scene of Custer's last stand. It was precipitated by a Federal government order that the Indians of the northern plains return to their reservations by January 31 of that year. The Sioux and Cheyenne, who had left their reservations because the terms of an earlier peace agreement with the government had been disregarded, decided to defy the ultimatum and rallied around Sitting Bull, Crazy Horse, and other famous chiefs. U.S. troops, called upon to enforce the order, included the Seventh Cavalry regiment under Lieutenant Colonel George A. Custer. In an engagement that has become legendary, Custer and some 225 soldiers in his immediate command, severely outnumbered, were surrounded in the **Valley of the Little Big Horn** and destroyed to a man. Seven remaining companies of the regiment suffered heavy casualties before the approach of reinforcements caused the Indians to withdraw. The national monument includes both the ridge where Custer and his men were annihilated and the area about 5 miles south of it where the other major action took place. A cluster of markers indicates the location where the last members of Custer's battalion are thought to have fallen. A visitor center contains maps, photographs, and exhibits that re-create the action. A national cemetery in the immediate area also houses the remains of soldiers killed in other Indian engagements. At Crow Agency, 3 miles north of the battlefield and headquarters of the vast Crow Indian reservation, an annual re-enactment of the famous 1876 en-

counter is usually held on the weekend after July 4. Visitors are attracted as well by the annual Crow Indian fair and rodeo, accompanied by dances and ceremonies. NR

For further information write: Superintendent, Crow Agency, MT 59022

FORT BENTON NATIONAL HISTORIC LANDMARK, *on the Missouri River*
Originally a fur-trading center (and even earlier a campsite for Captain William Clark), this historic old town enjoyed its finest period after the first steamboat arrived in 1859. From then until the rise of the railroads, Fort Benton was the terminus of busy river traffic on the Missouri. Historic remains include parts of the fort and of the old trading post and blockhouse. The **Fort Benton Museum** on Front Street, City Park, contains exhibits centering on fur and river traffic. NR

Museum open: June–Aug, Mon–Sat 10–noon, 1–5; Sun and holidays 1–5

FORT LOGAN, *17 miles northwest of White Sulphur Springs*
On this site stood a military post first established in 1869 to protect an area largely devoted to mining camps. NR

FORT PECK, *northeast Montana*
In 1867 an Indian agency and trading post were established here by Commander E. H. Durfee and Colonel Campbell K. Peck. This was during the height of fur-trading activity on the Missouri River, and Peck was also a pioneer in development of navigation of the river. Today on this site the huge Fort Peck Dam spans the Missouri. Assiniboin and Sioux Indians, resident on the reservation here, stage sun dances for tourists during July. NR

FORT UNION TRADING POST NATIONAL HISTORIC SITE. *See* NORTH DAKOTA

GREAT FALLS AND VICINITY
GREAT FALLS PORTAGE NATIONAL HISTORIC LANDMARK, *southeast at junction of U.S. 87, 89, and 91*
The spectacular falls in the Missouri River at this site were viewed by Meriwether Lewis and a party from the Lewis and Clark expedition on June 13, 1805, during the journey to the Pacific coast. At that time the falls necessitated a difficult month-long overland journey for the explorers; today they are an important source of hydroelectric power. NR

RUSSELL HOME AND STUDIO NATIONAL HISTORIC LANDMARK, *1217–19 4th Avenue*
Charles M. Russell, whose paintings depict Western life, occupied this house and log studio in his later years. His and other art works are on display, together with Indian artifacts. NR
Open: Tues–Sat 10–5, Sun 1–5

LEMHI PASS NATIONAL HISTORIC LANDMARK. *See* IDAHO

LOLO
TRAVELER'S REST NATIONAL HISTORIC LANDMARK, *1 mile south near U.S. 93*
On their way to the Pacific Meriwether Lewis and William Clark stopped here in the late summer of 1805 to make preparations for

crossing the Bitterroot Mountains. A party headed by Lewis explored the area further a year later, on the expedition's return journey. NR

LOLO TRAIL NATIONAL HISTORIC LANDMARK. *See* IDAHO, NEZ PERCE NATIONAL HISTORIC PARK

POMPEY'S PILLAR NATIONAL HISTORIC LANDMARK, *west of Pompey's Pillar on U.S. 10*

The great sandstone formation here was named by Captain William Clark, who carved his still-visible signature on it, July 25, 1806, on the return journey of the Lewis and Clark expedition from the Pacific. NR

PRYOR VICINITY

CHIEF PLENTY COUPS MEMORIAL, *1 mile west of Pryor on State 416*

Relics of Plenty Coups, a former chieftain of the Crow Indians, are on display in a museum here. NR

Open: summer, daily 8–5

ROSEBUD, *eastcentral Montana on the Yellowstone River*

On June 17, 1876, a band of Sioux and Cheyenne Indians, resisting confinement to reservation life, held off U.S. forces under General George Crook on this site.

STEVENSVILLE AND VICINITY

FORT OWEN, ½ *mile northwest of Stevensville*

The fort that stood on this location was one of the most prosperous trading posts in the area. It was established by Major John Owen in 1850. NR

ST. MARY'S MISSION CHURCH AND PHARMACY, *North Avenue in Stevensville*

Constructed in 1867 and still standing, this log church is the oldest mission in the Northwest. A museum in its rear houses mementos of its long history. NR

THREE FORKS OF THE MISSOURI NATIONAL HISTORIC LANDMARK, *northwest of Three Forks on the Missouri River*

This site, discovered in July, 1805, by Captain William Clark in the course of the Lewis and Clark expedition, is where the Gallatin River joins the Jefferson and Madison to form the Missouri. Lewis and Clark named the three streams, in addition to determining their function. The **Missouri Headwaters State Monument** is here. NR

VIRGINIA CITY HISTORIC DISTRICT NATIONAL HISTORIC LANDMARK, *55 miles southeast of Butte*

The discovery of gold at Alder Gulch in 1863 led to feverish mining activity—and to the rise of this colorful frontier city, which became closely associated with the gold strike, the lawlessness that it precipitated, and the vigilante bands formed to control outlaws. From 1865 to 1875 Virginia City was the territorial capital of Montana. Today it is an authentically reconstructed gold-rush ghost town. Among the restored attractions (open in the summer) are an assay office, blacksmith shop, general store, saloon, hotel, Wells Fargo office, and the territorial capitol. NR

Open: mid-June–Labor Day

NEBRASKA

BAYARD VICINITY
CHIMNEY ROCK NATIONAL HISTORIC SITE, *4 miles south off State 92*

Towering 500 feet above the nearby North Platte River, this rock column was a famous guidepost for trappers and traders and a campsite for westward-bound emigrants following the **Oregon Trail** route in covered wagons in the mid-19th century. Its weathered surface once bore the signatures of many pioneer travelers. NR

BEATRICE VICINITY
HOMESTEAD NATIONAL MONUMENT, *4 miles west on State 4*

The monument's site marks the claim of Daniel Freeman, one of the earliest settlers to file under terms of the national Homestead Act of 1862. The act entitled each American citizen or prospective citizen to make claim to 160 acres of unappropriated government land, which became his when he settled on the land and cultivated it for 5 years. In a larger sense the monument is in recognition of all homesteaders. Of particular interest are later Freeman buildings, the graves of Freeman and his wife, and the **Palmer-Epard Cabin,** a representative structure of the period erected nearby in 1867 and moved here in 1950. A visitor center displays historical objects. NR
Open: June–Aug, 8–5:30; rest of year, 8–4:30; closed holidays

BELLEVUE, *10 miles south of Omaha on the Missouri River*
Nebraska's oldest existing town, established about 1823 as a trading post, is now best known as the site of a Presbyterian mission for Indians, which was completed in 1858.

Top: Scotts Bluff National Monument near Gering. Left: Nebraska Statehood Memorial in Lincoln. Right: Chimney Rock, Oregon Trail landmark, near Bayard

CHADRON VICINITY

DAWES COUNTY PIONEERS SOCIETY MUSEUM OF THE FUR TRADE, 3½ *miles east on U.S. 20*

Besides tracing the history of the fur trade from about 1825, this museum in a restored trading post has an outstanding collection of early firearms.

Open: June–Aug, daily 8–6; rest of year by appointment

FORT CALHOUN VICINITY

FORT ATKINSON NATIONAL HISTORIC LANDMARK, *1 mile east via secondary road*

Between 1819 and 1827, when it was abandoned, Fort Atkinson was the westernmost link in a chain of United States forts designed to protect a rising fur trade from Indian attacks and the encroachment of British trading companies. It provided protection also for settlers on their way west, and beginning in 1825 it was the site of the **Upper Missouri Indian Agency.** Although there are no visible remains of the fort now, archaeological excavation beginning in 1956 has determined its physical layout and has disclosed valuable artifacts. NR

FORT ROBINSON VICINITY

FORT ROBINSON AND RED CLOUD AGENCY NATIONAL HISTORIC LANDMARK, *on U.S. 20*

A treaty of 1868 guaranteed the Sioux and other tribes food and supplies in return for lands ceded by the Indians to the United States. Provisions given the Oglala Sioux were issued at the Red Cloud Agency, moved to this site in 1873. The treaty did not bring tranquillity to the area, however; in 1874 Fort Robinson was set up to provide military protection for the agency, and the fort also served as a base for a number of subsequent Indian campaigns. Today the Red Cloud Agency buildings have disappeared, but structures dating from the 1880s and 1890s from Fort Robinson, which continued in active military service through World War II, still remain. A museum set up in the headquarters building of the fort by the Nebraska State Historical Society contains military items and exhibits tracing the history of the area from prehistoric times to the 1874–1940 period. NR

Open: Apr–Nov, daily 8–5, rest of year by appointment

GERING VICINITY

SCOTTS BLUFF NATIONAL MONUMENT, *3 miles west on State 92*

Scotts Bluff, which rises 800 feet above the surrounding North Platte valley floor and 4,649 feet above sea level, was named for a pioneer fur trapper who died in the vicinity about 1828. The monument on this site, overlooking the **Oregon Trail,** marks successive periods in the settlement of the West. After the fur traders came the migrants who from 1843 traveled along the Oregon Trail. Brigham Young and his company of Mormons followed not long after, and the discovery of gold in California in 1848 brought new waves of pioneers. Remains of the famous trail, worn by wagon wheels, are still visible. A visitor center tells the story of this westward movement, and the **Oregon Trail Museum,** at the base of the bluff, contains paintings by William Henry Jackson. In the decade beginning in 1860, nearby **Mitchell Pass** was used by riders of the pony express and by builders of the first transcontinental telegraph. NR

For further information write: Box 427, Gering, NE 69341

KEARNEY VICINITY
FORT KEARNY, 8 miles southeast on State 10
From 1848 to 1871, when it was abandoned, a Federal Army post stood on this site, offering protection to travelers following the Oregon Trail. Though none of the fort's structures survived, extensive research and excavation begun in 1960 have led to redevelopment of the area, including construction of a visitor center. The **Fort Kearney Museum** is located in the town of Kearney.

LINCOLN
BRYAN HOUSE (FAIRVIEW) NATIONAL HISTORIC LANDMARK, 4900 Sumner Street
This was the home of William Jennings Bryan, great orator and 3 times presidential candidate, during the years 1902–17, among the most important of his public life. Some original furnishings are in the house, among them Oriental items acquired on a round-the-world trip. The first floor was restored in 1962. NR
Open: June 1–Sept 1, Thurs–Sun 1–4; Oct–May by appointment

NEBRASKA STATEHOOD MEMORIAL, 1627 H Street
The memorial, thus designated officially in 1968, was the home of Thomas Perkins Kennard, one of three commissioners named by the state legislature in 1867 to select a capital for Nebraska, newly admitted to the Union. Kennard was largely responsible for the selection of Lincoln. The house, built in 1869 and recently restored, is thought to be the oldest surviving within the original 1867 boundaries of Lincoln. NR
Open: June–Aug, Tues–Sat 9–4, Sun 2–5; Sept–May, Tues–Sat 9–1, 2–4, Sun 2–5; closed holidays

NORTH PLATTE VICINITY
SCOUTS' REST RANCH, 3½ miles northwest via U.S. 30
Recently restored, this ranch was the home of Buffalo Bill Cody. Here he quartered and rehearsed his Wild West show and entertained such notables as General Philip Sheridan and Kit Carson.
Open: June–Labor Day, 8–9; rest of year, 8–5

OMAHA
MORMON CEMETERY, Northridge Drive and State Street
Some 600 Utah-bound Mormons died in this vicinity from disease and hardship during the winter of 1846–47 and lie buried here. A bronze monument, *Winter Quarters*, recalls that period. The history of the region is represented as well in several excellent museum collections. Indian and pioneer material is on display at **Joslyn Art Museum**, 2218 Dodge Street. The **Union Pacific Historical Museum**, 1416 Dodge Street, traces the growth of that famous railroad and of the West in general.

SCOTTSBLUFF VICINITY
HORSE CREEK TREATY MONUMENT, about 20 miles west
The monument unveiled here in 1929 commemorates the historic gathering of more than 10,000 Indians at Horse Creek in 1851. Organized by the Federal government and designed to establish peaceful agreements with respect to reservation boundaries and the privilege of crossing them, the conference resulted in the first Fort Laramie Treaty. Representatives included Shoshone, Sioux, Cheyenne, Assiniboin, Arapaho, Blackfeet, Crow, Mandan, Gros Ventre, and Arikari.

NEVADA

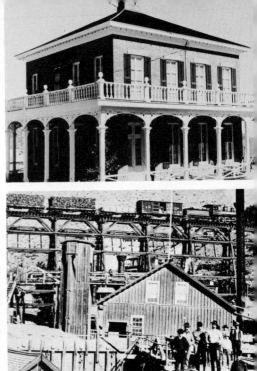

AUSTIN HISTORIC DISTRICT, *U.S. 50 below the crest of the Toiyabe Mountains*

During the 1860s Austin flourished briefly as a silver-mining boom town; at its peak, Austin boasted a population of 8,000 to 10,000 inhabitants and was Nevada's largest city after Virginia City (*see Virginia City Historic District*). Legend has it that silver was discovered in the area when a horse, in 1862, kicked over a rock, thereby revealing the ore. Austin's mines eventually yielded $50 million in ore. Many of Austin's old buildings are still in use—the **Lander County Courthouse,** raised in 1869; Nevada's oldest bank, built in 1862, and now a library; the **Gridley Store,** whose owner in 1864 raised a total of $275,000 for Union army relief by auctioning off a sack of flour. The ruins of **Stokes Castle,** built in 1879 by the financier Anson Phelps Stokes, are just outside the town. NR

BERLIN HISTORIC DISTRICT, *near Ione off State 21*

This site was formerly a camp in the Union Mining District, which was discovered in 1863 and over the next 17 years yielded about $1 million in gold and silver and 11,000 flasks of mercury. NR

CARSON CITY

Founded in 1858 on the site of a trading post established 7 years earlier, Carson City—named after scout Kit Carson—served as Nevada's territorial capital in 1861 and became the state capital in 1864. After the discovery of the Comstock Lode (*see Virginia City*), Carson City flourished as a supply point for mining and ranching communities in the vicinity. Today Carson City is the nation's smallest state capital after Juneau, Alaska. Erected in 1870–71, the original **Capitol Building** still houses the state legislature.

Left: ruins of Fort Churchill near Weeks. Top: the John W. Mackay Mansion in Virginia City. Right: photograph of an old Virginia City mining camp

DAYTON, *10 miles east of Carson City off U.S. 50*

Originally a trading post on the Carson River for California-bound pioneers, Dayton is one of Nevada's oldest settlements and the site of the first gold discovery. Gold was found in nearby **Gold Canyon** in 1850; this spurred prospecting in canyons to the west, culminating in the fabulous strikes at Gold Hill and Virginia City in 1859. Dayton subsequently became a stop on the pony express route and a milling center. Many old structures survive today.

GENOA

MORMON STATION STATE HISTORIC MONUMENT, *Carson Valley off U.S. 395*

The first permanent white settlement in Nevada was established here in 1849 when Hampden S. Beatie and 6 Mormon companions were sent from Salt Lake City by Brigham Young to found a trading post. Known as Mormon Station, it began to prosper as emigrants on the Humboldt section of the **California Trail** stopped to purchase supplies here. In 1851 a group of Salt Lake City businessmen led by John Reese expanded facilities at the post and built a fortified store and hotel. In subsequent years other settlers migrated to the area, which was renamed Genoa in 1855. In 1857 most of Genoa's Mormon population returned to Salt Lake City. Two years later Genoa was the scene of the first attempt at territorial government in Nevada. The stockade and trading post have been restored.
Open: May 1–Sept 30, daily 9–5

GOLDFIELD, *25 miles south of Tonopah on U.S. 95*

Following the discovery of silver at Tonopah (*see*), the spectacular gold strike made by prospectors in this area in 1902 created the community of Goldfield, which boomed from 1903 until 1918, boasted a population of 40,000, and was for a time the largest city in Nevada. Between 1903 and 1940 nearly $100 million in ore was produced here. A number of elegant stone buildings from Goldfield's heyday remain.

LAS VEGAS

LAS VEGAS MORMON FORT, *on N Las Vegas Blvd at Washington*

On June 14, 1855, 30 Mormon missionaries established a small settlement at this site, which subsequently developed into the town of Las Vegas. The Mormons built an adobe fort and houses, planted fields, and attempted to establish friendly relations with the local Paiute Indians. After the Mormons returned to Salt Lake City in 1857, the property was acquired by Octavius Decatur Gass, who developed **Las Vegas Ranch.** New prosperity came to Las Vegas in 1905 when the Los Angeles and Salt Lake Railroad decided to establish a station at the townsite. Today one of the Mormon houses stands to commemorate the 1855 pioneers. NR

TONOPAH, *at junction of U.S. 95 and 6*

The discovery of silver at Tonopah by the rancher Jim Belmont on May 19, 1900, initiated Nevada's second big mining boom, which ended a 20-year slump that had caused the state to lose a third of its population. Prospectors streamed into the area and discovered gold to the south in 1902 (*see Goldfield*). Tonopah soon became the nation's leading gold and silver producer—the mines yielded $200 million in ore—and acquired a population of thousands. The mines were depleted in the 1920s. A few original buildings still stand.

NEVADA

VIRGINIA CITY AND VICINITY

COMSTOCK LODE, *outside of town*

Discovered in 1859, the 2½-mile-long Comstock Lode—named after the prospector Henry Comstock, who staked part of the original claim—was one of the world's richest deposits of lode silver and gold and produced more than $300 million in high-grade ore. Wealth from the lode helped to build Virginia City and San Francisco, to finance the Civil War, and to make Nevada a state by 1864. Today the sites of 7 of the major mines are marked by large yellow dumps.

MACKAY MANSION, *129 D Street*

Erected in 1860 as headquarters for the Gould and Curry Mining Company—of which George Hearst, father of the publisher William Randolph, was half owner—this brick building was one of the few structures to survive the fire that razed most of Virginia City in 1875. It was subsequently the home of John W. Mackay, the richest man of the Comstock Lode (*see*). As "Boss" of the "Big Bonanza," the Consolidated Virginia Mine, Mackay made a fortune of more than $100 million.

Open: May 1–Oct 30, daily 10–5

VIRGINIA CITY HISTORIC DISTRICT NATIONAL HISTORIC LANDMARK

Founded in 1859, the year of the discovery of the Comstock Lode (*see*), Virginia City flourished for 20 years as the most prosperous mining metropolis in Nevada and the prototype for similar boom towns throughout the West. During the Civil War Comstock silver, shipped east from Virginia City's Wells Fargo office, helped finance the Union cause. Nevada's first newspaper, the *Territorial Enterprise* (founded at Genoa in 1857), on which Samuel Clemens and Bret Harte worked as reporters, was published at Virginia City. By 1876 it boasted a population of 30,000, 4 banks, 6 churches, 100 saloons, and the only elevator between Chicago and San Francisco. In 1873 the Consolidated Virginia Mine, the largest Comstock discovery of all, opened; it eventually yielded $234 million of ore. In 1875 a fire destroyed most of Virginia City, which was subsequently rebuilt. By 1880 the richest mines in the area were exhausted, and Virginia City began to decline. Today Nevada's largest ghost town has been restored to its 1870 appearance. Such structures as **Piper's Opera House** and **The Castle**, a Victorian mansion built in 1868 by Robert Graves, a millionaire mine superintendent, attest to Virginia City's former prosperity. NR

Opera house open: summer, daily 10–6. The Castle open: June–Oct, daily 11–5. Admission: 50¢

WEEKS VICINITY

FORT CHURCHILL NATIONAL HISTORIC LANDMARK, *U.S. 95A, 8 miles south of U.S. 50*

Consisting of adobe buildings, this outpost was erected on the **Overland Mail Route** in 1860 following a Paiute uprising and the resulting interruption of pony express mail service. Fort Churchill protected the first transcontinental telegraph, was a pony express stop, and during the Civil War served as the main supply depot for the Nevada Military District. Soldiers stationed here patrolled the overland routes from the Sierra to Austin and Ruby Valley, and into California's Owens Valley. By 1871 the post was abandoned. Only ruins remain. NR

NEW HAMPSHIRE

CANTERBURY

SHAKER VILLAGE, *12 miles north of Concord and west of State 106*
This Shaker colony, organized upon such religious tenets as celibacy, belief in visions, and the communal ownership of property, was established by Elder Clough in 1792. The village, whose white frame buildings have been restored, is now one of the 2 remaining Shaker communities in New England (*see also Hancock, Mass.*).
Open: Memorial Day–Labor Day, Tues–Sat, holidays 9–4

CHARLESTON

OLD FORT NO. 4, *on State 11, ½ mile west of junction with State 12*
In the spring of 1747 the northernmost fort in the Connecticut Valley was successfully defended by a 31-man garrison during a 3-day siege by a force of 700 French and Indians. In 1744 this area, comprising part of a land grant known as Township No. 4, was only sparsely populated, and a great log fort was begun to safeguard settlers against an imminent Indian attack. During the summer and fall of 1746 the colonists barricaded themselves in the fort, while Indians destroyed outlying buildings, crops, and livestock. After the 3-day battle in 1747 the enemy withdrew, never to attack again. During the Revolution, in 1777, General John Stark's army assembled at Fort No. 4 before the battle of Bennington, Vermont. Today the fort has been reconstructed according to drawings of 1746.
Open: June 13–Labor Day, daily 11–5; May 13–June 13, Labor Day–Oct 22, Sat–Sun 11–5

CONCORD, *central New Hampshire*

A tablet here marks the site where New Hampshire delegates assembled on June 21, 1788, and by a majority of 57 to 47 voted to

Top: the Mt. Washington Cog Railway. Left: a lithograph of the Macpheadris-Warner House in Portsmouth. Right: a contemporary view of Dartmouth Row

ratify the Federal Constitution, thus assuring its adoption. New Hampshire was the 9th and deciding state needed to carry the Constitution.

FRANKLIN PIERCE HOUSE, 52 South Main Street

Popularly known as Young Hickory of the Granite Hills, Franklin Pierce returned to his native state upon his retirement in 1857 as 14th President of the U.S.—and the only one from New Hampshire—and lived in this French-style Victorian mansion until his death in 1869. He lies buried in front of the Old North Cemetery. Open by appointment

STATE CAPITOL, intersection of Park and Main streets

The country's oldest State House in which the legislature still meets in its original chambers was constructed between 1816 and 1819 of Concord granite. Currently displayed in the rotunda are battle flags of the New Hampshire regiments in the Civil War. Open: Mon–Fri 8:30–5

CORNISH

SAINT-GAUDENS NATIONAL HISTORIC SITE, south of Plainfield off State 12A

The eminent American sculptor Augustus Saint-Gaudens spent the most productive years of his career on this estate, which he purchased in 1885 at the age of 37. He remodeled the old house, which had been built about 1800, landscaped the grounds, and converted the barn into a studio, where he produced such works as the standing Lincoln (1887), the Adams Memorial (1891), and the equestrian statue General William T. Sherman (1900). A group of promising young artists and other acquaintances of the sculptor soon came to work nearby and became known as the Cornish Colony. Today the house, grounds, and studios have been preserved. NR
For further information write: R.R. 2, Windsor, VT 05089

DERRY VICINITY

FROST HOMESTEAD NATIONAL HISTORIC LANDMARK, 2 miles southeast on State 28

The renowned and prolific American poet Robert Frost resided in this farmhouse (currently under restoration) from 1900 until 1909. During this period he engaged in farming and composed his first 2 volumes of verse, which included such works as "Death of the Hired Man" and "Trial by Existence." NR

EXETER, southeast New Hampshire

The first independent government among the colonies was established at Exeter on January 5, 1776, when a provincial congress issued a provisional declaration of independence, adopted a constitution providing for a house of representatives and a council, and recognized Meshech Weare as its first executive officer. This town, which was founded in 1638 by the Reverend John Wheelwright, served as the capital of the new state until 1808, when the seat of government was moved to Concord (see).

FRANKLIN

DANIEL WEBSTER BIRTHPLACE, off State 127

This frame cottage was the birthplace (1782) and boyhood home of Daniel Webster, eminent orator, congressman, and twice Secretary

of State. The house has been restored.
Open: last week in June–Labor Day, daily 9–6

HANOVER
DARTMOUTH COLLEGE
In 1769 the Congregationalist clergyman Eleazer Wheelock, with a gift of £10,000 from the Earl of Dartmouth, founded a college here for the Christian education of Indians "and other youths." The 9th oldest college in the nation preserves such notable structures as **Dartmouth Row,** 4 classroom buildings dating from 1784.

HILLSBORO VICINITY
PIERCE HOMESTEAD NATIONAL HISTORIC LANDMARK, *3 miles west on State 31*
Franklin Pierce, who was the nation's 14th President, during the ante-bellum period (1853–57), resided in this house from his infancy in 1804 until his marriage in 1834. The Federal-style structure was built in 1804 by Franklin's father, Benjamin Pierce, a general in the Revolution and twice governor of New Hampshire. NR
Open: last week of June–Labor Day, Tues–Sun. Admission: 50¢

MANCHESTER
GENERAL JOHN STARK MEMORIAL AND HOME, *2000 Elm Street*
This Cape Cod house was the childhood home of General John Stark, one of the Rogers Rangers who destroyed St. Francis, Quebec, during the French and Indian War in 1759, a hero of the Battle of Bunker Hill in June, 1775, and commander of the American militia during the battle of Bennington, Vermont, in August, 1777.
Open: May 15–Oct 15, Wed, Sun 1:30–4

MT. WASHINGTON COG RAILWAY, *Base Station Road, 6 miles off U.S. 302 from Fabyan-Bretton Woods*
The second steepest cog railway in the world, and the first of its kind, was conceived by Herrick and Walter Aiken and Walter Marsh; it was completed in 1869 at a cost of $139,500. Made safe by a toothed wheel and ratchet, this railway makes the 3-mile trip to the 6,293-foot summit at a grade of 1 foot in 4.
Trips: June 17–June 30, Sept 11–Oct 15, daily 11, 2:15; July 1–Sept 10, hourly 8–6. Round trip $7, children (6–12) $4

NEW CASTLE
FORT CONSTITUTION, *near intersection of State 1B and Wentworth Street*
Known at the time as Castle William & Mary, this 6-man British garrison was captured by several hundred New Hampshire patriots, who had been alerted by Paul Revere, on December 14–15, 1774, thus marking the first armed resistance of the Revolution. The powder and arms seized here were cached at Durham and later used by the colonists at the Battle of Bunker Hill. Today portions of the old fortress remain. At the U.S. Coast Guard station nearby is the **Fort Point Lighthouse,** erected in 1771 to replace a lantern hung at Castle William & Mary.

PORTSMOUTH AND VICINITY, *southeast New Hampshire*
Originally known as Strawbery Banke because of the wild strawberries found growing along the riverbanks, Portsmouth (as it was renamed in 1653) was founded in 1630 and was the first permanent

settlement on the Piscataqua River. Situated on an excellent harbor and possessing abundant timber resources, Portsmouth soon became a flourishing seaport town, where shipbuilding and other mercantile interests thrived during the 18th and 19th centuries. Preserved today along Portsmouth's winding streets are many reminders of its former prosperity. In the Old South End more than 30 early American buildings are being reconstructed as part of the **Strawbery Banke Restoration Project.** Representing a variety of architectural styles, the city's famous houses include the **Richard Jackson House** (NHL), erected in 1664 and the oldest extant frame dwelling in New Hampshire; the **Macpheadris-Warner House** (NHL), built between 1718 and 1723 in the early-Georgian style popular in the New England colonies; the high-Georgian **Wentworth-Gardner House** (NHL), built by ship's carpenters in 1760; and the late-Georgian **Moffat-Ladd House** (NHL), raised about 1764, which later was the home of William Whipple, a signer of the Declaration of Independence. Also in Portsmouth are the **John Paul Jones House,** where the Revolutionary naval hero lodged while his ships, the *America* and *Ranger,* were being fitted; and the **Governor John Langdon Mansion Memorial,** which was built in 1784 by the first pro tempore president of the U.S. Senate, a signer of the Constitution, and the man who informed George Washington of his election as President. About 2 miles south of town at Little Harbor is the rambling **Wentworth-Coolidge Mansion** (NHL), which, begun in 1695 and enlarged in 1730 and 1750, was the home and headquarters of Benning Wentworth, whom King George appointed the first royal governor of the province of New Hampshire in 1741. *Strawbery Banke open: late May–Oct 15, Mon–Sat 10–5, Sun 12–5; check individual houses*

RYE

ODIORNE'S POINT, *on State 1A just south of Seavey's Creek*
Pannaway Plantation, New Hampshire's first settlement, was established at this site in 1623. David Thompson, whose son, John, was the first child born in New Hampshire, and others who had come to colonize and develop trade, erected a manor house, smithy, cooperage, fort, and stages for drying fish. The village was subsequently abandoned in favor of Strawbery Banke, later renamed Portsmouth (*see*).

WILMOT

MASON'S PATENT, *along west side of State 14A just south of the Springfield town line*
A marker here commemorates the land grant given by authorities of the English Crown to Captain John Mason in 1629, which formed a portion of the colony of New Hampshire. (A royal grant of 1620 had given much of New Hampshire to the Council for New England.) Stretching from the Merrimack River on the west to the Piscataqua River on the north, Mason's grant was bounded by an arc, 60 miles distant from the sea, which became known as the Masonian curve and passes through the nearby town line between Wilmot and Springfield. New Hampshire's present boundaries were not determined until after conflicting land claims had caused serious border disputes with New York, Massachusetts, Vermont, and Canada throughout most of the pre-Revolutionary period. New Hampshire's western boundary was finally established at the west bank of the Connecticut River; its northern boundary was defined at the end of the French and Indian War.

NEW JERSEY

ALLAIRE

HOWELL IRON WORKS AT ALLAIRE, *Allaire State Park, State 524 and U.S. 9*

This 19th-century bog-iron furnace thrived until the discovery of coal and iron in Pennsylvania ended the demand for New Jersey's softer and more expensive bog iron. First operated by Benjamin B. Howell, the furnace was purchased in 1822 by James Allaire, a steam-engine manufacturer, who developed a self-contained model community for 500 employees of the rapidly expanding Howell Works. The pipes for New York City's first waterworks and the air chambers for Robert Fulton's *Clermont* were cast here. Allaire built kilns to make bricks for the 60 comfortable homes he erected for his employees, maintained a school and a stagecoach, and ran a company store. After the Howell Works closed in 1848, the village's inhabitants left. Restoration of the village is now under way; among the buildings open are the bakery, blacksmith and carpenter shops, general store, and manager's cottage.
Open: May–Aug, Mon–Sat 10–5, Sun 12–5; Sept–Apr, Tues–Sat 10–5, Sun 12–5

BATSTO

BATSTO VILLAGE, *State 542, 10 miles east of Hammonton*

This restored village was once an important iron- and glass-producing center. The Batsto Iron Works, built in 1766, was a major supplier of munitions for the American Army during both the Revolution and the War of 1812. The iron furnaces were closed in 1848, but until 1867 Batsto continued to thrive as a glass-producing com-

Top: George Washington rallying his men at the Battle of Princeton. Left: Thomas Edison's home in West Orange. Right: the blast furnace at Allaire

munity of nearly 1,000 people. Among the restored buildings are the ironmasters' mansion, gristmill, sawmill, blacksmith and wheelwright shops, and workmen's houses. NR
Open: Memorial Day–Labor Day, daily 10–6; rest of year, Mon–Fri 11–5, Sat, Sun, holidays 11–6

BURLINGTON

JAMES FENIMORE COOPER HOUSE, *457 High Street*
The famous author was born here in 1789. A year later his parents moved to New York. On display are Revolutionary and Civil War relics as well as a portion of the manuscript of *The Spy.*
Open Sun 3–5

JAMES LAWRENCE HOUSE, *459 High Street*
Lawrence, the naval hero of the War of 1812, was born here in 1781. During the Revolution his father was the town's Tory mayor. In the War of 1812 Lawrence was in command of the frigate *Chesapeake* when it engaged in battle with the British frigate *Shannon.* Mortally wounded, as he was carried below Lawrence uttered his famous words, "Don't give up the ship!" The Americans did surrender, but Lawrence's words became a motto of the United States Navy.
Open: Tues–Sat 10–12, 1–5, Sun 2–5; closed holidays

CALDWELL

GROVER CLEVELAND BIRTHPLACE, *207 Bloomfield Avenue*
The only U.S. President born in New Jersey, Cleveland was born in the first-floor back room of this house on March 18, 1837. The house was the manse of the Caldwell First Presbyterian Church, where Cleveland's father, Richard, was pastor. When Stephen Grover (the first name was soon dropped) was 3, the family moved to Fayetteville, New York. The house contains many of Cleveland's possessions, including the wooden cradle in which he was rocked, a chair he used in the White House, and a box containing some of the wedding cake from his White House wedding to Frances Folsom. **Westland** (NHL), the home in Princeton where he lived from 1897 until his death, is privately owned and not open.
Open: Tues–Sat 10–12, 1–5, Sun 2–5; closed holidays

CAMDEN

WALT WHITMAN HOME NATIONAL HISTORIC LANDMARK, *330 Mickle Street*
The famous poet lived here from 1884 until his death in 1892, at the age of 84. The house contains many of Whitman's furnishings and mementos, as well as clothing and books. NR
Open: Tues–Sat 10–12, 1–5, Sun 2–5; closed holidays

CAPE MAY HISTORIC DISTRICT
One of the oldest Atlantic coast resorts, Cape May in the 19th century attracted America's most prominent political and social figures. Presidents Lincoln, Grant, Pierce, Buchanan, and Harrison vacationed here, as did Horace Greeley, John Wanamaker, and wealthy society leaders. In the summer of 1847 a mob of admirers chased Henry Clay up and down the beach and when they caught him snipped pieces of his hair for souvenirs. In 1903 the first Ford agency got its first car from Henry Ford, who lost a beach race and had to sell the car to pay for his train fare back to Detroit. Many of the 19th-century structures, including the verandaed hotels that face the ocean, still stand. NR

ELIZABETH
BOXWOOD HALL, *1073 East Jersey Street*
Known also as the Boudinot Mansion, Boxwood Hall was the home from 1772 to 1795 of patriot and statesman Elias Boudinot. Boudinot served as first president of the Continental Congress and in that capacity signed the peace treaty with England. On April 23, 1789, General Washington stopped here for lunch on his way to his inauguration in New York as first President of the United States. In 1824 Major General the Marquis de Lafayette was an overnight guest here of General Jonathan Drayton, a signer of the Constitution, who bought Boxwood Hall from Boudinot in 1795. NR
Open: Tues–Sat 10–12, 1–5, Sun 2–5; closed holidays

FREEHOLD VICINITY

MONMOUTH BATTLEFIELD NATIONAL HISTORIC LANDMARK, *northwest on State 522*
Here, on June 28, 1778, the main British and American armies met for the last time in the war. After France entered the war on the American side, the British commander in chief, Sir Henry Clinton, was ordered to pull back his forces from Philadelphia to New York. Fearing a French naval attack if he made the retreat by sea, Clinton decided to risk the long march across New Jersey to Sandy Hook. His 12,000 troops and 1,500 plunder-laden wagons, strung out over 12 miles, made a tempting target for Washington's army, and on June 28 a force under Charles Lee attacked Clinton's rear guard. Then, inexplicably, Lee ordered a retreat. Not until Washington himself arrived with the main American force and relieved Lee of command did the Americans rally and hold off the counterattacking English. All day a fierce battle raged in sweltering heat. The Americans held, but night fell before they could form for their own counterattack, and during the night Clinton and his army slipped away. Washington had failed to deal the British a crushing blow or stop their retreat; but the Americans proved themselves a match for the best British troops. During the long day Molly Hays, the young wife of an artilleryman, carried pitchers of water to hot, thirsty Americans. As the soldiers saw her coming they called out, "Here comes Molly and her pitcher," which became shortened to "Molly Pitcher," the name by which she is known to history. The **Monmouth Battle Monument,** which commemorates the event, has a bronze bas-relief of Molly Pitcher at its base. NR

HADDONFIELD

INDIAN KING TAVERN, *233 Kings Highway East*
The Indian King was built in 1750 on Kings Highway, which had been laid out in 1686. The first New Jersey legislature met at the tavern in 1777 after having been driven out of Trenton by the British. While in session in the second-floor ballroom, the legislature adopted the Great Seal of New Jersey and passed a law substituting the word "state" for "colony" on all state papers. NR
Open: Tues–Sat 10–12, 1–5, Sun 2–5; closed holidays

HANCOCK'S BRIDGE

HANCOCK HOUSE
On March 21, 1778, a party of American rebels sleeping in Judge William Hancock's house were attacked by about 300 Loyalists under Major John Simcoe. About 30 patriots were bayoneted to death. The massacre was in reprisal for aid the Quaker community had given the American Army. Next to the house is a 200-year-old

cabin built of hand-hewn cedar planks. It is typical of those constructed by early Swedish settlers. NR

Open: Apr–Oct, daily 10–5; March, Sat and Sun 10–4:30

MORRISTOWN

 MORRISTOWN NATIONAL HISTORIC PARK

In January, 1777, and again in December, 1779, George Washington and the main body of the American Army established winter headquarters in Morristown. In 1777, after the surprising American victories at Trenton (*see Trenton Battle Monument*) and Princeton (*see Princeton Battlefield*), Washington's exhausted troops occupied farms and homes in and around the village from January until May. In 1779–80 the troops returned, settling in Jockey Hollow for the bitter winter while Washington and his wife moved into the home of Colonel Jacob Ford's widow. The **Ford Mansion**, at 230 Morris Street, Washington's headquarters, has been restored and has many of the original furnishings. Behind the house is the **Historical Museum**, which contains many of the general's letters and possessions as well as a collection of Revolutionary weapons and other historical objects and documents. **Fort Nonsense**, off Washington Street, built on Washington's orders in 1777 to defend supplies stored in Morristown, received its name from those who thought the purpose of the order was simply to give the troops something to do. **Jockey Hollow**, located 3 miles southwest of Morristown, contains the Continental Army campsites, reconstructed huts, and a reconstructed hospital. Also in Jockey Hollow is **Wick House**, a farmhouse used as headquarters by Major General Arthur St. Clair of the Pennsylvania Line. NR

Ford Mansion and museum open daily 10–5. Wick House open: Feb–Nov, daily 1–5; park closed holidays

PRINCETON

 NASSAU HALL NATIONAL HISTORIC LANDMARK, *Princeton University*

Completed in 1756 and named after King William the Third of the House of Nassau, Nassau Hall was built to house the College of New Jersey, which was chartered in 1746 and moved from Newark to Princeton in 1756. In 1776 the first New Jersey state legislature met here, and the first governor was inaugurated. The building was occupied by both British and American troops during the Revolution; in 1777 it was damaged by Washington's cannon in the Battle of Princeton (*see*). For several months in 1783 it was the new country's capitol, while the Continental Congress convened here and awaited the signing of a peace treaty with England. Alongside Nassau Hall and built in the same year is the former **President's House** (NHL) and Dean's House. NR

 PRINCETON BATTLEFIELD NATIONAL HISTORIC LANDMARK, *Princeton Battlefield State Park, State 583*

Here Washington's second New Jersey triumph over the British took place. After the American victory at Trenton on December 26, 1776 (*see Trenton Battle Monument*), Washington led his troops back to Pennsylvania, then on January 1 again crossed the now-frozen Delaware River to Trenton. By the next day, however, General Cornwallis had arrived with 8,000 fresh British troops, and Washington suddenly found himself in a deadly trap. The river had thawed behind him; the British were massed in front. Again Washington chose a bold plan: instead of attempting a retreat, he would plunge into New Jersey and hit the British garrison at Princeton. Early in the morning of January 3, 1777, while Cornwallis confidently waited to crush the rebels at daybreak, the American Army crept out of its camp. Orders were whispered, gun wheels were muffled in rags, cannon chains were held so they would not clank. At dawn, just outside Princeton, the rebels encountered Lieutenant Colonel Charles Mawhood's British regulars headed for Trenton. In the short, violent battle that followed, the Americans at first panicked, then recovered after Washington himself, mounted on a white horse, rode into the thick of battle and rallied his men. The British fled, and Washington led his men into Princeton, where at Nassau Hall (see) the rest of the British troops surrendered. Trenton and Princeton marked the end of British hopes for a quick victory. A monument at the battlefield commemorates the American success. NR

RINGWOOD

RINGWOOD MANOR NATIONAL HISTORIC LANDMARK, *Ringwood State Park, 3 miles east of Hewitt*
In the 18th and 19th centuries Ringwood was an important iron-producing center, and Ringwood Manor housed its famous iron-masters. During the Revolutionary War, when Robert Erskine, Washington's map maker, was ironmaster, Washington was a frequent visitor here. The original 1765 manor was partially destroyed by the British. In 1810 Martin Ryerson rebuilt it; from then until 1930 the 78-room mansion was occupied by Ryersons, Coopers, and Hewitts, the leading ironmaster families. They lived in luxury, and the valuable collection of furnishings and Americana they amassed is on display. NR
Open: May 1–Oct 31, Tues–Fri 10–4:30, Sat and Sun 10–5

RIVER EDGE

VON STEUBEN HOUSE, *Main Street*
Originally built by David Ackerman in 1695, this house was purchased and remodeled by the Zabriskie family about 1738. It was occupied by both British and American troops during the Revolutionary War, and in 1780 Washington briefly had his headquarters here. Because the Zabriskies were Tory sympathizers, the house was confiscated in 1783 by the state and given to General Von Steuben in appreciation for his services during the war. Von Steuben later sold it back to the Zabriskies. The house is furnished with colonial pieces. NR
Open: Tues–Sat 10–12, 1–5, Sun 2–5; closed holidays

ROCKY HILL

ROCKINGHAM, *County 518, 5 miles north of Princeton*
Known also as the Berrien Mansion, this 20-room house served as Washington's headquarters from August 23 to November 10, 1783. The Continental Congress, which had convened at Nassau Hall, Princeton University (see), to await the signing of a peace treaty with England, rented Rockingham for Washington so that he could attend the sessions. On November 2, 1783, the general composed his "Farewell Address to the Army" here, then delivered it from a second-floor balcony to troops assembled on the lawn below. While at Rockingham Washington and his wife, Martha, entertained many prominent patriots. The house has been restored, with period furnishings. NR
Open: Tues–Sat 10–12, 1–5, Sun 2–5; closed holidays

NEW JERSEY

SOMERVILLE

OLD DUTCH PARSONAGE, *65 Washington Place*

The congregation of the First Dutch Reformed Church built this house in 1751 as a parsonage for the Reverend John Frelinghuysen, founder of the Dutch Reformed Theological Seminary, which became Rutgers University. His successor, Jacob R. Hardenbergh, became a close friend of General Washington's; the general visited the parsonage often while staying across the street at Wallace House (*see*). Hardenbergh became first president of Queen's College (Rutgers). The parsonage, which contains some Dutch furnishings, has been moved from its original site on the Raritan River. NR

Open: Tues–Sat 10–12, 1–5, Sun 2–5; closed holidays

WALLACE HOUSE, *38 Washington Place*

Built in 1778 by John Wallace, this house was occupied from December, 1778, to June, 1779, by General Washington and his wife, while the Continental Army was stationed at Camp Middlebrook (now Somerville). The house is furnished with colonial objects and Revolutionary War relics, including Washington's campaign chest. NR

Open: Tues–Sat 10–12, 1–5, Sun 2–5; closed holidays

TRENTON

OLD BARRACKS, *South Willow Street*

This fine example of a colonial barracks was one of 5 units erected in 1758 by the Colonial Assembly to house colonial troops in the French and Indian War. During the Revolution they were occupied by British, Hessian, and American troops. Today the Old Barracks is furnished with colonial antiques. NR

Open: May–Sept, Mon–Sat 10–5, Sun 2–5; Sept–May, Mon–Sat 10–4, Sun 2–5

TRENT HOUSE NATIONAL HISTORIC LANDMARK, *539 South Warren Street*

Trenton's oldest house was built in 1719 by William Trent, New Jersey's first chief justice, after whom the city was named. Today the house contains period furnishings. NR

Open: May–Aug, Mon–Sat 10–5, Sun 1–5; Sept–Apr, Mon–Sat 10–4, Sun 1–5

TRENTON BATTLE MONUMENT, *North Broad Street and Brunswick Avenue*

This monument commemorates the first Battle of Trenton, fought on December 26, 1776, at which Washington's ragged American Army scored a significant victory. Washington planned to strike at Trenton in a surprise predawn attack. However, the Americans did not finish crossing from the Pennsylvania to the New Jersey side of the Delaware River until 4 A.M. on December 26 (*see McKonkey Ferry Museum*), and did not complete the 9-mile march to Trenton until well after daybreak. But the Hessian garrison stationed there was reeling from Christmas celebrations, and most were still sleeping when the Americans, split into 2 divisions, attacked about 8 o'clock. The surprise was complete, and the battle was over in less than three quarters of an hour. Colonel Rall, the Hessian commander, was killed; some 900 Hessians were taken prisoner. Only 4 Americans were wounded. The successful offensive gave the Army and the country the boost they needed. The British were disconcerted, and the rebels' cause no longer seemed hopeless (*see Princeton Battlefield*). The 150-foot-high battle monument marks the spot where General Nathanael Greene's division opened fire on the Hessians.

WASHINGTON CROSSING VICINITY

McKONKEY FERRY MUSEUM, *Washington Crossing State Park*
This restored colonial building represents the tavern where Washington rested briefly after his famous crossing of the Delaware River in 1776. After the American Army's crushing defeat in New York and its retreat across New Jersey and the Delaware River late in 1776, General Howe decided to end the British campaign for the winter rather than pursue Washington's tattered forces. Howe established a chain of British posts in New Jersey and sat back to wait for spring. Washington, however, decided on a desperate, daring offensive: needing an American victory to bolster troop morale and encourage re-enlistment, he decided to cross the flooded, ice-jammed, nearly impassable Delaware and surprise the British garrison at Trenton. On the night of December 25, in a gale-driven sleet, his main division of 2,400 men—shivering, thinly dressed, many of them shoeless—began to cross at McKonkey Ferry, 9 miles above Trenton. (The **Washington Crossing Site** is a National Historic Landmark.) Colonel John Glover's regiment of sailors and fishermen from Marblehead maneuvered every available boat back and forth across the swollen river, constantly fending off huge ice slabs. Not until 4 in the morning of December 26 was the crossing completed. Washington ended a short rest at the McKonkey Ferry House, and the march to Trenton and an important American victory began (*see Trenton Battle Monument*).
Open: Tues–Sat 10–12, 1–5, Sun 2–5; closed holidays

WAYNE

DEY MANSION, *199 Totowa Road*
Washington made his headquarters at the home of Colonel Theunis Dey during July, 1780. Late in July he moved his army up the Hudson River Valley. Then, after the discovery of Benedict Arnold's treachery, Washington moved his army back to New Jersey to guard himself against a kidnapping attempt. During October and November, 1780, he again made the Dey mansion his headquarters. The house has been restored and is furnished with 18th-century pieces. NR
Open: Tues, Wed, Fri 1–5, Sat, Sun 10–5

WEST ORANGE

EDISON NATIONAL HISTORIC SITE, *Main Street between Alden and Lakeside streets*
The site includes the home and the laboratory buildings where inventor Thomas Alva Edison lived and worked the last 44 years of his life. Erected in 1887, the laboratory complex, with its teams of workers, became the prototype for the modern industrial research laboratory. Today the buildings contain exhibits that include Edison's original tinfoil photograph, the first motion-picture camera and other movie apparatus, and early electric light and power equipment. There is also a replica of the "Black Maria," the world's first motion-picture studio. **Glenmont,** Edison's 23-room home, contains almost all the original furnishings as well as gifts from well-known people all over the world. The graves of Edison and his wife are behind the house. NR
House open: Mon–Sat 10–4. Lab open daily 9:30–4:30

NEW MEXICO

ABO NATIONAL HISTORIC LANDMARK, *3 miles west of Abó on U.S. 60 and secondary road*

Typifying the pueblos of the salinas—or salt lakes—east of the Manzano Mountains, Abó was occupied by the Tompiros tribe from about 1300 until it was destroyed by Apaches in the 1670s. Governor Juan de Oñate, the colonizer of New Mexico, first recorded the name "Abbó" on an expedition of 1598. During the first half of the 17th century, Abó became an important village on the principal route from the Rio Grande to the salt lakes. By the 1620s many of the Indians had been converted to Christianity; a large church was erected in the 1630s. The ruins of the adobe pueblo, church, and convent are preserved today. NR

ACOMA NATIONAL HISTORIC LANDMARK, *13 miles south of Casa Blanca on State 23*

Established about 1300, Acoma pueblo is believed to be the oldest continuously occupied settlement in the nation. In 1540 a detachment of soldiers led by Hernando de Alvarado from the Coronado expedition into New Mexico became the first Europeans to discover this thriving community. From their strategically situated mesa top, 357 feet above the fields that they worked below, the Indians of Acoma successfully resisted the Spanish for nearly a century, until the numerical superiority of the conquistadors forced them to surrender. The Franciscans founded the **San Estevan de Rey Mission** (NHL) at Acoma in 1629; it is in use today. A few families

Left: Palace of the Governors in Santa Fe Plaza. Right: the mission church at Taos Pueblo. Below: ruins of Fort Union outside Watrous

still live in the adobe houses at Acoma, and other Indians convene here for periodic festivals. NR
Open: daily, 1 hour after sunrise–1 hour before sunset

AZTEC RUINS NATIONAL MONUMENT, *1 mile north of Aztec on secondary road*

Erroneously called Aztec by European settlers, this pre-Columbian community—one of the largest in the Southwest—was actually built by ancestors of the present-day Pueblo Indians. Early in the 1100s Indian farmers scattered along the Animas River congregated in large villages and erected huge multistoried masonry dwellings that faced on plazas dominated by kivas, or ceremonial chambers. By the mid-1100s drought or other climatic conditions had forced the abandonment of Aztec and other large pueblos, and many of their occupants moved to the Mesa Verde area in southwest Colorado. About 1225 the descendants of the Indians who migrated to Mesa Verde returned to Aztec. During the severe drought of 1276–99, Aztec was abandoned permanently. Today a 3-story, 500-room **Pueblo** and a **Great Kiva** have been excavated. NR
For further information write: Box 101, Aztec Ruins, NM 87410

CHACO CANYON NATIONAL MONUMENT, *64 miles north of Thoreau on State 56*

This monument was the center of a Pueblo Indian culture that reached its peak between A.D. 1000 and 1100. The earliest inhabitants of this semiarid region were the Basket Maker Indians, who built circular pit houses in Chaco Canyon as early as A.D. 600. By 900 the pit houses had given way to multifamily dwellings, erected above the ground in rows or clusters of rectangular rooms. Most of these great apartment houses were mysteriously abandoned in the early part of the 13th century. Today the remains of 12 of the great pueblos, of which the **Pueblo Bonito**—with its 5 stories and 800 rooms capable of housing 1,000 persons—is the largest, and more than 400 smaller ruins are preserved in an area 8 miles long and 2 miles wide. Of the round subterranean kivas, chambers used for ceremonial or religious purposes, the most outstanding is the solitary **Casa Rinconada**, 64 feet in diameter. NR
For further information write: Box 156, Bloomfield, NM 87413

CHIMAYO VILLAGE

EL SANTUARIO DE CHIMAYO NATIONAL HISTORIC LANDMARK, *south, in Chimayo*

According to legend, a farmer, informed by a vision to dig up earth that reputedly had curative powers, uncovered a cross belonging to 2 priests who had been martyred at this site. The farmer placed the cross in a small adobe chapel that he built in 1816; the structure is currently a healing shrine visited by pilgrims.

CLAYTON VICINITY

RABBIT EARS (CLAYTON COMPLEX) NATIONAL HISTORIC LANDMARK, *north and west of town*

Rising above the level plains, this twin-peaked eminence was an important landmark for westbound travelers on the **Cimarron Cutoff** of the **Santa Fe Trail**. It was also a focal point for camps in the area and such year-round watering spots as **McNee's Crossing** (NHL), which was named after a scout who was murdered by Indians at this site in 1828 and which now contains a memorial marker. NR

NEW MEXICO

EL MORRO NATIONAL MONUMENT, *2 miles east of El Morro via State 53*
Rising 200 feet above the valley floor, this massive mesa point, known as El Morro ("headland") to the Spanish and later called Inscription Rock, served as a landmark and campsite for early travellers. Long before the arrival of the white man, ancient Zuñi Indians had carved petroglyphs on the rock. In 1605 Juan de Oñate, the colonizer and first governor of New Mexico, became the first European to leave an inscription in the soft sandstone. For the next 300 years explorers, soldiers, and settlers added their names and dates of stopovers. Today the rock symbolizes the cultural mixtures that made up the Southwest. NR
For further information write: Superintendent, Ramah, NM 87321

FORT UNION NATIONAL MONUMENT, *9 miles north of Watrous on State 477*
Fort Union was founded in 1851 near the point where the Santa Fe Trail's mountain route, leading across the Raton Pass, joined its other branch, the Cimarron Cutoff. It was the largest U.S. military post guarding the southwestern frontier during the 19th century. Garrisons stationed here protected travelers on the Santa Fe Trail and engaged in the Indian campaigns of the 1850s and 1860s. Fort Union also served as the principal quartermaster depot in the Southwest, dispatching supplies to other outlying posts in the territory. During the Civil War, in 1862, Union volunteers based at the fort ended the only serious Confederate threat to New Mexico and Colorado at the battle of Glorieta Pass (*see Santa Fe Vicinity*), 70 miles away. The fort was abandoned in 1891, and today only adobe ruins remain. NR
For further information write: Superintendent, Watrous, NM 87753

GILA CLIFF DWELLINGS NATIONAL MONUMENT, *47 miles north of Silver City on State 26 and 527*
Preserved at this monument are 5 cliff dwellings, comprising 35 rooms, which were built in natural caves in the face of an overhanging cliff by Pueblo Indians between A.D. 1272 and 1284. The masonry walls of the Gila conglomerate were made of stone from the formation exposed in the cliff. An example of a circular pit dwelling of the type built by the Mogollon Indians between A.D. 100 and 400, as well as an above-ground pueblo—the **TJ Ruin**—inhabited at the same time as the cliff dwellings, are found at the site. The settlement was abandoned about A.D. 1400, and this area eventually became the homeland of several bands of Apaches. NR
For further information write: Box 1320, Silver City, NM 88061

GRAN QUIVIRA NATIONAL MONUMENT, *1 mile east of Gran Quivira on State 10*
Situated on a high ridge in central New Mexico, this monument was a center of Mogollon Indian culture, which flourished from about A.D. 900 until 1672. About 1300 the Mogollon Indians gave up their single-family dwellings and began constructing communities resembling the pueblos of the Rio Grande Valley. By the 1600s the **Pueblo de las Humanas** was the largest in the region and the scene of Spanish missionary activity, as attested by the ruins of the Franciscan churches **San Buenaventura** and **San Isidro,** which stand nearby. Severe droughts, famine, and Apache raids that occurred between 1666 and 1670 destroyed much of the pueblo's population, and the village was abandoned between 1672 and 1675. NR
For further information write: Route 1, Mountainair, NM 87036

LOS ALAMOS AND VICINITY
BANDELIER NATIONAL MONUMENT, *12 miles south on State 4*
This monument preserves Indian ruins dating from the late Pueblo period between the 13th and 16th centuries A.D. After the disastrous droughts of the late 1200s, several Pueblo Indian groups left their ancient villages and settled here along the canyon-slashed slopes of the Pajarito Plateau, where they built and occupied large pueblos until about 1550. Today the 46-square-mile area of Bandelier National Monument is crossed only by trails. One of the most accessible features is the cliff ruins, or talus (rock debris) villages, extending for 2 miles along the base of the northern wall of Frijoles Canyon. The remains of such large pueblos as **Tyuonyi** and **Tsankawi** may also be visited. NR
For further information write: Superintendent, Los Alamos, NM 87544

LOS ALAMOS SCIENTIFIC LABORATORY NATIONAL HISTORIC LANDMARK, *Central Avenue*
Founded in 1943 on the remote Pajarito Plateau, the Los Alamos Scientific Laboratory was the home of the first atomic bomb, which was detonated some 200 miles to the south. The laboratory has since developed the hydrogen bomb and other nuclear weapons and has also contributed to the peaceful uses of nuclear energy. **Bradbury Science Hall**, nearby, contains exhibits on the applications of nuclear energy. NR
Bradbury Science Hall open: Mon–Fri 8–12, 1–5; closed holidays

MESILLA PLAZA NATIONAL HISTORIC LANDMARK, *on State 28*
On July 4, 1854, the American flag was raised over Mesilla Plaza, confirming the Gadsden Purchase Treaty, in which the United States acquired the southern route to California from the Rio Grande Valley. The village of Mesilla had been established on Mexican soil in 1850. After the realignment of the international boundary, the town played an influential role in the development of the Southwest by serving as capital of the territory that included New Mexico and Arizona, as a headquarters for the range cattle industry, and as a central point on the **Butterfield Overland Mail Route.** During the Civil War Mesilla was successively occupied by Confederate and Union forces. Today the plaza, with its church at one end and adobe buildings, retains much of its original appearance. NR

PECOS NATIONAL MONUMENT, *south of Pecos on State 63*
Pecos is a multistoried, 600-room quadrangular village built around a central plaza by Pueblo Indians during the 14th and 15th centuries. It served as the point of departure for Francisco Vásquez de Coronado's 1541 expedition to the legendary land of Quivira, as a landmark for other early explorers, and as a trading center for the Pueblo and Plains Indians. In the 1620s the Franciscans established the mission of **Nuestra Señora de Los Angeles de Porciúncula** at Pecos, which was then one of the largest pueblos in New Mexico. The mission was destroyed during the Pueblo Rebellion of 1680 and rebuilt after the Spanish reconquest of 1692–93. The population of Pecos began to decline in the middle of the 18th century as a result of disease and warfare with the Comanches, and the pueblo was abandoned by its last 17 occupants in 1838. Today the ruins of 2 major pueblos, the convent and church, and a restored kiva may be seen. NR
For further information write: Drawer 11, Pecos, NM 87552

PUNTA DE AGUA VICINITY

QUARAI NATIONAL HISTORIC LANDMARK, *1 mile south on secondary road*

Ruins of a Tiwas Indian pueblo and a church, **La Púrisima Concepción de Cuarac,** at this site commemorate Indian involvement in 17th-century controversies between church and state. Situated among the salt-lake pueblos east of the Manzano Mountains, Quarai was established in the 1300s; in the 1620s Franciscan priests founded a mission here. The Tiwas were discovered in a plot to revolt during a church-state squabble late in the 1660s. Quarai was abandoned in 1672 after repeated Apache raids. NR
Open daily 9–5

RATON PASS NATIONAL HISTORIC LANDMARK, *U.S. 85–87, Colorado-New Mexico border*

Crossing the Raton Mountains, this pass provided an alternate route to the Cimarron Cutoff segment of the **Santa Fe Trail.** During the Mexican War, the Raton Pass served as an invasion route into New Mexico. Later, during the Civil War, when Indian hostilities nearly halted traffic across the Cimarron Desert, most travelers were forced to take this hazardous passage, nearly 8,000 feet above sea level, through the mountains. NR

SANTA FE AND VICINITY

BARRIO DE ANALCO HISTORIC DISTRICT NATIONAL HISTORIC LANDMARK

One of the nation's oldest European settlements, this barrio, or district, was founded in the 1620s across the Santa Fe River from the side of town where prominent officials and citizens lived. Characterized by numerous examples of adobe construction, which merged Indian and Spanish building styles, the barrio continues to be an active working-class neighborhood. NR

GLORIETA PASS BATTLEFIELD NATIONAL HISTORIC LANDMARK, *10 miles southeast on U.S. 84–85*

The decisive Civil War battle in the Far West occurred at Pigeon's Ranch in Glorieta Pass on March 28, 1862. Texas volunteers under Brigadier General Henry H. Sibley had invaded New Mexico and launched an offensive against Fort Union (*see*) in order to gain control of Colorado's silver mines for the Confederacy. Clashing with Union troops under Colonel John P. Slough about 70 miles southwest of Fort Union, the Confederates almost had victory in their grasp when a Union flanking column succeeded in destroying the Confederate supply depot at the mouth of Apache Canyon. The Southerners were thus forced to withdraw from New Mexico. As a result, the Southwest from New Mexico to California was preserved for the Union. Today many of the key positions of the engagement may be identified. NR

PALACE OF THE GOVERNORS NATIONAL HISTORIC LANDMARK, *north side of the plaza*

The oldest public building in the United States was erected in 1610 by Governor Pedro de Peralta, who established Santa Fe as the capital of the Spanish Southwest. The building served as the Spanish seat of government for more than 2 centuries, except for the period of the Pueblo Rebellion of 1680, when the palace was seized by Indians and occupied until the reconquest in 1693. In 1821 the Mexican government took over the palace for official business.

General Stephen Watts Kearny raised the American flag at the building during the Mexican War of 1846. It subsequently housed 22 U.S. territorial governors. Today the palace has been restored and contains a museum devoted to the history of New Mexico. NR
Open: Tues–Sat 9–5, Sun, holidays 2–5

SANTA FE PLAZA NATIONAL HISTORIC LANDMARK
This historical heart of Santa Fe, founded as the Spanish capital of New Mexico in 1610 and the oldest seat of government in the United States, was the terminus of the **Old Santa Fe Trail**. The plaza is associated with such landmarks as the palace of the governors (*see*) and the nearby **Mission of San Miguel**, which was begun in 1610 and is one of the oldest churches in the country. NR
Mission of San Miguel open daily 8:30–11:30, 1–5:30

TAOS
BLUMENSCHEIN HOUSE NATIONAL HISTORIC LANDMARK, *Ledoux Street*
Ernest Blumenschein, who in 1898, along with Bert Philips, co-founded and led the Taos Art Colony, which inspired the modern art movement in the Southwest, resided in this adobe house. Through the efforts of Blumenschein and others, Taos became the most important art center west of the Mississippi River. NR
Open by appointment

CARSON HOUSE NATIONAL HISTORIC LANDMARK, *Kit Carson Avenue*
Kit Carson made this adobe house his residence from 1843, when he married the beautiful Josefa Jaramillo, until his death in 1868. During his colorful career, Carson earned renown as a mountain man, trapper, scout, and Indian fighter. Famous personalities of the day often rendezvoused at the Carson house, which today has been restored and contains a museum. Carson and his wife are buried in the cemetery in nearby **Kit Carson State Memorial Park**. NR
House open: summer, daily 7–7:30; winter, daily 8–5; closed holidays

TAOS PUEBLO NATIONAL HISTORIC LANDMARK, *3 miles north*
Built by the Tigua Indians, these 5-story communal dwellings—the tallest pueblo buildings in the Southwest—recall Indian resistance to Spanish rule during the 1600s. Spanish explorers had visited Taos Pueblo as early as 1540. Erected about 1598 near the entrance to the pueblo, the **Mission of San Geronimo** was destroyed and rebuilt twice before the Indian uprising of 1680. After reconquest, in 1694, the mission was re-established and continued to operate until 1847, when it was bombarded by American troops under Colonel Sterling Price during the Taos Rebellion. Only ruins of the mission remain. Taos Pueblo still houses about 1,400 Indians. NR

ZUNI VICINITY
HAWIKUH RUIN NATIONAL HISTORIC LANDMARK, *12 miles southwest, Zuñi Indian Reservation*
This Zuñi Indian pueblo, now in ruins, was the largest of the "Seven Cities of Cíbola," whose rumored wealth inspired Francisco Vásquez de Coronado's expedition into New Mexico in 1540. Háwikuh was the first village visited by Coronado, who found no gold but used the pueblo as his headquarters for several months. Ruins may be seen today. NR

NEW YORK

ALBANY

SCHUYLER MANSION NATIONAL HISTORIC LANDMARK, *Clinton and Schuyler streets*

> Philip Schuyler, Revolutionary War general, member of the Second Continental Congress, and U.S. senator, built this mansion (called The Pastures) in 1761–62. Here defeated British commander General John Burgoyne was held prisoner-guest following the Battle of Saratoga (*see*) in October, 1777. The house was also the scene of the 1780 wedding of Schuyler's daughter Elizabeth to Alexander Hamilton. NR
>
> *Open: Tues–Sat 9–5, Sun 12–5*

AMSTERDAM VICINITY

ERIE CANAL NATIONAL HISTORIC LANDMARK, *6 miles west on State 5*

> This 363-mile "ditch" between Albany and Buffalo, built in 1825, linked New York City and the Hudson Valley with the Great Lakes, thereby opening the Old Northwest to settlers and commerce. The canal cost an astonishing $7,143,789 to build, but it was such an immediate success that it paid for itself within a decade. Near Fort Hunter the ditch and locks of the original canal can be seen, along with locks from the improved 1841 canal and a modern lock from the New York State Barge Canal. NR

AUBURN

MILLARD FILLMORE MEMORIAL CABIN, *Washington Street*

> On January 7, 1800, Millard Fillmore, 13th President of the United States, was born in a log cabin very similar to this one. The actual cabin burned down in 1852.
>
> *Open: Apr–Nov, Tues–Fri 1–5, Sat 9–12, Sun 2–5*

Left: Erie Canal lock at Lockport. Top right: George Washington's Newburgh residence. Below: Hudson River view from the Battle Monument at West Point

SEWARD HOUSE NATIONAL HISTORIC LANDMARK, 33 *South Street*

This house, built in 1816, was the home of William H. Seward from 1824 until his death in 1872. Seward's long political career included service as state senator, governor of New York, U.S. senator, and Secretary of State under Presidents Lincoln and Andrew Johnson. The house is now a museum with special exhibits on "Seward's Folly," the 1867 purchase of Alaska. NR
Open: Mar–Dec, Mon–Sat 1–5; closed holidays

BATAVIA

HOLLAND LAND OFFICE NATIONAL HISTORIC LANDMARK, *131 West Main Street*

In 1791 Robert Morris, financier of the American Revolution and land speculator, bought 4 million acres of land extending west of the Genesee River from Lake Ontario to the Pennsylvania border. Morris sold about 3½ million acres of his land to the Holland Land Company, a group of Dutch financiers, in 1793. Joseph Ellicott, company surveyor and resident agent, built this Greek Revival office in 1815 and from here sent countless pioneers westward. NR
Open: Mon–Sat 10–5, Sun 2–5; closed holidays

BENNINGTON BATTLEFIELD NATIONAL HISTORIC LANDMARK, *State 67 near New York–Vermont line*

The American militia enjoyed 2 substantial victories here on August 16, 1777, when forces under John Stark, a hero of Bunker Hill, and subsequent reinforcements prevented valuable supplies from falling into British hands (*see also Bennington, Vermont*). The victories encouraged militia recruits and are credited with contributing considerably to Burgoyne's defeat at Saratoga. NR
Open daily 9–9

BREWERTON

FORT BREWERTON STATE HISTORIC SITE, *U.S. 11*

Only the earthworks remain of this small post, which protected the route between Albany and Fort Ontario (*see Oswego*) between the French and Indian War and Pontiac's Rebellion of 1763–66.
Open: Apr 1–Oct 31, daily during daylight hours

BUFFALO

THEODORE ROOSEVELT INAUGURAL NATIONAL HISTORIC SITE, *641 Delaware Ave*

On September 14, 1901, at 3:15 P.M., Theodore Roosevelt took the presidential oath of office in the library of this house, thus becoming the nation's 26th Chief Executive. Roosevelt came to the house of his friend Ansley Wilcox, a prominent lawyer, when word reached him that William McKinley had died of an assassin's attack. NR
Open: Mon–Sat 10–5, Sun 12–6

CROWN POINT

CROWN POINT STATE HISTORIC RESERVATION, *Route 8*

This site at the southern end of Lake Champlain contains the remnants of 2 forts—**Fort St. Frédéric** (NHL), built by the French in 1731, and **Fort Crown Point** (NHL), built by the British about 1760. The terrain between Lakes Champlain and George (*see also Ticonderoga*) and the Hudson River became the principal battleground during the French and Indian War. The British post, also called

Fort Amherst, is considered to be one of the finest examples of 18th-century military engineering in the country. Destroyed by fire in 1773, it was partially reconstructed when the Revolution began. Five great stonework bastions are intact, as well as the moat and walls. A museum is located near the ruins of Fort St. Frédéric.
Open: May 30–Sept 15, daily 8–4:30

FORT EDWARD

OLD FORT HOUSE, *27 Broadway*

Built in 1773, this frame house was a tavern and courthouse before the Revolution. During the war it was occupied by both sides and served as headquarters for Generals Schuyler, Arnold, Washington, Stark, and Burgoyne. It is now a historical museum.
Open: July–Aug, daily 1–5

FORT JOHNSON

OLD FORT JOHNSON, *State 5*

Sir William Johnson, British superintendent for Indian affairs, built this stately stone manor house in 1749. Originally called Mount Johnson, it was renamed during the French and Indian War when a palisade was built for protection. During the Revolution the house was confiscated by patriots, and the lead roof was stripped to be used for bullets. The restored house is now a museum. (*See also Johnson Hall in Johnstown.*)
Open: May–June, Sept–Oct, daily 1–5; July–Aug, Tues–Sat 10–5, Sun–Mon 1–5

HUNTINGTON STATION, LONG ISLAND

WALT WHITMAN HOUSE STATE HISTORIC SITE, *246 Walt Whitman Road*

On May 31, 1819, Walt Whitman was born in this simple 2-story farmhouse built by his father. The house features furnishings and paintings and a large collection of the poet's manuscripts, as well as paintings and sculptures of him.
Open daily 10–4

HYDE PARK

HOME OF FRANKLIN D. ROOSEVELT NATIONAL HISTORIC SITE, *U.S. 9*

On January 30, 1882, Franklin Delano Roosevelt was born in this beautiful frame house, which his father had bought in 1867. Through his long political career as state senator, assistant secretary of the Navy, vice-presidential candidate, governor of New York, and President of the United States, F.D.R. often returned here, and from 1933 to 1945 it was known as the Summer White House. On the 187-acre historic site are the main house, the presidential library and museum, and the Roosevelts' grave sites. NR
House open daily 9–5:30. Museum open daily 9–5; both closed Christmas

VANDERBILT MANSION NATIONAL HISTORIC SITE, *U.S. 9*

Called the symbol of an era, this magnificent 54-room Italian Renaissance palace is representative of the grand estates built by America's industrial millionaires in the post-Civil War years. Frederick W. Vanderbilt, grandson of the "commodore," had his mansion built in 1896 by McKim, Mead & White, the nation's foremost architects, at a cost of $660,000. NR
Open: Wed–Sun 9–5:30; closed Christmas

JOHNSTOWN

JOHNSON HALL NATIONAL HISTORIC LANDMARK, *139 Hall Ave*
This Georgian frame house was the residence of Sir William Johnson from 1763 until his death in 1774. As British superintendent of Indian affairs, Johnson was considered the most influential white man dealing with the Indians and helped keep the Iroquois on the British side during the French and Indian War. NR
Open: Tues–Sat 9–5; Sun 1–5

KATONAH

JOHN JAY HOMESTEAD STATE HISTORIC SITE, *off State 22*
When Supreme Court Chief Justice John Jay retired from public service in 1801, he came to this lovely clapboard farmhouse. One of the outstanding men of his time, Jay also served as president of the Continental Congress, negotiator and signer of the peace treaty with Great Britain, and governor of New York. Except for one new wing, the house remains as it was when Jay died here in 1829.
Open daily 9–5

KINDERHOOK VICINITY

VAN BUREN HOME NATIONAL HISTORIC LANDMARK, *east on State 9H*
Martin Van Buren, eighth President of the United States, lived in this Georgian house (called Lindenwald) from his retirement in 1841 until his death in 1862. A protégé of Andrew Jackson's, Van Buren served as state senator, U.S. senator, Secretary of State, and Vice President before his election as Chief Executive in 1836. A previous owner of the house employed Washington Irving as a tutor for his children, and it is said that Irving wrote some of his stories here. NR
Open by appointment

KINGSTON

CLINTON AVENUE HISTORIC DISTRICT
In 1658, following an Indian attack, Peter Stuyvesant ordered a stockade built to protect the founders of this Hudson River settlement. First called Esopus for a native tribe and then Wiltwyck, the village was named Kingston by the British. Along Clinton Avenue are the historic Senate House (*see*) and the **Academy Green,** where Stuyvesant signed a treaty with the Indians. NR

SENATE HOUSE STATE HISTORIC SITE, *312 Fair Street*
The first elected senate of the state of New York met in a room in this house on September 10, 1777. A month after that first meeting the British attacked Kingston and burned every house. The Senate House was repaired and used as a residence until the state purchased it in 1887. The chamber is now furnished as it was in 1777, and a regional historical museum adjoins the house. NR
Open: Mon–Sat 9–5, Sun 1–5

LAKE GEORGE VILLAGE VICINITY

FORT WILLIAM HENRY REPLICA, ½ *mile south of village on U.S. 9*
In 1755, during the French and Indian War, Sir William Johnson built this fort near the southern end of Lake George. After repeated assaults by the French, the post was captured in 1757 and destroyed by a force under Montcalm. Replicas of the barracks, stockade, and dungeon can be seen.
Open: May, June, Sept, Oct, daily 10–5; July–Aug, daily 9–10

LAKE GEORGE BATTLEFIELD PARK, ½ *mile south of village off U.S. 9*
This park commemorates the Battle of Lake George, an encounter on September 8, 1755, in which Sir William Johnson's British troops defeated French invaders from Fort St. Frédéric (*see Crown Point*). But Sir William let victory slip away by marching his men back to Albany. The park also contains the ruins of **Fort George,** a partially completed post begun in 1759, and a memorial to Saint Isaac Jogues, a French Jesuit missionary murdered in 1646.

LAKE PLACID
JOHN BROWN FARM STATE HISTORIC SITE, *4 miles south on State 73*
John Brown, self-styled liberator of the slave, was buried here on his farm following his execution for attempted seizure of the Federal arsenal at Harpers Ferry, Virginia, in October, 1859.
Open: Mon–Sat 9–5, Sun 1–5

LITTLE FALLS

HERKIMER HOME STATE HISTORIC SITE, *3 miles east off State 5S*
Nicholas Herkimer, son of a prosperous German immigrant, built this house overlooking the Mohawk River in 1764. At the outbreak of the Revolution, Herkimer was commissioned a brigadier general of the militia and soon became a national war hero when in August, 1777, he and 700 militiamen successfully repulsed the British at Oriskany (*see Rome*), Seriously wounded during the assault, Herkimer continued to inspire his troops. Eleven days later he died here. NR
Open: Mon–Sat 9–5, Sun 1–5

MOUNT McGREGOR
GRANT'S COTTAGE STATE HISTORIC SITE
Ulysses S. Grant came to this cottage high in the Adirondacks at the summit of Mount McGregor in June, 1885. Suffering from cancer of the throat, Grant hoped that the mountain air would ease his condition and enable him to finish his memoirs. On July 23, one week after he completed his book, Grant died. The house remains much as it was during the 18th President's 6-week stay. NR
Open: Tues–Sat 9–5, Sun 12–5

MOUNT VERNON

ST. PAUL'S CHURCH NATIONAL HISTORIC SITE
This Renaissance Revival church, begun in 1763 and completed in 1790, served for a time as headquarters for Hessian troops during the Revolution. The church was founded in 1665 when the settlement of Eastchester was established. NR

NEW PALTZ
HUGUENOT STREET HISTORIC DISTRICT NATIONAL HISTORIC LANDMARK
Called the oldest street in America with its original houses, this community reflects the 17th- and 18th-century Walloon and French Huguenot heritage of its early settlers. Of the 5 stone houses located on the street, only the **Jean Hasbrouck House** (NHL), begun in 1694, is open to the public as a museum. NR

NEW YORK CITY, THE BRONX

VALENTINE VARIAN HOUSE, *East 208th St and Bainbridge Ave*
Hessians captured this fieldstone house in 1776 and made it their

headquarters. Built by Isaac Valentine in 1758, it became the home of Isaac Varian, mayor of New York from 1839 to 1841. It is now the museum of the Bronx County Historical Society.
Open Sun 1–5

NEW YORK CITY, BROOKLYN
BROOKLYN BRIDGE NATIONAL HISTORIC LANDMARK
A landmark famous the world over for its beauty and design, this bridge was one of the first woven-wire cable suspension bridges ever constructed. Designed by John A. Roebling, the bridge spanned 1,595 feet between Manhattan and the city of Brooklyn and was opened in 1883 after 13 years of construction. Its design and execution, considered a marvel of engineering, were so outstanding that it was 50 years before a significantly longer bridge was built and 70 years before major reinforcements were required. NR

BROOKLYN HEIGHTS HISTORIC DISTRICT
Once the leading residential area of New York, Brooklyn Heights sits on a bluff overlooking the southern tip of Manhattan across the East River. Many of the buildings here were designed by the foremost architects of the pre-Civil War era. The district has been restored, and it now reflects much of its Victorian charm. NR

PLYMOUTH CHURCH OF THE PILGRIMS NATIONAL HISTORIC LANDMARK, *75 Hicks St*
Founded in 1847, this church gained fame as a center of the abolitionist movement in the years before the Civil War. Henry Ward Beecher, minister of the church, attracted the leading antislavery spokesmen of the day here, including William Lloyd Garrison, editor of the *Liberator*, Massachusetts Senator Charles Sumner, and poet John Greenleaf Whittier. NR

NEW YORK CITY, MANHATTAN
CASTLE CLINTON NATIONAL MONUMENT, *Battery Park*
Built in 1811 as part of the defenses of New York City in the imminent war with Great Britain, this fort served a variety of purposes. It was a U.S. military post until 1821, when it was ceded to New York City, which in turn leased it as a place for public entertainment. As **Castle Garden** the fort was the scene of outstanding events such as a reception for Lafayette in 1824 and the American debut of Jenny Lind in 1850. Five years later Castle Garden was converted to an immigrant landing depot. Between 1855 and 1889, when the depot closed, nearly 8 million immigrants passed through. From 1896 until 1941 the **New York City Aquarium** was housed here, and Castle Clinton is now being restored as a fort. NR
Open daily 9–4:30

CENTRAL PARK NATIONAL HISTORIC LANDMARK, *from 59th to 110th streets and from Fifth Avenue to Central Park West*
The 840 acres of landscaped wooded grounds was completed in 1876 according to the inspired designs of Frederick Law Olmsted and Calvert Vaux. The plans of the original roadways for horses and carriages and pedestrian walks have never had to be changed to accommodate the motorcar and the expanded population of the 20th century. The lakes, skating rinks, bandstands, carousel, zoos, free Shakespearean theater, and flower gardens are a few of the attractions that delight the visitor in Central Park.

CITY HALL NATIONAL HISTORIC LANDMARK, *City Hall Park,*
Broadway and Chambers St

>The seat of city government, an architectural masterpiece designed
by John McComb and Joseph Mangin and built in 1802–12, com-
bines a French classical plan with Federal details. The Declaration of Independence was read to the colonial army near this site
on July 9, 1776.
>*Open: Mon–Fri 9–4*

COOPER UNION NATIONAL HISTORIC LANDMARK, *4th Avenue*
and 7th Street

>In 1857 Peter Cooper, manufacturer, inventor, and philanthropist,
founded Cooper Union, an educational institution "for the advance-
ment of science and art." A pioneer in free public education, Cooper
Union offered a unique curriculum of general science combined
with practical training. Spokesmen for many important issues
addressed audiences here, and from this podium on February 27,
1860, Abraham Lincoln launched his campaign for the Republican
presidential nomination. NR

FEDERAL HALL NATIONAL MEMORIAL, *Nassau and Wall streets*

>The nation's first Capitol, Federal Hall was the site of the meeting of
the first Congress and the swearing-in of George Washington as the
first President on April 30, 1789. Built in 1703 as city hall, the building witnessed many famous events: the landmark trial of John Peter
Zenger for freedom of the press, the meeting of the Stamp Act
Congress of 1765, and the meetings of the government under the
Articles of Confederation. When Congress moved to Philadelphia,

*Left: the 305-foot Statue of Liberty overlooking New York Harbor. Right: New
York City's Cooper Union, with a statue of industrialist Peter Cooper in front*

Federal Hall fell into disrepair and was sold for salvage. The present structure, now a museum, was built in 1842 as a customhouse and subtreasury building. A statue dedicated in 1883 by Grover Cleveland celebrates Washington's inauguration. NR
Open daily 9–4:30

FRAUNCES TAVERN, *54 Pearl Street*
This building is a 1907 replica of the one Etienne de Lancey built in 1719. Originally his private residence, the house was converted to a tavern in 1763 by Samuel Fraunces. Here, 20 years later, George Washington delivered his famous farewell address to his officers. The tavern is now a restaurant and museum of the Revolution.
Open: Mon-Fri 10–4

GENERAL GRANT NATIONAL MEMORIAL, *Riverside Drive and West 122nd Street*
This 150-foot gray granite monument overlooking the Hudson River was built as a memorial to Ulysses S. Grant, supreme commander of the Union armies and 18th President of the United States. Familiarly known as Grant's Tomb, the memorial has exhibits relating to Grant's life and the Civil War. NR
Open daily 9–5

HAMILTON GRANGE NATIONAL MEMORIAL, *287 Convent Avenue*
Alexander Hamilton, first Secretary of the Treasury and a proponent of Federalism, lived in this house for the last 3 years of his life. A restoration program is in progress. NR
Open daily 9–4:30

A view of New York City from the East River, showing, from left to right, the Empire State Building, United Nations buildings, and the Chrysler Building

MORRIS-JUMEL MANSION NATIONAL HISTORIC LANDMARK, *160th St and Edgecomb Ave*

Built in 1765 by loyalist Roger Morris, this house served as head-quarters for George Washington from September 14 to October 18, 1776. From here on September 16 Washington directed the **Battle of Harlem Heights,** a successful rout of the British. After the war Morris' property was confiscated, and in 1810 Stephen Jumel bought the ruined house and restored it in the Federal style. NR

Open: Tues–Sun 11–4:30

NEW YORK PUBLIC LIBRARY NATIONAL HISTORIC LANDMARK, *Fifth Avenue at 42nd Street*

This imposing edifice, designed in the French Beaux-Arts style by Carrère & Hastings, was built (1898–1911) on the site of the United States' first world's fair, the Crystal Palace Exhibition (1853–58). The famous collection of more than 4½ million volumes, with specialties in American history and art, makes the library one of the best in the world. NR

Open: Mon–Fri 10–6

ST. PAUL'S CHAPEL NATIONAL HISTORIC LANDMARK, *Broadway between Fulton and Vesey streets*

Modeled after London's famous St. Martin's-in-the-Fields, this beautiful Georgian-style chapel, built in 1764–66, is the only colonial church left in New York. When the British occupied the city in 1776, Sir William Howe, commander in chief of British forces in America, and his staff worshiped here. A special congressional service was held in St. Paul's on April 30, 1789, following the swearing-in of George Washington as the nation's first President. NR

STATUE OF LIBERTY NATIONAL MONUMENT, *Liberty Island*

This colossal statue standing in New York Harbor has come to sym-bolize all that is good in America to millions of people around the world. Dedicated in 1886 by President Grover Cleveland, the statue was designed by Frédéric Auguste Bartholdi as a gift to the United States from the people of France to commemorate the alliance of friendship between the 2 countries. The famous poem at the base was written by Emma Lazarus. NR

Open: Nov–Apr, daily 9–5; May–Oct 9–6

THEODORE ROOSEVELT BIRTHPLACE NATIONAL HISTORIC SITE, *28 East 28th St*

This house, built in 1922, is an exact replica of the brownstone where Theodore Roosevelt was born and where he spent his boy-hood. Roosevelt began his political career in 1881 as a state senator and soon won nationwide attention for his exploits as assistant secretary of the Navy and as the organizer of the famous "Rough Riders." In 1901 Vice President Roosevelt succeeded to the Presidency on the death of William McKinley. NR

Open: Mon–Fri 9–4:30

UNITED NATIONS HEADQUARTERS, *42 East 48th Street at 1st Avenue*

The United Nations was created in 1945 as an instrument of world peace and unity. The headquarters occupies 18 acres along the East River and was the work of the world's leading architects and crafts-men. Guided tours are conducted daily every 15 minutes.

Open daily 9:15–5:15; closed Christmas and New Year's Day

NEW YORK CITY, QUEENS

OLD QUAKER MEETING HOUSE NATIONAL HISTORIC LAND-
MARK *137–16 Northern Boulevard*

> The only extant example of an ecclesiastical frame building in New
> York State, this meetinghouse, begun in 1694, is still in use today.
> Except for a brief period during the Revolutionary War when the
> British used it for a prison, hospital, and stable, the meetinghouse
> has served the Quaker community. NR
> *Open: Sun 2–4; other times by appointment*

NEW YORK CITY, STATEN ISLAND

CONFERENCE HOUSE NATIONAL HISTORIC LANDMARK, *Hylan
Boulevard*

> Admiral Lord Richard Howe, commander of the British fleet in
> America, met delegates from the Continental Congress here on
> September 11, 1776. The American representatives—Benjamin
> Franklin, John Adams, and Edward Rutledge—refused Howe's
> offer of amnesty and peace in exchange for a renunciation of the
> Declaration of Independence and the dissolution of Congress and
> its armies. NR
> *Open: Apr–Oct, Tues–Sun 10–5; Nov–March, Tues–Sun 10–4*

VOORLEZER'S HOUSE NATIONAL HISTORIC LANDMARK, *Arthur
Kill Road opposite Center Street*

> This clapboard house, built before 1696, is believed to be the oldest
> extant elementary-school building in the United States. The school
> dates from the period of Dutch settlement and is now part of the
> **Richmondtown Restoration,** a project that will include 40 buildings
> showing the evolution of an American village. NR
> *Open: Sun 2–5, otherwise by appointment*

NEWBURGH AND VICINITY

KNOX'S HEADQUARTERS, *4½ miles southwest on State 94*

> At various times from 1779 to 1782 General Henry Knox, chief of
> the Continental Artillery, made this colonial fieldstone house his
> headquarters. When Knox, who later became the first Secretary of
> War, left here for West Point (*see*), General Horatio Gates, com-
> mander under General Washington of the Continental Army at
> New Windsor (*see*), made this his headquarters.
> *Open: Mon–Sat 9–5, Sun 1–5*

NEW WINDSOR CANTONMENT STATE HISTORIC SITE, *1 mile
north of Vail's Gate on Temple Hill Road*

> The Continental Army, about 7,000 strong, was quartered here at a
> military village from the fall of 1782 until the spring of 1783.
> Consisting of 700 log houses built in rows and a large public build-
> ing known as the **Temple,** the camp was planned by Baron Von
> Steuben. Discontent among officers was rife, and General Washing-
> ton, headquartered at the nearby Hasbrouck House (*see*), came
> here to end the threat of a military dictatorship. When the camp was
> disbanded the log houses were sold; one has been returned. It is
> the only known extant camp structure built by Revolutionary
> soldiers. Also here are a replica of the Temple and a museum.
> *Open: April 15–Oct, Wed–Sun 9:30–5*

WASHINGTON'S HEADQUARTERS NATIONAL HISTORIC LAND-
MARK, *Liberty and Washington streets*

> From April, 1782, to August, 1783, George Washington made the

Jonathan Hasbrouck House his headquarters while the Continental Army was quartered at New Windsor (*see*). During this time Washington turned down proposals to declare himself king or military dictator of America and made public his belief in the subordination of military authority to civilian rule. Here too he established and conferred the Order of the Purple Heart for bravery by enlisted men. The house was purchased by New York State in 1850, making this the first historic property ever preserved by a state. NR
Open: Mon–Sat 9–5, Sun 1–5

NORTH WHITE PLAINS

WASHINGTON'S HEADQUARTERS (MILLER HOUSE), *Virginia Road*
During the **Battle of White Plains** on October 28, 1776, George Washington made this small frame house his headquarters. Three monuments in White Plains commemorate the battle.
Open: Feb 22–Nov, Wed–Fri 10–4; Sat, Sun 1–4; Tues by appointment

OSWEGO

FORT ONTARIO STATE HISTORIC SITE, *off U.S. 104*
Located at the mouth of the Oswego River overlooking Lake Ontario, this fort played a major role in the defense of this region from 1755, when the British constructed the first fort here. Captured and destroyed by the French a year later, the fort was rebuilt by the British and held by them during the Revolution. The post reverted to the Americans in 1796, only to be recaptured and destroyed by Great Britain during the War of 1812. A third fort was built here in 1839 and modernized during the Civil War. The post was abandoned by the Army in 1946 and is now being restored.
Open: March–Dec, Mon–Sat 9–5, Sun 1–5; closed holidays

OYSTER BAY, LONG ISLAND

RAYNHAM HALL, *20 West Main Street*
During the Revolution the British made this house their headquarters. The conspiracy between Major John André and Benedict Arnold to betray West Point was in large part uncovered here.
Open: Mon–Sat 10–12, 1–5, Sun 1–5; closed Tues

SAGAMORE HILL NATIONAL HISTORIC SITE, *Cove Neck Road*
Built as a summer residence by Theodore Roosevelt in 1884–85, this house soon became his permanent home. From 1901, when he assumed the Presidency on the death of William McKinley, until 1909, Sagamore Hill served as the Summer White House, and it was here on January 6, 1919, that Roosevelt died. NR
Open daily 9–5; closed Christmas and New Year's Day

PALMYRA

JOSEPH SMITH HOUSE, *Stafford Road*
In this frame house Joseph Smith, founder of the Mormon Church, spent his boyhood years. At nearby **Hill Cumorah** Smith had a miraculous visitation and received the "golden plates," which he translated in 1830 as the Book of Mormon.
Open daily 8–6

PLATTSBURGH VICINITY

PLATTSBURGH BAY NATIONAL HISTORIC LANDMARK, *east on Cumberland Bay*
On September 11, 1814, Captain Thomas Macdonough's fleet en-

gaged in a battle here that gave the Americans control of Lake Champlain, thereby thwarting an enemy takeover of New York State. Because of the defeat, a British army of 11,000 was forced to retreat to Canada, leaving behind a sizable cache of military supplies. NR

 VALCOUR BAY NATIONAL HISTORIC LANDMARK, *7 miles south on west shore of Lake Champlain*

An American fleet under Benedict Arnold was severely defeated here by a far superior British flotilla on October 11, 1776. However, the 7-hour battle and another engagement 2 days later delayed the British long enough that they decided to draw back to Canada for the winter. By the next year, the Americans had so increased their strength that they were able to win the Battle of Saratoga. NR

PORT CHESTER

BUSH HOMESTEAD, *479 King Street, John Lyon Park*

General Isaac Putnam made this Georgian house his headquarters from 1777 to 1778 while commanding troops in the Hudson Highlands. The house was built in 1740 by sea captain Abraham Bush.
Open Thurs 1:30–4:30

POUGHKEEPSIE

CLINTON HOUSE, *549 Main Street*

George Clinton, first governor of New York, lived in this house from 1777 to 1782, while Poughkeepsie was the state capital. In 1805 Clinton began an 8-year term as Vice President, serving under Presidents Jefferson and Madison.
Open Wed–Sat 9–5, Sun 1–5

REMSEN

BARON VON STEUBEN STATE MEMORIAL, *Starr Hill Road*

Known as the drillmaster of the American Revolution, Baron Frederick William von Steuben joined the Continental Army at Valley Forge in 1777 and converted the raggle-taggle troops into an effective fighting force. After the war New York granted him 16,000 acres, which he planned to develop into a settlement. He died in 1794 before much progress was made. Steuben is buried in a wooded grove here, and a replica of his log cabin has been constructed.
Open: April 15–Oct 15, Mon–Sat 9–5; Sun 1–5

RENSSELAER

FORT CRAILO NATIONAL HISTORIC LANDMARK, *Riverside Avenue*

In 1630 Kiliaen Van Rensselaer founded an 800,000-acre estate—the only successful patroonship established by the Dutch West India Company. Fort Crailo, the manor house of the estate, was built by Hendrick Van Rensselaer about 1704 and was occupied by the family until 1871. NR
Open: Tues–Sat 9–5, Sun 12–5

ROCHESTER

ANTHONY HOUSE NATIONAL HISTORIC LANDMARK, *17 Madison Street*

For the last 40 years of her life Susan B. Anthony, a leading crusader for women's rights, lived in this house, now a museum. NR
Open: Mon–Sat 11–4, Sun 1–5; closed Wed

NEW YORK

ROME AND VICINITY

 FORT STANWIX NATIONAL MONUMENT, *Spring Street*

The fort that originally stood on this site overlooking the **Oneida Carrying Place,** an important portage on the Mohawk River, was built in 1758. In 1777 an American garrison successfully held off a British siege, which prevented reinforcements from reaching General Burgoyne at Saratoga. Earlier, in 1768, the Iroquois had signed a treaty here by which they ceded to the British a vast parcel of land east of the Ohio River. The fort was abandoned in 1781 and razed soon after; a museum is now on the site. NR

Museum open: Tues–Fri 9–12, 1–4; Sun 1–4

ORISKANY BATTLEFIELD NATIONAL HISTORIC LANDMARK, *6 miles east of State 69*

The small battle that took place here on August 6, 1777, contributed significantly to the defeat and surrender of General John Burgoyne at Saratoga (*see*) in October. The 6-hour battle between militiamen on their way to relieve Fort Stanwix (*see*) and British troops is considered one of the bloodiest of the war. NR

Open: Mon–Sat 9–5, Sun 1–5

SACKETS HARBOR BATTLEFIELD STATE HISTORIC SITE

This small harbor on Lake Ontario was a center of naval operations during the War of 1812. The British twice attempted to capture the harbor, fighting a major battle here in May, 1813. Following the war the original defenses were dismantled; the present buildings were constructed in the 1840s.

Open: June–Sept, daily 9–5

SARATOGA NATIONAL HISTORICAL PARK, *30 miles north of Albany on U.S. 4 and State 32*

 Called the turning point of the Revolution, this battle served the British their first major defeat, encouraged colonial militia enlistments, and convinced the French that they should aid the Americans. By the opening of the campaign on September 19, 1777, General Horatio Gates had a force of more than 9,000 at his command, and after a series of battles (all outlined in the park) General John Burgoyne was forced to surrender on October 17 and return with his army to England. The loss of this army to the British was a decisive factor in the outcome of the war. NR

For further information write: Box 113C, Stillwater, NY 12170

SCHOHARIE

OLD STONE FORT, *1 mile north of Schoharie on North Main Street*

Built as a church in 1772 and converted during the Revolution, this fort was the scene of many British and Indian attacks.

Open: June–Aug, daily 10–5; May, Sept, Oct, Tues–Sat 10–5, Sun 12–5

STONY POINT VICINITY

STONY POINT BATTLEFIELD NATIONAL HISTORIC LANDMARK, *north on U.S. 9W and 202*

On July 15, 1779, one month after the British captured the unfinished fort at Stony Point, General "Mad" Anthony Wayne led a daring night attack to retake the post, thereby giving General Washington complete control of the Hudson. Wayne dismantled the fort, and only the earthworks remain, along with a museum. NR

Open: May–Oct, daily

TAPPAN

DE WINT HOUSE NATIONAL HISTORIC LANDMARK, *20 Livingston Street*

Four times during the Revolution George Washington made this house his headquarters. From here in the fall of 1780 Washington ordered the trial of British spy Major John André, who conspired with Benedict Arnold to betray West Point (*see*). NR
Open daily 10–4; closed Thanksgiving

TICONDEROGA

FORT MOUNT HOPE, *½ mile east of Ticonderoga*

Built during the French and Indian War to protect the La Chute River, a stream connecting Lakes George and Champlain, this post was occupied by both the British and Americans during the Revolution.
Open: May 27–Oct 15, daily 8–sunset

FORT TICONDEROGA NATIONAL HISTORIC LANDMARK, *1 mile northeast on State 73*

Because of its strategic location at the junction of Lakes George and Champlain, this outpost was a cornerstone of the defense of Canada and the Hudson River Valley. The French built star-shaped **Fort Carillon** in 1755, and Montcalm won a major battle here in 1758; but they abandoned it to the British the following year. During the Revolution the post changed hands many times, first falling to the Americans in May, 1775, when Ethan Allen and his Green Mountain Boys captured it. In 1777 it was retaken by the British and destroyed. The restored fort features an outstanding museum. NR
Open: May 15–June, daily 8–6; July–Aug, daily 8–7; Sept–Oct 15, daily 8–6

WEST POINT

UNITED STATES MILITARY ACADEMY NATIONAL HISTORIC LANDMARK

Since 1802, when the Academy was established by Congress, West Point has trained officers for the regular Army. Because of its commanding position above the Hudson River, General Washington insisted that a regular garrison be stationed here, and in 1778 defenses were constructed under the direction of Thaddeus Kosciusko, America's outstanding Polish ally. In 1780 an attempt was made by Benedict Arnold, then commander of the post, to betray the Point, but his plot was uncovered in time. Earlier in the Revolution a chain was strung across the Hudson to block passage of the British fleet; some links from that chain can be seen near **Battle Monument,** a memorial to regular Army men killed during the Civil War. NR

YOUNGSTOWN

OLD FORT NIAGARA NATIONAL HISTORIC LANDMARK, *Fort Niagara State Park on State 18*

Occupying a strategic point on Lake Ontario at the mouth of the Niagara River, Fort Niagara was first built by the French in 1678 and rebuilt in 1720. Six years later the present fort was built, and its capture was a fundamental objective during the French and Indian War and the War of 1812. Parts of the fort are preserved today along with the **Stone House,** a fortified French "chateau." NR
Open: summer, daily 9–8:45; winter, daily 9–4:30; spring and fall, daily 9–sunset

NORTH CAROLINA

ALAMANCE BATTLEGROUND STATE HISTORIC SITE, *4 miles south of Alamance on State 62*

> The encounter that occurred here on May 16, 1771, was one of the preludes to the Revolutionary War. Protesting principally against British economic policies, a band of colonists known as Regulators clashed with the royal colonial militia under Governor William Tryon. The Regulators were defeated, and 6 of their number were convicted of treason and hanged. There is a visitor center and museum. Also on this site is the **John Allen House** (NR), dating from about 1782, a frontier log dwelling recently moved from Snow Camp Community, its original location. NR
> *Open: Tues–Sat 9–5, Sun 1–5*

ASHEVILLE AND VICINITY

> **BILTMORE ESTATE NATIONAL HISTORIC LANDMARK,** *2 miles south on U.S. 25*
>
> The 19th-century French Renaissance mansion built here for George W. Vanderbilt is now a museum of art treasures and historic objects. The gardens were designed by Frederick Law Olmsted.
> *Open: Feb–Dec 15, 9–5. Admission: adults $3, children $1.50*

> **THOMAS WOLFE MEMORIAL,** *48 Spruce Street*
>
> The novelist's boyhood home, described (as Dixieland) in *Look Homeward, Angel,* has been restored and furnished with many original family possessions.
> *Open: May–Oct, Mon–Sat 10–12:30, 2–5:30, Sun 2–6. Admission: adults $1, children 50¢*

Left: Fort Raleigh on Roanoke Island. Right: Nathanael Greene statue near Greensboro. Below: a 1903 photo of the Wright brothers' flight at Kitty Hawk

ATLANTIC BEACH VICINITY

FORT MACON, *Bogue Point, 4 miles east on Fort Macon Road*

The site of Fort Macon, built between 1826 and 1834 and occupied by Confederate forces from the beginning of the Civil War until it was taken by Federal troops on April 24, 1862, is now a state park. The fort itself, pentagonal in design and deeply moated, has been restored and houses a museum. Fort Macon was garrisoned only intermittently in later years, notably during the Spanish-American War and World War II. The immediate area was also the site of several earlier forts, dating from the 1740s and constructed to protect Beaufort Inlet from the incursions of pirates and the Spaniards, who occupied and plundered Beaufort in 1747. NR

Open: Nov–Feb, 8–6; March–Oct, 8–7; Apr–Sept, 8–8; June–Aug, 8–9

BATH HISTORIC DISTRICT STATE HISTORIC SITE

In 1705 Bath became the first incorporated town of the province that became North Carolina. Of especial interest among restored structures is the **Palmer-Marsh House** (NHL), built before 1764 and the home of a prominent colonial official, Colonel Robert Palmer. The parish of St. Thomas Episcopal Church, oldest standing church in North Carolina and one of the oldest in the United States, was formed here in 1701. NR

Open: Tues–Sat 9–5, Sun 1–5. Admission: adults $1, children 50¢

CAROLINA BEACH VICINITY

FORT FISHER NATIONAL HISTORIC LANDMARK, *4 miles south on U.S. 421*

Fort Fisher was the largest earthwork fortification of the Confederacy and of vital importance to Southern forces, since it.kept the port of Wilmington open to blockade-runners almost until the close of the Civil War. Beginning in December, 1864, Federal naval forces began to bombard the stronghold; then on January 15, 1865, Federal troops stormed it and took possession. Soon nearby Wilmington was evacuated as well. Segments of the Fort Fisher earthworks remain, and a visitor center displays exhibits of the related Civil War action. NR

Open: Tues–Sat 9–5, Sun 1–5

CHAPEL HILL

OLD EAST NATIONAL HISTORIC LANDMARK, *University of North Carolina campus*

Old East was the first structure on the campus of the first state university in the United States, dating from 1795. Remodeling of the interior, in 1924, did not alter the building's original lines. Other early structures on the campus are **South (Main) Building, Old West, Person Hall,** and **Playmakers Theater.** NR

DURHAM VICINITY

BENNETT PLACE STATE HISTORIC SITE, *intersection of State 1313 and 1314*

A farmhouse on this site, now reconstructed, is where the Civil War ended to all intents and purposes. Here, on April 26, 1865, General Joseph E. Johnston met with General W. T. Sherman and surrendered some 90,000 Confederate forces in North Carolina, Georgia, and Florida. This was 17 days after Lee's surrender to Grant at Appomattox. NR

Open: Tues–Sat 9–5, Sun 1–5

DUKE HOMESTEAD AND TOBACCO FACTORY NATIONAL HISTORIC LANDMARK, ¼ *mile north on Guess Road and east on State 1025*
The restored frame home of the tobacco pioneer Washington Duke, and birthplace of his sons Benjamin and James, dates from 1851. The Dukes organized the American Tobacco Company in 1890. Near the house is a small log structure that served as the Dukes's first tobacco factory. NR
Open: Apr–Sept, Sun 2:30–5:30

EDENTON, *northeast North Carolina on an inlet of Albemarle Sound*

On October 25, 1774, a group of Edenton women gathered to forswear tea drinking in protest against the British tax on tea and related levies. Thought to be the earliest instance of political activity on the part of American women, the event is commemorated by the bronze **Teapot Memorial** on Colonial Avenue facing the courthouse green. Of interest too are **Chowan County Courthouse** (NHL), **Cupola House** (NHL), **Iredell House** (NR), **Barker House,** and **St. Paul's Episcopal Church.**
Open: Tues–Sat 10–4:30, Sun 2–5. Admission (tour of 5 buildings): adults $2, children and students 50¢

FLAT ROCK VICINITY

CARL SANDBURG HOME NATIONAL HISTORIC SITE, ¼ *mile west*
Connemara was the last home of the noted writer; here he lived from 1945 until his death in 1967, and here he wrote his last works, including the autobiography *Always the Young Strangers* and the novel *Remembrance Rock.* The structure dates from 1838 and was built by Christopher G. Memminger, who served as secretary of the treasury for the Confederacy. Restoration of the home, to include Sandburg's personal and literary effects, has been a recent development. NR
Open daily 8–4:45; closed holidays

GREENSBORO VICINITY

GUILFORD COURTHOUSE NATIONAL MILITARY PARK, *6 miles northwest near U.S. 220*
A 233-acre park occupies the area where a significant battle of the Revolutionary War took place on March 15, 1781. Though the British under Lord Cornwallis won the battle, it was the hollowest of victories. Cornwallis lost approximately a fourth of his troops in the encounter of Guilford Courthouse with a largely inexperienced American force commanded by General Nathanael Greene. Far from furthering the British campaign to subdue the Southern areas preparatory to a major thrust against the colonial armies of the North, the battle here was sufficiently costly to foreshadow Cornwallis' surrender at Yorktown, Virginia, later in the year. The park includes markers and monuments relating to the action; exhibits and an audio-visual program at the visitor center further explain this historic place, and there are also self-guiding walking trails. NR
Open: June–Aug, daily 8:30–6; Sept–May, daily 8:30–5. For further information write: Box 9334, Plaza Station, Greensboro, NC 27408

HALIFAX HISTORIC DISTRICT, *bounded by St. David Street, Roanoke River, the Owens House drainage ditch, and the Magazine Spring Gut*

Of special historical interest in the district is **Constitution House,** now relocated from its original site in Halifax and restored. Here, on April 4, 1776, delegates to the provincial congress met and

appointed a committee to consider "the usurpation and violences attempted and committed by the King and Parliament of Britain against America." Eight days later the committee's findings were adopted by the congress; the report, which became known as the Halifax Resolves, authorized local delegates to the Continental Congress to vote for independence from Britain—the first such official action of any colony. On November 12, 1776, Constitution House was the site of North Carolina's first constitutional convention. A state constitution was drawn up, and Richard Caswell was elected governor by ordinance. A marker locates the site of the **Colonial Courthouse,** where the Halifax Resolves and the first state constitution were ratified. Several historic homes and a colonial cemetery are located in the district as well. NR
Open: Tues–Sat 9–5, Sun 1–5

KINSTON VICINITY
C.S.S. *NEUSE* STATE HISTORIC SITE, *2 miles west off U.S. 70A*
The hull of the Confederate ram *Neuse,* the largest remaining naval vessel of the Southern forces, is on display under a protective roof, and an adjoining visitor center exhibits articles recovered from the hull. The ironclad gunboat saw only brief action before being blown up in 1865, in the Neuse River, to prevent its falling into the hands of Union forces. The recovery operation began in 1961; since 1964 the hull has been in its present location. Another state historic site in the immediate area is the **Grave of Richard Caswell,** North Carolina's first governor.
Open: Tues–Sat 9–5, Sun 1–5

KITTY HAWK
WRIGHT BROTHERS NATIONAL MEMORIAL, *Kill Devil Hills*
On December 17, 1903, the Wright brothers, Orville and Wilbur, launched the first successful flight of a power-driven passenger-carrying airplane. Though the craft was in the air only about 12 seconds and traveled but 120 feet, the event was historic in the most literal sense: it proved the possibility of aviation and spurred a wholly new means of travel. In addition to the memorial itself, there are markers that indicate the takeoff and landing spots. There are also a reproduction of the 1903 craft and structures representing the Wrights' camp as they prepared for the flight. NR
Open daily 8:30–5

LENOIR VICINITY
FORT DEFIANCE, *north on State 268*
Built during colonial days, Fort Defiance originally was an outpost designed to protect the scattered settlers from Indian raids. In 1789 General William Lenoir built his home on the site of the old fort and gave his residence the fort's name. This large farmhouse has been lived in continuously by descendants of the builder, who had a leading role in the frontiersmen's victory over the British at Kings Mountain (South Carolina) in 1780, and who later had a distinguished career as a North Carolina public official. NR

LEXINGTON VICINITY
DANIEL BOONE MEMORIAL PARK, *off State 703*
Boone Park contains the site of a cabin built by the noted pioneer. A **Museum of Relics** is housed in the reproduction of a log cabin, and nearby is a cave that is said to have been used by Boone as a refuge from Indians.

NORTH CAROLINA

MOUNT GILEAD VICINITY

TOWN CREEK INDIAN MOUND NATIONAL HISTORIC LAND-
MARK, 4½ miles southeast on State 73

Indians of the late prehistoric period, with a Mississippian-in-
fluenced culture, established a ceremonial village here, probably
in the first half of the 16th century. Parts of it have been reconstructed, and there is a museum with exhibits of the culture of the
original builders. Of particular interest are a restored temple atop
an earth mound, a priest's dwelling, a burial house, and a palisade
surrounding the area of the temple. NR
Open: Mon–Sat 9–5, Sun 1–5

MURPHY

FORT BUTLER SITE, on U.S. 64

A marble shaft indicates the site of Fort Butler, which was constructed in 1838 when the Cherokee Indians were being systematically removed from their lands in the Southeast and resettled
farther west. Forts such as this were established as points for
gathering the Indians preparatory to the westward march.

NEW BERN

TRYON PALACE, *George Street between Eden and Metcalf streets*

Built between 1767 and 1770 and largely destroyed by fire in 1798,
this magnificent colonial mansion, now restored, was built for
William Tryon, royal governor of North Carolina. It also served as
the first state capitol (until 1794). The Tryon complex includes the
John Wright Stanly House, completed in the 1780s by Stanly,
merchant and patriot, and visited by Washington, Lafayette, and
Nathanael Greene.
Open: Tues–Sat 9:30–4, Sun 1:30–4. Admission: $2, children $1

NEWTON GROVE VICINITY

BENTONVILLE BATTLEGROUND STATE HISTORIC SITE, *2 miles
north on County 1008*

The largest land action on North Carolina soil was this Civil War
engagement, March 19–21, 1865, in which nearly 90,000 troops
participated. General Lee had decided that Sherman's army must
not be permitted to march northward and join Grant in Virginia.
The Bentonville battle was the South's last offensive strategy.
Though outnumbered eventually, Confederate forces under
General Joseph E. Johnston scored some initial successes against
Sherman here; a stalemate occurred, however, when a second wing
of Sherman's forces joined the action. Sherman continued on to
Goldsboro, North Carolina, where reinforcements were waiting.
After their losses at Bentonville, Confederate armies were even
more in need of replacements, and the Southern strategy of stopping
Sherman had failed. The site includes the restored **Harper House**
(NR), a residence used as a field hospital by both North and South
at different times in the action; a substantial portion of the battlefield earthworks; a Confederate cemetery; and a visitor center-
museum. NR
Open: Tues–Sat 9–5

OCRACOKE ISLAND, *barrier beach between the Atlantic Ocean and Pamlico
Sound*

This area was said to be a favorite hideout of the notorious pirate
Blackbeard. **Teach's Hole,** near Ocracoke Inlet, the passage connecting Pamlico Sound with the Atlantic at the southwest end of

the island, was where Blackbeard met his end in November, 1718. During the American Revolution Pamlico Sound was used for transporting munitions and supplies to colonial forces fighting the British.

PINEVILLE

JAMES K. POLK BIRTHPLACE STATE HISTORIC SITE, *12 miles south of Charlotte on U.S. 521 and State 51*

A log house and outbuildings thought to be similar to the original ones were reconstructed in 1967, and there is also a visitor center with exhibits centering on the life of Polk, 11th President of the United States. He was born here on November 2, 1795, and resided here until he was 11, when the family moved to Tennessee.
Open: Tues–Sat 9–5, Sun 1–5

RALEIGH

ANDREW JOHNSON BIRTHPLACE, *Pullen Park*

Andrew Johnson, 17th President of the United States, was born on December 29, 1808, in a small house originally situated on Fayetteville Street in Raleigh. Later it was moved to East Cabarrus Street; shortly after its purchase and presentation to the city, the structure was removed to its present site in Pullen Park. Johnson resided in Raleigh until 1826. The house has been preserved in its original form; the present furnishings, though not the property of the Johnson family, are representative of the period in which the future President lived there.
Open: Sun–Fri 2–5. Admission: adults 25¢, children 10¢

ROANOKE ISLAND, MANTEO VICINITY

FORT RALEIGH NATIONAL HISTORIC SITE, *4 miles north on U.S. 158*

This is the scene of the earliest English attempts to establish colonies within the present limits of the United States. With a patent to explore the New World, Sir Walter Raleigh sponsored the first of 2 settlements on this site in 1585. This did not prosper, in part because of difficulties with Indians, in part because the colonists' main activity was directed more toward locating riches than toward establishing a new home. They returned to England in 1586 with the aid of Sir Francis Drake, leaving behind a small detachment to hold the fort. But when an enlarged company under Raleigh's patronage returned to Roanoke Island in 1587, those who had remained could not be found. This was the beginning of a series of mysteries surrounding the second colonization attempt, which resulted in the so-called Lost Colony. It was here that Virginia Dare became the first child born of English parents in the New World. The going proved difficult again, and Governor John White returned to England for help later in 1587. But England's preoccupation with the threat of a Spanish invasion made it impossible to obtain aid for the colony; when White returned in 1591, he "found the houses taken down and the place very strongly enclosed with a high palisade of great trees, with curtains and flankers, very fortlike." The fate of the 116 settlers of the Lost Colony was never determined and has remained the source of much speculation. But historical records of Fort Raleigh, constructed by the first colonists and rebuilt by the second contingent of 1587, and subsequent archaeological evidence have made possible reconstruction of the original earth fort. Within the present 144-acre area there are portions of the settlement sites of both 1585 and 1587. Other points

of interest are an **Elizabethan Garden** and a visitor center containing excavated artifacts. At nearby **Waterside Theater** during the summer months, Paul Green's symphonic drama *The Lost Colony*, based on the history of the area, is presented. NR
Open: July–Aug, 9–6; Sept–June, 8:30–5. For further information write: Box 457, Manteo, NC 27954

SOUTHPORT VICINITY
BRUNSWICK HISTORIC DISTRICT, *adjacent to Orton Plantation, off State 133 between Wilmington and Southport*
This site contains 2 points of interest from different times in American history. Brunswick Historic District (NR) comprises the remains of the colonial town of Brunswick, which was captured and held for 3 days in 1748 by Spanish privateers and which later became a Southern focal point for resistance to British control of the colonies. By the time of the Revolution, Brunswick had become a leading port for the export of naval stores and lumber to Europe and the West Indies. In 1776 the town was burned by British troops. It was never resettled or restored, but subsequent excavation located foundations of some 60 buildings and uncovered artifacts of scientific and historical interest. Of particular interest are the ruins of **St. Philip's Church.** In 1862 the town site was traversed by a Confederate stronghold, **Fort Anderson.** The fort held out until February, 1865, shortly after the fall of Fort Fisher (*see Carolina Beach*). Well-preserved earthworks are still visible, and from them the visitor can survey the entire area and its legacy from 2 periods of history.
Open: Tues–Sat 9–5, Sun 1–5

STATESVILLE VICINITY
FORT DOBBS SITE, *Fort Dobbs Road*
This was a frontier outpost of the colony of North Carolina during the French and Indian War, completed in 1756 and in use until after the Cherokee Indian attacks of 1759 and 1760. The fort was abandoned officially in 1764, though the actual date of its dismantling has been subject to dispute. Interest in restoration of Fort Dobbs spans more than a century and a half. Archaeological investigation begun in 1969 uncovered the cellars under the central building and the moat in front of the palisades surrounding that building. At the same time numerous artifacts from the period of the French and Indian War were found. Long-range plans call for increasing the land in the vicinity of the fort site and for developing it as both a historic and a recreational area. Meanwhile, earthworks of the old fort are visible. NR
Open daily

TRYON VICINITY
BLOCK HOUSE SITE, $\frac{1}{2}$ *mile off U.S. 176*
Located just within the North Carolina boundary, this one-story structure dates from pre-Revolutionary times. It was originally a trading post; later, instead of serving as a commercial contact with the Indians, it offered protection against the Cherokees. NR

WAXHAW VICINITY
ANDREW JACKSON BIRTHPLACE SITE, *reached by U.S. 521 from North Carolina 75 or South Carolina 5*
Both Carolinas have long claimed to be the birthplace of Andrew Jackson, seventh President of the United States. From his infancy

Jackson lived principally with relatives across the border in South Carolina. But the small North Carolina town of Waxhaw, near the South Carolina line, makes its claim with a monument at the site of **McCamie Cabin,** outside Waxhaw. Jackson, who won fame both as soldier and politician, was born on March 15, 1767.

WILMINGTON AND VICINITY

BURGWIN-WRIGHT HOUSE (CORNWALLIS HOUSE), *3rd and Market streets*

Built in 1772 by John Burgwin, merchant and city and state official, this famous structure served as the headquarters of Lord Cornwallis in 1781.

Open: March 15–April, Mon–Fri 9–4, Sat 11–4, Sun 2–4; May–March 14, Mon–Fri 9–4. Admission: adults $1, children and students 25¢

MOORES CREEK NATIONAL MILITARY PARK, *25 miles northwest on State 210*

On February 27, 1776, North Carolina patriots won a significant victory over Loyalist forces who were on their way to rendezvous with a British expeditionary squadron. The clash occurred at Moores Creek Bridge. The outcome, achieved despite a Loyalist superiority in numbers, helped to prevent a full-scale British invasion of the Southern colonies. It also led to a North Carolina decision, on April 12, 1776, to instruct its delegation to the Continental Congress to vote for independence (*see Halifax*). And it provided moral support for the colonists in their quest for freedom from British rule. Moores Creek National Military Park, established in 1926 and covering 50 acres, contains a visitor center with exhibits describing the battle. Battlefield tours also are conducted from the visitor center. NR

Open daily 8–5; closed Christmas. For further information write: Superintendent, Currie, NC 28435

U.S.S. *NORTH CAROLINA* BATTLESHIP MEMORIAL, *south via U.S. 17, 74, 76, and 421*

One of the most active of American warships in the Pacific during World War II, the U.S.S. *North Carolina* is now a memorial on the Cape Fear River. Open to the view of visitors are the main deck and secondary decks, gun turrets and bridge, and crew quarters. The history of the battleship is mirrored in the ship's museum. A sound and light production, *The Immortal Showboat,* based on the ship's history, is given nightly during the summer.

Open daily 8–sunset. Admission: adults $1, children (6–11) 25¢

WINSTON-SALEM

OLD SALEM HISTORIC DISTRICT NATIONAL HISTORIC LANDMARK

The town of Salem was founded in 1766 by a Moravian colony and was consolidated with Winston in 1913. Now authentically restored, Old Salem is an outstanding example of an 18th-century German community. The more than 30 restored structures include **Salem Tavern** (NHL), built in 1784 and visited by George Washington in 1791, and **Single Brothers House** (NHL), erected in 1768–69 (and enlarged in 1786) of German half-shingle construction as a dwelling for unmarried males over 14. NR

Open: weekdays 9:30–4:30, Sun 1:30–4:30. Admission (tour of entire district): adults $3.50, students $1.25

NORTH DAKOTA

ABERCROMBIE VICINITY

FORT ABERCROMBIE STATE HISTORIC SITE, *east off U.S. 81*

This first Federal fort in what is now North Dakota was built in 1858 Before it was abandoned in 1877, Fort Abercrombie experienced two attacks by Sioux Indians in 1862, including a 5-week siege. The original guardhouse still stands, together with restored blockhouses and a museum, in a state park.

Open: June–Aug, daily 9–9; May, Sept, Oct, daily 9–5

BUFORD VICINITY

FORT BUFORD STATE HISTORIC SITE, *Buford*

Situated near the confluence of the Yellowstone and Missouri rivers, this Army post was in active service from 1866 until 1895, when it was abandoned. It played an important part in quelling Indian disturbances in the area; it was here, in 1881, that Sitting Bull and his band of Sioux followers surrendered following their escape into Canada. Among the surviving structures, administered by the state historical society, are the original stone powder magazine and the officers' headquarters, now a museum.

FORT UNION TRADING POST NATIONAL HISTORIC SITE, *west of Buford*

For nearly 40 years, from the time of its construction in 1828 by a subsidiary of John Jacob Astor's thriving American Fur Company, Fort Union was the most important fur-trading post on the upper

Left: Theodore Roosevelt in the 1880s. Top: blockhouses at Fort Lincoln outside Mandan. Below: buffalo in Theodore Roosevelt National Memorial Park

Missouri River. The Indians of the area brought beaver and buffalo hides in abundance, despite strained relations between them and the white traders due to the introduction of whiskey and then smallpox to the tribes. This early prosperity was heightened by the arrival of the first steamboat, the *Yellowstone,* up the Missouri in 1832. By the outbreak of the Civil War the Army's need for a northern fort had led it to purchase the post. Fort Union was dismantled, and its materials were used in the building of nearby Fort Buford (*see*). Plans for reconstruction of Fort Union have been announced, based in part on the work of such artists as John James Audubon, Karl Bodmer, and George Catlin, who had visited it. Meanwhile the National Park Service provides guided tours of the site. NR
Open in summer

ELLENDALE VICINITY
WHITESTONE BATTLEFIELD STATE HISTORIC SITE, *28 miles northwest off U.S. 281*
A monument and museum are on the site of the last major battle between Federal forces, under General Alfred Sully, and the Sioux Indians east of the Missouri River. The encounter, on September 3–5, 1863, broke Sioux power in the area.
Open: May 15–Oct 15, Mon–Sat 9–4, Sun and holidays 9–7

FORT TOTTEN VICINITY
FORT TOTTEN STATE HISTORIC SITE, *south of Fort Totten*
Originally a Federal military outpost and in active service as such from 1867 to 1890, Fort Totten then became an Indian agency for a reservation that is still home for more than 6,000 Sioux and Chippewa. It was constructed to protect the overland route from southern Minnesota to western Montana and to facilitate the placing of Sisseton and Wahpeton Sioux on a reservation. Fort Totten is one of the best-preserved outposts in the West; 15 original buildings remain, and the site of the cavalry square now serves as the center of the reservation. Historical and wildlife museums are maintained, and programs of Indian dances are offered. NR
Open: June–Sept, daily 8–5

MANDAN VICINITY
FORT ABRAHAM LINCOLN STATE PARK, *4½ miles south of Mandan*
Here, in reconstructed form, are remains of an Indian village and a Federal fort, which occupied the area at different times. There is also a museum, which tells their stories. **Slant Village,** a Mandan community probably dating from the 17th century, is represented by 5 earth lodges, one furnished as the Indians had it, together with tools and other relics. Three blockhouses of the fort (originally named Fort McKeen and constructed in 1872, primarily to protect engineers and workers of the Northern Pacific Railroad) also are on view. Fort McKeen, renamed Fort Abraham Lincoln, became a combined infantry and cavalry post; from these headquarters Custer and the Seventh Cavalry departed in 1876 on their ill-fated Little Big Horn expedition. The fort was abandoned in 1891.
Museum open: May–Nov, daily 9–5

FORT RICE STATE HISTORIC SITE, *22 miles south of Mandan*
For 13 years, beginning in 1864, this fort was garrisoned to protect navigation on the Missouri River. In 1868 it was the scene of a peace council attended by Federal officials and representatives of the Sioux Indians. Several blockhouses have been restored.

NORTH DAKOTA

MARMARTH VICINITY

FORT DILTS STATE HISTORIC SITE, *between Marmath and Rhame*
A plot containing the grave of 8 Federal soldiers and the ruins of
a sod fortification is at this locale. The men were killed in the
defense of a wagon train bound for the Montana gold country when
it was attacked by Sioux Indians in 1864. The hastily constructed
"fort" was named for Jefferson Dilts, a scout for the ill-starred
expedition, who is buried here.

MEDORA AND VICINITY

CHATEAU DE MORES STATE HISTORIC SITE, ½ *mile southwest*
In 1883 a Frenchman intent on founding a cattle empire in the
Badlands established the town of Medora. The Marquis de Mores'
venture did not succeed: only traces of his short-lived meat-packing
establishment survive. But his 26-room frame chateau still stands,
with many original furnishings and other of his belongings.
Open daily 8–5, weather permitting

THEODORE ROOSEVELT NATIONAL MEMORIAL PARK, *headquarters in Medora*
Though primarily noted for its natural beauty, this 70,000-acre
park in the Badlands has an important historical association.
Theodore Roosevelt came to the area in 1883, first to hunt and then
to ranch for a 4-year period. Two Roosevelt ranches were on the
site—the **Maltese Cross** and **Elkhorn**—and the park preserves the
locale of the headquarters of his Elkhorn Ranch. The park is a
memorial to his work in behalf of conservation. NR
Visitor center open: summer, 8–8; rest of year, 8–5

MENOKEN VICINITY

MENOKEN INDIAN VILLAGE SITE NATIONAL HISTORIC LAND-
MARK, 1¼ *miles north of Menoken, Verendrye State Park*
Investigation of this site has established that it is the place where
Pierre de La Vérendrye, the first non-native explorer of the area,
first made contact with the Mandan Indians, in 1738. Excavation
has determined the placement of principal features of the fortifications and has turned up valuable artifacts. NR

PEMBINA, *northeast corner of state, 22 miles northeast of Cavalier*
Pembina State Park includes the site of the first trading post in what
is now North Dakota, built by Charles Chaboillez, a representative
of the North West Company, in 1797–98. In the early years fur
traders were the principal occupants of the area. Then in 1812
Scottish pioneers, sponsored by William Douglas, Earl of Selkirk,
arrived to found the earliest white settlement in the present area
of the state. Just north of the town a marker indicates the site of the
first church and first school (1818). Just south is the locality of **Fort
Pembina,** a military reservation maintained from 1870 to 1895.
Pembina State Museum records the history of this region.
Museum open: Memorial Day–Sept 15, daily 9–5

WASHBURN VICINITY

FORT MANDAN STATE HISTORIC SITE, *14 miles west of Washburn*
The Lewis and Clark expedition spent the winter of 1804–5 here
among the friendly Mandan Indians; here it was that a young Shoshone girl named Sacagawea, or Bird Woman, joined the expedition,
which she served as a guide. The buildings were destroyed by the
Sioux in 1805, but a replica of the fort has been constructed.

OHIO

BOLIVAR VICINITY

FORT LAURENS SITE, ¼ *mile south of Bolivar near State 212*

For about a year, beginning late in 1778, the United States maintained a small military base here, its only fort in the present area of Ohio during the Revolutionary War. Fort Laurens was intended both as a protection against Indians and as a precaution against a possible British strike from the west. An 81-acre state memorial marks the site. NR

Memorial museum open: Mar–Nov, Tues–Sun 9:30–5

CANTON

WILLIAM McKINLEY MEMORIAL, *7th Street, NW*

Located in a memorial park, the tomb, a domed monument, and a historical center with exhibits of McKinley's adult life are visited annually by many tourists. NR

Open: Tues–Sun 9–5

CHILLICOTHE VICINITY

MOUND CITY GROUP NATIONAL MONUMENT, *4 miles north on State 104*

This area was the cultural center of one of the most remarkable prehistoric civilizations in the Americas—that of the Indians now called Hopewell. Much of southern Ohio has a Hopewellian legacy; this site is among the most famous localities where excavation (begun here in 1846) has produced a wealth of artifacts. The site contains 24 burial mounds within a 13-acre earthen enclosure. The remains date from about 1000. NR

Visitor center open: June–Labor Day, 8–6; rest of year, 8–5

Top left: Great Serpent Mound near Locust Grove. Below: Schoenbrunn Village near New Philadelphia. Right: Perry's Victory Memorial at Put-in-Bay, Lake Erie

OHIO

CINCINNATI

HARRIET BEECHER STOWE HOUSE, *2950 Gilbert Avenue*
Originally the property of Lyman Beecher, the house is now a museum dedicated to his daughter, the author of *Uncle Tom's Cabin;* the museum features material on the blacks of Ohio.
Open: June–Sept 15, Sat, Sun, and holidays 10–5

WILLIAM HOWARD TAFT HOME, *2038 Auburn Avenue*
The man who became our 27th President and later Chief Justice spent the first 25 years of his life in this 2-story brick structure, which dates from about 1840 (NR). Also in Cincinnati is the **Taft Museum**, 316 Pike Street, built in 1820, an outstanding example of Federal architecture that contains rare paintings and other art objects. It was presented to the city by Mr. and Mrs. Charles P. Taft.
Home open daily 9–5

CLEVELAND

DUNHAM TAVERN, *6709 Euclid Avenue*
Originally built as a farmhouse in 1832, the frame structure was more famous as a stopping place on the Buffalo–Cleveland–Detroit stage road. Restored as a stagecoach inn, it is one of the oldest buildings in the city proper and now houses a museum collection devoted to early Americana.
Open: Tues–Sun 12:30–4:30; closed holidays

GARFIELD MONUMENT, *Lakeview Cemetery off Euclid Avenue*
The tomb of the twentieth President, James A. Garfield, is here, together with a monument to him.

DAYTON

DUNBAR HOUSE NATIONAL HISTORIC LANDMARK, *219 North Summit Street*
Paul Laurence Dunbar, who rose from poverty to "poet laureate" of black America, returned home to Dayton to spend the last three years (1903–6) of his life in this house, now a state memorial. Personal belongings of the noted poet, novelist, and short-story writer are on display here. NR
Open: June–Sept, Wed–Sun 10–5

DEFIANCE

FORT DEFIANCE SITE, *Washington and Fort streets*
In 1794, on a site that is now a city park, General Anthony Wayne constructed this short-lived outpost, which was in ruins when General William Henry Harrison built **Fort Winchester,** nearby above the west bank of the Auglaize River, in 1812. The Fort Winchester Memorial Bridge is now on the site of this second outpost. Opposite the site of Fort Defiance, on the north bank of the Maumee River, is the locality believed to be the birthplace of the Indian chief Pontiac.

EAST LIVERPOOL VICINITY

U.S. PUBLIC LAND SURVEY NATIONAL HISTORIC LANDMARK, *at eastern edge of town*
On the Ohio-Pennsylvania boundary (also in Beaver County, Pennsylvania) is the beginning point of the United States Public Land Survey. Here in 1785 Thomas Hutchins, first geographer to the United States, initiated the rectangular land survey system, which was employed thereafter in surveying the vast public domain, out of which came 31 states. NR

EATON VICINITY

FORT ST. CLAIR SITE, *1 mile west via State 122*

This small fort, built in 1791–92 by General James Wilkinson, was in the area that was the scene of Indian resistance to American occupation of the land north and west of the Ohio River. In 1792 militia under the command of Major John Adair fought a battle with Miami Indians under Chief Little Turtle here. Archaeological excavation determined the site of the supply fort named St. Clair; it is on an 89-acre plot that is now a state memorial. NR
Open daily during daylight hours

FORT JEFFERSON

FORT JEFFERSON SITE, *State 121*

The locality of still another outpost that served this area in pioneer days is now a state memorial. The fort was built by forces of General Arthur St. Clair in 1791. NR
Open daily during daylight hours

FORT RECOVERY

FORT RECOVERY SITE, *near intersection of State 49 and 119*

The site of this outpost, now a state memorial, was the scene of a major Indian victory over American expansion westward. Forces under General Arthur St. Clair had moved from newly constructed Fort Jefferson (*see*) to this site in 1791; on November 3 and 4 they engaged the Indians and suffered the loss of some 900 men before falling back to Fort Jefferson. In 1793 General Anthony Wayne, determined to avenge the rout, returned to the battleground and built the fort he named Recovery to signify American reoccupation of the area. On June 30, 1794, an Indian force attacked a supply detachment encamped just outside Fort Recovery; this time the American troops were able to make an orderly withdrawal to the fort and to withstand an Indian assault. The encounter marked a turning point in the Indians' ill-fated attempt to repel the white man's expansion into this area. The partially restored fort includes 2 blockhouses with a connecting stockade wall. A museum re-creates the action here and at other points in the territory of the Indian wars of the 1790s. NR
Memorial open daily during daylight hours. Museum open: March–Nov, Tues–Sun 9:30–5

FREMONT

FORT STEPHENSON SITE, *Croghan, Arch, and High streets*

On August 2, 1813, American forces under Major George Croghan successfully defended Fort Stephenson, built in that year, against British and Indian attack in the last battle of the War of 1812 on Ohio soil. Though greatly outnumbered, Croghan and his men made effective use of a single cannon by shifting it from position to position. The site of the fort is now Fort Stephenson Park, which contains a public library; on the library lawn is displayed the famous cannon, dubbed Old Betsy. A museum in the library displays Indian and pioneer relics.
Open: Mon–Fri 9:30–8:30, Sat 9:30–6; closed Wed afternoons in summer

HAYES HOME NATIONAL HISTORIC LANDMARK, *1337 Hayes Ave*

Spiegel Grove, the 25-acre estate of the 19th President of the United States, Rutherford B. Hayes, includes the 1859 Victorian family residence and a historical museum and extensive presidential

library. A monument marks the graves of Hayes and his wife. NR
*Home open: Sun–Tues 2–5, Wed–Sat 9–5. Library-museum open:
Mon–Sat 9–5, Sun and holidays 1:30–5*

GNADENHUTTEN

GNADENHUTTEN MASSACRE SITE, *1 mile south*
Some 90 Christian Indians were slaughtered by drunken American
militiamen in the Indians' mission huts and cabins on March 8,
1782. The bodies of the martyrs are buried here, and there is a
museum on the grounds, which are a state memorial. NR

GREENVILLE

FORT GREENVILLE SITE, *West Main Street and Public Square*
Built in 1793 as winter quarters for the American forces of General
Anthony Wayne, this fort, though short-lived, was the site of significant negotiations between the Federal government and Indian
tribes. From these dealings, in 1795, came the Treaty of Greenville; as a result of Wayne's victory at Fallen Timbers (*see Maumee*),
the Indians ceded much of the Northwest Territory.

LANCASTER

SHERMAN HOUSE NATIONAL HISTORIC LANDMARK, *137 East
Main Street*
Here is the birthplace of General William T. Sherman and his
brother, Senator John Sherman. The restored building contains a
re-creation of the general's Civil War field tent and other exhibits.
Open: June–Oct, Tues–Sun 9:30–5

LEBANON VICINITY

FORT ANCIENT NATIONAL HISTORIC LANDMARK, *7 miles southeast on State 350*
Prehistoric Indian earthworks are here in a hilltop area. Though
the original construction was by people of the Hopewell culture,
the name of the site, which has the appearance of a fortification,
applies to a group that occupied it at a later time. A museum has
exhibits of Hopewell and other prehistoric Indian cultures. NR
Open: March–Nov, Tues–Sun 9:30–5

LOCUST GROVE VICINITY

SERPENT MOUND NATIONAL HISTORIC LANDMARK, *4 miles
northwest on State 73*
The Great Serpent Mound, occupying a hill crest parallel to Brush
Creek, is the largest serpent effigy mound in the United States,
nearly a quarter mile in length. It was also one of the first areas to
be set aside because of its prehistoric associations and scientific
value. Excavations have determined the plan of its construction by
the Adena Indians between 1000 B.C. and A.D. 700. NR
Museum open: Apr–Oct, daily during daylight hours

MARIETTA

CAMPUS MARTIUS MUSEUM, *corner of Second and Washington streets*
Marietta, the oldest settlement in Ohio and the first permanent one
in the Northwest Territory under the Ordinance of 1787, is the home
of the pioneer museum Campus Martius. Among the old buildings
on display is the **Ohio Company Land Office** (1788), now restored.
The home of Rufus Putnam (1788), leader of the pioneer band who
first settled here in April, 1788, is also on display. NR
Open: Mon–Sat 9–5, Sun 1–5

MARION

HARDING HOME NATIONAL HISTORIC LANDMARK, *380 Mount Vernon Avenue*

> From the front porch of this modest house, Harding conducted the campaign that resulted in his election as our 29th President. Most of his adult life was spent in the restored structure. A museum behind it includes pertinent historical material. NR
> *Open: Mon–Sat 10–5, Sun 10–6*

MAUMEE VICINITY

FALLEN TIMBERS BATTLEFIELD NATIONAL HISTORIC LANDMARK, *2 miles west on U.S. 24*

> American forces under General Anthony Wayne defeated the Indians and supporting Canadian militia here on August 20, 1794. As a result came a treaty signed (1795) at Greenville (*see*), which established United States sovereignty in the Northwest Territory and furthered its expansion in the area that became Ohio. NR

MENTOR

GARFIELD HOME NATIONAL HISTORIC LANDMARK, *1059 Mentor Avenue*

> Forty years before Warren Harding's "front porch" campaign, James A. Garfield used much the same technique in running successfully for the Presidency. Lawnfield, constructed in 1832, was his base. Now the Garfield residence has been restored, including a bedroom and study containing Garfield's personal belongings. NR
> *Open: May–Oct, Tues–Sat 9–5, Sun and holidays 1–5*

MILAN

EDISON BIRTHPLACE NATIONAL HISTORIC LANDMARK, *9 Edison Drive*

> The noted inventor Thomas A. Edison was born in this brick cottage in 1847, 6 years after its construction, and spent the first 7 years of his life here. The dwelling contains some Edison mementos and a few original furnishings. NR
> *Open: Feb 11–March 31, Fri–Sat 9–5, Sun 1–5; Apr 1–Dec 1, Tues–Sat 9–5, Sun 1–5*

MOUNT NEBO

WILLIAM HENRY HARRISON TOMB, *State 128 near North Bend*

> The ninth President of the United States, who earlier had a distinguished military career, is buried here. NR

NEW PHILADELPHIA VICINITY

SCHOENBRUNN VILLAGE, *1 mile southeast on U.S. 250*

> This state memorial is a reproduction of a village, the first Moravian mission settlement for Indians in Ohio, built in 1772 at the invitation of the Delaware chief King Netawatwes. NR
> *Open: March–Apr, Oct–Nov, daily 9–5; May–Sept, 9–6*

NEWARK

NEWARK EARTHWORKS NATIONAL HISTORIC LANDMARK, *Mound Builders State Memorial, State 79*

> The Newark vicinity is especially rich in prehistoric Indian earthworks dating from about 650 B.C. This example of Hopewellian construction contains an effigy mound in the shape of an eagle. A museum is devoted to Ohio Indian art. NR
> *Open: March–Nov, Tues–Sun 9:30–5*

OHIO

NILES

NATIONAL WILLIAM McKINLEY BIRTHPLACE MEMORIAL, *40 North Main Street*

A museum and library built near the site of his birthplace (now demolished) are dedicated to President William McKinley, a native of Niles.

Open: June–Aug, Tues–Sun 1–4

OXFORD

McGUFFEY HOUSE NATIONAL HISTORIC LANDMARK, *401 East Spring Street*

In the period of his residence here, 1833–36, William Holmes McGuffey wrote the first 3 of his 6 *Eclectic Readers*, pioneer American educational works. The furnishings include the octagonal table at which he worked. NR

Open: Tues–Sun 2–4:30; Sat 9–11, 2–4:30

PERRYSBURG VICINITY

FORT MEIGS NATIONAL HISTORIC LANDMARK, *1.3 miles southwest*

A restored portion of the War of 1812 fort, built by General William Henry Harrison, is here in the form of a state memorial. NR

Open daily during daylight hours

POINT PLEASANT

GRANT BIRTHPLACE, *U.S. 52 and State 232*

The frame cottage in which Ulysses S. Grant was born on April 27, 1822, is now a state memorial, furnished in period pieces.

Open: Apr–Oct, Tues–Sun 9:30–5

PUT-IN-BAY, SOUTH BASS ISLAND

PERRY'S VICTORY AND INTERNATIONAL PEACE MEMORIAL NATIONAL MONUMENT

Near Put-in-Bay, at the Battle of Lake Erie, American forces under Commodore Oliver Hazard Perry won a highly significant victory on September 10, 1813, over a British naval squadron. Not only did it gain control of the lake for the United States, but it opened the way for a successful advance into Canada of Army forces led by General William Henry Harrison. The combined naval and land successes greatly strengthened American claim to the Old Northwest, which was secured by the Treaty of Ghent in 1814. The signing 3 years later of the Rush-Bagot Agreement, which limited the number of warships on the Great Lakes, was the first stage in eventual permanent disarmament of the boundary between the United States and Canada. The memorial, which is on a 21-acre site on the island in Lake Erie, thus commemorates accomplishments of both war and peace. NR

Open daily Apr–Oct

ZOAR HISTORIC DISTRICT, *bounded by Fifth Street, Foltz Street, First Street, and rear lines of properties fronting on West Street*

In 1817 members of a German pietist sect established a village that became an example of communal enterprise. Zoar ceased to exist as such in 1898, but the physical nucleus of the community remains, including the residence of its leader, Joseph Baumeler (Bimeler). A garden follows the Biblical description of the New Jerusalem. NR

Open: Apr–Oct, Tues–Sun 9:30–5

OKLAHOMA

BARTLESVILLE VICINITY

NELLIE JOHNSTONE NO. 1, *13 miles southwest in Johnstone Park*

Drilled in 1897, this oil well was the first commercially important well to be discovered in Oklahoma. A replica stands today. NR

CHEYENNE VICINITY

WASHITA BATTLEFIELD NATIONAL HISTORIC LANDMARK, *northwest on U.S. 283*

This battlefield was the scene of Lieutenant Colonel George A. Custer's attack on the sleeping Cheyenne village of Chief Black Kettle, the "Peace Chief," on November 27, 1868. Custer's tactics here demonstrated the effectiveness of winter-long campaigns, a strategy devised by General Philip H. Sheridan against the southern Plains Indians, who were driven to reservations set aside for them by the following spring. The massacre also set the stage for Custer's fate at the Battle of the Little Bighorn, in Montana, 8 years later. Today the **Black Kettle Museum** near the site commemorates those slain. NR

Open daily 9–5; closed holidays and Mondays from late Oct to late Apr

CLAREMORE

WILL ROGERS MEMORIAL, *1 mile west on State 88*

Will Rogers, the world-renowned humorist and one of Oklahoma's most beloved sons, planned to erect a home at this site. Born in neighboring Oologah in 1879, Rogers made a successful stage career out of his experiences as an Oklahoma cowboy; his writings earned him the epithet "cowboy philosopher." This memorial contains Rogers' grave and personal belongings. The **Will Rogers Birthplace** (NR) is preserved at the Will Rogers State Park at Oologah.

Top left: Cherokee Supreme Court Building at Tahlequah. Below: Will Rogers Birthplace at Oologah. Right: Old Stone Corral at Fort Sill near Lawton

OKLAHOMA

CLEO SPRINGS VICINITY
HOMESTEADER'S SOD HOUSE, *4 miles north on State 8*
Erected in 1894 by Marshall McCully, who came to Oklahoma during the great land rush of 1893, this structure is the only extant original homesteader sod house in the state. The house now contains furnishings typical of 1907, the year Oklahoma achieved statehood. NR
Open: Tues–Fri 9–5, Sat–Sun 2–5

FORT GIBSON NATIONAL HISTORIC LANDMARK
Founded in 1824, this Army frontier post for 16 years acted as custodian of the Cherokee, Seminole, and Creek Indians, who had been forcibly transported from their homelands in the Southeast to Indian Territory in Oklahoma. During this period the log fort protected these tribes from hostile Plains Indians. Abandoned before the Civil War, Fort Gibson was occupied by Union troops during the war and remained reactivated until 1889. The log stockade and many buildings have been reconstructed. NR
Open daily, daylight-saving time 9–7, standard time 9–5

GEARY VICINITY
JESSE CHISHOLM GRAVE SITE, *8 miles northeast*
Buried here is Jesse Chisholm, a mixed-blood Cherokee trader and guide, who in 1867 established the famous cattle-drive route that bears his name. The **Chisholm Trail** ran from the Nueces River in east Texas north through Indian Territory (Oklahoma), and into Kansas—the rail terminal where cattle were shipped east. NR

GUTHRIE, *central Oklahoma on U.S. 77*
The focal point of the land run of 1889, which opened unassigned land in the heart of the Indian Territory to white settlement, Guthrie subsequently became capital of the Oklahoma Territory, created in 1890, and the first state capital when Oklahoma entered the union in 1907. The capital was moved to Oklahoma City in 1910.

LAWTON VICINITY
FORT SILL NATIONAL HISTORIC LANDMARK, *north on U.S. 66, 277, and 281*
Established in 1869 by General Philip Sheridan, this military reservation played an important role in controlling Indian tribes of the southern plains for more than 2 decades. From 1870 to 1878 Fort Sill served as the Kiowa-Comanche Agency. Today the fort is headquarters of the U.S. Army Field Artillery. Surviving buildings of the old post include the **Old Stone Corral** and the **Old Chapel**, both built in 1870. The **Old Post Guardhouse**, where Geronimo and other rebel warriors were detained, contains historical exhibits. NR
Open daily 8:30–4:30; closed Jan 1–2, Dec 24–25

NIDA VICINITY
FORT WASHITA NATIONAL HISTORIC LANDMARK, *southwest on State 199*
Constructed in 1842 near the junction of the Washita and Red rivers, this outpost was established by Zachary Taylor to protect the Chickasaw Indians in the recently created Indian Territory (1830) and to serve as a stopping place for travelers along the **Southern Overland Trail.** The fort was subsequently a base for the exploration of the Southwest. During the Civil War Fort Washita was occupied by Confederate troops. Standing today are the well-preserved and

partially restored commissary warehouse, 2 barracks, quartermaster storehouse, and officers' quarters. NR
Open: Tues–Fri 9–5, Sat–Sun 2–5

OKMULGEE

CREEK NATIONAL CAPITOL NATIONAL HISTORIC LANDMARK
Constructed in 1878, this Victorian edifice served as the capitol of the Creek Indian nation and is symbolic of the Creeks' successful assimilation of white institutions. In their homeland of Georgia and Florida this tribe had developed a form of representative government, which, after their removal to Oklahoma, they remodeled along the lines of the Federal government. Known as the Old Creek Indian Council House today, the capitol contains a museum with displays of Indian craftwork and weapons. NR
Open: June–Aug, Mon–Sat 9–5, Sun 1–5; Sept–May, closed Mon

SALLISAW VICINITY

SEQUOYA'S CABIN NATIONAL HISTORIC LANDMARK, *11 miles northeast on State 101*
This one-room log cabin was erected in 1829 by the famous Indian Sequoya, inventor of the Cherokee alphabet. A native of the Appalachian region where Tennessee, Georgia, and North Carolina converge, Sequoya in the early years of the 19th century became intrigued with the idea that white men communicated with each other through writing, and he set out to devise an alphabet for his tribe. After 12 years of experimenting, Sequoya, in 1821, produced an alphabet or syllabary consisting of 84 characters—each representing a syllable—from which any Cherokee word could be written. Ahyoka, Sequoya's daughter, was the first to use the alphabet, and soon it became widely employed among Cherokees. Sequoya moved with other Cherokees to eastern Oklahoma in 1829, and he subsequently promoted migration to the area. His cabin is now maintained as a shrine. NR
Open daily 9–5

TAHLEQUAH

CHEROKEE NATIONAL CAPITOL NATIONAL HISTORIC LANDMARK
Erected about 1869 in the capital city of the Cherokee Indian nation, this brick Victorian structure is a monument to the Cherokees' ability to adjust their culture to a changing environment. Realizing that their survival depended on peaceful coexistence with the white man's world, the Cherokees, as early as 1765, founded schools to educate their children. The tribe adopted a republican form of government in 1820 and in 1821 became the only American Indian group to publish a code of laws. The capitol currently serves as the Cherokee County Courthouse. Other Cherokee government buildings in Tahlequah include the **Supreme Court Building,** raised in 1844, and the **National Prison,** constructed in 1879. The **Cherokee Female Seminary** is now the administration building of Northeastern State College and houses Indian artifacts. NR
Female Seminary open: Mon–Fri 9–5

TISHOMINGO

CHICKASAW COUNCIL HOUSE, *on courthouse grounds*
Raised in 1856 in the former capital of the Chickasaw nation, this log cabin served as the tribe's first capitol building.
Open: Tues–Fri 9–5, Sat–Sun 2–5

OREGON

ASTORIA AND VICINITY

FORT ASTORIA NATIONAL HISTORIC LANDMARK, *15th and Exchange streets*

In 1811 John Jacob Astor, founder of the Pacific Fur Trading Company, sponsored an expedition to the Columbia River in an attempt to break the British fur trading monopoly. The "Astorians" erected an outpost at this site, the first white settlement in the Oregon Country. During the War of 1812 rumors of an attack by British men-of-war caused the post to be abandoned. Fort Astoria was restored to the United States in 1815, and it subsequently played an important role in the settlement of Oregon. Today a portion of Fort Astoria has been reconstructed. NR
Open daily

FORT CLATSOP NATIONAL MEMORIAL, *4½ miles south near U.S. 101*

Captains Meriwether Lewis and William Clark established their winter headquarters of 1805–6 on this site at the mouth of the Columbia River after their epoch-making exploratory journey across the North American continent. Fort Clatsop was named after a tribe of friendly local Indians, who often came to the camp to visit and trade. Detailed journals kept by Lewis and Clark during their stay at the fort provided the earliest published accounts of the Pacific Northwest, spurring interest in the area and resulting in the eventual creation of the Oregon Territory in 1849. Today a replica of the fort has been built according to Clark's original drawings. NR
For further information write: Supt, Box 604–FC, Astoria, OR 97103

FORT STEVENS MILITARY RESERVATION, *10 miles west off U.S. 101*

Founded by the U.S. Army in 1863, during the Civil War, to prevent

Left: Presbyterian Church in Jacksonville. Top right: Fort Clatsop National Memorial near Astoria. Below: Fort Dalles Surgeon's Quarters at The Dalles

Confederate gunboats from entering the mouth of the Columbia River, Fort Stevens was the longest-active military post within the present borders of Oregon. Named after General Isaac Ingalls Stevens, first governor of Washington, the post was active until 1884; in 1898 it was reactivated and subsequently enlarged. On June 21, 1942, Fort Stevens, which was being used as an Army training base, became the only military installation in the continental United States to be fired upon by the enemy during World War II, when shells from a Japanese submarine fell within 200 yards of Battery Russell. The fort was released by the military in 1947. Today many of the structures of the Upper Fort survive. NR

SAMUEL ELMORE CANNERY NATIONAL HISTORIC LANDMARK, *on the waterfront at the foot of Flavel Street*
 The nation's oldest continuously operated salmon cannery was erected in 1881 at a time when Astoria was the world's leading salmon producer (1876–87). Standing today are the original cannery, storage building, and bunkhouse, which housed Chinese laborers. Other parts of the plant have been modernized and are still in use. NR
 Conducted tours: Mon–Fri 8–11, 1–4; advance notice requested

BURNS VICINITY
PETE FRENCH ROUND BARN, *50 miles southeast at Diamond Station*
 Erected about 1884 and containing a masonry corral for exercising horses during the bitterly cold winters, this barn stands as a landmark to the era when cattlemen from California were expanding north into the open rangeland of southern Oregon. After the Civil War U.S. Army regulars had removed the Indian threat from that part of Oregon east of the Cascades. In 1872 Pete French migrated from the Sacramento Valley to the Blitzen Valley, where he became a prominent rancher; before his death in 1897 he controlled 130,000 acres and 30,000 head of cattle. NR

THE DALLES
FORT DALLES SURGEON'S QUARTERS, *15th and Garrison streets*
 Raised in 1857, this Gothic Revival building is the only surviving structure of the military post that from 1856 until the mid-1860s commanded the gateway between Indian territory east of the Cascades and the Willamette Valley. Named for a series of rapids that interrupted navigation on the middle Columbia River, The Dalles was first settled by Methodist missionaries in 1837. The mission was subsequently sold to Dr. Marcus Whitman, whose massacre by the Cayuse Indians in 1847 near Walla Walla, Washington, brought an end to missionary activity in the area. In 1850 the property was incorporated into the Fort Dalles Military Reservation. Fort Dalles was the principal base of operations in the vicinity during the period of Indian uprisings; it was abandoned by the military in 1867. NR
 Open: May 1–Sept 30, Wed–Mon 9–5; rest of year, Wed–Fri, Sun 1–5, Sat 10–5

FORT KLAMATH VICINITY
FORT KLAMATH SITE, *near junction of State 62 and 232*
 Established in 1863 and garrisoned by militia and U.S. Army regulars for 27 years, this military post protected settlers in the Klamath Lakes region east of the Cascades from hostile Indians. It became the center of operations during the Modoc War of 1872–73 (*see also*

California, Lava Beds National Monument). In 1864 a Federal order created the Klamath Indian Reservation to the south of the fort for the Klamath, Modoc, and Yahooskin Snake tribes. In 1870 a band of renegade Modocs, led by Captain Jack, left the reservation and entrenched themselves in the Lost River country of the northern California border. Two years later troops from Fort Klamath were sent to return the Indians, and after a prolonged campaign they captured the band. The leaders of the insurrection were executed at Fort Klamath. None of the approximately 40 buildings of the fort survives today. A replica of the **Guardhouse** stands at the site. NR

GOVERNMENT CAMP AND VICINITY
OREGON TRAIL MARKER, *west on U.S. 26 at Laurel Hill*

A marker at this site in the Cascade Mountains designates the point where the Oregon Trail began following an Old Indian trail in order to detour the Columbia River rapids and Mount Hood to the Willamette Valley. Extending for some 2,000 miles from Independence, Missouri, to the mouth of the Columbia River, this famous emigrant route was first traced by explorers and trappers in the early decades of the 19th century. The Oregon Trail became a deeply rutted highway during the great westward migration of the 1840s and 1850s, when thousands of pioneers in wagon trains made the perilous passage over it in what was one of the greatest treks of recorded history. Oregon's fertile Willamette Valley was the destination of most travelers.

JACKSONVILLE HISTORIC DISTRICT NATIONAL HISTORIC LAND-MARK, *on State 238*

Founded in 1852 after gold was discovered nearby, this mining boom town flourished for 32 years as the county seat and principal distribution, financial, and trading center of southern Oregon. Jacksonville began its decline in 1884 after it was bypassed by the California and Oregon Railroad. Preserved and little altered today are many of the commercial and residential structures reflecting Jacksonville's importance as a mid-19th-century inland business community. These buildings include the **C. C. Beekman Bank,** which opened in 1853 and saw $31 million in gold pass over its counters before it closed in 1880; the **U.S. Hotel,** built in 1884; and the **Wells Fargo Office,** churches, and the courthouse, which was raised in 1883 and currently houses the **Jacksonville Museum** containing pioneer relics. NR

Museum open: July 1–Labor Day, Mon–Sat 9–9, Sun 12–9; rest of year Mon–Sat 9–5, Sun 12–5; closed holidays

LA GRANDE AND VICINITY
WALLOWA LAKE STATE PARK, *78 miles east off State 82*

The Wallowa region of northeastern Oregon was the homeland of the band of Nez Perce Indians led by the famous Chief Joseph. Although a U.S. treaty of 1855 had established a reservation in the area where Oregon, Washington, and Idaho adjoined, after gold was discovered in the vicinity in 1860 a new treaty of 1863 relegated the Indians to a smaller reservation. In 1877 the threat of government action finally forced the Joseph band to leave the Wallowa Valley. The Indians retreated to Idaho, where they began the Nez Perce War, the last and most extensive war in the Pacific Northwest (*see also Idaho, Nez Perce National Historical Park*). An Indian cemetery containing the grave of Chief Joseph's father may be seen at the northern end of the lake.

OREGON CITY
DR. JOHN McLOUGHLIN HOUSE NATIONAL HISTORIC SITE,
713 Center Street, McLoughlin Park
> This house belonged to Dr. John McLoughlin, a founder of Oregon
> City in 1829. Chief factor of the Hudson's Bay Company, from
> 1824 to 1846 he controlled the Columbia District, a vast area in-
> cluding British Columbia, Washington, Oregon, Idaho, and parts of
> Montana. During his administration McLoughlin won acclaim for
> preventing major Indian uprisings, helping settlers, expanding the
> fur trade, and encouraging the development of agriculture and
> husbandry in the Oregon Country. Restored today, the McLoughlin
> House is one of the few extant pioneer dwellings in the region. NR
> *Open: summer, Tues–Sun 10–5; winter, Tues–Sun 10–4*

PORTLAND AND VICINITY
BYBEE-HOWELL HOUSE, *Howell Park Road, Sauvie Island*
> Built in 1856, this Greek Revival residence is the oldest extant
> structure on historic **Sauvie Island,** which was first recorded in
> the journals of Lewis and Clark. The house has been restored.
> *Open: May–Oct, daily 11–5*

CHAMPOEG STATE PARK, *28 miles south off I-5*
> A monument at this site commemorates the inhabitants of the
> Willamette Valley who, on May 2, 1843, gathered here and voted to
> organize themselves into a community governed by law, thus
> establishing the first effective civil government in the Oregon
> Country. Both American and French-Canadian settlers, who had
> jointly occupied the area since 1818, took part in the 52 to 50 tally.
> The provisional government served until 1849, when Oregon
> became a U.S. territory. During the 1850s Champoeg, situated
> above the falls of the Willamette River, flourished as an important
> trading and transportation center. Champoeg was destroyed in the
> flood of 1861 and was never rebuilt. One house, which survived
> and has been reconstructed today, belonged to the prominent
> Oregon pioneer Robert Newell, who operated a farm, general store,
> warehouse, and steamboats. The **Champoeg Pioneer Museum** con-
> tains historical exhibits.
> *Newell House open: Feb 1–Nov 30, Tues–Sun 8–8. Museum open
> daily 8–5*

SALEM
PARSONAGE OF THE METHODIST MISSION AND JASON LEE
HOME, *Thomas Kay Historical Park*
> These restored buildings are the only remaining structures of the
> Methodist Mission, which was founded in 1834 by Rev. Jason Lee
> and a group of missionaries. They subsequently spurred interest in
> the settlement of the Oregon Country, took part in organizing a
> provisional government (*see Champoeg State Park*), and established
> Oregon Institute—later Williamette University—the first institution
> of higher education west of the Rockies. The original mission station
> to the Indians was built 10 miles north of present-day Salem on the
> Willamette River, and satellite stations soon sprang up in other
> areas. In 1841 the center of operations was moved to the Chemeketa
> Plain, where Salem's first buildings, including Superintendent
> Lee's home and the parsonage for Gustavus Hines, preacher-in-
> charge and director of the Indian Manual Labor Training School,
> were raised.
> *Open: May 24–Sept 3, Sun, Wed, Fri 1:30–4:30*

PENNSYLVANIA

ALLENTOWN
ZION REFORMED CHURCH, *Hamilton and Church streets*

Liberty Bell Shrine, in the church basement, contains a replica of the Liberty Bell, housed where the original bell was kept hidden for safekeeping in 1777 and 1778, during the period of British occupation of Philadelphia. The church where the original bell was kept dated from 1773; the present structure, built on the site of the first one, was completed in 1888.

Open: Mon–Sat 11–4, Sun 2–4; Oct 15–Apr 15, closed Tues

ALTOONA VICINITY
HORSESHOE CURVE NATIONAL HISTORIC LANDMARK, *5 miles west on State 193*

The feat of providing a railroad passage through the Allegheny Mountains, so important to westward expansion, was made possible by this ingenious engineering design, a landmark in its time and still one today. Upon completion in 1854, Horseshoe Curve joined the eastern and western divisions of the Pennsylvania Railroad. The entire course of the famous curve can be viewed from this site. NR

AMBRIDGE
OLD ECONOMY NATIONAL HISTORIC LANDMARK, *State 65*

Within this borough, from 1825 to 1905, was the prosperous industrial community named Economy, which was settled as a religiously motivated utopian experiment by the followers of the German immigrant George Rapp. Community gardens and 17 original Economy buildings are still clustered within a small area. They include the **Great House** (1825), home of Rapp, leader of the

Left: site of Lincoln's address in Gettysburg National Cemetery. Top right: Washington's headquarters at Valley Forge. Below: Ephrata Cloister

Harmony Society, which established the community; the **Music Hall**; and shops. NR

Open: Mon–Sat 8:30–5, Sun 1–5; closed holidays. Admission: adults 50¢

BAUMSTOWN VICINITY

DANIEL BOONE HOMESTEAD, *off U.S. 422*

The famous frontiersman was born in a log house here on November 2, 1734. Sometime in the 18th century it was replaced by the present stone structure, which has been restored and serves as a museum devoted to Boone and to pioneer life in general.

Open: May–Oct, Mon–Sat 8:30–5, Sun 1–5; Nov–Apr, Mon–Sat 9–4:30, Sun 1–4:30

BEDFORD

FORT BEDFORD PARK AND MUSEUM, *123 Pitt Street*

Located in a building patterned on early blockhouses, the museum contains a large scale model of Fort Bedford, constructed on this site about 1758 and originally named Fort Raystown. **Espy House,** now a bakery, was where President Washington maintained headquarters in 1794, when troops were assembled here to put down the Whiskey Rebellion.

Museum open: Apr–Oct, daily 10–9

BETHLEHEM, *eastern Pennsylvania off U.S. 22*

This historic city was settled by Moravians from Bohemia and Saxony, beginning in 1741. Twenty-one structures in the center of Bethlehem remain from the pre-Revolutionary War period, and a walking tour of these begins at the site of **First House,** 427 Main Street (adjacent to Hotel Bethlehem). First House, a log building erected in 1741 as Bethlehem's first structure, was demolished in 1823. Still standing are **Gemein Haus** (now the Moravian Museum of Bethlehem), 66 West Church Street, completed in 1742; **Single Brethren's House** (1748), 89 West Church Street; **Widow's House** (1768), 53 West Church; **Sisters' House** (1744–73), 44–50 West Church; and **Old Chapel** (1751), 64 West Church. Significant buildings also remain from the period 1776–1876; many of these are on the route of a riding tour originating at Hotel Bethlehem.

For further information write: Historic Bethlehem, Main and Church streets, Bethlehem, PA 18018

CARLISLE

CARLISLE INDIAN SCHOOL NATIONAL HISTORIC LANDMARK, *U.S. 11*

During the 40 years of its existence, 1879–1918, Carlisle Indian School, located at **Carlisle Barracks,** was an outstanding educational facility for American Indians. Among its surviving buildings, now part of the Army War College, is **Thorpe Hall,** named for the legendary athlete Jim Thorpe, Carlisle's most famous alumnus. Carlisle Barracks itself dates from 1757; during the Revolutionary War it was a munitions center. In 1951 the Army War College was located here. Also on the grounds are the old **Hessian Guardhouse,** now a museum, and the **Omar N. Bradley Museum.** NR

Bradley Museum open: May–Oct, Tues–Sun 1:30–4:30. Hessian Guardhouse open: May–Oct, Sat–Sun 1–4:30

GRAVE OF MOLLY PITCHER, *Old Graveyard, South Street*

The heroine of the Battle of Monmouth in 1778 (*see New Jersey*), a resident of Carlisle, is buried here, along with other Revolutionary notables.

OLD WEST NATIONAL HISTORIC LANDMARK, *Dickinson College campus*

The heart of the campus of this historic school is the U-shaped building known as Old West, which was designed by Benjamin H. Latrobe and constructed between 1804 and 1822. NR

CHADDS FORD VICINITY

BRANDYWINE BATTLEFIELD NATIONAL HISTORIC LANDMARK, *Brandywine Battlefield Park, on U.S. 1*

Here, on September 11, 1777, the British scored a decisive victory over Washington's forces and were thus able to march on to Philadelphia. Washington's headquarters have been reconstructed, and so has the **Gilpin House** (NR), which was occupied by Lafayette. Also in this area are **Chad House** (NR), off State 100, an old stone structure, and **Birmingham Friends Meetinghouse**, 1245 Birmingham Road, which was used as a hospital after the battle. NR

CHESTER

WILLIAM PENN LANDING SITE, *Penn and Front streets*

On October 28, 1682, William Penn stepped ashore here and renamed the city, which, as Upland, was first settled about 1645. NR

CORNWALL

CORNWALL FURNACE NATIONAL HISTORIC LANDMARK, *off U.S. 322*

The charcoal furnace here, in operation from 1742 until 1883, stands as a representative of the type of facility that produced most of America's iron during that period. In the Revolution, cannon and other munitions were cast here for American forces. Nearby Cornwall mine, still in use, is the oldest iron mine in continuous operation in the United States, and the nation's deepest open-cut mine. East of the furnace is a village of miners' houses dating from the 1860s. NR
Open: May–Oct, Mon–Sat 8:30–5, Sun 1–5; Nov–Apr, Mon–Sat 9–4:30, Sun 1–4:30. Admission: adults 50¢, children (under 12) free

EPHRATA

EPHRATA CLOISTER NATIONAL HISTORIC LANDMARK, *junction of U.S. 322 and 222*

Led by Johann Conrad Beissel, a group of Seventh-Day German Baptists settled this town about 1730 as a communal, semimonastic religious society. The religious orders were virtually extinct by the end of the 18th century, but the society's buildings, known as Ephrata Cloister, were occupied by members until about 1934. Still standing are the **Saal**, constructed in 1740 as a community house; **Saron**, or Sisters' House, 1742–43; Beissel's log dwelling; the **Almonry**, or alms and bake house; an academy dating from 1837; and cottages. NR
Open: summer, Mon–Sat 8:30–5, Sun 1–5; winter, Mon–Sat 9–4:30, Sun 1–4:30. Admission: 50¢

ERIE

FLAGSHIP *NIAGARA* AND PROW OF U.S.S. *WOLVERINE, foot of State Street*

The exhibits here are in one sense memorials to Erie as a shipbuilding center. The reconstruction of the *Niagara* on view is not

only patterned on Commodore Perry's second flagship in the Battle of Lake Erie (1813) but contains a sizable section of the original keel. The *Niagara* made a major contribution to the American victory in this decisive battle of the War of 1812. The U.S.S. *Wolverine*, built and launched at Erie in 1843, was the nation's first iron-hulled warship. The prow is all that remains of it.
Niagara *open: summer, Tues–Sat 8:30–5, Sun 1–5; winter, Tues–Sat 9–4:30, Sun 1–4:30.* Wolverine *open daily 8:30–4:30*

WAYNE BLOCKHOUSE, *Third and Ash streets*
This structure is a replica of the one in which General Anthony Wayne died in 1796 while commanding troops opposing the Indians of the Northwest. It was built over the site of his original grave. Subsequently his remains were transferred to Wayne.
Open: May 30–Labor Day, daily 9–11:30, 1–4:30, 5:30–9; after Labor Day, by appointment only

ESSINGTON
THE PRINTZHOF NATIONAL HISTORIC LANDMARK, *Taylor Avenue and Second Street, Governor Printz Park*
New Sweden was the first permanent white settlement in what eventually became the colony of Pennsylvania. It was founded in 1638 as a commercial venture for Sweden in the New World (*see also Wilmington, Delaware, Fort Christina*), and in 1643 the first royal governor, Johan Printz, established his home (Printzhof) and a fort on Tinicum Island in the Delaware River. The foundations of his house, together with colonial and Indian relics, were uncovered by archaeological excavations dating from the 1930s (NR). A mile north of this site is **Morton Homestead,** on the banks of Darby Creek, Prospect Park Borough. This restored log and stone structure is among the oldest surviving buildings in Pennsylvania.
Printzhof open daily during daylight hours. Morton Homestead open: summer, Tues–Sat 8:30–5, Sun 1–5; winter, Tues–Sat 9–4:30, Sun 1–4:30

GETTYSBURG
GETTYSBURG NATIONAL MILITARY PARK, *visitor center on State 134*
Seeking a decisive victory here on Northern soil, the Confederate forces of General Robert E. Lee received instead a setback from which they never fully recovered. The battle, July 1–3, 1863, pitted Lee's Army of Northern Virginia against the Army of the Potomac, commanded by Major General George G. Meade. Thirty miles of road traverse areas of the park where fighting occurred in this famous battle, which turned the tide of the Civil War; along the way are more than 1,400 monuments, statues, and markers, and four observation towers. Within the park is the site where Lincoln delivered the Gettysburg Address on November 19, 1863, to dedicate nearby **Gettysburg National Cemetery.** Guided tours are available, and among other noteworthy locales are the **Eternal Light Peace Memorial, Meade's Headquarters,** the **High Water Mark Monument,** and **Devil's Den** (a Confederate stronghold). Near the park are the **National Civil War Wax Museum,** the **Gettysburg National Museum,** the **Hall of Presidents,** and the **Lincoln Room Museum.** On the southwest edge of the park is **Eisenhower National Historic Site,** the general's farm, which is not open to the public at the present time. NR
For further information write: Supt, Gettysburg, PA 17325

PENNSYLVANIA

HARMONY, *western Pennsylvania, 12 miles southwest of Butler*
> The Harmony Society of George Rapp (*see Ambridge*) had its first settlement here, beginning in 1805. Some of the early buildings still stand, and the original settlers' graves are in the cemetery.

HARRISON CITY VICINITY
BUSHY RUN BATTLEFIELD NATIONAL HISTORIC LANDMARK, *2 miles east on State 993*
> The battle here, August 5–6, 1763, was important in quelling Indian raids on British colonial outposts and in opening western Pennsylvania to settlement. Going to the relief of Fort Pitt, a British force under Colonel Henry Bouquet routed the Indians, then engaged in a series of raids known as the Pontiac War or Pontiac's Rebellion, after the Ottawa chief. Plaques and a small museum on the site explain the action. NR
> *Open daily during daylight hours*

JOHNSTOWN VICINITY
ALLEGHENY PORTAGE RAILROAD NATIONAL HISTORIC SITE, *U.S. 22*
> For more than 20 years from the time of its completion in 1834, the Pennsylvania Canal between Philadelphia and Pittsburgh was the state's main transportation line west. A vital part of this project was construction of a railroad, from Hollidaysburg to Johnstown, linking the eastern and western divisions of the canal—a 36-mile stretch through the Alleghenies that required 10 inclined planes and a 901-foot tunnel for the laying of track. To traverse this stretch, travelers and cargo were transferred from barges to specially designed railroad cars. NR

JOHNSTOWN FLOOD NATIONAL MEMORIAL, *intersection of U.S. 219 and State 869*
> On May 31, 1889, following a period of steady rain, an earthen dam gave way here and permitted millions of tons of water to sweep down the valley of the Little Conemaugh River. The flood devastated Johnstown and surrounding communities. Both the disaster and the national organization of relief that came in its wake are commemorated by the memorial at the site of the old dam. NR

LANCASTER
BUCHANAN HOUSE NATIONAL HISTORIC LANDMARK, *1120 Marietta Avenue*
> This brick structure, built in 1828 and named Wheatland (NR), was the residence of the 15th President of the United States, James Buchanan, from 1849 to 1868. Buchanan memorabilia are on view. Also of interest in this area are the **Amish Farm and House,** 6 miles east on U.S. 30, and·the **Amish Homestead,** 3 miles east on State 462. Tours are conducted through both.
> *Buchanan House open: March 15–Nov, Mon–Sat 9–5, Sun 10–5. Admission: $1*

LIGONIER
FORT LIGONIER, *junction of U.S. 30 and State 711*
> On view is a restoration of the fort that was a British stronghold during the French and Indian War and the time of the Indian uprising under Pontiac. The original fort stood from 1758 to 1765, and that period is the basis of displays in a museum here.
> *Open: March–Nov, daily 9–dusk. Admission: adults $1*

MASON-DIXON MONUMENT. *See* DELAWARE

MORGANTOWN VICINITY
    HOPEWELL VILLAGE NATIONAL HISTORIC SITE, *10 miles northeast of Morgantown Interchange of the Pennsylvania Turnpike*
        This village (1770–1883) represents the beginnings of America's iron and steel industry, employing charcoal furnaces. It was founded by Mark Bird just prior to the Revolution and supplied cannon and shot for the Army. Among the structures on view are the ruin of an anthracite furnace, a charcoal hearth, the ironmaster's house, and a blacksmith shop. All were important in Hopewell's role as an ironmaking center. NR
        Open: March–Oct, daily 9–6; Nov–Feb, daily 8–5; closed holidays

MORRISVILLE VICINITY
    PENNSBURY MANOR, *on Delaware River south of Bordentown Road*
        The mansion and gardens of William Penn, complete with outbuildings, have been completely re-created on the foundations of the original, built in 1683.
        Open: summer, Mon–Sat 8:30–5, Sun 1–5; winter, Mon–Sat 9–4:30, Sun 1–4:30. Admission: 50¢

NAZARETH, *eastern Pennsylvania, 6 miles northwest of Easton*
        Among the surviving buildings that reflect the community's past as a Moravian center are **Gray Cottage** (1740), on Ephrata Place; **George Whitefield House,** East Center and New streets, now housing the Moravian Historical Society Library and Museum; and **Nazareth Hall,** Hall Square, formerly a Moravian school for boys.

NORRISTOWN VICINITY
    VALLEY FORGE NATIONAL HISTORIC LANDMARK, *Valley Forge State Park*
        Suffering from hardship, hunger, and a succession of defeats, the army commanded by General George Washington arrived at the scene of this historic encampment on December 19, 1777. Though the winter was a bitter one, the army emerged in the spring as a rejuvenated force capable of coping with British regulars. Remains of trenches, earthworks, and other fortifications are visible, along with restored soldiers' huts. Other attractions of the park are the stone house used by Washington as headquarters and the parade ground. Also at Valley Forge are the restored quarters of Baron Frederick Von Steuben, who contributed much to the army's transformation here. There are conducted tours of the park, of **Washington Memorial Chapel,** on State 23, and of the adjoining **Valley Forge Museum,** both of which contain historic treasures. NR
        Park visitor center open daily 9–5

NORTHUMBERLAND
    PRIESTLEY HOUSE NATIONAL HISTORIC LANDMARK, *Priestley Avenue*
        Joseph Priestley, the English clergyman and chemist who discovered oxygen, settled in the United States in 1794 in search of a haven for political and religious dissenters. His home in Northumberland was built in the same year, and there he resided until his death in 1804. The frame structure has been restored. NR
        Open: summer, Tues–Sat 8:30–5, Sun 1–5; rest of year, Tues–Sat 9–4:30, Sun 1–4:30; closed holidays. Admission: 50¢

PHILADELPHIA

ACADEMY OF MUSIC NATIONAL HISTORIC LANDMARK, *Broad and Locust streets*

This is the oldest auditorium for music, still retaining its original form and purpose, in the United States. It was built in 1857; throughout this century it has been the home of the Philadelphia Orchestra. NR

AMERICAN PHILOSOPHICAL SOCIETY HALL NATIONAL HISTORIC LANDMARK, *Independence Square*

The brick building, now restored, dates from 1789. The society whose home this is traces its origin to 1768. Benjamin Franklin was the first president of the organization, which is the oldest learned society in the United States. NR

ARCH STREET MEETINGHOUSE, *302–338 Arch Street*

Dating from 1804, this is the city's oldest meetinghouse of the Society of Friends. It was built on land given by William Penn and first used as a cemetery. NR

BARTRAM HOUSE NATIONAL HISTORIC LANDMARK, *54th St and Eastwick Avenue*

The home of John Bartram (1699–1777), pioneer American botanist, stands here amid his even more famous gardens, where he cultivated rare and exotic plants. The stone structure was built in 1731 and is now furnished with period pieces. NR
Open daily 8–4; closed Christmas. Admission: 25¢

The Betsy Ross House and an 18th-century engraving of Independence Hall in Philadelphia

BETSY ROSS HOUSE, *239 Arch Street*
The restored brick building, originally built about 1700, is reputed to be the birthplace of the American flag. The claim has been disputed, and so has the fact of Betsy Ross's residence here, but the structure is still a mecca for tourists and scholars alike.
Open daily 9:30–5:15; closed Christmas

 CARPENTERS' HALL, *320 Chestnut Street*
Included in Independence National Historical Park (*see*), this brick structure was built in 1770 as a guildhall by the Carpenters' Company, which still owns and maintains it. The First Continental Congress met here in September, 1774. NR
Open daily 10–4; closed holidays

CHRIST CHURCH, *2nd Street between Market and Filbert streets*
George Washington and Benjamin Franklin were among the notables who worshiped at this church, built between 1727 and 1754. The Georgian colonial building is an outstanding example of church architecture of the period. The church burial grounds at 5th and Arch streets contain the graves of Franklin and his wife, Deborah. The church is part of Independence National Historical Park. NR
Open daily 9–5; Sun services at 9 and 11

CONGRESS HALL, *6th and Chestnut streets*
Built between 1787 and 1789 as the Philadelphia County Courthouse, this brick structure served as the meeting place of the U.S. Congress from 1790 to 1800. It was the scene of George Washington's second inaugural address and his Farewell Address, and of John Adams' induction as second President of the United States. It is part of Independence National Historical Park.
Open daily 9–5; closed Dec 25 and Jan 1

DESHLER-MORRIS HOUSE, *5442 Germantown Avenue*
President George Washington resided here briefly during the summers of 1793 and 1794, when yellow fever forced the government to move out of the main part of Philadelphia. It is included in Independence National Historical Park. NR
Open: Tues–Sun 1–4; closed holidays. Admission: 25¢

ELFRETH'S ALLEY HISTORIC DISTRICT NATIONAL HISTORIC LANDMARK, *between 2nd and Front streets*
This oldest unchanged and continuously occupied street in the city is an authentic slice of colonial Philadelphia, containing 17th- and 18th-century workingmen's homes and a museum. On the first Saturday in June some of the homes are open. NR

FIRST BANK OF THE UNITED STATES, *116 South 3rd Street*
Erected between 1795 and 1797, this is thought to be the oldest bank building in the United States. It now houses the visitor center of Independence National Historical Park.
Open: July–Aug, daily 9–4:30; Sept–June, Mon–Fri 9–4:30

GERMANTOWN HISTORIC DISTRICT NATIONAL HISTORIC LANDMARK, *Germantown Ave between Windrim Ave and Upsal St*
Originally settled in 1683 by Netherlanders, Germantown received a large contingent of emigrants from Germany in the first half of the 18th century. Some 50 buildings dating from the 18th and early

19th century are still standing in this district, including homes, churches, taverns, and a school. NR

GLORIA DEI (OLD SWEDES') CHURCH NATIONAL HISTORIC SITE, *Swanson Street between Christian and Water streets*
This oldest existing church building in Philadelphia was constructed between 1698 and 1700 by Swedish colonists. Still in active service, it is also of great interest architecturally. NR
Open weekdays 9–5

INDEPENDENCE NATIONAL HISTORICAL PARK, *bounded by Walnut, 6th, Chestnut, and 2nd streets*
Independence Hall, at 6th and Chestnut streets, is the principal gem of the collection of historic treasures located within this district. Constructed between 1732 and 1756 as the Pennsylvania State House, it is the home of the Liberty Bell; here, on July 4, 1776, the Declaration of Independence was adopted, a year following the gathering of the Second Continental Congress in the same building, and it was here in 1787 that the Constitutional Convention presided over by Washington created the U.S. Constitution. Here, too, in 1775, Washington accepted the post of Commander in Chief of the American Army. Independence Park components, not all situated within the area indicated above, also include the First Bank of the United States, Carpenters' Hall, American Philosophical Society Hall, Congress Hall, Christ Church, Gloria Dei Church, and the Deshler-Morris House (all of which are described separately in this section), together with the **Second Bank of the United States, Library Hall, Old City Hall** (used by the U.S. Supreme Court from 1791 to 1800), the **Bishop White House, St. Joseph's Church, St. George's Church,** and Mikveh Israel Cemetery. *For further information write: Supt, 313 Walnut St, Philadelphia, PA 19106*

LOGAN HOME, STENTON, NATIONAL HISTORIC LANDMARK, *18th and Cortland streets*
This brick house, built in 1730, was the residence of James Logan, William Penn's secretary, who became Philadelphia's mayor in 1722. During the Revolution it was used as headquarters by George Washington and Sir William Howe. NR
Open: Tues–Sat 1–5

OLD FORT MIFFLIN, *Marina and Penrose Ferry roads*
Begun in 1771 and incomplete at the outbreak of the Revolution, this fort site was held by 300 American troops when General William Howe's British forces took Philadelphia in September, 1777. After a 6-day siege the patriots retreated across the Delaware River into New Jersey. The British were then enabled to receive supplies from upriver. Fort Mifflin was rebuilt in 1798 by Pierre L'Enfant, the planner of Washington, D.C. NR

THE PENNSYLVANIA HOSPITAL NATIONAL HISTORIC LANDMARK, *8th and Spruce streets*
In operation since 1752, and at its present site since 1756, this is the country's oldest established hospital. NR

U.S.S. *OLYMPIA* **NATIONAL HISTORIC LANDMARK,** *Pier 40, foot of Chestnut Street*
The cruiser that served as Commodore Dewey's flagship at Manila

Bay is the oldest steel-hulled American warship afloat. NR
*Open: Apr–Oct, daily 10–5; Nov–Mar, Tues–Sun 10–4. Admission:
$1, children (under 12) 50¢*

WALNUT STREET THEATRE NATIONAL HISTORIC LANDMARK,
9th and Walnut streets
One of the nation's oldest playhouses in continuous operation, the
Walnut Street Theatre was completed in 1809. NR

PITTSBURGH
FORKS OF THE OHIO NATIONAL HISTORIC LANDMARK, *Point
Park*
Within this park are the sites of 2 historic outposts: **Fort Duquesne,**
built by the French in 1754 and taken by the British in 1758, and
nearby **Fort Pitt,** constructed by the British. The blockhouse just
outside Fort Pitt, built in 1764, still stands. NR

QUARRYVILLE VICINITY
FULTON BIRTHPLACE NATIONAL HISTORIC LANDMARK, *8
miles south on U.S. 222*
A stone farmhouse now occupies the site where Robert Fulton, who
designed the first wholly successful American steamboat, was born
in 1765. NR
*Open: summer, Tues–Sat 8:30–5, Sun 1–5; rest of year, Tues–Sat,
9–4:30, Sun 1–4:30*

TITUSVILLE VICINITY
DRAKE WELL NATIONAL HISTORIC LANDMARK, *Drake Well
Memorial Park, 3 miles southeast on State 36*
A replica of the first derrick used by Edwin L. Drake, oil pioneer,
and a museum are on this site, where in 1859 Drake drilled the
world's first successful oil well. NR
*Open: summer, Mon–Sat 8:30–5, Sun 1–5; rest of year, Mon–Sat
9–4:30, Sun 1–4:30; closed holidays. Admission: 50¢*

UNIONTOWN VICINITY
FORT NECESSITY NATIONAL BATTLEFIELD, *11 miles east on U.S.
40*
Here, on July 3, 1754, the French and Indians forced the surrender
of colonial troops commanded by Lieutenant Colonel George
Washington in the opening engagement of the French and Indian
War. Reconstructions of the fort's stockade and entrenchments
have been made on their original sites. Also here are **Mount Washington Tavern,** built about 1818 and now a museum, and the grave
of General Edward Braddock, who was killed in 1755 in another
engagement with the French. NR
Open: Mon–Sat and holidays 9–5; May–Oct, Sun 10–6

YARDLEY VICINITY
WASHINGTON CROSSING STATE PARK NATIONAL HISTORIC
LANDMARK, *between Yardley and New Hope on the Delaware River*
The park commemorates one of the great moments of the American
Revolution, the Christmas-night crossing of the Delaware River
by General George Washington and his troops for the capture of
Trenton in 1776—a victory that did much to keep alive America's
quest for ultimate independence. The point of embarkation of his
main force is marked. (*See also New Jersey, Washington Crossing.*)
NR

RHODE ISLAND

COVENTRY

NATHANAEL GREENE HOMESTEAD, 48 Taft Street, Anthony Village

General Nathanael Greene, George Washington's second in command during the Revolution, resided in this house, which was erected in 1774 and has been referred to as the Mount Vernon of the North.

Open: Wed, Sat, Sun 2–5, and by appointment; closed Dec 1–Feb 1

KINGSTON VICINITY

GREAT SWAMP FIGHT MONUMENT, *west off State 138*

This obelisk commemorates the decisive battle of King Philip's War, which was fought here on December 19, 1675, between 3,000 Narraganset Indians and 1,000 New Englanders. Beginning in 1662, Metacom, son of Sachem Massasoit and known to the colonists as King Philip, began forming a league of New England tribes. In 1675 the war that threatened New England's very existence began when the Indians attacked Swansea, Massachusetts, and subsequently overran the Connecticut Valley. During the Great Swamp Fight, 80 settlers and 1,000 Indians were slain. The war dragged on for 18 more months until Philip's remaining force lost the Battle of Bridgewater Swamp in 1676, and Philip was murdered by another Indian near Mount Hope.

NEWPORT

MIANTONOMI MEMORIAL PARK, *bounded by Housing Authority property and Girard and Hillside avenues and Admiral Kalbfuss Road*

This site was included in a land grant purchased from the Narraganset Indians in 1638. Rhode Island settlers used the 120-foot-tall hill here as a lookout, for beacons, and for public executions. In 1776 Colonel Israel Putnam erected fortifications at the site, which were subsequently seized by the British during their 3-year occupation of Newport. NR

Left: Hunter House in Newport. Center: steeple of the First Baptist Meeting-house in Providence. Right: interior of the Touro Synagogue in Newport

NEWPORT HISTORIC DISTRICT NATIONAL HISTORIC LAND-MARK, *bounded by Van Zandt Ave, Farewell, Sherman, High, Thomas, Golden Hill, Thames, Marsh, and Washington sts*

Built at the height of Newport's prosperity as a seaport, these mid-18th-century public and private structures represent the most advanced examples of academic Georgian architecture produced in the colonies. Many of the buildings reflect the work of the master carpenter Richard Munday or the distinguished architect Peter Harrison. Completed by Munday in 1742, the **Old Colony House** (NHL) initially housed the general assembly of Rhode Island colony; on July 20, 1776, the acceptance of the Declaration was read from its balcony, and during the Revolution George Washington attended a banquet in the great hall with the Comte de Rochambeau; the Federal Constitution was ratified at the building in 1790, and the state legislature met here from 1790 until 1900. The **Brick Market** (NHL), a commercial edifice with an open arcade on the ground floor, was built by Harrison between 1762 and 1772 and was used at various times as a theater and as a town and city hall. Other structures of the period include the **Hunter House** (NHL), erected in 1748 for Deputy Governer Jonathan Nichols, and several small dwellings and shops. NR

Old Colony House open: July–Labor Day, daily 9:30–4; rest of year, Mon–Fri 9:30–12, 1–4, Sat 10–5. Brick Market open: Mon–Sat 10–5. Hunter House open: Memorial Day–Oct 1, daily 10–5

OLD STONE MILL, *Touro Park*

There are 2 prevalent theories about the origin of this Newport landmark: some maintain that it was built by Norsemen 7 centuries ago; others believe that the mysterious tower dates from 1673.

ORIGINAL U.S. NAVAL WAR COLLEGE NATIONAL HISTORIC LANDMARK, *Coaster's Harbor Island*

A college offering advanced professional courses for naval officers was founded at this site in 1884. Alfred Thayer Mahan, who served as an early president of the college, made important contributions to this country's naval policies and doctrines. The building in which Mahan taught is currently the commandant's headquarters. NR

REDWOOD LIBRARY NATIONAL HISTORIC LANDMARK, *50 Bellevue Avenue*

Designed by Peter Harrison in 1748, this structure is the nation's oldest library building in continuous use. The library was an outgrowth of a philosophical society established in 1730, to which Abraham Redwood donated funds for the acquisition of books in 1747. NR

Open: Mon–Sat 10–6

TOURO SYNAGOGUE NATIONAL HISTORIC SITE, *85 Touro Street*

Designed in the Georgian style by the noted architect Peter Harrison and dedicated in 1763 by the Reverend Isaac Touro, this synagogue—the oldest in America—attests to Rhode Island's long tradition of religious freedom. As early as 1647, Roger Williams proclaimed religious liberty in a code of laws for his colony. In 1658 Sephardic Jews originally from Spain and Portugal settled in Newport. By the mid-18th century Jewish merchants, shippers, and craftsmen were contributing to Newport's prosperity as a bustling seaport. After the Revolution, when many of Newport's public buildings were destroyed, the synagogue was used for town meetings (1781) and for sessions of the general assembly (1781–84). George Washington visited Touro Synagogue in 1790 and presented the congregation with a letter of recognition. The restored synagogue is still used as a house of worship. NR

For further information write: 85 Touro Street, Newport, RI 02840

TRINITY EPISCOPAL CHURCH NATIONAL HISTORIC LANDMARK, *141 Spring Street*

Erected in 1725–26 by master carpenter Richard Munday, Trinity Church is one of the best-preserved colonial churches in America. Surmounted with a bishop's miter weathervane, the church contains the nation's only extant 3-tiered pulpit. NR

Open: June 15–Labor Day, daily 10–5; rest of year by appointment

VERNON HOUSE NATIONAL HISTORIC LANDMARK, *46 Clarke Street*

Raised in the 1750s by Metcalf Bowler, who later became chief justice of the Rhode Island supreme court, this Georgian frame house was bought in 1773 by shipowner William Vernon, who served as president of the Eastern Navy Board during the Revolution. In 1780–81, the Comte de Rochambeau, commander of America's French allies, used the residence as his headquarters during his occupation of Newport. NR

Open by appointment

WANTON-LYMAN-HAZARD HOUSE NATIONAL HISTORIC LANDMARK, *17 Broadway*

Erected in 1675, the oldest house in Newport was the residence of several early colonial governors and later of British officials. Occupied by Martin Howard, the Tory stamp master in 1765, the house suffered damage during the Stamp Act riots of that year. Today the structure has been restored. NR

Open: July 1–Labor Day, daily 10–5

PAWTUCKET

OLD SLATER MILL NATIONAL HISTORIC LANDMARK, *Roosevelt Avenue*

Established by Samuel Slater in 1793, this waterpower-operated mill was the birthplace of the nation's cotton textile industry, as well as the factory system of manufacturing. Slater had worked in an English textile plant and had memorized the factory layout; upon immigrating to the United States, Slater set up his mill and reconstructed the complicated textile machinery. Today the original structure contains a museum of industrial technology. NR

Open: Feb–Dec, Tues–Sat 10–5, Sun 2–5; closed holidays

PORTSMOUTH

BUTTS HILL FORT, *off Sprague Street*

This spot was the scene of the only engagement fought on Rhode Island soil during the Revolution. Generals Lafayette, Hancock, Greene, and Sullivan took part in an unsuccessful attempt to drive the British from Aquidneck Island. Old redoubts are still visible.

FOUNDERS' BROOK, *off Boyd's Lane*

Rhode Island's second settlement—originally called Pocasset— was established at this site in 1638 by Anne Hutchinson, who had been expelled from Boston, along with her husband and a few followers, because of her heretical beliefs. Mrs. Hutchinson was the nation's first woman to found a town. On **Pudding Rock** is a bronze tablet inscribed with the "Portsmouth Compact," which established the settlement's truly democratic form of government.

PROVIDENCE

FIRST BAPTIST MEETINGHOUSE NATIONAL HISTORIC LANDMARK, *North Main Street*

This meetinghouse was completed in 1775 for the country's oldest Baptist congregation, which was organized in 1638 by Roger Williams. Brown University commencements have traditionally been held here. NR
Open: May 1–Oct 31, Mon–Sat 10–4; Nov 1–Apr 30, Mon–Sat 11–3

GOVERNOR STEPHEN HOPKINS HOUSE, *Benefit and Hopkins streets*

Stephen Hopkins, 9-time governor of Rhode Island between 1755 and 1768 and a signer of the Declaration of Independence, resided in this house. George Washington twice visited the dwelling. NR
Open: Wed, Sat 1–4, or by appointment

ROGER WILLIAMS NATIONAL MEMORIAL, *Old Town*

This memorial honors the contributions of Rhode Island founder Roger Williams to the growth of religious freedom in America. Banished from the Massachusetts Bay Colony in 1636 because of his religious nonconformity, Williams came to this site beside a spring and founded the settlement of Providence, which he named "for God's merciful providence unto me in my distress." Here Williams won the friendship of the Narraganset Indians and established a government based on such "democraticall" principles as the consent of the governed, the separation of church and state, and religious liberty. NR

STATE CAPITOL, *situated on a hill north of the Civic Center*

Designed by McKim, Mead and White and begun in 1895, this impressive building of white Georgia marble contains Rhode Island's original parchment charter, granted by King Charles II in 1663. NR
Open: Mon–Fri 8:30–4:30

UNIVERSITY HALL, BROWN UNIVERSITY, NATIONAL HISTORIC LANDMARK, *Brown University Campus*

Constructed in 1770–71, University Hall is the oldest building at Brown University. The nation's seventh-oldest college, originally called Rhode Island College, was chartered at Warren in 1764 and relocated to its present site 6 years later. During the Revolution University Hall was used as a hospital and barracks. Early in the 19th century the structure was associated with the famous American educator Horace Mann, who graduated from Brown in 1819. The edifice presently houses administrative offices. NR

SAUNDERSTOWN

STUART BIRTHPLACE NATIONAL HISTORIC LANDMARK, *Gilbert Stuart Road*

Gilbert Stuart, the celebrated artist best known for his portraits of George Washington painted from life, was born in this house in 1755 and resided here until 1761. Stuart studied in London under artist Benjamin West and later had such distinguished subjects as John Adams, John Quincy Adams, and Thomas Jefferson. NR
Open: Sat–Thurs 11–5

SOUTH CAROLINA

BEAUFORT. *See* PORT ROYAL ISLAND

BETHANY VICINITY

KINGS MOUNTAIN NATIONAL MILITARY PARK, *northwest on State 161*

On October 7, 1780, Lord Cornwallis' campaign to secure the area south of Virginia for Great Britain met a setback in a Revolutionary War encounter between American mountain frontiersmen and Loyalist troops under Major Patrick Ferguson, a British regular. The Loyalist force was routed and Ferguson was killed. The scene of the action was near the border separating the Carolinas. Exhibits of the battle are on display in a park headquarters building. NR
Open: Mon–Sat 8:30–5, Sun 9:30–5:30; closed holidays

CAMDEN VICINITY

CAMDEN BATTLEFIELD NATIONAL HISTORIC LANDMARK, *5 miles north on U.S. 521 and 601*

One of the oldest inland towns in the state, Camden was also the scene of much Revolutionary War action. From the middle of 1780 the British occupied it, and the Battle of Camden, August 16, 1780, resulted in a resounding British victory over American forces under General Horatio Gates—a victory made the more costly by the death in combat of Baron Johann de Kalb, the Americans' German champion. General Nathanael Greene, Gates's successor, advanced on Camden the following April but felt unequal to the task of attacking it; 2 miles north, at **Hobkirk Hill**, the British again defeated the Americans on April 25, 1781. But continuing militia raids forced Lord Francis Rawdon, the British commander, to burn Camden and to evacuate it the following month. The fortifications were destroyed, but a stone monument marks the battlefield site. More

Left: Cowpens National Battlefield Monument near Chesnee. Top right: Fort Sumter in Charleston Harbor. Below: Dock Street Theater in Charleston

recently, restoration of a portion of historic Camden has been begun, with the object of reconstructing the area where in 1780–81 Camden was the main British supply post for their southern operations. NR

CHARLESTON AND VICINITY
DOCK STREET THEATER, *135 Church Street*
This is the first building in the United States designed solely for theatrical purposes. Opened in 1736, it was damaged twice by fire; reopened in 1937, after extensive reconstruction, it is still used by a local troupe.

FORT MOULTRIE, *Sullivan's Island, West Middle Street*
The first Fort Moultrie, one of three on this site, was a small structure of palmetto logs and sand. It was the scene of an important Revolutionary War battle, June 28, 1776, when some 400 American patriots under Colonel William Moultrie defeated a British squadron of 9 ships and forestalled British occupation of the South. Originally called Fort Sullivan, it was renamed for the commander of the victorious patriot forces. The present fort, built between 1807 and 1811, was partially destroyed in the Civil War, but the original walls and powder magazine are intact. In the 1830s, when the Federal government was seeking to relocate the Seminole Indians, the Seminole leader Osceola was captured and confined in Fort Moultrie, where he died in 1838 and where his grave remains. Edgar Allan Poe, a soldier here in 1828, wrote the poem "Israfel" on Sullivan's Island and also used the locale as the setting for "The Gold Bug." Development of coastal artillery led to the construction of **Battery Jasper** here in 1898. Fort Moultrie was deactivated in 1947 and is now administered as part of Fort Sumter National Monument (*see*).
Open: Apr–Oct, daily 8–5; Nov–March, Wed–Sun 8–5

FORT SUMTER NATIONAL MONUMENT, *Charleston Harbor*
Construction of this historic fortress was begun in 1829 and continued until 1860, when South Carolina seceded from the Union. On April 12, 1861, Confederate artillery fire over Fort Sumter signaled the start of the Civil War. In the same year Confederate forces seized Fort Sumter and held it until their evacuation on February 17, 1865. Meanwhile, with nearby Fort Moultrie (*see*), it was a key to the defense of Charleston against Union onslaughts; for a 20-month period beginning in 1863, Fort Sumter was the scene of a continual siege as Federal forces sought to capture it by naval and land attacks. Finally the approach of General Sherman's army forced the Confederate withdrawal from both forts and other installations in the Charleston area. After the conflict between the states, Fort Sumter was repaired and garrisoned; its gun emplacements, like those of Fort Moultrie, reflect changes in coastal artillery dating from the period of the Spanish-American War. Following its retirement from active service, Fort Sumter was partially restored. Tour boats to the fort leave from the foot of Calhoun Street on Lockwood Drive. The grounds include a museum and visitor center from which tours are conducted. NR
For further information write: Box 428, Sullivan's Island, SC 29482

HEYWARD-WASHINGTON HOUSE NATIONAL HISTORIC LANDMARK, *87 Church Street*
Built in 1770, this brick Georgian town house was the home of Thomas Heyward, Jr., a signer of the Declaration of Independence.

In 1791 President Washington occupied the house while visiting Charleston. NR
Open: Mon–Sat 10–5, Sun 2–5. Admission: adults $1, children 50¢

MIDDLETON PLACE NATIONAL HISTORIC LANDMARK, *northwest on State 61*

In 1741 Henry Middleton, who later became president of the Continental Congress, began extensive landscaped gardens on his estate under the direction of an English landscape designer. The gardens, famous for their flowering camellias and azaleas, are the oldest landscaped gardens in America. There is a family tomb on the estate in which Arthur Middleton, a signer of the Declaration of Independence, is buried. In the restored stable yard demonstrations of colonial crafts are given. NR
Open daily all year. Admission: adults $2.50, students $1.50

POWDER MAGAZINE, *79 Cumberland Street*

Dating from 1713, this is the oldest public building in Charleston. It was used as a munitions warehouse during the Revolutionary War and now houses a museum of furniture and wearing apparel. NR
Open: Sept–July, Tues–Sat 9:30–4; closed holidays. Admission: adults 50¢

ST. MICHAEL'S EPISCOPAL CHURCH NATIONAL HISTORIC LANDMARK, *corner of Meeting and Broad streets*

Completed in 1752, this notable Episcopal church is designed after St. Martin's-in-the-Field of London. During the Revolution the British seized the bells in the tower and shipped them to England. Among those who worshiped here were George Washington, the Marquis de Lafayette, and Robert E. Lee. NR

SITE OF OLD CHARLES TOWNE, *State 171, on the west bank of the Ashley River*

The site of the state's first permanent settlement is now a historic park (NR). In April, 1670, a colony of English settlers was established at Albemarle Point, due west of the city's present location, and named Charles Towne in honor of King Charles II. As part of the South Carolina tricentennial in 1970, a 200-acre site was developed to include the original 10-acre area of the colony, complete with reconstructed stockade, redoubt, and trenches. Across the Ashley, a section of old Charleston noted for its architectural value forms Charleston Historic District (NHL). The magnificent Georgian and Federal town mansions reflect the great wealth that Charlestonians amassed before the Revolution from rice and indigo plantations and from cotton thereafter.

CHESNEE VICINITY

COWPENS NATIONAL BATTLEFIELD SITE, *2 miles southeast of U.S. 221*

Here, on January 17, 1781, American forces, including a nucleus of Army regulars and a larger number of militia, decisively defeated a superior British detachment commanded by Colonel Banastre Tarleton. The Americans were commanded by Brigadier General Daniel Morgan, and the engagement was a calculated, and successful, attempt to divert part of Lord Cornwallis' British forces while American troops in the Carolinas were being reorganized under the command of General Nathanael Greene. In less than an hour the battle, which took place in a cow pasture, was over with only 350 of Tarleton's 1,150 cavalrymen escaping from the colonials' surprise counterattack on both their flanks. NR

For further information write: Box 31, Kings Mountain, SC 28086

CLEMSON

CALHOUN HOUSE NATIONAL HISTORIC LANDMARK, *Clemson University campus*

John C. Calhoun, Secretary of War under President James Monroe and Vice President under John Quincy Adams and Andrew Jackson, resided in this house from 1825 until his death in 1850. It was here that he wrote his *South Carolina Exposition and Protest*, which set forth the doctrine of nullification and epitomized his promotion of the Southern cause in the growing controversy that resulted in the Civil War. Calhoun named the structure, dating from 1803, Fort Hill for a fort built in this area in 1776. Many of the Calhouns' original furnishings are on view. NR

Open: Tues–Sat 10–noon, 1–5:30, Sun 2–6

COLUMBIA

ARCHIVES BUILDING, *1420 Senate Street*

State records from 3 centuries are housed here. The **Confederate Relic Room and Museum** contains a variety of military equipment.

Open daily except holidays, 9–9

GOVERNOR'S MANSION, *800 Richland Street*

The building was constructed in 1855 as officers' barracks of Arsenal Academy; it was converted into a house in 1868 and first occupied as such by Robert K. Scott, a Reconstruction governor. Then for a brief period it was a boarding house. From 1879, when the mansion underwent renovation, it has served as the governor's residence. NR

Open: Mon–Fri 9–5, by appointment

WOODROW WILSON BOYHOOD HOME, *1705 Hampton Street*

This was the home of Woodrow Wilson from 1872 to 1875. It was built for the father of the future President, a teacher of theology at the Presbyterian seminary in Columbia, and was the family residence until Professor Wilson accepted the ministry of a church in Wilmington, North Carolina, in 1875. The restored structure includes some of the original furnishings.

Open: Tues–Sat 10–1, 2–4, Sun 2–5. Admission: adults $1

CROSS ANCHOR VICINITY

SITE OF THE BATTLE OF MUSGROVE'S MILL, *2½ miles outside Cross Anchor on State 56*

Here, near the North Carolina border, American forces won a minor victory in the Revolutionary War on August 19, 1780. Shortly before attacking the British post at Musgrove's Mill, the Americans learned that their adversaries' ranks had been reinforced. Their horses too worn to retreat, the Americans engaged the enemy hastily, depleted the British force, and then withdrew. The scene of this engagement is indicated by a battle marker and monument.

EUTAWVILLE VICINITY

EUTAW SPRINGS BATTLEGROUND PARK, *2 miles east on State 6 and 45*

Near the end of the Revolutionary War, an American force under

General Nathanael Greene engaged the British here, September 8, 1781, in an attempt to delay reinforcements destined to join Lord Cornwallis' army. The British losses forced them to retire to Charleston for the rest of the war. NR

GEORGETOWN VICINITY

HOPSEWEE PLANTATION NATIONAL HISTORIC LANDMARK, *12 miles south on U.S. 17*

Typical of the low-country rice plantation house, Hopsewee was the birthplace of Thomas Lynch, Jr., a signer of the Declaration of Independence. Thomas Lynch, Sr., was en route to Philadelphia to sign the document when he died. NR

Open: Tues–Fri 10–5. Admission: adults $1.50, students 50¢

LANCASTER VICINITY

ANDREW JACKSON STATE HISTORICAL PARK, *8 miles north on U.S. 521*

Named for the seventh President, whose birthplace is in this vicinity, the park contains a museum housing frontier relics of the period 1750–1850.

Open: Tues–Sat 9–5, Sun 1–5

NINETY SIX VICINITY

OLD NINETY SIX AND STAR FORT, *2 miles south between State 248 and 27*

Old Ninety Six was the scene of the first bloodshed of the Revolution in the area that is now South Carolina. In November, 1775, a band of 562 patriots commanded by Colonel Andrew Williamson defeated a royalist force, although they were greatly outnumbered. The town, oldest white settlement in western South Carolina, was built around a trading post that had been established about 1730. It moved from the original location to a point 2 miles distant, where the first railroad arrived in 1855. The name "Ninety Six" derived from the supposed distance between it and the Indian village Keowee. During the Revolutionary War British troops under Lieutenant J. H. Cruger captured Star Fort, at the site of Old Ninety Six. On May 12, 1781, an American force under General Nathanael Greene began a 28-day siege of the stronghold, but the attack was abandoned when a British army commanded by Lord Rawdon approached. Having no artillery, Greene had set out to tunnel his way under Star Fort. Traces of the tunnel, which was dug under the direction of the Polish engineer Thaddeus Kosciusko, are still visible, and relics of the action and of frontier life have been unearthed. NR

PARRIS ISLAND

JAN RIBAULT MEMORIAL

This memorial marks the attempt in 1562 by French Huguenots to plant a settlement on the Sea Islands. They named it **Charlesfort,** and though it lasted only a year it represented one of France's challenges to Spain's claim to all of North America.

PENDLETON HISTORIC DISTRICT

Laid out in 1790, Pendleton is one of the oldest towns in the northwestern part of the state. In its early years it was the scene of much trade, especially in carriages, cabinets, and ironwork. In the vicinity is **Hopewell,** which was the plantation abode of the Revolutionary War hero General Andrew Pickens. Beneath an oak on the Hopewell grounds, the Treaty of Hopewell was negotiated in 1785 by Pickens and representatives of Indian tribes of the area. Under terms of the agreement, the Indians surrendered their rights to extensive areas of what is now the Carolinas, Georgia, and Tennessee. NR

PORT ROYAL ISLAND

BEAUFORT ARSENAL, *713 Craven Street*
Built originally in 1776, this structure was rebuilt in 1852 on the site of the first Beaufort courthouse. It houses 2 brass trophy guns taken from the British in 1779; they were seized by Union soldiers in 1861 but returned in 1880. The **National Military Cemetery** on Boundary Street contains the graves of 12,000 Union troops who died in the South during the Civil War, together with the remains of a small number of Confederate soldiers. The **Beaufort Historic District** (NR) preserves the atmosphere of this picturesque Sea Island port, whose history dates back to 1520, when Spanish explorers first visited here. Most of the surviving buildings are from early in the 19th century.

FORT FREDERICK, *in Port Royal*
Erected by the British in 1718, this is the oldest fort constructed of tabby (lime with shells, gravel, and stone) in the United States. It has now been restored.

SPARTANBURG

FOSTER'S TAVERN, *191 Cedar Spring Road*
Built between 1801 and 1808, this was an overnight stopping place on a well-traveled stage route serving Virginia, North Carolina, and Georgia. John C. Calhoun was one of the notables who stayed here. NR

SUMMERTON

SITE OF FORT WATSON
This Revolutionary War fort was built atop an Indian mound by the British. It was captured in 1780 by General Francis Marion, whose men, lacking artillery, constructed in a single night a log tower higher than the fort, and from the tower fired on the fort.

SUMMERVILLE VICINITY

OLD DORCHESTER HISTORICAL STATE PARK, *6 miles south on State 642*
On this site a town was established in 1696 by a colony from Dorchester, Massachusetts. It was in existence about 50 years, and among the ruins on view are an old fort (**Fort Dorchester**) and the tower of **St. George's (Anglican) Church.** NR
Open daily during daylight hours

SUMTER VICINITY

STATEBURG HISTORIC DISTRICT
This pre-Revolution community was founded by General Thomas Sumter, who led American troops against the British and who later was a U.S. congressman and senator; he is buried here. Another point of historic interest is **Borough House,** built in 1758, which was used during the Revolution by General Nathanael Greene and Lord Cornwallis. Among the house's treasured possessions are letters from Sumter and Robert E. Lee. On the grounds is an ancient tree, **Spy Oak,** from which Tory spies were hanged. NR

SOUTH DAKOTA

CUSTER VICINITY
CRAZY HORSE MEMORIAL, *5 miles north off U.S. 16*

Sculptor Korczak Ziolkowski is currently at work on a colossal memorial to the Sioux Indian chief Crazy Horse. An entire granite mountain is being carved into a likeness of the chief astride his horse. The completed sculpture will stand 563 feet high and 641 feet long. Visitors may view the blasting in progress from an observation platform. The sculptor's home and studio and a gallery of his other works are open to the public.

Open daily 6:30 A.M.–dark. Admission: $2 per car

GORDON STOCKADE, *3 miles east in Custer State Park on U.S. 16*

The Custer expedition to the Black Hills in the summer of 1874 reported the likelihood of a gold strike; true to form, prospectors were not long in arriving. The first group, led by John Gordon, erected this stockade, now restored, as protection against Indians in the winter of 1874–75. Mementos of General Custer are contained in the **Way Museum** in Custer. The state park named for Custer contains one of the country's largest buffalo herds, and visitors can also see, each July, a pageant re-creating the Black Hills gold discovery, staged near the site of the original 1874 strike.

DEADWOOD HISTORIC DISTRICT NATIONAL HISTORIC LANDMARK

Rich in tradition, just as it was once rich in more material respects, Deadwood is today a resort and trading center and still a hub of mining traffic. Soon after the discovery of gold in the Black Hills in 1874, the town attracted valuable human assets in the persons of Wild Bill Hickok, Calamity Jane, and Deadwood Dick, who resided here and now rest in **Boot Hill Cemetery** on Mount Moriah, 500 feet above the main street, which is set in a gulch. This famous main street still numbers among its original structures the saloon where Deadwood Dick was shot down by Jack McCall. A **Wax Museum** in Old Towne Hall on Lee Street re-creates the area's

Left: Deadwood City. Top right: Mount Rushmore National Memorial near Keystone. Below: model of Chief Crazy Horse sculpture near Custer

colorful history. Among the relics in **Adams Memorial Hall Museum** is the first locomotive in the Black Hills, which arrived, by bull team, in 1879. During the first weekend in August, a rodeo and pageant recall pioneer days. On the western edge of town, **Broken Boot Gold Mine**, in operation from 1878 to 1904, offers underground tours from May 15 to September 15, weather permitting. *Wax museum open: June 1–Oct 1, daily 8–6. Adams museum open: June 15–Sept 15, daily 8–8; rest of year, 9–noon, 1–5*

KEYSTONE VICINITY

MOUNT RUSHMORE NATIONAL MEMORIAL, *3 miles west off U.S. 16A*

Carved in the granite of Mount Rushmore are likenesses of the heads of 4 American Presidents, George Washington, Thomas Jefferson, Abraham Lincoln, and Theodore Roosevelt, each between 60 and 70 feet in height. They are the work of the sculptor Gutzon Borglum. The memorial is best viewed under morning light; from June 1 to Labor Day, floodlights illuminate the sculpture at night, and evening programs in the amphitheater recount the philosophies of the four Presidents and the history of the memorial project. NR
Open daily throughout the year

LEAD

HOMESTAKE MINE, *on U.S. 14A and 85*

This largest gold-producing mine in the Western Hemisphere has been in operation since 1878. Tours of its surface operations are conducted.
Open: June–Aug, Mon–Sat 8–5, Sun 8–4; May, Sept, Oct, Mon–Sat 8–3:30

MOBRIDGE VICINITY

BURIAL SITE OF SITTING BULL, *off U.S. 12*

The noted Sioux chief Sitting Bull met his death at the hands of Indian police on December 15, 1890, during the so-called Messiah War (*see Wounded Knee*), at a point near here. His body was taken to Fort Yates, North Dakota, for burial at that time, but it was moved here, to the site of former Indian villages, in 1953.

PIERRE VICINITY

OAHE MISSION SCHOOL AND CHAPEL, *west side of Missouri River atop east end of the Oahe Dam*

In 1877 the Oahe Congregational Church was erected by Thomas L. Riggs to serve as a school and church for the Indians and settlers of the territory. Riggs was the son of the man who had created a written language and dictionary for the Dakota Indians. For the next 37 years Riggs continued his missionary work in the small chapel. In 1964 the small building with a belfry was moved from its original site in Peoria Bottom, which was then inundated by the waters of Oahe Dam. Today the church, atop the largest earthen structure in the country, is available for Sabbath and wedding services.

SITE OF OLD FORT PIERRE, *3 miles above the mouth of Bad River on west side of the Missouri*

The vicinity of the mouth of the Bad River was a strategic spot in the fur trade on the Upper Missouri and as such was the site of 3 trading posts. In 1817 Joseph La Framboise built a "house of dry wood" to trade with the Dakotas; **Fort La Framboise** lasted until 1819. Then in 1822 the Columbia Fur Company built **Fort Tecumseh,** which remained in operation until 1832, when it was replaced by **Fort Pierre.** Pierre Chouteau built the cottonwood stockade when the fur trade was at its peak. The first steamboat, the *Yellowstone,* to ply the Upper Missouri brought supplies and, over the years, many important guests—George Catlin, Karl Bodmer, John C. Frémont, John James Audubon. By the 1850s the fur trade had waned—the silk stovepipe had replaced the beaver hat—and the days of the mountain men were over; so the American Fur Company sold the post to the military in 1855. But the old stockade was in such poor repair that the U.S. Army was never able to use it as a garrison, and it vanished without a trace.

VERENDRYE HILL AND MONUMENT, *overlooking Fort Pierre, opposite Pierre on the Missouri River at its confluence with the Bad River*
The first documented visit of the white man to this region was that of the French explorers Louis and François Vérendrye in 1743. On March 30 of that year, they buried a lead plate inscribed with a claim to the territory in the name of the King of France. The plate was discovered by chance in 1913 and is now part of the collection of the South Dakota Historical Society Museum in Pierre. A monument marks the site of the discovery.

SISSETON VICINITY
FORT SISSETON, *20 miles west of Sisseton*
In what is now a state park stands the restoration of the oldest existing fort in South Dakota. This Federal outpost was built in 1864, primarily to provide protection against the Sioux for wagon trains; it was abandoned as a military base in 1888. Its original name, Fort Wadsworth, was changed to Sisseton in 1876.

WOUNDED KNEE BATTLEFIELD NATIONAL HISTORIC LANDMARK, *on Pine Ridge Indian Reservation*
A museum and a mass grave containing the bodies of Chief Big Foot and more than a hundred of his Sioux followers mark the site of the last significant armed encounter between Indians and United States forces. Having been systematically deprived of their land and way of life, the Indians had turned in desperation to a "messiah craze," the principal ritual of which was a ghost dance, introduced by a Nevada Paiute named Wovoka. His vision of a land where the buffalo were restored and the white men driven out led to a religious fervor that swept through tribes in many parts of the West. Big Foot and his band of Sioux were on their way to a mass Indian revival gathering when the encounter occurred, December 29, 1890. U.S. troops overtook them; Big Foot seemed prepared to accept arrest, but he and his followers escaped, only to be overtaken again at Wounded Knee Creek. While they were disarming the Indians, resistance caused troops of the Seventh Cavalry to return the Sioux fire. The result was more a massacre than a battle. The poorly equipped Indians were soon routed, and those who fled were pursued and cut down. In the spring of 1973 Wounded Knee became a dramatic symbol of Indian dissatisfaction with their treatment by the U.S. government. A group of Indians occupied the town and were held under siege for 70 days by Federal marshals while they attempted to negotiate their grievances with government officials. NR
Open: May–Sept, daily 8–5:30

CHATTANOOGA VICINITY

CHICKAMAUGA AND CHATTANOOGA NATIONAL MILITARY PARK, *9 miles south on U.S. 27*

This park was the scene of 2 fierce Civil War battles fought in September and November, 1863, for control of Chattanooga, a strategic railroad junction and gateway to the heart of the Confederacy. On September 18 the Union Army of the Cumberland— about 58,000 men—clashed with some 66,000 Confederate troops under Braxton Bragg at **Chickamauga Creek** in Georgia. The fighting continued until the Confederates pierced the Union defenses on September 20, forced the Federal army to retreat into Chattanooga, and laid siege to the city. George H. Thomas assumed command of the Union army, which was subsequently reinforced by troops under Generals Joseph Hooker, William T. Sherman, and Ulysses S. Grant, who became the overall commander. On November 23 Grant began his offensive; intense fighting occurred at **Orchard Knob,** and on November 24 the so-called Battle above the Clouds took place at **Lookout Mountain,** which the Confederates finally evacuated. On November 25 the Army of the Cumberland scaled the heights of **Missionary Ridge** in one of the great charges of the war and forced the Confederates to retreat into northwest Georgia. Chattanooga and most of Tennessee were then under Union control. NR

For further information write: Supt, Fort Oglethorpe, GA 30742

COLUMBIA

JAMES K. POLK HOUSE NATIONAL HISTORIC LANDMARK, *West 7th and South High streets*

James K. Polk, 11th President of the United States (1845–49), spent several years as a youth in this house. Polk served as Speaker of the House of Representatives in 1835 and as governor of Tennessee from 1839 to 1841. The house contains Polk memorabilia. NR

Open: Mon–Sat 9–12, 1–5, Sun 1–5; closed Christmas

Left: New York monument at Chickamauga National Military Park at Chattanooga. Center: engraving of Andrew Jackson. Right: The Hermitage in Nashville

CUMBERLAND GAP NATIONAL HISTORICAL PARK. *See* KENTUCKY

DAYTON COURTHOUSE, *east Tennessee on U.S. 27*
>This courthouse was the scene of the world-famous Scopes or "Monkey" Trial, which took place in July, 1925. High-school teacher John T. Scopes was being prosecuted by the state of Tennessee for teaching Darwinian evolution to a biology class, in defiance of a statute that forbade the act of creation to be explained in public schools in terms other than the literal account in Genesis. The renowned attorney Clarence Darrow unsuccessfully defended Scopes, who was convicted and released on a technicality, while William Jennings Bryan successfully conducted the prosecution.

ELIZABETHTON VICINITY
>SYCAMORE SHOALS NATIONAL HISTORIC LANDMARK, *3 miles west on the Watauga River*
>A monument commemorates the 900 patriot backwoodsmen from Kentucky and Tennessee who mustered and trained at this site in 1780 before taking part in the Revolutionary Battle of Kings Mountain, South Carolina (*see*), in which they prevailed over 1,100 Loyalist troops. Here, five years earlier, the Cherokee Indians had ceded lands along the Watauga and in Kentucky to the colonies. NR

FORT DONELSON NATIONAL MILITARY PARK, *1 mile west of Dover on U.S. 79*
>The first major Federal victory of the Civil War occurred at this site on the Cumberland River on February 16, 1862, when some 27,000 Union troops, aided by gunboats, under Ulysses S. Grant defeated approximately 18,000 Confederates. After 3 days of fighting, General Simon B. Buckner, the Confederate commander in charge, surrendered the stronghold in accordance with Grant's terms for an "unconditional and immediate surrender." The 14,000 Confederate prisoners of war turned over to the North represented the largest number of men ever to surrender at one time in North America. Grant's decisive victory dealt the Confederacy a mortal blow by opening 2 avenues into the heart of the South by way of the Tennessee and Cumberland rivers. The victory also raised flagging Union morale and made the nation aware of Grant's considerable military abilities. Preserved in this park are the earthworks of the fort, Confederate river batteries, a reconstructed powder magazine, and 2 miles of trenches. Adjacent to the site is the **Fort Donelson** (Dover) **National Cemetery.** NR
>*For further information write: Superintendent, Dover, TN 37058*

FRANKLIN VICINITY
>FRANKLIN BATTLEFIELD NATIONAL HISTORIC LANDMARK, *south on U.S. 31*
>One of the bloodiest battles of the Civil War occurred at this site on November 30, 1864, between the Confederate Army of Tennessee under General John B. Hood and Federal forces under John M. Schofield and his field commander, General Jacob D. Cox. Much of the fighting raged around the nearby **Carter House** (NHL), which Cox held at his headquarters. The battle took a staggering human toll: the Confederates suffered 6,252 casualties and lost 6 generals, one of whom was John C. Carter; the Union suffered 2,326 casualties. Hood's failure to penetrate Union lines anticipated his final defeat at Nashville 2½ weeks later. NR
>*Carter House open: May–Sept, daily 9–5; rest of year, daily 9–4*

GREENEVILLE
ANDREW JOHNSON NATIONAL HISTORIC SITE, *Depot Street*
This site commemorates Andrew Johnson, who rose from humble origins to become the 17th President of the United States. In a distinguished and controversial career, Johnson, who started out as an impoverished tailor, served as alderman, mayor, state legislator, congressman, governor, and U.S. senator. In 1864 Johnson was selected as Abraham Lincoln's running mate and upon Lincoln's assassination, he succeeded to the Presidency. During his term in office, Johnson became the only President in U.S. history to be impeached. After a long and stormy trial in Congress, only one vote kept him in office. Preserved here are the house where Johnson lived from 1831 to 1851, the tailor shop where he worked, a later homestead, and his grave. NR
For further information: Supt, Depot St, Greeneville, TN 37743

HOHENWALD VICINITY
MERIWETHER LEWIS MONUMENT, *7½ miles east on Natchez Trace Parkway and State 20*
Captain Meriwether Lewis, leader of the first overland expedition to the Pacific Ocean in 1804–6, met a mysterious death from gunshot wounds at **Grinder's Inn,** which stood alongside the Natchez Trace—a former Indian trail that became a famous pioneer highway—on October 11, 1809. Lewis, governor of the Louisiana Territory, was traveling from Mississippi to Washington, D.C., in order to resolve personal financial difficulties. En route, Lewis showed signs of "mental derangement" and is believed to have committed suicide. A broken column marks Lewis' grave beside the Natchez Trace; a tablet designates the site of Grinder's Inn.

JONESBORO HISTORIC DISTRICT, *northeast Tennessee on U.S. 411*
In 1779 Tennessee's oldest community was established at this site, and 5 years later the short-lived state of Franklin was organized here on lands that North Carolina had ceded to the nation; John Sevier served as its first and only governor (1785–88). When Tennessee was admitted to the Union in 1796, Jonesboro was the scene of the constitutional convention and the first 2 meetings of the general assembly before the capital was relocated to Greeneville. Andrew Jackson began his law practice at Jonesboro in 1788. NR

KINGSPORT VICINITY
LONG ISLAND OF THE HOLSTON NATIONAL HISTORIC LANDMARK, *South Fork of the Holston River*
This island was the scene of several significant events in the exploration and settlement of the old Southwest. It marked the beginning of Daniel Boone's **Wilderness Road** through the Cumberland Gap, over which more than 200,000 settlers traveled between 1775 and 1795. The Revolutionary Battle of **Long Island Flats,** in which Cherokee resistance to the Americans was broken, occurred a short distance to the north in 1776. NR

KNOXVILLE
BLOUNT MANSION NATIONAL HISTORIC LANDMARK, *200 W Hill Avenue*
One of the first frame houses west of the Alleghenies was erected in 1792 by William Blount, who served as governor of the United States territory south of the River Ohio and was instrumental in gaining statehood for Tennessee in 1796. Blount had fought in the

Revolution, had been a signer of the Federal Constitution, was a
founder of Blount College, which became the University of Tennessee, and acted as superintendent of Indian Affairs for the
Southern Department. NR
Open: May–Nov 1, Tues–Sat 9:30–12, 1–5; Sun 2–5; closed holidays

MEMPHIS AND VICINITY

BEALE STREET HISTORIC DISTRICT NATIONAL HISTORIC
LANDMARK, *Beale Street from Main to 4th Street*
The unique jazz form known as the blues originated in this district
early in the 1900s. Here in Pewee's Saloon, W. C. Handy composed
and played his celebrated "Memphis Blues" (1909) and "St. Louis
Blues" (1914). Formerly lined with saloons, nightclubs, and
theaters, Beale Street is now undergoing an urban renewal project
to re-create its past. NR

CHUCALISSA INDIAN TOWN, *5 miles south on U.S. 61, then 4½ miles
west on Mitchell Road in Fuller State Park*
This was one of several Indian villages that flourished between
A.D. 900 and the early 1600s along the eastern shore of the Mississippi River from the present site of Memphis some 40 miles into
Mississippi. Hernando de Soto encountered these communities
when he explored the area in 1541, but the towns were deserted by
the time the French passed through the region in 1673. Restored
today, the village contains a temple mound, thatched huts, an
excavated cemetery group with 40 burials on display, and a museum.
Open: Tues–Sat 9–5

NASHVILLE AND VICINITY

FORT NASHBOROUGH, *1st Ave North between Church and Broadway*
Nashville grew up around the site of Fort Nashborough, which was
founded in 1780 on a bluff overlooking the Cumberland River by a
group of pioneers led by James Robertson. People from nearby
settlements convened at Fort Nashborough and adopted the
Cumberland Compact, which provided for the government of the
area. The fort has been reconstructed near its original site.
Open daily 9–4; closed Jan 1 and Dec 25

THE HERMITAGE NATIONAL HISTORIC LANDMARK, *12 miles
east on U.S. 70N*
Andrew Jackson, who began his career as a frontier militia commander and became the nation's seventh President, built The
Hermitage in 1819 and resided there until his death in 1845. In the
Creek Indian War of 1813, Jackson earned a major general's commission and in 1815 became the hero of the Battle of New Orleans,
the final engagement of the War of 1812. Jackson served 2 terms as
President (1829–37). He and his wife, Rachel, are buried at The
Hermitage. Across the road stands **Tulip Grove** (NR), a plantation
house erected in 1836 by Mrs. Jackson's nephew Andrew Jackson
Donelson. NR
Open daily 9–5; closed Dec 25

STATE CAPITOL, *between 6th and 7th avenues North on Charlotte*
This Greek Revival edifice was designed by the eminent architect
William Strickland and built between 1845 and 1855 with the aid
of prison labor. The Tennessee General Assembly had selected
Nashville as the permanent state capital in October, 1843.
Open: Mon–Fri 8–4:30, Sat 9–2

OAK RIDGE

X-10 REACTOR, OAK RIDGE NATIONAL LABORATORY, NATIONAL HISTORIC LANDMARK

The manufacture of the atomic bomb was made possible when the world's first full-scale nuclear reactor began operating here on November 4, 1943. The **American Museum of Atomic Energy** depicts the peacetime uses of the atom and includes a scale model of the X-10. NR

Museum open: Mon–Sat 9–5; Sun 12:30–6:30; closed holidays

SHILOH NATIONAL MILITARY PARK, *10 miles south of Savannah and Adamsville, via U.S. 64 and State 22*

The first major western engagement of the Civil War occurred at this site on April 6–7, 1862. After the fall of Forts Henry and Donelson (*see Fort Donelson National Military Park*), Confederate General Albert Sidney Johnston withdrew his troops from Kentucky and most of Tennessee and concentrated about 40,000 men at Corinth, Mississippi. Grant pursued Johnston and stopped with approximately 40,000 men at **Pittsburgh Landing,** 23 miles north of Corinth, to await reinforcements led by General Don Carlos Buell. Johnston decided to thwart Grant's plan by attacking the Federals at the site of **Shiloh Church** on April 6. Johnston was mortally wounded at the **Peach Orchard** and was succeeded in command by General P. G. T. Beauregard. That night Buell's army arrived and increased Grant's force to almost 62,000 men. The next day Grant launched a counterattack and finally forced the Southerners to retreat unpursued to Corinth. The Union victory was an important milestone in the campaign aimed at securing control of the Mississippi River, and it directly led to the capture of Corinth by the Federals that May. The Union dead were buried at the adjoining **Shiloh (Pittsburgh Landing) National Cemetery.** NR

For further information write: Superintendent, Shiloh, TN 38376

STONES RIVER NATIONAL BATTLEFIELD, *3 miles northwest of Murfreesboro*

One of the bloodiest engagements of the Civil War took place at this site from December 31, 1862, until January 2, 1863, between the Union Army of the Cumberland under Major General William S. Rosecrans and the Confederate Army of Tennessee under General Braxton Bragg. Although the Confederates took the early offensive, Union artillery halted their drive on January 2, and Bragg's forces finally retreated to Tullahoma on January 3. Neither side could claim a decisive victory. The Union dead are buried in the adjoining **Stones River (Murfreesboro) National Cemetery.** NR

For further information write: Box 1039, Murfreesboro, TN 37130

VONORE VICINITY

FORT LOUDOUN NATIONAL HISTORIC LANDMARK, *1½ miles north off U.S. 411*

This fort was erected in 1756–57 during the French and Indian War by colonists from South Carolina to impede the progress of the French in the Mississippi Valley and to serve as a gesture of friendship to England's allies, the Cherokee Indians. Following maltreatment by the settlers, however, the Cherokees blockaded Fort Loudoun and forced it to surrender in August, 1760: the soldiers were massacred or captured, and the Indians subsequently burned the fort. Today the stronghold is being reconstructed. NR

Open daily 9–5

TEXAS

ALBANY VICINITY

FORT GRIFFIN STATE HISTORIC PARK, *15 miles north on U.S. 283*
Erected in 1867 on the Clear Fork of the Brazos to replace Fort
Belknap (*see Newcastle*), Fort Griffin defended the area from hos-
tile Indians. The military post served as the base of operations
for the famous raids, directed by Generals Ranald Mackenzie and
Nelson Miles, against the nomadic tribes of the Staked Plain of the
Texas Panhandle. By 1881 the frontier had been pushed westward,
and Fort Griffin was abandoned. Only ruins survive today. NR

AMARILLO VICINITY

ALIBATES FLINT QUARRIES AND TEXAS PANHANDLE PUEBLO
CULTURE NATIONAL MONUMENT, *35 miles north off State 136,
overlooking Lake Meredith*
From approximately 12,000 years ago until the arrival of the Europeans, Indians came to this site to quarry flint, from which they
fashioned multicolored tools and weapons. Excavations here have
revealed that Ice Age hunters used flint spear points and knives for
slaughtering the mammoth, giant bison, sloth, and tapir. Indians of
the Texas Panhandle Pueblo culture, who settled in the area about
1300, traded their flint weapons and implements for Minnesota
pipestone, Pacific Ocean shells, and Arizona painted pottery.
Today the remains of 2 late pre-Columbian pueblos, as well as flint
chips, quarry blanks, and chipped stone artifacts, may be seen. NR
*Open to the public on weekends by prior arrangements; write:
Box 326, Sanford, TX 79078*

AUSTIN

FRENCH LEGATION, *East and San Marcos streets*
In 1841 the French minister to the Republic of Texas erected and
occupied this building. The structure is the only legation in the

*Left: Fort Davis National Historic Site. Top right: Lyndon B. Johnson Boyhood
Home in Johnson City. Below: the Alamo in San Antonio*

continental United States (with the exception of those in Washington, D.C.) to be constructed by a foreign government. NR
Open: Tues-Sun 1-5

GOVERNOR'S MANSION, *11th and Colorado streets*
Raised in 1856 for Governor Elisha M. Pease, this stately Greek Revival mansion still houses Texas governors. NR
Open: Mon-Fri 10-noon; closed holidays

STATE CAPITOL, *north end of Congress Avenue*
Designed by Elijah E. Myers and completed in 1888, this pink granite State House is second in size only to the U.S. Capitol in Washington, D.C. Austin became capital of Texas during the Republic in 1839, retaining its status when statehood was granted in 1845. NR
Open daily 8:30-4:30

BEAUMONT VICINITY
LUCAS GUSHER, SPINDLETOP OIL FIELD NATIONAL HISTORIC LANDMARK, *3 miles south on Spindletop Road*
On January 10, 1901, the modern petroleum age literally "blew in" at this site when Anthony F. Lucas struck a gusher, which spouted forth a geyser of oil for 6 days at the rate of 75,000 barrels a day. Soon after the event, derricks dotted the area, refineries were built, and the population of Beaumont tripled. By 1927 Texas was the nation's leading petroleum producer. Today a monument, well pump, and replica of a wooden derrick remain at the site. NR

BROWNSVILLE
FORT BROWN NATIONAL HISTORIC LANDMARK, *foot of Elizabeth Street*
Established in 1846 by General Zachary Taylor on the north side of the Rio Grande, across from Matamoros, Mexico, Fort Brown garrisoned troops during the Mexican War. Afterward it defended the international border and protected Brownsville from Indians in the 1850s, and during the Civil War it played a key role in the contest for Brownsville, which changed hands several times. Later in the century William C. Gorgas, who became Surgeon General of the U.S. Army in 1914, began his study of yellow fever at Fort Brown's post hospital. Today Fort Brown's surviving buildings house Texas Southmost College. NR

RESACA DE LA PALMA BATTLEFIELD NATIONAL HISTORIC LANDMARK, *just north on Parades Line Road*
On May 9, 1846, General Zachary Taylor's American forces and the Mexican army under General Mariano Arista met here in an engagement that marked the end of fighting in Texas during the Mexican War. The battle was the continuation of an artillery duel that had begun the previous day at nearby Palo Alto and was the first significant skirmish of the Mexican War. Defeated, the Mexicans were forced to retreat across the Rio Grande. Taylor's victory paved the way for his invasion of Mexico. NR

DENISON
DWIGHT D. EISENHOWER BIRTHPLACE STATE HISTORIC SITE, *Lamar Avenue and Day Street*
Dwight D. Eisenhower, 34th President of the United States, was born in this white frame house on October 14, 1890. The structure

has been restored to its 1890 appearance.
Open: June 1–Labor Day, daily 8–6:30; rest of year, Tues–Sun 10–5

EL PASO AND VICINITY
CHAMIZAL NATIONAL MEMORIAL, *on Cordova Island in the Rio Grande*

This memorial symbolizes the peaceful conclusion of a long-standing boundary dispute between the United States and Mexico. Ever since the Treaty of Guadalupe Hidalgo of 1848 made the Rio Grande the international boundary between the 2 countries, the river has steadily shifted its course to the south and has caused Mexico to lose territory. The terms of the Chamizal Treaty of 1963 provide that the Rio Grande will be rerouted to place all Mexican lands once again south of the river. This memorial will include displays on the history of the settlement of El Paso. NR
For further information write: 1426 Southwest Center, El Paso, TX 79901

MISSION NUESTRA SENORA DEL CARMEN, *in the Ysleta section of town*

In 1681, during the Indian revolt along the upper Rio Grande in New Mexico, Spanish refugees and Indian converts fled to this vicinity, where they established the oldest settlement—Ysleta del Sur—and earliest mission, originally known as Corpus Christi de la Ysleta, in Texas. Today the mission has been restored, and many of Ysleta's old adobe structures survive.

FORT DAVIS NATIONAL HISTORIC SITE, *Fort Davis, in Limpia Canyon off State 17 and 118*

Founded in 1854 by order of Jefferson Davis, Secretary of War, to protect travelers on the San Antonio-El Paso Road, a segment of the Overland Trail to California, Fort Davis played a major role in the defense system of western Texas. Federal troops garrisoned here patrolled the area, escorted wagon trains and stagecoaches, and pursued raiding Comanches and Apaches. During the Civil War, in 1861, Fort Davis was occupied by Confederate troops, who evacuated the post in 1862. Fort Davis was subsequently destroyed by Apaches. Federal forces consisting of the black troops of the 9th and 10th Cavalry and the 24th and 25th Infantry returned and rebuilt the post in 1867, and in the next 18 years they compiled a successful record against hostile Indians and outlaws. The soldiers' most impressive achievement was the 1879–81 campaign against Chief Victorio and his Warm Springs Apaches, who were finally driven into Mexico, thus ending the Indian wars in Texas. Fort Davis was abandoned in 1891. Of the 50 buildings that once stood at the site, 16 adobe and red stone officers' residences, 2 troop barracks, warehouses, and the hospital are preserved today. NR
For further information write: Superintendent, Fort Davis, TX 79734

FREDERICKSBURG HISTORIC DISTRICT, *central Texas on U.S. 290*

In 1846 German immigrants led by John O. Meusebach established this settlement in the Texas hill country, which they named in honor of Frederick the Great of Prussia. Meusebach in 1847 signed a treaty with the Comanches, which brought everlasting peace to the colony. Preserved are many *fachwerk* (stucco-covered timber construction) residences, as well as structures known as Sunday houses, which were built by families who lived too far from town to attend church and return home the same day. NR

TEXAS

GOLIAD VICINITY

PRESIDIO NUESTRA SENORA DE LORETO DE LA BAHIA
NATIONAL HISTORIC LANDMARK, *2 miles south off U.S. 183*
Strategically situated on the route connecting the province of Texas
with Mexico, this Spanish frontier fort was established in 1749 to
protect nearby missions and subsequently played a key role in the
history of the area. During the Hidalgo Revolt in 1812—in which
Mexicans fought for independence from Spain—the Gutierrez-
Magee expedition seized the outpost and held it for a year. Later,
during the Texas Revolution, in October, 1835, Colonel James
Walter Fannin captured the presidio and made it his command
headquarters in the struggle against Mexico. Forced to surrender
after the Battle of Coleto Creek, on March 19, 1836, Fannin and his
342 men were imprisoned in the presidio, and under direct orders
of Mexican President Santa Anna, they were executed nearby on
Palm Sunday, March 27, 1836, in violation of the capitulation terms
that they would be treated as prisoners of war. "Remember Goliad"
thus became a rallying cry for Texas independence. A historical
museum is on the premises, and the graves of Fannin and his men
are south of the presidio. NR
Open daily 9–5

GROESBECK VICINITY

OLD FORT PARKER STATE HISTORIC SITE, *4 miles north on State 14*
Constructed in 1834 by members of the Parker clan as a private fort
to protect 8 or 9 families, this stronghold was the scene of a brutal
massacre by hundreds of Comanches in 1836. Five members of the
Parker family were killed, and 9-year-old Cynthia Ann Parker and 4
other persons were taken into captivity. Cynthia grew up with the
Indians, married a Comanche chief, and became the mother of
Quanah Parker, the last great Comanche chief. In 1860 Cynthia was
recaptured and returned to her kinsmen. Unable to adjust to white
civilization, Cynthia and her daughter, Prairie Flower, died 4 years
later. Today Old Fort Parker has been restored. About a mile away,
in **Fort Parker Memorial Cemetery,** are the graves of those slain
in 1836.
Open during daylight hours

HOUSTON VICINITY

SAN JACINTO BATTLEFIELD NATIONAL HISTORIC LANDMARK,
21 miles east off State 225
Led by Sam Houston, Texans won their independence from
Mexico in a decisive engagement fought at this site on April 21,
1836. The Americans overwhelmed Santa Anna's numerically
superior Mexican forces here. This victory enabled the Republic
of Texas to be fully independent and precipitated Texas' annexation by the United States in 1845. Today a 570-foot-high granite
monument, containing a museum of Texas history, commemorates
the battle. NR
Open: June–Labor Day, daily 9:30–5:30; closed Mon rest of year

U.S.S. *TEXAS, in San Jacinto Battleground State Historic Park*
Launched just before World War I, this battleship saw action in
that war and in World War II, at which time she served as flagship
during the D-day invasion commanded by Dwight D. Eisenhower
in 1944. Permanently berthed today, the ship is the world's only
remaining vessel of the dreadnought class.
Open: Sept 1–April 30, Tues–Sun 11–5; rest of year, Tues–Sun 11–6

TEXAS

HUNTSVILLE

SAM HOUSTON MEMORIAL PARK, ½ *mile south on west side of U.S. 75 business route*

> This park commemorates General Sam Houston, hero of the Battle of San Jacinto (*see Houston, San Jacinto Battlefield*), first president of the Lone Star Republic (1836–38, 1841–44), and governor of the state of Texas (1859). After Texas seceded from the Union in 1861, Governor Houston was removed from office because of his refusal to recognize the Confederacy. Preserved here are the general's home of 1847, his "**Steamboat House**," built in 1858 and modeled after a Mississippi steamboat, his **Law Office**, and a museum.
> *Open daily 9–5; closed holidays*

JACKSBORO VICINITY

FORT RICHARDSON NATIONAL HISTORIC LANDMARK, *1 mile southwest off U.S. 281*

> Established in 1867, Fort Richardson was the northernmost of a group of forts founded after the Civil War to protect the Texas frontier from Comanche and Kiowa Indian depredations. A massacre near the outpost in 1871 and the punishment of those chiefs responsible instigated Indian uprisings in the area that culminated in the Red River War of 1874. Fort Richardson was abandoned in 1878. Surviving buildings include the hospital, which houses a museum. NR
> *Museum open: Tues–Sun 10–6. Grounds open during daylight hours*

JOHNSON CITY AND VICINITY

LYNDON B. JOHNSON NATIONAL HISTORIC SITE, *15 miles west in Stonewall off U.S. 290 on Park Road 49*

> This site in the Texas hill country includes the **Birthplace** and **Boyhood Home** of Lyndon Baines Johnson, 36th President of the United States. The son of Sam Ealy Johnson, Jr., a Texas legislator, and Rebekah Baines Johnson was born in a 2-bedroom farmhouse on the banks of the Pedernales River in 1908. When Lyndon was 5, his parents moved to a Victorian frame house in nearby Johnson City to provide a better education for their children. Lyndon lived here until his graduation from high school in 1924. After an active political career as congressman (1937–49), senator (1949–60), Vice President (1960–63), and President (1963–69), Johnson retired to the LBJ Ranch near his birthplace. After his death in 1973, Johnson was buried in a family plot beside the Pedernales. The birthplace has been reconstructed and the boyhood home restored. Both structures contain family heirlooms. NR
> *Birthplace open: Tues–Sat 10–5:30. Boyhood Home open daily 10–5:30*

KINGSVILLE VICINITY

KING RANCH NATIONAL HISTORIC LANDMARK, *west off State 141*

> The largest and best-known ranch in the continental United States was founded early in the 1850s by Captain Richard King, who purchased a 75,000-acre tract, one of the original Spanish land grants, on Santa Gertrudis Creek. Here was developed the Santa Gertrudis breed of cattle, the first strain to originate in the Western Hemisphere. Today the ranch has grown to more than 1,250,000 acres. A 12-mile loop drive passes ranch headquarters, stables, and other interesting sights. NR
> *Drive open daily 6:30–6*

LA GRANGE
MONUMENT HILL STATE HISTORIC SITE, *3 miles southwest on U.S. 77*
This memorial tomb contains the bodies of men slain in the ill-fated Mier Expedition of 1842. After Mexicans had invaded the Republic of Texas that year, a retaliatory expedition, under General Somerwell, was sent into Mexico. Outnumbered by Mexican forces, 250 Texans surrendered at Mier on the lower Rio Grande. As punishment for an escape attempt, one tenth of the Texans—chosen by lot—were shot. The tomb also contains the remains of 41 soldiers, led by Captain Nicholas Dawson, who were massacred by Mexicans at Salado Creek near San Antonio the same year.
Open: May–Aug, daily 8–8; rest of year 8–5

NAVASOTA
WASHINGTON-ON-THE-BRAZOS STATE HISTORIC PARK, *off State 90 at Washington and 7 miles southwest*
The Texas declaration of independence and constitution were signed in a building—now reconstructed—at this site beside the Brazos River in 1836. A provisional government was established here as well. A museum contains exhibits on Texas history.
Open: Wed–Sun 10–5

NEWCASTLE VICINITY
FORT BELKNAP NATIONAL HISTORIC LANDMARK, *3 miles south on State 251*
Established in 1851, this military post was one of the largest forts in a chain of defenses erected before the Civil War to protect travelers and settlers in northern Texas from marauding Comanche and Kiowa Indians. After 1858 the outpost was a stop on the Butterfield Overland Mail Route. Evacuated by Federal troops at the outbreak of the Civil War, Fort Belknap was subsequently occupied by the Texas Frontier Regiment, which continued campaigns against the Indians. Abandoned in 1867, Fort Belknap today preserves its arsenal and several reconstructed buildings. NR
Open: Sat–Thurs 9–5

PORT LAVACA VICINITY
FORT SAINT LOUIS SITE, *head of Lavaca Bay*
This is the site of the former Fort Saint Louis, founded in 1685 under the French flag by René Robert Cavelier, Sieur de La Salle. While searching for the mouth of the Mississippi, La Salle had mistakenly landed at the head of Lavaca Bay, where he established this base of exploration. La Salle was murdered by one of his own men farther inland near the present town of Navasota in 1687. In 1689 Fort Saint Louis was attacked by Indians and reduced to ruins. A Spanish force under Alonso de León rescued the few survivors. NR

SAN ANGELO
FORT CONCHO NATIONAL HISTORIC LANDMARK, *south of town*
Constructed in 1867 at the forks of the Concho River, where several east-west trails converged to avoid the Staked Plain to the north and the desert to the south, Fort Concho served as the point of departure for most southern expeditions to the Far West. The commanders garrisoned here included Colonel Ranald Mackenzie, leader of the famous Mackenzie's Raiders, whose daring exploits against the Comanche and Kiowa Indians eventually paved the way for the peaceful settlement of the area. Deactivated in 1889, Fort

Concho now has many well-preserved structures. NR
Open: Mon–Sat 9–5, Sun 1–5

SAN ANTONIO

THE ALAMO NATIONAL HISTORIC LANDMARK, *Alamo Plaza*

Originally known as Mission San Antonio de Valero, San Antonio's earliest mission was established in 1718 and converted into a fortress after 1793. The Alamo was the scene of the famous Texas Revolution battle of March 6, 1836, in which a force of 188 Americans under Colonel William B. Travis was slaughtered by Santa Anna's Mexican army of 5,000. Texas had declared its independence from Mexico in 1836, and the group under Travis, including Colonel James Bowie and Davy Crockett, took a "victory or death" oath to defend San Antonio to the last man. The Mexican army began its siege of the Alamo on February 24. After repeated assaults, the walls of the Alamo were finally scaled on March 6, and all the defenders were massacred. Not only did the event cause Santa Anna many casualties and delay the Mexican invasion of Texas for 2 weeks, but it served to stiffen Texas resistance under the rallying cry "Remember the Alamo" and allowed the Texans to achieve victory that April at San Jacinto (*see San Jacinto Battlefield*). NR
Open: Mon–Sat 9–5:30; Sun and holidays 10–5:30; closed Dec 24–25

ESPADA AQUEDUCT NATIONAL HISTORIC LANDMARK, *Espada Road, just east off U.S. 281S*

Built over Piedras Creek in 1740 by Franciscans of the nearby Mission San Francisco de la Espada, the Espada aqueduct was part of an extensive irrigation system constructed between 1731 and 1745. The network included a dam over the San Antonio River and an *acequia* (irrigation ditch) and served the 5 missions in the San Antonio vicinity. The remaining 5-mile section of the aqueduct, which still functions, is the only extant Spanish structure of its type in the United States. NR

MISSION NUESTRA SENORA DE LA PURISIMA CONCEPCION DE ACUNA NATIONAL HISTORIC LANDMARK, *807 Mission Road*

Established on the Angelina River among the Hasiuais Indians of East Texas in 1716, this mission was relocated to its present site on the San Antonio River in 1731. For more than 20 years Franciscan

Missions Purisma Concepcion and San José in San Antonio

fathers and Indians labored to erect a massive stone church, which, completed in 1755, boasted walls almost 4 feet thick, twin bell towers, and a cupola. Today the mission is the oldest unrestored stone church in the nation. NR

SAN JOSE MISSION NATIONAL HISTORIC SITE, 6¼ miles south on U.S. 281

San José y San Miguel de Aguayo was one of the most important missions on the northern frontier of New Spain during the 18th century. Founded in 1720 by Captain Juan Valdez, lieutenant general of the province of Texas, at the urging of Franciscan Fray Antonio Margíl de Jesus, the mission grew rapidly. By the middle of the 18th century San José was a thriving community with some 2,000 Indian convert residents caring for 3,000 head of livestock and producing 3,000 bushels of corn annually. Today San José is one of the best-preserved examples of mission architecture. NR
For further information: 6539 San Jose Dr, San Antonio, TX 78214

SPANISH GOVERNOR'S PALACE NATIONAL HISTORIC LANDMARK, 105 Military Plaza

Constructed in 1749 to house commandants of the Presidio of Béxar, this aristocratic edifice after 1772 became headquarters of the Spanish government in Texas. In 1820 Moses Austin came to this building to secure the right to colonize Spanish Texas with United States citizens. The palace has been restored. NR
Open: Mon–Sat 9–5, Sun and holidays 10–5

LA VILLITA, between South Presa and South Alamo streets

The "little village" is an authentic restoration of San Antonio's earliest community, which was established by 1722 around the Mission San Antonio de Valero (*see San Antonio, the Alamo*). Although the settlement was initially populated by poor Spanish soldiers and their Indian wives, La Villita became a fashionable residential district after 1819 when it was spared the ravages of a flood that destroyed most of San Antonio. One of the best-known adobe dwellings here belonged to General Perfecto de Cos, who at his home on December 9, 1835, signed the Articles of Capitulation after the Texans had captured San Antonio from the Mexicans. This humiliating incident probably influenced Cos' brother-in-law Santa Anna to spare no pity for the Texans at the Alamo in 1846, when he recaptured the town.

SAN FELIPE

STEPHEN F. AUSTIN STATE HISTORIC PARK, Park Road 38

In 1823 Stephen F. Austin established the first Anglo-American colony in Texas in this area. The community of San Felipe de Austin was the scene of the conventions of 1832 and 1833, and the consultation of 1835, which spearheaded the drive for Texas independence. The park contains a replica of Austin's log cabin, where he conducted colony affairs, as well as a statue of him.

WECHES

MISSION TEJAS STATE HISTORIC PARK, southwest off State 21

In 1690 an expedition headed by Alonso de León established San Francisco de Los Tejas, the first Spanish mission in east Texas, at this site on the Neches River in order to prevent French encroachment in the area. The mission was named after the Tejas Indians, a local intertribal confederacy. A replica stands today.

UTAH

BEAVER VICINITY

OLD COVE FORT, *junction of I-15 and State 14*

Erected in 1867, just after the outbreak of the Black Hawk Indian War, this fort was built, under the auspices of Brigham Young, to protect travelers on the Salt Lake-Pioche stage line route as well as the newly installed telegraph line. NR

Open: Easter–Oct, Mon–Fri 8–6

FAIRFIELD

CAMP FLOYD STATE HISTORICAL SITE, ½ *mile west of State 73*

Established in 1858 by Federal troops who had been sent to Utah under the command of Colonel Albert Sidney Johnston to suppress Mormon insurgents, Camp Floyd became the largest Army encampment in the United States. At its peak of activity in 1858–59, the post garrisoned from 2,400 to more than 3,000 soldiers at any one time. Troops stationed here escorted emigrant trains to California, captured outlaws, and provided protection from Indians. Before it was abandoned in 1861, the installation helped bolster Utah's flagging economy by serving as a marketplace for Mormon goods and providing a cheap source of needed commodities. Camp Floyd also represented the first sizable Gentile community in Utah and signaled the demise of Mormon isolation from the rest of the nation. Today the **Stagecoach Inn** (NR), built by John Carson for travelers and military personnel, and the **Commissary** have been restored; the **Johnston Army Cemetery** contains the bodies of the 84 men who died at Camp Floyd.

Stagecoach Inn open: April 1–Oct 31, daily 9–6

FILLMORE

TERRITORIAL CAPITOL, *Center Street between Main and 1st West*

Dedicated in 1855, this incompleted one-wing structure served briefly as Utah's first territorial capitol. The 1855 session of the

Top left and right: statue of Joseph Smith and aerial view of Temple Square in Salt Lake City. Below: the Golden Spike Ceremony at Promontory Summit

legislature was held in the State House; 2 succeeding legislatures convened here for one day apiece in 1856 and 1858, but the legislators readily adjourned to the more comfortable accommodations of Salt Lake City, 150 miles away. The building now houses pioneer relics. NR

Open daily 8–8

HOVENWEEP NATIONAL MONUMENT. *See* COLORADO

PROMONTORY SUMMIT

GOLDEN SPIKE NATIONAL HISTORIC SITE, *31 miles west of Brigham City via State 83*

A stone monument commemorates the completion of the nation's first transcontinental railroad at this site near the northern shore of Great Salt Lake on May 10, 1869. Here the rails of the Central Pacific, which had laid track eastward from Sacramento, were joined in a ceremony with the rails of the Union Pacific, which had laid track westward from Omaha. Extending across 1,773 miles of wilderness, the railroad had taken approximately 6½ years to build after Congress passed the Railroad Act of 1862, appropriating Federal funds for its construction. The completion of the railroad signified the breaching of the far western frontier and the establishment of a new era of trade, commerce, and political intercourse between the Atlantic and Pacific coasts. NR

For further information: Box 639, Brigham City, UT 84302

ST. GEORGE

BRIGHAM YOUNG WINTER HOME AND OFFICE, *Dixie State Park, U.S. 91*

Mormon President Brigham Young used this house, erected in 1872, each year from 1873 until shortly before his death in 1877. Young had directed Mormon pioneers to colonize St. George, which boasted a mild climate, in 1861 and had dedicated a temple there in 1871. NR

Open: June–Aug, daily 8–7; Sept–May, daily 9–5; closed holidays

SALT LAKE CITY AND VICINITY

BEEHIVE HOUSE, *75 East South Temple Street*

This Greek Revival mansion, surmounted with a beehive-shaped cupola—the traditional Mormon symbol of industry—was erected in 1854 for Brigham Young, president of the Mormon Church and first governor of the Utah Territory. In the mansion Young housed his large family and entertained prominent travelers and dignitaries of the day, including President Ulysses S. Grant. The building served as the official residence of presidents of the Mormon Church from 1893 until 1918. NR

Open: Mon–Sat 9–5

BINGHAM CANYON OPEN PIT COPPER MINE NATIONAL HISTORIC LANDMARK, *16 miles southwest on State 48*

The world's earliest and largest open pit copper mine was established here in 1904. By 1919 its output had made Utah the nation's fourth-ranking copper producer. The mine's yield is still considerable. NR

COUNCIL HALL (OLD CITY HALL), *2nd, North, and State streets*

Dedicated in 1866 at a gala ceremony attended by Brigham Young and other dignitaries, this structure served for nearly 30 years as

Salt Lake City Hall and the meeting place of the territorial legislature. Relocated to its present site, the building currently contains period paintings and furnishings. NR
Open: summer, Mon–Fri 8:30–6, Sat–Sun 9:30–6; rest of year, Mon–Fri 8:30–5

EMIGRATION CANYON NATIONAL HISTORIC LANDMARK, *east edge of town on State 65*

On July 24, 1847, the Mormon leader Brigham Young and his followers took this passage through the Wasatch Mountains to the Salt Lake Valley. From an eminence just north of the mouth of Emigration Canyon, Young realized that the valley before him was the destined homeland of his people and allegedly uttered: "It is enough. This is the *right* place. Drive on." Today the massive granite "This Is the Place Monument" stands at the site of Young's prophesy. NR
Visitor center open: summer, 7–10; winter, 10–6

TEMPLE SQUARE NATIONAL HISTORIC LANDMARK, *bounded by Main Street and North, West, and South Temple*

This walled square in the heart of Salt Lake City attests to the Mormon achievement of creating a "Kingdom of Zion" out of the Utah desert. On July 28, 1847, 4 days after his arrival in the Salt Lake Valley, Mormon leader Brigham Young came to this site between 2 forks of a small mountain stream and declared, "Here will be the temple of our God." The 10 acres composing Temple Square were marked off, and Salt Lake City soon grew up around the square. Dominating the area is the monumental gray granite **Temple,** which was designed by noted pioneer architect Truman O. Angell and took 40 years to erect (1853–93). The scene of sacred and secret Latter Day Saint ritual, the temple is closed to the public. Other edifices in Temple Square include the **Tabernacle,** completed in 1867, which boasts the world's largest domed roof, and the semi-Gothic **Assembly Hall,** raised in 1882. The **Sea Gull Monument** commemorates the summer of 1848, when hordes of crickets attacked the Mormons' crops; a flock of sea gulls providentially appeared and devoured the crickets. Preserved also is the **Osmun Deuel Log Cabin,** built in 1847, the oldest extant house in Salt Lake City. During the winter of 1849–50 it served as the office of Captain Howard Stansbury, who surveyed the Great Salt Lake. NR
Temple Square gates open: summer, 6–11; winter, 8–11. Bureau of Information Building open daily 9–5

SANTA CLARA

JACOB HAMBLIN HOME, *Dixie State Park, west of town on U.S. 91*

Jacob Hamblin, a Mormon missionary to the Indians renowned for his peacemaking achievements, as well as a colonizer, trail blazer, and scout, built this fortress-house of solid rock in 1863. In 1854 Hamblin and other Mormon pioneers established on the southern frontier of the Utah Territory a mission and outpost, which grew into the community of Santa Clara. Hamblin subsequently used Santa Clara as a base of missionary activity among the Hopis and Navajos of southern Utah, Nevada, and northern Arizona. Hamblin also served as a guide for Major John Wesley Powell's government survey of the Colorado River and assisted emigrant trains across the treacherous southwest desert. Today the Hamblin Home has been restored. NR
Open: May–Oct, daily 8–7; Nov–Apr, Tues–Sun 9–5

VERMONT

BENNINGTON

 BENNINGTON BATTLE MONUMENT, *Monument Circle off U.S. 7*
Erected in 1891, this 306-foot-tall monolith commemorates the victory, on August 16, 1777, of the Continental Army over the British at the Battle of Bennington, which was a prelude to the British defeat at Saratoga 2 months later. A detachment of British and Hessians, led by Colonel Friedrich Baum, had been sent by General John Burgoyne to Bennington to seize military stores, which the British needed in their attempt to cut New England off from the other colonies. General John Stark of New Hampshire led the Americans into the engagement, exclaiming, "There are the Red Coats and they are ours, or this night Molly Stark sleeps a widow!" Stark's troops defeated Colonel Baum's forces in their fortified redoubts near Bennington. The Green Mountain Boys, under Colonel Seth Warner, assisted in the rout by repulsing a British relief force just over the New York-Vermont state line (*see New York, Bennington Battlefield*). NR
Open: Apr 1–Nov 12, daily 9–6

FAIRFIELD

CHESTER A. ARTHUR BIRTHPLACE, *off State 36 or 108*
Chester A. Arthur (1830–86), the nation's 21st President, was born on the site of this one-story clapboard house. Vice President Arthur assumed the Presidency upon the death of President James A. Garfield on September 19, 1881. The house has been reconstructed from photographs of the original.
Open: June–Sept

HUBBARDTON

 HUBBARDTON BATTLEFIELD AND MUSEUM, *junction of Castleton-Hubbardton Road and Old Military Road*
On July 7, 1777, the only Revolutionary War battle fought entirely in Vermont occurred at this site, where colonial troops performed one of the most successful rear-guard actions in American military

Left: overall view of village of Plymouth Notch, birthplace of Calvin Coolidge.
Right: Bennington Battle Monument

annals. Defeated at Ticonderoga, General Arthur St. Clair and his American troops retreated into Vermont and left a detail of a few hundred men, including Colonel Seth Warner and his Green Mountain Boys, at Hubbardton to form a rear guard. Here pursuing British regulars and German mercenaries were met by the Americans, who retired to positions atop Monument Hill until they disengaged the enemy and rejoined the main force. Brought to a standstill, the British suffered such heavy losses that they retreated to Ticonderoga. A museum on the premises reconstructs the battle electronically. NR

Open: Memorial Day–Oct 15, Mon–Sat 8–4, Sun 9–5

MIDDLEBURY

WILLARD HOUSE NATIONAL HISTORIC LANDMARK, *Middlebury College campus*

In 1814 Emma Willard, a pioneer in the women's education movement, opened the Middlebury Female Seminary in this house. The curriculum included such courses, not customarily offered to young ladies, as mathematics, history, and languages. Emma Willard's 1819 address to the New York legislature has been termed the "Magna Charta of female education." The house is currently the admissions office for **Middlebury College,** which was founded in 1800. NR

MONTPELIER

VERMONT STATE HOUSE NATIONAL HISTORIC LANDMARK, *State Street*

Dedicated in 1859, this granite and marble State House, surmounted by a statue of Ceres, replaced 2 earlier structures. In 1805 Montpelier had become "the permanent seat of the Legislature for holding all their sessions." Inside the building today are a statue of Ethan Allen and a brass cannon captured from Hessians in the 1777 Battle of Bennington. NR

Open: Mon–Fri 8–4:30, Sat–Sun 10–12, 1–5; July–Labor Day, Mon–Fri 8–9, Sat–Sun 8:30–4:30

ORWELL

MOUNT INDEPENDENCE, *3 miles off State 22-A*

Jutting out from the Vermont shoreline into Lake Champlain, directly opposite Fort Ticonderoga, this wooded bluff was once fortified as part of the area's defensive complex. When Ethan Allen captured Fort Ticonderoga on May 10, 1775, a float bridge between the 2 posts was constructed. On July 6, 1776, the British retook Ticonderoga, and the retreating patriot forces under General Arthur St. Clair crossed the bridge to Mount Independence on their way to Rutland via Hubbardton (*see Hubbardton Battlefield and Museum*). NR

PLYMOUTH NOTCH

COOLIDGE HOMESTEAD NATIONAL HISTORIC LANDMARK, *off State 100A*

A dramatic event unparalleled in American annals occurred at this house at 2:47 A.M. on August 3, 1923, when Vice-President Calvin Coolidge, upon the death of President Warren G. Harding, took the oath of office, administered by his father (a Vermont notary public), to become the 30th President of the United States. Calvin Coolidge had lived in this white frame house from 1876, when he was 4, until 1887; during his public career he often returned to visit his

beloved boyhood home. The event of 1923 was the only time in the nation's history that a President was sworn in by his own father under such unique circumstances. Today this house has been restored, as have the **Calvin Coolidge Birthplace**, the church he attended, across the street, and the **Wilder House**, next door, the birthplace of the President's mother, Josephine Victoria Moor. NR
Open: May 15–Oct 15, daily 9–6

RIPTON VICINITY

FROST FARM (HOMER NOBLE FARM) NATIONAL HISTORIC LANDMARK, *3 miles east, 1 mile north off State 125*
Robert Frost, author of 11 volumes of poetry, recipient of 4 Pulitzer Prizes, and one of America's most popular poets, spent his summers at this farm from 1940 until his death in 1963. During this period he published 5 volumes of poems and took part in the 1961 inauguration of John F. Kennedy. The cabin Frost occupied currently contains his personal possessions. NR
Open by appointment

SHELBURNE

S.S. *TICONDEROGA* NATIONAL HISTORIC LANDMARK, *Shelburne Museum, 7 miles south of Burlington on U.S. 7*
Launched in 1903, the steel-hulled S.S. *Ticonderoga* plied the waters of Lake Champlain until 1953 and is now the nation's only basically unaltered side-paddle-wheel steamboat. The former excursion boat is currently displayed in the **Shelburne Museum,** an outdoor museum of New England life over a span of 3 centuries. NR
Museum open: May 15–Oct 15, daily 9–5

STRAFFORD

MORRILL HOMESTEAD NATIONAL HISTORIC LANDMARK, *south of the common*
Constructed between 1848 and 1851, this Gothic Revival cottage belonged to Justin Smith Morrill, author of the Morrill Acts passed by Congress in 1862 and 1898, which established land grant colleges. This legislation was probably the most important achievement of the Federal government in the field of higher education during the 19th century. Morrill served in the House of Representatives from 1855 to 1867, and in the Senate from 1867 to 1898. NR
Open: Memorial Day–Labor Day, Tues–Sun

WINDSOR

OLD CONSTITUTION HOUSE, *16 North Main Street*
On July 8, 1777, delegates from the New Hampshire Grants (the name given to the area that is now Vermont) met at this tavern, operated by Elijah West, and adopted the first constitution of the "free and independent State of Vermont." This document was the first of its kind in the nation to prohibit slavery and establish universal manhood suffrage. By the authority of the constitution, Vermont became a republic, independent not only of Great Britain but of the other states as well, and for the next 14 years it coined its own money, ran its own post office, and carried on diplomatic relations with foreign governments. In 1791 Vermont became the 14th state and the first to be admitted to the Union under the Federal Constitution. Known as the Birthplace of Vermont today, the Constitution House has been preserved and restored. NR
Open: May 15–Oct 15, daily 10–5

VIRGINIA

ACCOTINK VICINITY

POHICK CHURCH, *2 miles southwest on U.S. 1*

Vestrymen of this historic church, completed in 1773, include George Washington, George Mason, and George William Fairfax. The building was restored after suffering Civil War damage. NR
Open daily; Sunday service at 11 A.M.

ALEXANDRIA AND VICINITY

ALEXANDRIA HISTORIC DISTRICT NATIONAL HISTORIC LANDMARK

This district comprises nearly 100 blocks in the heart of the original town, which was established in 1748. George Washington was one of the surveyors of the district, which reflects Alexandria's position as the leading seaport and commercial center of northern Virginia for approximately 100 years, from about 1750 to the outset of the Civil War. Both historically and architecturally, many of the district's buildings merit close attention. The most important of them are described individually below. NR

 CARLYLE HOUSE, *123 North Fairfax Street*

The merchant John Carlyle had this famous house built in 1752. It was a center of political and social activity in colonial America. Here, in 1755, General Braddock met with the council of British colonial governors to map his campaign against the French and Indians; at the same time he made Colonel George Washington a member of his staff. Here, too, was the scene of the Fairfax Resolves, drawn up by George Mason in protest against British taxation shortly before the outbreak of the Revolution. The house has been restored and furnished with original materials. NR
Open: summer, daily 10–5; rest of year, daily 10–4. Admission: adults 50¢, children 30¢

Left: Mount Vernon. Top right: the Rotunda at University of Virginia in Charlottesville. Below: lithograph of Lee's surrender to Grant at Appomattox

CHRIST CHURCH NATIONAL HISTORIC LANDMARK, *116 N Washington Street*
>   The family pews of George Washington and Robert E. Lee adjoin in this structure, built between 1767 and 1773 and little changed now. Washington bought a pew when the church opened; Lee was confirmed here in 1853 and attended regularly. NR
>   *Open: weekdays 9–5, Sun 2–5; Sunday services at 8 and 10:30*

FORT BELVOIR, *9 miles south on U.S. 1*
>   On the grounds of this active military post, earlier called Fort Humphreys, are the ruins of **Belvoir,** the mansion house established in 1741 by Lord (Thomas) Fairfax. George Washington was a frequent visitor here after the property was inherited by his friend George William Fairfax. Belvoir was demolished by the British in 1814.

FORT WARD PARK, *4301 West Braddock Road*
>   Located outside the Alexandria Historic District, this 40-acre park contains a partial restoration of one of a chain of forts erected hastily by Federal authorities in defense of Washington, D.C., soon after the outbreak of the Civil War. Fort Ward, begun in September, 1861, was a major defensive post; its northwest bastion has been restored, complete with mounted guns. An officers' hut and museum were built from specifications furnished by Mathew Brady photographs; the museum contains an important collection of Civil War material. The park also has an amphitheater.
>   *Open: Mon–Sat 9–5, Sun 12–5; closed holidays*

FRIENDSHIP FIRE COMPANY, *107 South Alfred Street*
>   The enginehouse that served this company, a volunteer corps formally organized in 1774, is now a museum of early fire-fighting equipment and part of the Alexandria Historic District. It contains a replica of an engine that was presented to the company in 1774 by George Washington, who was one of the first members and in 1799 honorary captain.
>   *Open: Mon–Sat 9:30–5*

GADSBY'S TAVERN NATIONAL HISTORIC LANDMARK, *128 North Royal Street*
>   This famous old inn, now restored, comprises 2 adjoining buildings erected in 1752 and 1792. Originally it was called City Tavern, and for many years it was both a social and a political center. Here, in 1754, George Washington set up an enrolling office for volunteers in his first command, and then a headquarters during the French and Indian War. From the tavern steps in 1799 he reviewed Alexandria troops in one of the last acts of his military career. John Paul Jones, Lafayette, and Baron de Kalb are others who used the inn, located in the Alexandria Historic District. NR
>   *Open daily 9:30–5*

GUNSTON HALL NATIONAL HISTORIC LANDMARK, *19 miles south on George Washington Parkway and U.S. 1*
>   This was the home of George Mason, Revolutionary leader and constitutional authority who wrote the Virginia Declaration of Rights (1776). The structure, built between 1755 and 1758, is also an outstanding example of colonial architecture. Restored in 1920, Gunston Hall is now a historic house museum. NR
>   *Open daily 9:30–5. Admission: adults $1.50, school-age children 50¢*

PRESBYTERIAN MEETING HOUSE, *321 South Fairfax Street*
Dating from 1774 and located within the Alexandria Historic District, this building served as a meeting place for American patriots. Eulogies for George Washington were delivered here. In the adjoining cemetery is the Tomb of the Unknown Soldier of the American Revolution.
Open daily

ROBERT E. LEE BOYHOOD HOME, *607 Oronoco Street*
The Georgian mansion here was the home of Robert E. Lee during 9 of his first 18 years. He was 5 when the Lee family moved into the house in 1812. Located within the Alexandria Historic District, the structure contains antiques and Lee memorabilia. Earlier the house was the scene of the courtship of George Washington Parke Custis, adopted grandson of George Washington, and Mary Fitzhugh. In 1831 the only child of that union, Mary Custis, became Mrs. Robert E. Lee.
Open daily 9–5. Admission: adults $1, children (under 12) 25¢

STABLER-LEADBEATER APOTHECARY SHOP, *107 South Fairfax Street*
The Lee family were among Alexandria notables who used the facilities of this shop, located in the Alexandria Historic District. A marker indicates the spot where Robert E. Lee was making a purchase when Lieutenant J. E. B. Stuart delivered to him orders to suppress John Brown's raid on Harpers Ferry in 1859. The shop, built in 1792, contains ledgers and prescription files bearing the names of famous early customers.
Open: Mon–Sat 10–5

WASHINGTON NATIONAL MASONIC MEMORIAL, *King and Callahan streets*
The memorial is 333 feet in height and stands on a hill overlooking the old section of Alexandria along the Potomac. Items on display include the family Bible of George Washington and a clock that was stopped at the time of his death.
Open daily 9–5

APPOMATTOX VICINITY
APPOMATTOX COURT HOUSE NATIONAL HISTORICAL PARK, *3 miles northeast on State 24*
To all intents, the Civil War ended here on April 9, 1865, with Lee's surrender of the Army of Northern Virginia to Grant. The long march to Appomattox had begun 7 days earlier for Lee's veteran but starving and badly outnumbered forces. Grant's cracking of the Richmond and Petersburg defense lines was followed by pursuit of Lee's army. Realizing that further combat would be in vain, Lee sought a meeting with Grant; the surrender took place in the **Wilmer McLean House.** This structure, dismantled in 1890, has now been reconstructed on its original site. The nearby courthouse also has been rebuilt, and other buildings in the area, including **Meeks General Store,** the **Woodson Law Office, Clover Hill Tavern** (not open to public), **County Jail,** and private homes, have been restored to their approximate 1865 appearance. The courthouse contains a museum and auditorium where audio-visual programs are presented. NR
Open: Labor Day–June 15, daily 8:30–4:45; rest of year, 8:30–6:45. Admission: $1 per car

ARLINGTON VICINITY
ARLINGTON NATIONAL CEMETERY
Within Arlington National Cemetery are the graves of noted Americans, including Presidents Taft and Kennedy, Oliver Wendell Holmes, Generals John J. Pershing and George C. Marshall, and Admirals Robert E. Peary and Richard E. Byrd. Points of interest include the **Confederate Memorial, Marine Corps War Memorial,** and **Tomb of the Unknown Soldier,** containing the remains of veterans of the world wars and Korean conflict. On a hilltop site the **Custis-Lee Mansion** (NR), also known as Arlington House, was constructed between 1802 and 1817 by George Washington Parke Custis, grandson of Martha Washington. His daughter, Mary Ann Randolph Custis, married Robert E. Lee here in 1831, and the house was the scene of most of their life together. The house and grounds were seized by Federal forces in 1861 in the move to fortify approaches to Washington, D.C. Four years later the area was converted into a national cemetery. The mansion, now restored as a memorial to Lee, contains some original furnishings, together with furnishings from Mount Vernon and personal effects of George Washington.
Custis-Lee Mansion open: Apr–Labor Day, daily 9:30–6; rest of year, daily 9:30–4:30. Admission: adults 50¢

ASHLAND VICINITY
PATRICK HENRY HOUSE (SCOTCHTOWN) NATIONAL HISTORIC LANDMARK, *10 miles northwest on State 685*
Henry lived here from 1771 to 1777, a historic period in the life of one of the most influential Americans of his time. (His "Give me liberty, or give me death" speech to the Virginia Convention dates from 1775.) Following Henry as owner was John Payne, father of Dolley Payne, who later married James Madison: Scotchtown was thus her childhood home. The restored structure, originally erected about 1719, is one of the oldest plantation houses in the country and is of great interest architecturally. NR
Open: Apr–Oct, Mon–Sat 10–5, Sun 2–5. Admission: adults $1

CHANCELLORSVILLE. See FREDERICKSBURG, FREDERICKSBURG AND SPOTSYLVANIA NATIONAL MILITARY PARK

CHARLES CITY VICINITY
BERKELEY, *on James River 22 miles east of Richmond on State 5*
Built in 1726 by Benjamin Harrison II, father of a signer of the Declaration of Independence, this was the birthplace of William Henry Harrison, ninth President of the United States. It is claimed that this was the site of the first official Thanksgiving observance, in 1619. The plantation was plundered by British forces in 1781; during the Civil War General McClellan was quartered here.
Open daily 8–5. Admission: adults $1.50, children (under 12) 75¢

CHARLOTTESVILLE AND VICINITY
ASH LAWN, *2 miles beyond Monticello on State 53*
The estate of James Monroe was designed for him in 1798 by his neighbor Thomas Jefferson. Original Monroe furnishings and period pieces are on view. Like other historic estates in the area, Ash Lawn reflects many aspects of early American life and society. The grounds, with boxwood gardens and a 300-year-old oak, are especially noteworthy.
Open daily 7–7. Admission: adults $1, children 40¢

MICHIE TAVERN, 2½ *miles southeast on State 53*
Now restored as a museum, this famous inn was built about 1735 and subsequently enlarged. An early proprietor was Major John Henry, father of Patrick Henry. Among the famous guests were Jefferson, Madison, Monroe, Jackson, and Lafayette.
Open daily 9–5. Admission: adults $1, children (6–12) 50¢

MONTICELLO NATIONAL HISTORIC LANDMARK, 2 *miles south on State 53*
Not only was this the home of Thomas Jefferson for more than 50 years, it was virtually a lifetime project of his. It was built to his designs between 1769 and 1809, and its many inventive touches reveal his remarkable architectural skill. Richly furnished, the brick house in Roman Revival style contains many of his personal belongings. Jefferson is buried here. NR
Open: March–Oct, daily 9–4:30; Nov–Feb, daily 8–5. Admission: adults $1.50, children (6–12) 50¢

SHADWELL, *4 miles east*
Near the village of Shadwell is the site of Shadwell estate, where Thomas Jefferson was born in 1743. The residence was Jefferson's home until 1770, when it burned.

UNIVERSITY OF VIRGINIA, *university campus*
The university was founded by Thomas Jefferson in 1819 and designed by him as well. The focal point of his architectural plan was the **Rotunda** (NHL), adapted from the Pantheon in Rome and begun as the university library in 1822. It was destroyed by fire in 1895 and restored in 1898; meanwhile it had served as a banquet hall to honor Lafayette during a visit in 1824, and then as a Confederate military hospital. Extending southward from the Rotunda is the "academical village" of colonnades, arcades, faculty pavilions, and student dormitories. The **University of Virginia Historic District** (NR) is bounded on the north by University Avenue, on the south by Jefferson Park Avenue, on the east by Hospital Road, and on the west by McCormick Road.

COLONIAL HEIGHTS
LEE HEADQUARTERS (VIOLET BANK), *at Arlington Avenue*
The second of 2 historic houses bearing the name Violet Bank served Robert E. Lee as headquarters from June through October, 1864. A distinctive feature of the grounds is an old and large magnolia, or "cucumber tree." The restored structure is now a museum project housing Civil War mementos. The first building on the site dated from 1770 and was Lafayette's headquarters in 1781. It burned in 1810.
Open: June–Oct, daily 10–4.

COLONIAL NATIONAL HISTORICAL PARK. *See* VIRGINIA BEACH, CAPE HENRY; JAMESTOWN; YORKTOWN

CUMBERLAND GAP NATIONAL HISTORICAL PARK. *See* KENTUCKY

FREDERICKSBURG AND VICINITY
FREDERICKSBURG AND SPOTSYLVANIA NATIONAL MILITARY PARK, *Fredericksburg and the area in Spotsylvania County to the west and southwest*
The 3,672-acre park includes parts of 4 major Civil War battlefields

(Fredericksburg, Chancellorsville, the Wilderness, and Spotsylvania Court House); Fredericksburg National Cemetery; the Stonewall Jackson Memorial Shrine, Guinea, Virginia (earlier Guiney's Station), the house in which Jackson died; and historic Salem Church. At Fredericksburg, December 11–13, 1862, General Ambrose E. Burnside's Army of the Potomac sought to dislodge Confederate forces under Lee from their entrenched positions on the heights west and south of the town. The attempt ended in failure and in the dismissal of Burnside from his ill-fated command. His successor, General Joseph Hooker, was no more successful at Chancellorsville, where in May, 1863, Union forces were turned back again by Lee; in action concluding on May 4 and 5, Lee concentrated his troops against Hooker at Salem Church, 4 miles west of Fredericksburg, and forced the Union commander to retreat across the Rappahannock. The Confederates' success was costly, however, for Jackson had been mistakenly fired on by his own men on the night of May 2, and he died 8 days later. The Wilderness (May 5–7) and Spotsylvania Court House (May 9–19) action in 1864 was more indecisive, as Grant attempted to move Union forces between Lee and Richmond; though not successful, Grant's strategy substantially weakened his adversary and set the pattern for the war of attrition in the months ahead. Two visitor centers, each containing a museum, are in the park: in Fredericksburg on U.S. 1 at the foot of Marye's Heights, and on the Chancellorsville battlefield 10 miles west of Fredericksburg on State 3. NR
For further information write: Box 679, Fredericksburg, VA 22401

HUGH MERCER APOTHECARY SHOP, *Caroline and Amelia streets*
Among the business places with historic associations is the shop of Hugh Mercer, physician and later an officer in the American Army during the Revolution. He operated the apothecary shop, where Washington was a visitor, between 1771 and 1776. It has been restored to its original appearance and contains relics of medicine and pharmacy.
Open: March–Nov 14, daily 9–5; Nov 15–Feb, daily 9–4:30. Admission: adults 60¢, students 35¢

KENMORE NATIONAL HISTORIC LANDMARK, *1201 Washington Avenue*
This is a mid-18th-century brick house built by Fielding Lewis for his bride, Betty, sister of George Washington. Lewis served in the Virginia House of Burgesses and from 1775 as commissioner of a factory that produced small arms for the state militia. The structure retains its original interiors as well as very striking plasterwork ceilings and chimneypieces. NR
Open: March–Nov 15, daily 9–5; Nov 16–Feb, daily 9–4:30. Admission: adults $1.25, students 60¢

MARY WASHINGTON HOUSE, *1200 Charles Street*
Erected in 1770, it was purchased by George Washington 2 years later for his mother, who resided here until her death in 1789. In 1781 Lafayette visited her at her home; in the same year Washington and Rochambeau stopped here on their way to Yorktown. On March 12, 1789, Washington bade her goodby before leaving for his inauguration. Among the 18th-century furnishings are some that belonged to Mrs. Washington. The garden contains boxwood thought to be planted by her. Nearby are **Meditation Rock,** a quiet spot often visited by Mary Washington, and her burial place and monument,

on Washington Avenue at the end of Pitt Street.
Open: March–Nov 15, daily 9–5; Nov 16–Feb, daily 9–4:30. Admission: adults 75¢, students 35¢

MASONIC LODGE NO. 4, A.F. & A.M., *Princess Anne and Hanover streets*

George Washington was made a Mason in this lodge on November 4, 1752. The building at this location has been the home of the lodge since 1812, and it contains the Bible used in the Washington ceremony and the minute book recording the event. Lafayette received honorary membership here in 1824.

MONROE LAW OFFICE NATIONAL HISTORIC LANDMARK, *908 Charles Street*

James Monroe, who had studied law with Thomas Jefferson for 3 years beginning in 1780, opened this brick office in 1786. Here, until 1789, the future President practiced law during a period away from government service. In 1961 the 1758 structure was enlarged to include a library and museum housing his books and much of his correspondence. Also on display are furnishings bought by the Monroes in France during his period as ambassador there and later used in the White House. Of particular interest is a Louis XVI desk with secret compartments, on which he signed the document that became known as the Monroe Doctrine. The library and museum are part of the University of Virginia. NR
Open daily 9–5. Admission: adults 75¢, students 35¢

RISING SUN TAVERN NATIONAL HISTORIC LANDMARK, *1306 Caroline Street*

The Washington family's association with Fredericksburg includes this famous building, constructed in 1760 by Charles Washington, youngest brother of George. It became a center of political life, especially when Southern delegates to the Continental Congress gathered on their way to Philadelphia. In 1777 a group including Thomas Jefferson and George Mason outlined the bill that Jefferson later set forth as the Statute of Virginia for Religious Liberty. The structure's assembly room, since destroyed by fire, was the scene of a "peace ball" in 1781 to celebrate the victory at Yorktown; it was attended by George Washington, Lafayette, Rochambeau, and other notables. NR
Open: March–Nov 15, daily 9–5; Nov 16–Feb, daily 9–4:30. Admission: adults 75¢, students 35¢

WASHINGTON BIRTHPLACE NATIONAL MONUMENT, *38 miles east via State 218, U.S. 301, State 3 and 204*

The birthplace of George Washington was on a 150-acre tract that fronted on Popes Creek. Here between 1722 and 1726 his father, Augustine Washington, built the house in which the first President of the United States was born on February 22, 1732. The child spent his first 3 years here, then returned when he was 11 to study surveying. The house burned during the Revolutionary War. On its site a Memorial Mansion was constructed in 1932, not as a restoration of the original but as a representation of a typical Virginia plantation house of Washington's time. The monument also contains a colonial frame kitchen, a commemorative shaft of granite, the Washington family burial plot, and the site of the home (1664) of George's great grandfather, John Washington. NR
Open daily 9–5. Admission: 50¢ per person or $1 per vehicle

HAMPTON VICINITY
FORT MONROE NATIONAL HISTORIC LANDMARK, *Old Point Comfort*

The present fort, still in active service, was built between 1819 and 1834 on the site of military installations dating from 1609, when the Jamestown settlers fortified the area against possible Spanish attack. Union forces were in control of Fort Monroe throughout the Civil War, when it played an important role as the Federal stronghold nearest the Confederate capital. Their control was challenged dramatically by the Confederate ironclad C.S.S. *Virginia* (earlier the *Merrimac*) in 1862 in a 2-day engagement culminating in the inconclusive encounter between it and the Union ironclad *Monitor*. Between 1865 and 1867 Jefferson Davis was imprisoned at Fort Monroe. Three casements of the old fort have been converted into a museum. NR

Open daily 8–5

JAMESTOWN NATIONAL HISTORIC SITE, *Jamestown Island*

After stopping briefly at Cape Henry (*see Virginia Beach*), the colonists who established the first permanent English settlement in America built Jamestown beginning on May 13, 1607. It was the capital of the colony of Virginia from 1607 to 1698; it also was the scene of the meeting of the Virginia House of Burgesses in 1619— the first representative legislative assembly in the New World. All the Jamestown area excluding the National Historic Site (which is privately administered) is included in Colonial National Historical Park. The only part of the settlement remaining above ground is **Old Church Tower**, dating from about 1640. But the visitor can see foundations of houses and public buildings (including three State Houses), remains of streets, and a variety of artifacts, all recently uncovered through archaeological research. Other early Jamestown landmarks and personages are visible through representations, including paintings and statues. **James Fort, Powhatan's Lodge,** and replicas of the ships that brought the colonists are among the representations in Jamestown Festival Park. NR

Open daily during daylight hours. For further information write: Superintendent, Yorktown, VA 23490

Left: Old Church Tower at Jamestown. Right: Fort Monroe at Hampton

VIRGINIA

KILMARNOCK VICINITY

CHRIST CHURCH NATIONAL HISTORIC LANDMARK, *3 miles south on State 3*
> Dating from 1732, this is one of the finest and best-preserved colonial churches in the state. It was erected on the land of—and at the expense of—Robert "King" Carter, a leading public official of the colony of Virginia whose descendants included even more illustrious figures. The tombs of Carter and 2 of his wives are here. NR

LEXINGTON

BARRACKS, VIRGINIA MILITARY INSTITUTE, NATIONAL HISTORIC LANDMARK, *north edge of Lexington on U.S. 11*
> Part of the original barracks wall, dating from the mid-19th century, has been incorporated in the present-day cadet barracks of this school, which trained Stonewall Jackson and George C. Marshall (NR). In addition, an 1848 building that served as a tailor shop and then as a hospital is still in use. The school's **Jackson Memorial Hall** contains a well-known mural of the Battle of New Market (*see*). The **George C. Marshall Memorial Research Library** houses the personal papers of Marshall and other material related to his career as soldier and government official.
> *Marshall Library open: summer, Mon–Sat 9–5, Sun 1–5; academic year, Mon–Sat 9–4, Sun 1–4*

JACKSON HOME, *8 East Washington Street*
> The house here, the only home ever owned by Stonewall Jackson, is now a museum containing his personal possessions and original furnishings. Jackson's grave is in the Lexington cemetery renamed in his honor.
> *Jackson home open daily 9–5*

LEE CHAPEL NATIONAL HISTORIC LANDMARK, *Washington and Lee University campus*
> The chapel contains the vault in which Robert E. Lee and members of his family are buried. It also houses the office he used while he served the school as its president (1865–70). The university complex includes the **President's House**, designed by Lee; adjacent to the university is **Lee Memorial Church**.
> *Lee Chapel open: Apr–Sept, Mon–Sat 9–5, Sun 2–5; Oct–March, Mon–Sat, 9–4, Sun 2–4*

MANASSAS NATIONAL BATTLEFIELD PARK, *26 miles southwest of Washington, D.C., on State 234*
> The first and second Battles of Manassas (or Bull Run) resulted in important early Confederate victories. In the first, July 21, 1861, Jackson distinguished himself and gained the epithet "Stonewall." The second, August 28–30, 1862, was the key to Lee's first invasion of the North. NR
> *For further information write: Box 350, Manassas, VA 22110*

MIDDLETOWN VICINITY

CEDAR CREEK BATTLEFIELD AND BELLE GROVE NATIONAL HISTORIC LANDMARK, *on I-81 between Middletown and Strasburg*
> Belle Grove, a limestone house, dates from the end of the 18th century. It was the scene of the honeymoon of James and Dolley Madison. General Philip Sheridan used it as headquarters, and here his forces were surprised by Confederates under General

Jubal Early, October 19, 1864. From Winchester, where he was when the Battle of Cedar Creek (or Belle Grove) began, Sheridan made his famous ride to rejoin his army, which he rallied and led to still another victory over Early. NR

Open: Apr–Oct, Mon–Sat 10–4, Sun 1–5. Admission: adults 50¢, children (under 12) 25¢

MOUNT VERNON NATIONAL HISTORIC LANDMARK, *7 miles south of Alexandria on George Washington Memorial Parkway*

As a home site, this was patented by the Washington family in 1674. Lawrence Washington, half-brother of George, built the estate in his period of residence, beginning in 1743. George took possession in 1754, enlarged the main house, built a group of outbuildings, and landscaped the grounds, which now contain his grave. He resided in Mount Vernon until his call to lead American Revolutionary forces, again following the war, and finally during the period between the end of his Presidency (1797) and his death (1799). This famous estate is a treasure house, historically speaking—a repository of Washington memorabilia and a source of much information about early American life and society. NR

Open: March–Sept, daily 9–5; Oct–Feb, daily 9–4. Admission: adults $1.25, children (6–11) 50¢

NEW MARKET

NEW MARKET BATTLEFIELD PARK, *1½ miles north via Exit 67, I-81, on State 305*

The park here honors the contribution of youthful cadets of Virginia Military Institute to the Confederate victory of General John C. Breckinridge's troops over Federal forces in the Battle of New Market, May 15, 1864. On the grounds is **Bushong House**, which was used as a field hospital following the action. An exhibition hall re-creates Civil War history. NR

Open daily 9–5. Admission: adults $1, children (7–13) 50¢

NORFOLK

 ST. PAUL'S EPISCOPAL CHURCH, *St. Paul Boulevard and City Hall Avenue*

Dating from 1739, this was the only major building to survive the British burning of Norfolk in 1776. A British cannonball is still embedded in the south wall. **Fort Norfolk** (1794) served the Americans against the British in the War of 1812; early in the Civil War it was a Confederate fortress.

Open: Mon–Sat 10–4:30, Sunday services at 8, 11, and 5

PETERSBURG VICINITY

FIVE FORKS BATTLEFIELD NATIONAL HISTORIC LANDMARK, *12 miles west on County 627 at Church Road*

In this decisive engagement, April 1, 1865, Lee's last supply line in his defense of Richmond and Petersburg was cut. He dispatched General George E. Pickett to keep Federal forces from the Southside Railroad, but General Philip Sheridan's Union troops severed this vital supply route and forced Lee to withdraw from Richmond. NR

PETERSBURG NATIONAL BATTLEFIELD, *southeast, south, and southwest*

The 10-month Petersburg campaign, beginning in June, 1864, and ending at Five Forks (*see*), was an ultimately successful Union

effort to take this city, the vital depot through which supplies for the Confederate defense of Richmond flowed. Grant's dogged siege gradually constricted Lee's forces and supplies by rail. Petersburg's fall on April 3, 1865, thereby dooming Richmond, made Lee's surrender at Appomattox (*see*) inevitable. Still visible are many original earthworks used in the campaign; nearby is **Poplar Grove National Cemetery,** where many of the dead lie. NR
Open: June–Labor Day, 8–9; rest of year, 8–5

RICHMOND AND VICINITY

MARSHALL HOUSE NATIONAL HISTORIC LANDMARK, *9th and Marshall streets*

John Marshall, one of the most influential holders of the office of Chief Justice of the U.S. Supreme Court (1801–35), was owner of this brick house for 45 years and spent much of his life in it. The structure was built in 1790; an additional bedroom was provided in 1810. NR
Open: Feb–Oct, Mon–Sat 10–5, Sun 2–5; Nov–Jan, Mon–Sat 10–4:30, Sun 2–4:30

RICHMOND NATIONAL BATTLEFIELD PARK

The fall of the Confederate capital, Richmond, on April 3, 1865, was preceded by 7 Union drives. McClellan's **Peninsular Campaign of 1862** came close to success. Eventually Grant's siege of Petersburg (*see*), 1864–65, resulted in the surrender of that key supply base and of Richmond. A complete tour of the related battlefields (of 1862 and 1864–65) requires a 78-mile drive; an abundance of earthworks and historical artifacts remain. The park's headquarters visitor center is at 3215 East Broad Street; other such centers are at 2 of the major combat sites, **Cold Harbor,** where Lee's repulse of Grant, June 3, 1864, caused the latter to concentrate his primary attention on Petersburg thereafter, and **Fort Harrison.** NR
For further information write: 3215 E Broad St, Richmond, VA 23223

ST. JOHN'S EPISCOPAL CHURCH NATIONAL HISTORIC LANDMARK, *East Broad Street between 24th and 25th streets*

Built in 1740–41, this was the scene of Patrick Henry's "Liberty or death" speech in 1775. The area in which it is located, one of the oldest in **Richmond,** is a **National Historic District.** NR
Open: Mon–Sat 10–4, Sun after services to 4

STATE CAPITOL (CONFEDERATE CAPITOL) NATIONAL HISTORIC LANDMARK, *Capitol Square*

This famous building, designed by Thomas Jefferson and Louis Clérisseau after the ancient Corinthian temple in Nîmes, France, the Maison Carrée, has been the state capitol for almost 200 years, and it was also the Confederate capitol during the years (1861–65) when Richmond was the capital of the Confederacy. It was built between 1785 and 1792; wings were added in 1904–5. In the Old Hall, Aaron Burr's treason trial was conducted in 1807. In the rotunda is the figure of George Washington by Jean Antoine Houdon; on the grounds of Capitol Square is the equally famous Washington Monument executed by Thomas Crawford from designs by Robert Mills. NR
Open: Mon–Fri 8:15–5, Sat and holidays 9–5; May–Sept, Sun 9–5; Oct–April, Sun 1–5; closed Dec 25

WHITE HOUSE OF THE CONFEDERACY NATIONAL HISTORIC LANDMARK, *Clay and 12th streets*

Brockenbrough House, erected in 1818, served as the executive mansion of the Confederacy, the residence of President Jefferson Davis for 4 years. Since 1893 it has been a Civil War museum; it is now known as the Confederate Museum. NR

Open: Mon–Sat 9–5, Sun 2–5. Admission: adults $1, children (7–12) 50¢

ROCKY MOUNT VICINITY

BOOKER T. WASHINGTON NATIONAL MONUMENT, *16 miles east on State 122*

Part of the original Burroughs Plantation, where Washington was born in 1856, has been restored, and includes a replica of the slave cabin where he spent his earliest days. The noted educator wrote of his beginnings in *Up from Slavery*, his autobiography. NR

Open: Apr–May and Labor Day–Oct, Mon–Fri 8–4:30, Sat–Sun 9:30–6; June–Labor Day, Mon–Fri 8–6, Sat–Sun 9:30–6; Nov–March, daily 8–4:30

STAUNTON

WILSON BIRTHPLACE NATIONAL HISTORIC LANDMARK, *N Coalter Street*

Woodrow Wilson, 28th President of the U.S., was born in the Greek Revival manse here in 1856. Among the original possessions on display are the family Bible and the bookcase bought by Wilson with the first money he earned. NR

Open: June–Aug, Mon–Sat 8:30–5, Sun 9–5; Sept–May, daily 9–5; Dec–Feb, closed Sun. Admission: adults $1, children 50¢

STRATFORD

STRATFORD HALL NATIONAL HISTORIC LANDMARK, *3 miles north on State 214*

This outstanding example of early Georgian architecture, built between 1725 and 1730, was the birthplace of Robert E. Lee. It was the birthplace as well of Richard Henry Lee and Francis Lightfoot Lee, both signers of the Declaration of Independence. NR

Open daily 9–4:30. Admission: adults $2, children 50¢

VIRGINIA BEACH

CAPE HENRY, *reached via U.S. 60 through Fort Story Military Reservation*

Before the establishment of Jamestown (*see*), first lasting English settlement in America, the colonists of that historic venture landed here, on April 26, 1607. They remained for 4 days, then sailed up the James River to make their settlement. The site of the first landing, at Cape Henry, now part of Colonial National Historical Park, is marked by a **Memorial Cross**. The nearby **Cape Henry Lighthouse** (NHL), in operation 1792–1881, was the first one authorized by the U.S. government. NR

WILLIAMSBURG AND VICINITY

CARTER'S GROVE NATIONAL HISTORIC LANDMARK, *⅛ mile southeast of the intersection of U.S. 60 and State 667*

This imposing Georgian mansion, which has been described as "the most beautiful house in America," was built between 1750 and 1753 and was remodeled and enlarged in 1927–28. The original

owner was Carter Burwell, grandson of the noted Virginia land-
holder and colonial official Robert "King" Carter. NR
Open: March–Nov, daily 9–5. Admission: adults $1.75, students $1

WILLIAMSBURG HISTORIC DISTRICT NATIONAL HISTORIC
LANDMARK, *bounded by Francis, Waller, Nicholson, N England,
Lafayette, and Nassau streets*
> Originally settled in 1632 as Middle Plantation, Williamsburg
> was renamed in 1699, when it succeeded Jamestown as capital of
> the colony of Virginia. Restoration of a very famous historic district
> (Colonial Williamsburg) in a historic city began in 1927 and has
> striven to re-create the environment of the period when Williams-
> burg was a flourishing capital city (until 1799). Of particular his-
> torical interest are 3 reconstructions of buildings destroyed by fire
> and now used for exhibition purposes: the **Colonial Capitol,** Duke
> of Gloucester Street, on the foundations of the original (1705)
> building; **Governor's Palace,** Palace Green, home of Virginia's
> royal governors in colonial days; and **Raleigh Tavern,** adjoining the
> capitol, a center of social activity and then a meeting place for
> patriots as the Revolutionary era neared. Five structures separately
> designated National Historic Landmarks are within this district
> (itself an NHL): the **Wren Building** (1702), on the campus of the
> College of William and Mary, built on original designs by Sir
> Christopher Wren and now restored; **Bruton Parish Church** (1712–
> 15), on Duke of Gloucester Street; the **Peyton Randolph House**
> (1715–24), Nicholson Street, most of whose interiors are original;
> **James Semple House** (about 1780), Francis Street, thought to have
> been designed by Thomas Jefferson; and **Wythe House** (1752),
> Palace Green, home of George Wythe (noted jurist and civic official
> and a signer of the Declaration of Independence) and headquarters
> for George Washington before the siege of Yorktown and for
> Rochambeau afterward. All but the Semple House are accessible
> to the public. NR
> *Bruton Parish Church open: Mon–Sat 10–5; services Sun. Other
> buildings can be visited individually or as part of a tour; informa-
> tion available at Information Center, northeast of the Governor's
> Palace*

WINCHESTER
JACKSON HEADQUARTERS NATIONAL HISTORIC LANDMARK,
415 North Braddock Street
> This Gothic Revival house was headquarters for General Thomas J.
> (Stonewall) Jackson just before his Shenandoah Valley campaign
> of 1862, which threatened the security of Washington. Now a
> museum, it contains many of Jackson's personal possessions. NR
> *Open daily 9–5. Admission: adults 60¢, children 25¢*

YORKTOWN BATTLEFIELD, *Colonial National Historical Park on U.S. 17*
> Here, on October 19, 1781, American independence was virtually
> secured with the successful conclusion of the American-French
> siege of Lord Cornwallis' British forces. Earthworks, mounted
> cannon, and other relics of the action have been preserved, and
> **Moore House,** where the articles of capitulation were drafted, has
> been restored. A visitor center at the eastern end of **Colonial Park-
> way** is the starting point of a self-guided tour. **Yorktown National
> Cemetery** is part of this site. NR
> *For further information write: Supt, Yorktown, VA 23490*

WASHINGTON

BREMERTON

U.S.S. *MISSOURI, moored in west end of Puget Sound Naval Yard*

On September 2, 1945, in Tokyo Bay, this battleship was the scene of the signing of the formal instrument of surrender by Japan to the Allied Powers, thus ending World War II. Launched in 1944, the *"Mighty Mo"* saw action in the Pacific at Iwo Jima, Okinawa, and other areas. The ship subsequently served in the Korean War. Today a brass plaque on the "surrender deck" commemorates the event. NR

Open: summer, daily 10–8; rest of year, Mon–Fri 12–4, Sat–Sun 10–4

CHINOOK VICINITY

CHINOOK POINT NATIONAL HISTORIC LANDMARK, *4 miles southeast on U.S. 101 in Fort Columbia Historical State Park*

In 1792 the American sea captain Robert Gray discovered the Columbia River—the fabled Great River of the West long sought by explorers—at this site. Gray's find gave the United States a valid claim to the Pacific Northwest, territory likewise claimed by the British until the Oregon Treaty of 1846 fixed the Canadian boundary at the 49th parallel. In the 1800s Chinook Point served as a landmark for navigating the dangerous entrance to the Columbia. **Fort Columbia** was one of 3 military posts established here during the Spanish-American War. The **Commanding Officer's House** and other structures still stand. NR

Interpretive center open: May 1–Oct, daily 8–dusk

LEWIS AND CLARK CAMPSITE STATE PARK, *2 miles south on U.S. 101*

Captains Meriwether Lewis and William Clark, on their epoch-making trek across North America, first recorded the breakers of

Left: the totem pole in Pioneer Square Historic District in Seattle. Right: Fort Simcoe officer's row near Yakima

the Pacific Ocean at this site, where they camped from November 15 to 24, 1805. After a 17-month journey, the expedition entered the present state of Washington on October 11, 1805, and canoed down the Snake and Columbia rivers, portaging dangerous rapids along the way. (Today the **Lewis and Clark Trail Highway** follows their approximate route from Clarkston, at the Idaho border, to Ilwaco, at the mouth of the Columbia.) On November 17, Clark and 11 men left this campsite and proceeded along the beach to **Cape Disappointment** and the Pacific, thus achieving their principal goal. NR

EAST WENATCHEE VICINITY
PANGBORN-HERNDON MEMORIAL, *3 miles northeast*
This basalt column commemorates the first nonstop trans-Pacific flight from Japan to the United States. On October 5, 1931, aviators Clyde Pangborn and Hugh Herndon II took off in a small single-engine plane from Sabishiro Beach, Japan, flew 4,558 miles, and landed at this site 41 hours and 31 minutes later. NR

LONGVIEW
MONTICELLO CONVENTION SITE, *bounded by 18th, Maple, and Olympia avenues*
The leaders of the Cowlitz Valley and Puget Sound areas gathered at this site on November 25, 1852, and petitioned Congress to divide the Oregon Territory and create a separate government north of the Columbia River. The following March, Congress acceded to their wishes and established the Territory of Washington.

LYLE AND VICINITY
HORSETHIEF LAKE STATE PARK, *6 miles east on Highway 14*
One of the richest archaeological sites in the nation, this area at the Long Narrows of the Columbia River was a famous Indian camp-site where, in the summer, various tribes would peacefully assemble to trade, gamble, and absorb one another's culture. Indians came from miles away to fish for salmon, which were abundant at this point on the Columbia. The district was also the gateway between 2 distinct geographical sections of the Oregon Country: Indians from the wet, lush coastal region would come here to barter dried clams, canoes, seashells, and baskets for furs, robes, and dried meats brought by Indians from the arid plains to the east. Today such debris accumulations as **Wakemap Mound** reveal a wealth of artifacts, some of which originated as far away as Minnesota. Many pictographs and petroglyphs may be seen on the cliffs. NR

LYONS FERRY VICINITY
MARMES ROCK SHELTER NATIONAL HISTORIC LANDMARK, *1 mile north on west side of Palouse River*
Excavations at this rock shelter—considered to be the most outstanding archaeological site uncovered in the Northwest—have revealed the earliest burials in the Pacific Northwest. Skeletons found here date from as early as 5600 b.c. Cultural materials have been discovered in the 8 geological strata that have been excavated. NR

MUKILTEO
MUKILTEO (POINT ELLIOT TREATY SITE), *on State 525*
A popular Indian gathering place, this beach was the scene of the signing of treaties by 82 leaders of 22 Indian tribes with Governor

Isaac Stevens in 1855. Among the Indians present was Chief Sealth (*see Suquamish, Chief Seattle's Grave*).

PORT GAMBLE HISTORIC DISTRICT NATIONAL HISTORIC LANDMARK

Founded in 1853 on Puget Sound, this company-owned town was one of the first and most important lumber-producing centers on the Pacific Coast. The California gold rush of 1848, by creating a market for timber for towns and cities to support mining operations, precipitated the rise of the lumber industry in the Northwest. Lumberjacks soon pushed into the heavily forested areas of Washington and built towns like Port Gamble, whence sailing vessels would carry cargoes of wood to San Francisco. Still an active sawmill town, Port Gamble preserves many of its Greek Revival, Victorian, and New England-style structures of the mid-1800s. NR

PORT TOWNSEND AND VICINITY

FORT FLAGLER STATE PARK, *on north end of Marrowstone Island*

This coastal artillery post was founded, along with Forts Casey and Worden, late in the 1890s to guard the entrance—at Admiralty Inlet—to Puget Sound and prevent hostile naval vessels from attacking such prime targets as the Bremerton Navy Yard and the cities of Seattle and Tacoma. The fortification is representative of a type of coastal defense installation that played a key role in national military strategy prior to the advent of airplanes and nuclear weapons. After World War I coastal forts became obsolete. Fort Flagler was reactivated as a training base during World War II. Today gun batteries and a display shelter are at the site.

ROSALIA VICINITY

STEPTOE BATTLEFIELD, ½ *mile south on U.S. 195*

At this site on May 17, 1858, approximately 156 American soldiers under Lieutenant Colonel E J. Steptoe suffered one of the most significant defeats incurred by the Army at the hands of the Indians in the area. Taking refuge in the nearby hills, the soldiers fended off a series of attacks by large numbers of Spokane, Palouse, and Coeur d'Alêne Indians. At nightfall, under cover of darkness, the Americans retreated with their wounded toward Fort Walla Walla.

SAN JUAN ISLAND NATIONAL HISTORIC PARK, *reached by auto ferry from Anacortes, 75 miles north of Seattle*

This park commemorates the final and peaceful settlement of the Oregon Boundary Dispute, which lingered from the signing of the Oregon Treaty in 1846 until 1872. While establishing the 49th parallel as the boundary between the U.S. and Canada, the Oregon Treaty had left unclear the matter of ownership of San Juan Island, which was located "in the middle of the channel which separates the continent from Vancouver's Island." British and Americans subsequently occupied the disputed island jointly. The conflict reached a climax in 1859 during the "Pig War," which resulted when an American killed a foraging pig belonging to an employee of the Hudson's Bay Company, and reprisals were feared. British and American troops were thereupon dispatched to San Juan Island to maintain the peace. Hostilities were prevented, and in 1872 the dispute was arbitrated: the island was given to the U.S. Today the blockhouse, commissary, barracks and other buildings of the British camp still stand. Only foundations and vestiges of defense works remain at the American camp. NR

For further information write: Box 549, Friday Harbor, WA 98250

WASHINGTON

SEATTLE

PIONEER SQUARE HISTORIC DISTRICT, *First Avenue at James Street*

This area was the heart of Old Seattle, which was first settled across Elliott Bay at Alki Point in 1851 and relocated in 1852 to its present site. A fine natural harbor and a vast expanse of virgin forest combined to make the new community—named Seattle after a local Indian chieftain, Sealth (*see Suquamish*)—an excellent setting for its first industry, a sawmill opened in 1853 by Henry L. Yesler. The mill cut timber for export and employed most of the town's early settlers. The road down which logs were rolled to the mill gave rise to the expression "skid road." Seattle prospered and within a half century became the major city of the Northwest. Although a fire in 1889 (the year Washington achieved statehood) burned down Seattle's docks and most of its business district, the town was soon rebuilt with late-Victorian structures, which are still preserved today. A 60-foot totem pole marks the area. NR At the foot of Densmore Street is docked the **Wawona** (NR), which once held the world's record of codfish caught by a single ship.

SPOKANE VICINITY

SPOKANE HOUSE, *9 miles northwest in Riverside State Park*

This is the site of the former fur trading post Spokane House, which was established in 1810 as the North West Company's western outpost in the Columbia Basin and was the first permanent white settlement in Washington. Over the next 16 years Spokane House was the only trading post west of the Rockies that was the scene of activity of 3 different companies; in 1812 John Jacob Astor's Pacific Fur Company founded a rival post near Spokane House, which was purchased by the North West Company a year later; in 1821 the North West Company merged with the Hudson's Bay Company, which subsequently administered Spokane House until it was abandoned in 1826. Today an interpretative center stands on the site.

SUQUAMISH

CHIEF SEATTLE'S GRAVE, *Suquamish Memorial Cemetery, off State 305*

The grave and marker here commemorate the Indian Chief Sealth—or "Seattle," as he was called by the early settlers—whose lifetime (1786–1866) spanned the period of exploration and settlement of the Puget Sound area. During the Indian uprisings of 1855, Sealth remained friendly with the settlers; in gratitude for his loyalty, the settlers named their new community Seattle.

TACOMA

FORT NISQUALLY GRANARY NATIONAL HISTORIC LANDMARK, *Point Defiance Park*

Erected in 1843 and the oldest extant structure in Washington, this granary was part of Fort Nisqually, a Hudson's Bay Company trading post established in 1833 and the first permanent white settlement on Puget Sound. Occupied by the British until 1869, Fort Nisqually served as a communications and supply depot for Hudson's Bay Company posts in British Columbia, and in 1840 it became headquarters of the Puget Sound Agricultural Company, a Hudson's Bay subsidiary. Today the granary and **Factor's House** have been moved from their original site 15 miles away and restored, and the other buildings have been reconstructed. NR

TOLEDO AND VICINITY

COWLITZ MISSION, *2½ miles east off I-5 on old U.S. 99*

Founded in 1838 by Fathers Blanchet and Demers, who originally held church services for settlers in rude dwellings at this site, the Cowlitz Mission is the oldest mission in the Northwest.

VANCOUVER

FORT VANCOUVER NATIONAL HISTORIC SITE, *E Evergreen Blvd*

Established in 1824 and relocated to its present site in 1829, Fort Vancouver for 2 decades served as headquarters and depot for all operations of the British-owned Hudson's Bay Company west of the Rocky Mountains and was the political, social, economic, and cultural center of the Pacific Northwest. The fur trading post was administered by Chief Factor John McLoughlin, who was instrumental in creating the Hudson's Bay Company's vast commercial empire. At the height of its prosperity, from 1844 to 1846, the fort contained 22 major buildings. After the Treaty of 1846 between the U.S. and Great Britain, which fixed the southern Canadian boundary at the 49th parallel, Fort Vancouver became part of American territory and declined in importance. In 1849 the site became a U.S. Army camp, and it is still in use. Today the original stockade and buildings are outlined on the site, and the north wall and gate as well as a portion of the east wall have been restored. NR

For further information write: Supt, Vancouver, WA 98661

WALLA WALLA VICINITY

WHITMAN MISSION NATIONAL HISTORIC SITE, *7 miles west off U.S. 410*

This is the site of the Waiilatpu Mission to the Cayuse Indians, which was founded in 1836 by Dr. Marcus and Narcissa Whitman and was active until 1847, when the Indians massacred the Whitmans' and 11 other missionaries. Taking the route to the Northwest that became known as the **Oregon Trail,** Narcissa Whitman and Eliza Spalding became the first American women to cross the continent overland. At Waiilatpu the Whitmans introduced Christianity to the Cayuse, taught them the rudiments of agriculture and letters, and treated their diseases. Early in the 1840s the mission became an important way station on the Oregon Trail. In 1847 a measles epidemic killed half the Cayuse tribe, who had no resistance to the white man's disease, and provoked the tragic and violent attack that ended Protestant missionary work in the Pacific Northwest. Indians destroyed the mission in 1848. Today the graves of the Whitmans and outlined building sites may be seen. NR

For further information write: Supt, Route 2, Walla Walla, WA 99362

YAKIMA AND VICINITY

FORT SIMCOE HISTORICAL STATE PARK, *38 miles southwest at western end of State 220*

Established as one of the 2 (along with Fort Walla Walla) regular Army posts in the interior of the Washington Territory following a flare-up of Indian hostilities late in 1855, Fort Simcoe served as an advance post for the Ninth Regiment of U.S. Infantry under Major Robert Selden Garnett from 1856 until 1859. Built on the site of an old tribal meeting place, Fort Simcoe was subsequently used as an Indian agency and school on the Yakima Indian Reservation. The **Commandant's House,** 3 captains' dwellings, and a blockhouse have been restored, and other structures reconstructed.

Open daily 8–5

WEST VIRGINIA

BEVERLY VICINITY

RICH MOUNTAIN BATTLEFIELD, *6 miles south of Elkins off U.S. 250*
On July 11, 1861, Federal troops under General George B. McClellan decisively defeated a Confederate force under General Robert Garnett, leaving the area of West Virginia to the crest of the Alleghenies open to the Union. The battlefield here includes ruins of **Hart House**, which was built by Joseph Hart, son of a signer of the Declaration of Independence, and used as a field hospital during the Rich Mountain action.

CARNIFEX FERRY BATTLEFIELD STATE PARK, *7 miles southwest of Summersville*
A Union force commanded by General William S. Rosecrans defeated Confederate troops under General John B. Floyd here on September 10, 1861. Still visible are trenches and graves of the fallen.

CHARLES TOWN

JEFFERSON COUNTY COURTHOUSE, *George and Washington sts*
The abolitionist John Brown was tried here and convicted of treason following his raid on the government arsenal at Harpers Ferry (*see*) in October, 1859. He was hanged in Charles Town on December 2, 1859.
Open: May–Oct, Sat–Sun noon–5

CHARLESTON

SITE OF FORT LEE, *1202 East Kanawha Boulevard*
Colonel George Clendenin established Fort Lee in 1788, and around it grew the modern city of Charleston. From the time of the fort's erection until 1795, Daniel Boone resided here.

Left: Jefferson County Courthouse at Charles Town. Top right: Grave Creek Mound at Moundsville. Below: Harpers Ferry National Historical Park

STATE CAPITOL, *Kanawha Boulevard, East*
The **State Museum**, housed in the basement of this building, contains an important collection on pioneer life. Among the relics are a rifle of Daniel Boone's and spectacles that belonged to Aaron Burr.
Open: Mon–Sat 9–5, Sun 1–5

CHESAPEAKE & OHIO CANAL NATIONAL MONUMENT. See DISTRICT OF COLUMBIA *and* MARYLAND

CLARKSBURG
JACKSON BIRTHPLACE SITE, *328 West Main Street*
A bronze plate marks the site of a brick house where General Thomas J. "Stonewall" Jackson was born on January 21, 1824.

LOWNDES MUNICIPAL PARK, *entrance on Second Street*
Traces of old earthworks built by Federal forces during the Civil War, when the city was an important Union supply base, are still visible on Lowndes Hill here.

DROOP VICINITY
DROOP MOUNTAIN BATTLEFIELD STATE PARK, *west side of U.S. 219 between Droop and Hillsboro*
Union forces under Brigadier General William W. Averell defeated a Confederate army led by Brigadier General John Echols here on November 6, 1863, ending important Southern resistance in the state. Breastworks, graves, and monuments remain. NR

FORT ASHBY, *South Street in Fort Ashby*
Built in 1755, under the direction of George Washington, this was one of a chain of frontier outposts designed to protect the trans-Allegheny frontier. It has been restored faithfully. NR
Open: June–Aug, Thurs 11–4

HARPERS FERRY NATIONAL HISTORICAL PARK, *in Harpers Ferry*
This historic town developed from a settlement begun in 1733. In 1796 a Federal arsenal was built, and it was the abolitionist John Brown's raid on the arsenal, October 16–17, 1859, that stirred an entire nation. Seeking to establish both a stronghold for a frontal attack on the institution of slavery and a refuge for blacks, Brown and 18 followers seized several strategic points before a troop of Marines, commanded by Colonel Robert E. Lee, quelled the insurrection. Brown was routed from the enginehouse where he had barricaded himself. Tried in Charles Town (*see*), he was convicted of treason and hanged. The park includes a district within Harpers Ferry that contains a visitor center, together with separate areas in **Loudoun Heights, Bolivar Heights** (both in West Virginia), and **Maryland Heights** (Maryland). High points of a walking tour include the **Master Armorer's House** (1859), restored home of the chief gunsmith of the armory, now a museum of gunmaking; **Brown's Fort,** the fire-engine house used by Brown on the armory site; and **Harper House** (1775–82), also restored, the oldest surviving structure within Harpers Ferry. NR
For further information write: Box 117, Harpers Ferry, WV 25425

MOUNDSVILLE
GRAVE CREEK MOUND NATIONAL HISTORIC LANDMARK, *Tomlinson Avenue and 9th Street*
One of the largest Indian burial mounds in the United States and

the site of extensive excavation, this is representative of thé Adena
culture of about 500 B.C. NR
Open: Apr–Dec, daily 11–6. Admission: adults 50¢

PIERCE VICINITY
FAIRFAX STONE HISTORICAL MONUMENT, *northeast*
The marker indicates the boundary between West Virginia and
Maryland, which was established by a Supreme Court decision
settling a dispute between the states. The original Fairfax Stone
was placed a mile south of here about 1747 to mark the westernmost
corner of the huge estate of Lord Fairfax, given to him by royal grant.
NR

POINT PLEASANT BATTLEGROUND, *confluence of the Ohio and Kanawha rivers*
Following the French and Indian War, the English government
sought to discourage colonists from settling the land west of the
Allegheny Mountains. The move was not successful, to the displeas-
ure of the Indians, who resented the encroachment. The murder of
an Indian family precipitated the Battle of Point Pleasant. In
retaliation, an Indian force under the Shawnee chief Cornstalk
engaged 1,100 Virginia militiamen commanded by General Andrew
Lewis on October 10, 1774. The fierce fight resulted in the Indians'
decisive defeat and in the breaking of their power in the Ohio Valley. Three frontier forts were built in this vicinity between 1774 and
1786. Located in **Tu-Endie-Wei Park** are a monument to the Battle
of Point Pleasant; monuments to Cornstalk and "Mad Ann" Bailey,
a noted frontierswoman and scout; and **Mansion House,** dating from
1797, the oldest house in the Kanawha valley, now restored as a
museum. NR
Open: Apr–Nov, daily 9–5

WHEELING
INDEPENDENCE HALL, *16th and Market streets*
Built about 1854 as a customhouse, this building became West
Virginia's first capitol. Here was held the constitutional convention
that drew up the laws of the state upon its admission to the Union
in 1863. Earlier, most of the sessions of the legislature of the restored government of Virginia had met here, and during the Civil
War arms and ammunition for Federal forces were stored inside. NR

SITE OF FORT HENRY, *Main Street between 11th and Ohio streets*
A bronze plaque indicates the site of the outpost established in
1774, 5 years after the first settlement in the Wheeling area. The
fort originally was known as Fincastle; it was renamed in 1776 to
honor Patrick Henry. As Fort Henry, it was an important base during
the Revolutionary War; although peace had been consummated by
September, 1782, the so-called last battle of the Revolution occurred
here when a force of British and Indians attacked the fort but
retired after an unsuccessful 2-day siege.

WHITE SULPHUR SPRINGS
PRESIDENTS' COTTAGE MUSEUM, *on the grounds of Greenbrier Resort*
This white cottage, built in 1816, has housed 14 vacationing U.S.
Presidents. It served as a summer white house for Martin Van
Buren, John Tyler, and Millard Fillmore.
Open: Apr–Nov, Mon–Sat 10–12, 1–4:30